Kālachakra Tantra
Rite of Initiation

Kālachakra Tantra
Rite of Initiation
For the Stage of Generation

A commentary on the text of
Kay-drup Ge-leg-bel-sang-bo by
Tenzin Gyatso, the Fourteenth Dalai Lama,
and the text itself

Edited, translated and introduced by
Jeffrey Hopkins

New enlarged edition with index

Wisdom Publications • Boston

Wisdom Publications
199 Elm Street, Somerville MA 02144 USA

Enlarged edition with index, 1999
Revised edition, 1989
First published, 1985

Library of Congress Cataloging in Publication Data

Bstan-'dzin-rgya-mtsho, Dalai Lama XIV, 1935–
Kālachakra tantra : rite of initiation : for the stage of generation : a commentary on the text of Kay-drup-ge-lek-bel-sang-bo / by Tenzin Gyatso, the Fourteenth Dalai Lama, and the text itself ; edited translated and introduced by Jeffery Hopkins. — New enl. ed.
p. cm.
Includes bibliographical references and index.
ISBN 0-86171-151-3 (pbk. : alk. paper)
1. Kālacakra (Tantric rite)—China—Tibet. 2. Tripiṭaka. Sūtrapiṭaka. Tantra. Kālacakratantra—Criticism, interpretation, etc. I. Hopkins, Jeffrey. II. Mkhas-grub Dge-legs-dpal-bzaṅ-po, 1385–1438. III. Tripiṭaka. Sūtrapiṭaka. Tantra. Kālacakratantra. English & Tibetan. IV. Title.
BQ8921.K34B77 1999
294.3'438—dc21

99-18615

ISBN 0-86171-151-3

04 03 02 01 00
6 5 4 3

Set in 10 on 12½ point Palatino by Character Graphics of Somerset, England and printed and bound by Eurasia Press of Singapore.

Contents

Preface

This book is concerned with a rite of initiation for the *Kāla-chakra (Wheel of Time) Tantra,* a Buddhist tantra of the Highest Yoga Tantra class. It presents the series of initiations authorizing practice of the first of two stages involved in the tantra, the stage of generation – the period of imaginative appearance as an ideal being. A system of daily practice required of those who have received initiation is also included. Discussed are the process of preparing the student for initiation and the actual stages of the seven initiations that authorize practice of visualization of a practitioner as a deity – or ideal, altruistically active being – in a mandala, an ideal environment.

This is the first time that a tantric initiation ritual has been explained in detail in a Western language. The initiation ritual is translated, interspersed with commentary from His Holiness the Dalai Lama, temporal and spiritual leader of Tibet, mainly from a ceremony conducted in Wisconsin in 1981. The Kālachakra initiation was offered for the first time in the West by His Holiness the Dalai Lama during July of 1981 (the year of the Iron Bird) at Deer Park, a small rural site outside of Madison, Wisconsin, that is the home of a Tibetan Buddhist monastery and temple. The initiation was organized and sponsored by the Deer Park Buddhist Center and friends, a Buddhist organization under the direction of the Venerable Geshe Sopa.

During the process of the initiation, the Dalai Lama, as is customary, gave copious commentary detailing the proper attitude and motivation of the recipient and the individual steps of visualization and of reflection on profound and subtle topics that are at the heart of the initiation, or authorization, process. His explanations offered during the ceremony, as well as others given privately to me in preparation for serving as his translator, bring the basic initiation ceremony to life, rich with meaning and contextualization. The special tantric techniques for transforming body, speech, and mind into completely altruistic expression are thereby made lucid and accessible to interested readers.

The Introduction first describes the general Great Vehicle view on purification into a state of altruistic service as well as the special tantric practice of deity yoga that is founded on compassion and realization of emptiness. Next, it describes the process of initiation for the stage of generation, outlining and explaining the many steps in the ritual. It also provides background on the history of the *Kālachakra Tantra* and introduces the authors and texts.

I would like to thank Elizabeth Napper for making numerous editorial suggestions on the entire manuscript, Gareth Sparham for typing the translation of the ritual text, and Karen Saginor and Daniel Cozort for proof-reading the galleys. As is detailed in the ninth chapter of the introduction, I have attempted, through consulting lamas competent in the tradition, to keep errors of translation and interpretation to a minimum; I ask for readers' forebearance for those undiscovered.

Jeffrey Hopkins
Charlottesville, Virginia

Technical Note

The names of Tibetan authors, orders, and places are given in "essay phonetics" for the sake of easy pronunciation; for a discussion of the system used, see the Technical Note at the beginning of my *Meditation on Emptiness*, pp.19-22.

Transliteration of Tibetan in parentheses and in the glossary is done in accordance with a system devised by Turrell Wylie; see "A Standard System of Tibetan Transcription", *Harvard Journal of Asiatic Studies*, Vol. 22, 1959, pp.261-7. For Sanskrit citations, *ch*, *sh*, and *ṣh* are used instead of the more usual *c*, *ś*, and *ṣ* for the sake of easy pronunciation by non-specialists; *chh* is used for *ch*.

Publisher's Acknowledgment

The Publisher gratefully acknowledges the generous help of the Hershey Family Foundation in sponsoring the printing of this book.

Introduction
by Jeffrey Hopkins

1 *Altruistic Purification*

In Buddhism, liberation is always *from* a state that needs healing and *to* a healed state of release and greater effectiveness.[1] Buddha is viewed as like a physician; practitioners are like patients taking the medicine of Buddha's doctrine in order to be cured from a basic illness and to achieve a state of health necessary for widely effective altruistic endeavor.

According to explanations standard in Tibetan Buddhism,[2] even in the Low Vehicle[3] schools of tenets – Great Exposition School[4] and Sūtra School – in which the mental and physical continuum of an enlightened being is said to be completely severed at the time of death, there is a period, subsequent to enlightenment, of far more effective interaction with others, as was the case with Shākyamuni Buddha. According to the Great Vehicle schools of tenets – the Mind Only School and the Middle Way School – which hold that the continuum of mind never ends, the primary aim of Bodhisattvas is to bring about the welfare of other sentient beings and the means to accomplish this is their own enlightenment, the gaining of authentic freedom. For, with the attainment of a Buddha's enlightenment, there is gained a limitless, unending, spontaneous capacity to help others effectively.

What distinguishes someone as a Bodhisattva is to engender an altruistic intention to become enlightened, which, through training, has become so spontaneous that it is as strong outside as it is within meditation. This is called *bodhichitta,* literally "mind of enlightenment" but more like "mind toward enlightenment", "mind directed toward enlightenment". As Maitreya's *Ornament for Clear Realization (mngon rtogs rgyan, abhisamayālaṃkāra)* says:[5]

> Mind generation is asserted as a wish for complete
> Perfect enlightenment for the sake of others.

This has been formulated into a definition of *bodhichitta* or, as I translate it, "altruistic intention to become enlightened":

> a main mental consciousness induced by an aspiration for [bringing about] others' welfare and accompanied by an aspiration to one's enlightenment.[6]

It is an attitude endowed with two aspirations, the first for others' welfare and the second for one's own highest enlightenment as a Buddha, the latter being seen as a means for accomplishing the first. Even though one's own enlightenment must be accomplished first in order to bring about others' welfare, service to others is prime in terms of motivation.

The enlightenment of a Buddha is seen as a means to bring about others' welfare because a Buddha, being omniscient, knows all possible techniques for advancement and knows in detail the predispositions and interests of other beings. Between the two bodies of a Buddha, Truth Body and Form Body[7] (the latter including the Complete Enjoyment Body and the Emanation Body), Bodhisattvas primarily seek Form Bodies, since it is through physical form that the welfare of others can be accomplished, this being mainly through teaching what is to be adopted in practice and what is to be discarded in behavior. Though Truth and Form Bodies necessarily accompany each other and thus are achieved together, the Bodhisattvas' emphasis is on achieving Form Bodies in order to appear in myriad forms suitable to the interests and dispositions of trainees and to teach them accordingly.

Some Bodhisattvas' motivation is described as like that of a king, for they see themselves as first becoming enlightened and then helping others. Others' motivation is described as like that of a boatman since they strongly want to arrive at the shore of the freedom of Buddhahood in the company of everyone else. Again, others' motivation is described as like that of a shepherd in that they want to see others safely enlightened before they become enlightened, like a shepherd returning home at the rear of the flock. The only realistic mode is said in Tibetan traditions to be the first, the king-like motivation, since there is no state superior to Buddhahood for accomplishing others' welfare. Hence, the description that Bodhisattvas put off final enlightenment as Buddhas in order to be of greater service to sentient beings is considered to be an exaggerated statement expressing the greatness of their altruistic, shepherd-like motivation.

Buddhahood, with such altruistically oriented knowledge and activity, is the final aim – "final" in the sense that it is the path of no more learning, there being no further development of new levels of understanding or compassion. It is a beginning in the sense that for the first time one can serve others to one's full capacity, forever, unceasingly, as long as there are beings who need to be helped, and that is forever.

This heroic effort to bring about others' welfare is conceived in terms of there being (1) a basis for such purification and transformation within us, (2) objects of purification, (3) a path that serves as a means of purification, and (4) a fruit of that purification.

THE BASIS OF PURIFICATION

The basis of purification is the Buddha nature, which is viewed in two ways. One is the clear light nature of the mind, a positive phenomenon, and the other is the emptiness of inherent existence of the mind, a negative phenomenon, a mere absence of inherent establishment of the mind, which is a precondition for its transformation. Both of these aspects are said to be expressed in the famous statement from Dharmakīrti's *Commentary on (Dignāga's) "Compendium [of Teachings] on Valid Cognition" (tshad ma rnam 'grel, pramāṇavarttika)*:[8]

> The nature of the mind is clear light.
> The defilements are adventitious.

"Adventitious" *(glo bur ba)* here does not mean "uncaused" but instead means that the defilements do not subsist in the very nature of the mind. Since desire, hatred, and ignorance do not reside in the very nature of the mind – because the nature of the mind is clear light – the defilements can be removed without destroying the mind.

The clear light nature of the mind in its first sense as a positive phenomenon is also emphasized in Maitreya's *Sublime Continuum of the Great Vehicle (rgyud bla ma, uttaratantra)*, but it has its fullest exposition in Highest Yoga Tantras such as the *Guhyasamāja Tantra* and the *Kālachakra Tantra*. In these systems it is described as the fundamental innate mind of clear light – fundamental in the sense that its continuum exists forever, that is to say, both while one is afflicted and, after enlightenment, while unafflicted. It also is described as the all-good *(kun tu bzang po, samantabhadra)* and as the basis-of-all *(kun gzhi, ālaya)* in that it is the basis of all the phenomena both of cyclic existence and of nirvana.[9] At first, it may seem surprising that a system emphasizing suffering as much as Buddhism does should also have a doctrine of a basic goodness or basic purity of the mind, but such a foundation is essential for the radical transformation of the condition of suffering into a state of freedom.

The second way of conceiving the Buddha nature is as the absence of inherent existence[10] of the mind. This does not refer to a non-existence of the mind, nor does it refer to its lacking definition or nature, for the definition of consciousness is "that which is luminous and knowing".[11] Rather, it refers to the mind's not existing under its own power, the mind's not being established by way of its own character, the mind's not existing from its own side. This is the emptiness of the mind, which is an existent quality of the mind while at the same time being the final nature of the mind. For instance, when analyzing to determine whether a table exists in its own right, one investigates whether it is exactly the same as its parts or completely different from its parts (one of these two being required if the table *exists in its own right*), one does not find such a table, but rather finds a non-finding of the table. This non-finding is the emptiness of the table. Its emptiness is a mere absence of the table's existing from its own side; this emptiness exists and can be realized, first conceptually and eventually directly.

In terms of the mind, its emptiness also can be settled by way of many approaches, examining its production by causes, its production of effects, its relationship with the beginning, middle, and end of a moment of mind, and so forth. When, through these approaches, one realizes the emptiness of inherent existence of the mind, one can for the first time understand that the mind, and other phenomena, are falsities, appearing to exist in their own right but not existing in their own right. The conflict between appearance and fact is understood, this distortion being seen as having two aspects. One is the false appearance even to non-conceptual sensory perception of objects as if they inherently exist; the other is conceptual assent to that false appearance. This error is endemic in that not only do we innately, without any training, conceive phenomena to exist in their own right but also, even in raw sense perception, phenomena appear in a false aspect due to faults embedded deep in our minds (though not in the nature of the mind).

From this point of view all phenomena except emptiness are called *saṃvṛti-satya,* "truths-for-a-concealer", truths for a concealing consciousness, *saṃvṛti* being primarily understood as that which covers, that which obscures. "Truth" here is specified as meaning that which exists the way it appears, and only an ignorant consciousness takes objects such as tables or a mind to exist the way they appear. These objects are truths for ignorance; they are objects that are taken by ignorance to exist the way they appear.

For a non-Buddha, only emptinesses exist the way they appear in direct perception and thus emptinesses are the only truth; this does not mean that other phenomena do not exist. Both emptinesses and all other phenomena exist, objects of knowledge – existents – being what are divided into two classes: truths-for-a-concealer and ultimate truths. Emptinesses are ultimate truths in that they are objects of an ultimate consciousness and exist the way they appear in direct perception. However, an ultimate consciousness is not the final consciousness, a Buddha's omniscient consciousness, but is a non-conceptual "reasoning consciousness", so called because it is gained from having analyzed, through approaches such as those mentioned above, whether an object exists from its own side or not.

Thus, both the clear light nature of the mind and the emptiness of inherent existence of the mind are the Buddha nature, the nature of the mind that allows for transformation into Buddhahood. The Buddha nature is, therefore, the basis of purification and transformation in that it is that from the company of which defilements are removed.

THE OBJECTS OF PURIFICATION

The defilements that are removed are primarily the two types of distortion just mentioned; they are called afflictive obstructions and obstructions to omniscience. The afflictive obstructions prevent liberation from cyclic existence, the round of powerless, repeated birth, aging, sickness, and death. The primary afflictive obstruction is the ignorance conceiving that phenomena – persons and other phenomena – inherently exist, but also included are the unsalutory consciousnesses that such ignorance induces – desire, hatred, pride, enmity, belligerence, miserliness, laziness, and so forth. All of these depend on ignorance for their very existence; without ignorance and with wisdom they cannot exist. They are called afflictions *(nyon mongs, klesha)* because they afflict, they distort oneself. The most common illustration is the distortion of the face that anger brings about, but not just desire and hatred are afflictions/distortions; ignorance is the basic affliction. It is the basic bondage, the basic distortion. From its superimposition of an exaggerated status of phenomena, and entirely dependent upon it, the other distortions arise, seeming to be in the very fabric of life but actually not.

An even deeper distortion is the second type of object to be purified, the obstructions to omniscience. This is described as the *appearance* of objects as inherently existent and can only be removed after the afflictive obstructions have been eradicated. Since the primary motivation of Bodhisattvas is to help others, they mainly want to remove the obstructions to omniscience, for these are what prevent full knowledge of liberative techniques and subtle knowledge of others' minds; however, they must first remove the afflictive obstructions, subsequent to which they can gradually do away with the basic false appearance of phenomena that prevents, obstructs, and hinders knowledge of all.

THE MEANS OF PURIFICATION

Based on its twofold analysis of the nature of the mind, Great Vehicle Buddhism holds the belief that these basic errors can be removed. However, discussion, dialogue, and argument are not sufficient for their removal. Although discussion and so forth are important aspects of many persons' gaining the wisdom that phenomena do not inherently exist, realization that arises merely from such is not sufficient. A powerfully concentrated mind is also necessary. The path of developing a wisdom consciousness realizing the absence of inherent existence to the point where it can serve as an actual antidote to the afflictive obstructions depends upon developing one-pointed concentration and then alternating such one-pointed, fixed concentration with analytical meditation so that eventually analytical meditation, rather than harming stabilizing meditation, serves to induce a greater degree of stabilizing meditation, and vice versa. It is said that a calm abiding of the mind – a stability of mind – that is induced, not by stabilizing meditation, but by analytical meditation, far exceeds that induced only by stabilizing meditation.

Still, such a meditative stabilization that is a union of calm abiding and special insight is also not sufficient. The emptiness of inherent existence, which is the object of this consciousness of meditative stabilization, is being seen through the medium of a conceptual image called a meaning-generality. Gradually, the meaning-generality of emptiness is removed, one's consciousness and the emptiness of inherent existence that is its object become less and less dualistic, and finally one achieves direct perception of emptiness in a totally non-dualistic cognition. It is non-dualistic in five senses:

1 there is no conceptual appearance
2 there is no sense of subject and object – subject and object are like fresh water poured into fresh water
3 there is no appearance of inherent existence
4 there is no appearance of conventional phenomena; only emptiness appears
5 there is no appearance of difference – although the emptinesses of all phenomena in all world systems appear, they do not appear to be different.[12]

Even this degree of perception of emptiness only removes artificially gained afflictive obstructions, that is, apprehensions of inherent existence gained through the fortification of study, analysis, and systems of philosophy. It is not sufficiently powerful to remove the innate afflictive obstructions – the ignorance, desire, and so forth that even animals and babies have. For this, repeated meditation on the reality already seen is needed; one must re-enter direct perception of emptiness again and again. Much like washing dirty clothing, the grosser levels of dirt are cleansed first, and then gradually the more subtle.

In time, all of the afflictive obstructions are removed, but this process is not sufficient to remove the obstructions to omniscience, which are primarily the appearance of objects as if they exist in their own right and the predispositions in the mind that bring about this false appearance. The same wisdom consciousness must be sufficiently empowered and enhanced through the Bodhisattva practice of the altruistic deeds of giving, ethics, and patience in what are described as limitless ways over a limitless period of time. Attitudes of altruism and the concordant deeds that such motivation induces finally somehow empower the wisdom consciousness so that it can remove the basic distortion, the false appearance of phenomena. In the sūtra system presentations, this entire process is said to take three periods of "countless" eons. In Highest Yoga Tantra, it is greatly enhanced through utilizing subtler levels of consciousness such that Buddhahood can be accomplished in one lifetime.

THE FRUITS OF PURIFICATION

Although in this way the distortions of desire, hatred, and the ignorance conceiving objects to exist in their own right are removed, love, compassion, faith, and so forth are not thereby extricated because they do not depend for their existence on ignorance, no matter how much they may at times become involved with ignorance, afflictive desire, and so forth, and thus they are not removed when ignorance is removed. Love and compassion have valid cognition as their support, and since it is a quality of the mind that, once developed, such mental phenomena do not require the same effort for their production again, they can be developed limitlessly.[13]

The most basic distortions impeding full development – the obstructions to omniscience that are the appearance of objects as if they exist in their own right – are removed when altruism and altruistic deeds so enhance wisdom that no trace of false appearance remains. In this sense, altruism is in the service of wisdom, but also wisdom is in the service of altruism in that, concordant with Bodhisattvas' fundamental motivation, the full enlightenment gained through this more advanced type of wisdom allows complete, spontaneous, altruistic display in forms more numerous than the sands of the Ganges to help sentient beings in accordance with their interests and dispositions.

Buddhahood is not a state of total non-dualism as was the case with meditative equipoise on emptiness. Out of the five dualisms listed above, three exist in Buddhahood. There is no conceptual appearance, but there is a sense of subject and object in terms of realizing conventional phenomena, although not in the perspective of the omniscient consciousness's realization of emptiness, which is totally non-dualistic. There is no appearance of inherent existence but conventional phenomena appear – it is not that just emptiness appears – and thus there is appearance of difference; both the emptinesses of all phenomena in all world systems appear and those phenomena also appear. Within totally non-dual realization of the emptiness of inherent existence, a Buddha also perceives conventional phenomena, acting in myriad ways to bring about others' attainment of the same state. This is freedom from bondage and freedom for effective altruistic endeavor.

2 *Deity Yoga: The Special Tantric Technique*

Because people are of different capacities, dispositions, and interests, Shākyamuni Buddha taught many different paths.[14] He set forth sūtra and tantra; within sūtra, he taught four different schools of tenets – Great Exposition School, Sūtra School, Mind Only School, and Middle Way School – and within tantra, he set out four different sets of tantras – Action, Performance, Yoga, and Highest Yoga (literally "Unsurpassed Yoga").[15]

Within the four schools of the sūtra system he described three varieties of paths – for Hearers,[16] Solitary Realizers,[17] and Bodhisattvas. Each of the four schools has internal subdivisions, and the four divisions of tantra also contain many different types of processes and procedures of meditation. The result is that there are many different levels of commitment – ranging from the assumption of tantric vows down to the assumption of only the refuge vow – many different paths and many different styles.[18]

To appreciate the special distinctiveness of tantra, it is necessary to determine the difference between the sūtra and tantra vehicles, and to do that, first it is necessary to settle the difference between the vehicles in sūtra – the Hearers' Vehicle, Solitary Realizers' Vehicle, and Bodhisattvas' Vehicle or Great

Vehicle – and then consider the further division of the latter into its sūtra and tantra forms.

THE DIFFERENCE BETWEEN THE SŪTRA VEHICLES

"Vehicle" *(theg pa, yāna)* has two meanings:

1 Since *yā* means to go, and *na* indicates the *means* of going, a vehicle is comprised of those practices which carry one to a higher state – those practices which when actualized in the mental continuum cause manifestation of a higher type of mind.
2 Somewhat unusually, "vehicle" can also refer to the destination – that place or state at which one is aiming. This is because just as a vehicle can bear or carry a certain load, so the state of Buddhahood – the goal of the Bodhisattva Vehicle – can bear or carry the welfare of all sentient beings, whereas the state of a Low Vehicle Foe Destroyer *(dgra bcom pa, arhan)*[19] can bear much less.[20]

Since "vehicle" has these two meanings, the distinction between the two Buddhist Vehicles – Hearer and Solitary Realizer (being Low Vehicle) and Bodhisattva (or Great Vehicle) – must occur either within the sense of vehicle as the means by which one progresses or within the sense of vehicle as the destination or state to which one is progressing, or both.

In the interpretation of Low Vehicle and Great Vehicle according to the Middle Way Consequence School,[21] considered to be the acme of philosophical systems by most Tibetan schools, there is a tremendous difference between the two in the sense of vehicle as that to which one is progressing. In the Low Vehicle, practice culminates in one's becoming a Foe Destroyer, one who has overcome the foe of ignorance but is not omniscient and thus is not a Buddha. Unlike a Buddha, a Foe Destroyer does not have the ability spontaneously to manifest in various forms in order to help all beings. Since the states of being a Buddha and a Foe Destroyer are very different, there is a significant difference between the Low and Great Vehicles in the sense of vehicle as that to which one is progressing: the respective goals of Buddhahood and Foe Destroyerhood.

With this difference in goal, there must also be a difference in the two vehicles in the sense of the practices by which one progresses to these goals. The difference between the Low and Great Vehicles in terms of the means of progress can occur in only two places – method or wisdom, these two comprising the entire path, in that method mainly produces the Form Body of a Buddha and wisdom mainly produces the Truth Body.[22] In the Consequence School's interpretation, the Low and Great Vehicles do not differ with respect to wisdom in that both require realization of the subtle emptiness of inherent existence of *all* phenomena such as body, mind, head, eye, wall, consciousness, etc.[23] Although the Low and Great Vehicles do differ in terms of *how* wisdom is cultivated – how many reasonings one uses for getting at the subtle emptiness, Bodhisattvas using myriad reasonings and Hearers and Solitary Realizers only a few[24] – in terms of the object of the wisdom consciousness, the subtle emptiness of inherent existence, there is no difference between the emptiness a Low Vehicle practitioner realizes and the emptiness a Mahāyānist realizes. In this sense there is no difference in wisdom.

Since wisdom in the Low and Great Vehicles does not differ in terms of the type of emptiness being cognized, the difference between the two vehicles must lie in method.[25] "Method" here specifically means motivation and the deeds that it impels. No matter how much compassion a Low Vehicle practitioner may have, his or her primary motivation is to release oneself from cyclic existence.[26] However, in the Great Vehicle the primary motivation is the *altruistic* aspiration to highest enlightenment[27] induced by great love and compassion in which one takes on the burden of the welfare of all beings. Thus, there is a significant difference between the Low and Great Vehicles in terms of method, even though not in wisdom.[28]

Hence, the Low and Great Vehicles differ in both senses of vehicle, as the means by which one progresses as well as that to which one progresses.

THE DIFFERENCE BETWEEN THE PERFECTION VEHICLE AND THE MANTRA VEHICLE

In the Great Vehicle itself, there are two vehicles – the Perfection Vehicle and the Mantra (or Tantra) Vehicle.[29] The Perfection Vehicle is sūtra Great Vehicle, and the Mantra Vehicle is mantra or tantra Great Vehicle.

Do the sūtra Great Vehicle and the tantra Great Vehicle differ in the sense of vehicle as that to which one is progressing? The goal of the sūtra Great Vehicle is Buddhahood, and Tantrayāna cannot have another goal separate from Buddhahood as there is no attainment higher than the Buddhahood that is described in sūtra as attainment of the Truth and Form Bodies. Sūtra describes a Buddha as a being who has removed all obstructions and attained all auspicious attributes, a being who has no movement of coarse winds or inner energies;[30] thus such Buddhahood has to include the attainments of even Highest Yoga Mantra,[31] the primary aim of which is to stop the movement of all coarse winds and manifest the most subtle consciousness – the mind of clear light – simultaneously appearing in totally pure form.[32] Hence, the Vajradharahood often mentioned as the goal of tantra and the Buddhahood described in sūtra are the same.[33]

There being no difference between the Perfection Vehicle and Mantra Vehicle in terms of the goal – the destination – they must differ in the sense of vehicle as the *means* by which one progresses. They must differ either in terms of method or wisdom or both. If the difference lay in wisdom, there would be many problems because the Perfection Vehicle contains Nāgārjuna's Middle Way teachings on emptiness, and there would have to be some other more subtle emptiness than that which Nāgārjuna establishes with many different reasonings in the twenty-seven chapters of his *Treatise on the Middle Way (dbu ma'i bstan bcos, madhyamakashāstra),* whereas there is none. Thus there is no difference between sūtra and tantra in the view, which here refers to the objective view, that is, the object that is viewed *(yul gyi lta ba)* – emptiness or ultimate truth – not the realizing consciousness, since sūtra Great Vehicle and Highest Yoga Tantra do differ with respect to the subtlety of the consciousness realizing emptiness. Specifically, in Highest Yoga Tantras such as the *Kālachakra Tantra*, more subtle, enhanced consciousnesses are generated to realize the same emptiness of inherent existence. Still, because the object realized is the same whether the consciousness is more subtle or not, the "objective view" is the same.[34]

In this way, between the sūtra and tantra Great Vehicles there cannot be any difference in the factor of wisdom in terms of the object that is understood by a wisdom consciousness. Hence, the difference again has to lie in method.

In both the sūtra and tantra Great Vehicles, the basis of method is the altruistic intention to become enlightened for the sake of all sentient beings; because of this, the motivational basis of the deeds of the path is the same. The other main factor of method has to do with the deeds induced by that motivation. In sūtra Great Vehicle these are the practices induced by the altruistic aspiration – the perfections of giving, ethics, and patience. However, since these are also practiced in tantra, the difference cannot be found there either. Furthermore, tantra has an even greater emphasis than sūtra on the deeds of the perfections in that a tantric practitioner is committed to engage in them at least six times during each day.[35]

Moreover, the distinction could not be made on the basis of speed of progress on the path because within the four tantra sets – Action, Performance, Yoga, and Highest Yoga Tantra – there are great differences in speed and in sūtra Great Vehicle there are five different modes of progress, slow to fast. In addition, the difference must not lie in some small or insignificant feature, but in an important one.[36]

The profound distinction occurs in the fact that in tantra there is meditation in which one meditates on one's body as similar in aspect to a Buddha's Form Body whereas in sūtra Great Vehicle there is no such meditation. This is deity yoga,[37] which all four tantra sets have but sūtra systems do not. Deity yoga means to imagine oneself as having now the Form Body of a Buddha; one meditates on oneself in the aspect of a Buddha's Form Body,[38] imagining oneself as an ideal, altruistically active being now.

In the Perfection Vehicle there is meditation similar in aspect to a Buddha's Truth Body – a Buddha's wisdom consciousness. A Bodhisattva enters into meditative equipoise directly realizing emptiness with nothing appearing to the mind except the final nature of phenomena, the emptiness of inherent existence; the wisdom consciousness is fused with that emptiness. Even though, unlike their tantric counterparts, sūtra Bodhisattvas do not specifically imagine that the stage of meditative equipoise *is* a Buddha's Truth Body,[39] meditation similar in aspect to a Buddha's Truth Body does occur in the sūtra system in the sense that the state of meditative equipoise on emptiness mimics a Buddha's exalted wisdom consciousness in its aspect of perceiving the ultimate. However, the sūtra Perfection Vehicle does not involve meditation similar in aspect to a Buddha's *Form* Body. There is meditation on Buddhas and so forth as objects of offering, etc., but there is no meditation on oneself in the physical body of a Buddha.[40]

Such meditative cultivation of a divine body is included within the factor of method because it is mainly aimed at achieving a Buddha's Form Body. In the sūtra system the sole means for achieving a Buddha's Form Body is, on the basis of the altruistic intention to become enlightened, to engage in the first three perfections – giving, ethics, and patience – in "limitless" ways over a "limitless" period of time, specifically three periods of "countless" great eons ("countless" being said to be a one with fifty-nine zeros). Though the Mantra Vehicle also involves practice of the perfections of giving, ethics, and patience, it is not in "limitless" ways over "limitless" periods of time. Despite emphasis on the perfections, practice in "limitless" ways over "limitless" time is unnecessary because one is engaging in the additional technique of meditation on oneself in a body similar in aspect to a Buddha's Form Body.[41] In other words, in the tantric systems, in order to become a Buddha more quickly, one meditates on oneself as similar in aspect to a Buddha in terms of both body and mind. This practice is significantly distinctive and thus those systems which involve it constitute a separate vehicle, the Tantra Great Vehicle.

In deity yoga one first meditates on emptiness and then uses that consciousness realizing emptiness – or at least an imitation of it – as the basis of emanation of a Buddha. The wisdom consciousness itself appears as the physical form of a Buddha. This one consciousness thus has two parts – a factor of wisdom and a factor of method, or factors of (1) ascertainment of emptiness and (2) appearance as an ideal being – and hence, through the practice of deity yoga, one *simultaneously* accumulates the collections of merit and wisdom, making their amassing much faster.[42]

The systems that have this practice are called the *Vajra* Vehicle because the appearance of a deity is the display of a consciousness that is a *fusion* of wisdom understanding emptiness and compassion seeking the welfare of others – an inseparable union symbolized by a vajra, a diamond, the foremost of stones as it is "unbreakable".[43] Since the two elements of the fusion – compassionate method and penetrating wisdom – are the very core of the Perfection Vehicle, one can understand that sūtra and tantra, despite being different, are integrated systems. One can understand that compassion is not superseded by but essential to tantra and that the wisdom of the Perfection Vehicle is not forsaken for a deeper understanding of reality in the Tantra Vehicle.

Summary

Let us summarize the points made in this discussion. The difference between the vehicles must lie in the sense of vehicle as that by which one progresses or that to which one progresses. The Low Vehicle differs from the Great Vehicle in both. The destination of the lower one is the state of a Hearer or Solitary Realizer Foe Destroyer and of the higher one, Buddhahood. Concerning "vehicle" in the sense of means by which one progresses, although there is no difference in the wisdom realizing the subtlest nature of phenomena, there is a difference in method – Low Vehicle not having and Great Vehicle having the altruistic mind of enlightenment (that is, the altruistic intention to become enlightened) and its attendant deeds.

Sūtra and tantra Great Vehicle do not differ in terms of the goal, the state being sought, since both seek the highest enlightenment of a Buddha, but there is a difference in the means of progress, again not in wisdom but in method. Within method they differ not in the basis or motivation of the deeds, the altruistic intention to become enlightened, nor in having the perfections as deeds, but in the additional technique of deity yoga. A deity is a supramundane being who himself or herself is a manifestation of compassion and wisdom. Thus, in the special practice of deity yoga one joins one's own body, speech, mind, and activities with the exalted body, speech, mind, and activities of a supramundane being, manifesting on the path a similitude of the state of the effect.

DIFFERENCE BETWEEN THE FOUR TANTRA SETS

Within the Mantra Vehicle, there are many ways of differentiating varying numbers of tantra sets. D̄zong-ka-b̄a, in his *Great Exposition of Secret Mantra,* follows a system of division into four tantra sets – Action Tantra, Performance Tantra, Yoga Tantra, and Highest Yoga Tantra.[44] These four are differentiated not (1) by way of their *object of intent* since all four are aimed at bringing about others' welfare, nor (2) by way of the *object of attainment* they are seeking since all four seek the full enlightenment of Buddhahood, nor (3) by way of merely having different types of *deity yoga* since all four have many different types of deity yoga but are each only one tantra set.

Some say that the four tantra sets are for the different castes; however, the trainees of all four tantra sets are drawn from all levels of society, and, furthermore, not all persons of any level of society are suitable as practitioners of tantra. Others say that the four tantra sets are for persons following particular non-Buddhist deities; however, it is not necessary to take up a non-Buddhist system that has what, for Buddhism, is a wrong view on the status of persons and other phenomena before entering into the Mantra Vehicle; also, absurdly, someone who initially assumed Nāgārjuna's view of the emptiness of inherent existence could not be a main trainee of any tantra set if it were necessary first to assume a wrong view.

Others, seeing that tantra involves the usage of desire, hatred, and ignorance in the path in order to overcome those and seeing that practices are geared for persons having one or the other affliction predominant among their negative states, say that the four tantra sets are for persons dominated by particular types of afflictive emotions. However, although a certain afflictive emotion in a tantric practitioner may be predominant in the sense of being stronger than the other afflictive emotions, tantrists are simply not dominated by afflictive emotions. Rather, they are especially motivated by compassion, intent on the quickest means of attaining highest enlightenment in order to be of service to others. With regard to trainees of Highest Yoga Tantra, the Seventh Dalai Lama Ḡel-sang-gya-tso *(bskal bzang rgya mtsho,* 1708-57) says in his *Explanation of the Rite of the Guhyasamāja Mandala (gsang 'dus dkyil 'khor cho ga'i rnam bshad):*[45]

> Some see that if they rely on the Perfection Vehicle and so forth, they must amass the collections [of merit and wisdom] for three countless great eons, and thus it would take a long time and involve great difficulty. They cannot bear such hardship and seek to attain Buddhahood in a short time and by a path with little difficulty. These people who claim that they, therefore, are engaging in the short path of the Secret Mantra Vehicle are [actually] outside the realm of Mantra trainees. For to be a person of the Great Vehicle in general one cannot seek peace for oneself alone but, from the viewpoint of holding others more dear than oneself, must be able, for the sake of the welfare of others, to bear whatever type of hardship or suffering might arise. Since Secret Māntrikas are those of extremely sharp faculties within followers of the Great Vehicle, persons who have turned their backs on others' welfare and want little difficulty for themselves are not even close to the quarter of Highest Secret mantra . . . One should engage in Highest Yoga Tantra, the secret short path, with the motivation of an altruistic intention

> to become enlightened, unable to bear that sentient beings will be troubled for a long time by cyclic existence in general and by strong sufferings in particular, thinking, "How nice it would be if I could achieve right now a means to free them!"

Even though the path of the Mantra Vehicle is quicker and easier, a practitioner cannot seek it out of fearing the difficulties of the longer, Sūtra path. Rather, the quicker path is sought due to being particularly moved by compassion; a Mantra practitioner wants to achieve enlightenment sooner in order more quickly to be of service to others. The Dalai Lama has said in public lecture that proper contemplation of the difficulties and length of the Sūtra path generates greater determination and courage; this must be because contemplating one's own altruistic activity over great periods of time undermines the thresholds of impatience, anger, and discouragement. It is a ridiculous position that the trainees of Mantra, who are supposed to be the sharpest of all Bodhisattvas, would be discouraged in the face of a long path and, from that depression, seek a short path. The altruism of Māntrikas is even more intense than that of practitioners of the Perfection Vehicle.

In this vein, D̄zong-ka-b̄a, in refuting the position of the Indian scholar Alaṃkakalasha that the *Guhyasamāja Tantra* is taught to those in the merchant caste whose desire and hatred are great but whose ignorance is slight, says:[46]

> In general, the chief trainees of the Great Vehicle must have strong compassion. In particular, the chief trainees of Highest Yoga wish to attain Buddhahood extremely quickly in order to accomplish the welfare of others due to their being highly moved by great compassion. Therefore, it is nonsense to propound that they must have very great hatred.

Similarly, the Mongolian savant J̄ang-ḡya Rol-b̄ay-dor-jay *(lcang skya rol pa'i rdo rje*, 1717-86) says in his *Clear Exposition of the Presentations of Tenets, Beautiful Ornament for the Meru of the Subduer's Teaching (grub pa'i mtha'i rnam par bzhag pa gsal bar bshad pa thub bstan lhun po'i mdzes rgyan):*[47]

> It is said in the precious tantras and in many commentaries that even those trainees of the Mantra Vehicle who have low faculties must have far greater compassion, sharper faculties, and a superior lot than the trainees of sharpest faculties in the Perfection Vehicle. Therefore, those who think and propound that the Mantra Vehicle was taught for persons discouraged about achieving enlightenment over a long time and with great difficulty make clear that they have no penetration of the meaning of tantra. Furthermore, the statement that the Mantra Vehicle is quicker than the Perfection Vehicle is in relation to trainees who are suitable vessels, not in terms of just anyone. Therefore, it is not sufficient that the doctrine be the Mantra Vehicle; the person must be properly engaged in the Mantra Vehicle.

Far from being taught for those who are unable to proceed on the Perfection Vehicle, the four tantras were expounded for persons of particularly great compassion, and thus the position that the four tantra sets are for persons dominated by different types of afflictive emotions such as desire or hatred is impossible.

Others say that the four tantra sets are for persons holding the views of the four schools of Buddhist tenets. This position is equally unfounded since the Mantra Vehicle is part of the Great Vehicle both from the viewpoint of school of tenet – the view of the Mind Only School or of the Middle Way School being required – and from the viewpoint of path, a Bodhisattva's altruism being necessary.[48]

Rather, the four tantra sets are differentiated by way of their main trainees being of four very different types. Their main trainees have (1) four different ways of using desire for the attributes of the Desire Realm in the path and (2) four different levels of capacity for generating the emptiness and deity yogas that use desire in the path.

1 *Four Ways of Using Desire in the Path*

Based on descriptions of the four tantra sets found in Highest Yoga Tantras, it is said that in Action Tantra the desire involved in male and female looking or gazing at each other is used in the path; in Performance Tantra the desire involved in male and female smiling at each other is used in the path; in Yoga Tantra the desire involved in male and female embracing and touching each other is used in the path, and in Highest Yoga Tantra the desire involved in sexual union is used in the path. When desire arising from looking, smiling, holding hands or embracing, and sexual union is used in the path in conjunction with emptiness and deity yogas, desire itself is extinguished. Specifically, desire such as for sexual union leads to sexual union and, thereby, the generation of a blissfully withdrawn consciousness that the practitioner then uses to realize emptiness. The realization of the emptiness of inherent existence, in turn, destroys the possibility of desire.

The process is compared to a worm's being born from moist wood and then turning around and eating the wood. In putting together the example and the exemplified, the wood is desire; the worm is the blissful consciousness; the consumption of the wood is the blissful consciousness's destruction of desire through realizing emptiness. The reason why a blissful consciousness is used is that it is more intense, and thus realization of emptiness by such a consciousness is more powerful.

The process is most easily explained in Highest Yoga Tantra. In Highest Yoga Tantra, consciousnesses are divided into the gross, the subtle, and the very subtle. According to the system of the *Guhyasamāja Tantra,* a Highest Yoga Tantra that is parallel in importance to the *Kālachakra Tantra,* the most subtle is called the fundamental innate mind of clear light; the subtle are three levels of consciousness called the minds of radiant white, red (or orange), and black appearance; the gross are the five sense consciousnesses and the mental consciousness when not manifesting one of the above subtler levels. Through stopping the gross levels of consciousness, the more subtle become manifest. The first to manifest is a mind of radiant white appearance ("radiant" means vivid, not radiating from a center to the outside) that is described as like a clear night sky filled with moonlight, not the moon shining in empty space but space filled with white light. All conceptuality has ceased, and nothing appears except this radiant white appearance. When that mind ceases, a more subtle mind of radiant red or orange increase dawns; this is compared to a clear sky filled with sunlight, again not the sun shining in the sky but space filled with red or orange light. When this mind ceases, a still more subtle mind of radiant black near-attainment dawns; it is called "near-attainment" because one is close to manifesting the mind of clear light. The mind of black near-attainment is compared to a moonless, very black sky just after dusk when no stars shine; during the first part of this phase it is said that one remains conscious but then becomes unconscious in thick blackness. Then, with the three pollutants of the white, red, black appearances cleared away, the mind of clear light dawns; it is the most subtle level of consciousness.

The various systems of Highest Yoga Tantra seek to manifest the mind of clear light, also called the fundamental innate mind of clear light, by way of different techniques. One of these techniques is to use blissful orgasm (but without emission) to withdraw the grosser levels of consciousness, thereby manifesting the most subtle level of mind. This very powerful and subtle mind is then used to realize the emptiness of inherent existence, thereby enhancing the power of the path-consciousness realizing emptiness so that it is more effective in overcoming the obstructions to liberation and the obstructions to omniscience. This is how the desire for sexual union is used in the path in Highest Yoga Tantra; in this tantra set, the usage of desire in the path is explicitly for the sake of enhancing the wisdom consciousness realizing emptiness by way of actually generating subtler and thus more powerful consciousnesses that realize it. The difficulty of using an orgasmic blissful consciousness to realize anything indicates that it would take a person of great psychological development and capacity to be able to utilize such a subtle state in the path. It also indicates how, without the contextualization of how and why sexual union is used in the path, the practice could be mis-used or misinterpreted.

In the three lower tantras, it is said that even though such subtler consciousnesses are not generated from the desire involved in looking, smiling, and touching, the blissful consciousnesses that are generated are nevertheless used in realizing emptiness. In this way, the Mongolian scholar Nga-w̄ang-b̄el-den *(ngag dbang dpal ldan,* born 1797) says in his *Presentation of the Grounds and Paths of the Four Great Secret Tantra Sets, Illumination of the Texts of Tantra (gsang chen rgyud sde bzhi'i sa lam gyi rnam bzhag rgyud gzhung gsal byed):*[49]

> The three lower tantras involve using in the path the bliss that arises upon looking at, smiling at, and holding hands with or embracing a meditated Knowledge Woman [consort]; however, this is not done for the sake of generating a special subject [a subtle consciousness] realizing emptiness, for such is a distinguishing feature only of Highest Yoga Tantra. Nonetheless, most of [D̄zong-ka-b̄a's] followers explain that this does not mean that the bliss [consciousness] that arises upon looking, smiling, and so forth does not realize emptiness.

The utilization of the subtlest level of consciousness allows Highest Yoga Tantra to be faster for someone who is capable of practicing it, and thus only through Highest Yoga Tantra is it possible to achieve Buddhahood in one lifetime.

2 *Four Capacities for Practice*

In addition to the four different ways of using desire for the attributes of the Desire Realm in the path, the four tantra sets correspond to four different levels of capacity for generating the emptiness and deity yogas that use desire in the path. The tantric path centers around emptiness yoga and deity yoga, and practitioners have different needs or mind-sets with relation to successfully implementing these yogas. Those who make use of a great many external activities in actualizing emptiness and deity yogas are trainees of Action Tantra. However, this does not mean that Action Tantra lacks yoga, for it has a complex and very powerful yoga for developing a meditative stabilization that is a union of calm abiding and special insight;[50] rather, it means that the main trainees of Action Tantra also engage in many ritual activities such as bathing, for they find that these activities enhance their meditation.

Those who equally perform external activities and internal meditative stabilization are trainees of Performance Tantra; those who mainly rely on meditative stabilization and use only a few external activities are trainees of Yoga Tantra. Those who do not make use of external activities and yet have the capacity to generate the yoga of which there is none higher are trainees of Highest Yoga Tantra.

Still, Highest Yoga Tantra involves a great deal of ritual as will be seen in the initiation ritual and daily practice rite translated in this book; the point being made here perhaps is that Highest Yoga Tantra does not involve ritual bathing and so forth in the way that Action Tantra, etc., do.

This division of the four tantra sets by way of the capacity of their main trainees refers to their *ability* to generate the main yogas – the emptiness and deity yogas – of their respective systems within an emphasis on external activities, with balanced emphasis on external activities and internal meditative stabilization, with emphasis on meditative stabilization, and with no such external activities. The division is not made merely by way of persons who are *interested* in such paths, for some persons become interested in paths that they do not presently have a capacity to practice. As D̄zong-ka-b̄a says:[51]

> Also, though trainees in general are more, or less, interested in external activities and in cultivation of yoga, there are instances of interest in a path that does not fit a person's faculties; thus, the main trainees of the four tantra sets cannot be identified through interest.

SUMMATION

The distinctive tantric practice of deity yoga, motivated by great compassion and beginning with emptiness yoga, is carried out in different ways in the four tantra sets. Various levels of desire – involved in looking, smiling, touching, and sexual union – are utilized by the respective main trainees in accordance with their disposition to styles of practice – emphasizing external activities, balancing external activities and meditative stabilization, emphasizing meditative stabilization, or exclusively focusing on meditative stabilization. The techniques are geared to the levels of capacity of trainees as they proceed in their practice over the continuum of lifetimes, the variety of vehicles and forms being a representation of Buddha's compassionate knowledge. All tantric systems are built on a foundation of altruistic motivation and require the Bodhisattvas' altruistic deeds.

3 *Motivation: The Thirty-Seven Practices*

To enact deity yoga, it is necessary to receive initiation, and to do that, it is necessary to have, as the foundation of the path, experience of some degree of compassion and the realization of emptiness. Therefore, it is customary for a lama, preceding an initiation, to lecture on the stages of the path common to both the sūtra and tantra paths. At the Kālachakra initiation in Madison in 1981, His Holiness the Dalai Lama first lectured for three days in a large auditorium on recognition of the suffering nature of life, generation of an altruistic intention to become enlightened, and the view of the emptiness of inherent existence. An eloquent example of this type of teaching, necessary and integral to tantric practice (not just a precursor) is to be found in the Dalai Lama's *Kindness, Clarity, And Insight*[52] in the chapter entitled "The Path to Enlightenment" (pp.118-156).

The emphasis on recognizing suffering and generating compassion is not just brought over from sūtra practice but is essential to tantra itself. The Initiation Chapter of the *Kālachakra Tantra* (stanza 12) speaks eloquently about suffering:

> In the womb there is the suffering of dwelling in the womb; at birth and while a child there is also suffering.
>
> Youth and adulthood are filled with the great suf-

ferings of losing one's mate, wealth, and fortune, as well as the great suffering of the afflictive emotions.
The old have the suffering of death and again the fright of the six transmigrations such as the Crying and so forth.
All these transmigrating beings, deluded by illusion, grasp suffering from suffering.

(For the Dalai Lama's commentary on this, see pp. 196-197) Also, the compiler of the tantra, Mañjushrīkīrti, illustrates his compassion with protective wishes:[53]

Just as those of the lineage of sages along with Ravi came to attain knowledge-wisdom from this [tantra],
So may sentient beings dwelling in the three forms of cyclic existence become the same through the kindness of the *Kālachakra* [*Tantra*].

And:

In just the way that my mind-vajra dwells throughout the earth for the sake of liberating sentient beings,
So may it dwell in the three forms of cyclic existence of sentient beings through the force of Kālachakra.

And:

May the Bodhisattvas above [the earth] who supremely frighten the demi-gods dwelling in the class of demons,
The wrathful kings as well as their consorts who dwell in the directions and intermediate directions in the worlds of humans,
And the kings of hooded serpents under the earth who at all times bind up the groups of evil spirits and unvirtuous ones –
May all of them protect unknowing worldly beings in all respects each day.

Still, despite the fact that compassion is the basic motivation for the practice of tantra and integral to its practice, the best presentations of how to cultivate compassion are found in the Sūtra Great Vehicle. A famous example of advice on how to cultivate both compassion and the attitudes that are necessary prerequisites to it is the *The Thirty-Seven Practices (lag len so bdun ma)* by a scholar of the Sa-gya order of Tibetan Buddhism known as the Bodhisattva Tok-may-sang-bo *(rgyal sras thogs med bzang po,* 1245-1369).[53a] since it easily gives a feeling for the humble and altruistic attitudes that motivate a Bodhisattva's endeavors, a translation of these renowned stanzas is included here.

THE THIRTY-SEVEN PRACTICES

By the Bodhisattva Tok-may-sang-bo

Homage to Avalokiteshvara.

Respectful homage always through the three doors of body, speech, and mind
To the supreme lamas and the protector Avalokiteshvara
Who though perceiving that all phenomena have no going or coming
Make effort single-pointedly for the welfare of transmigrators.

The perfect Buddhas, the sources of help and happiness,
Arise from having practiced the excellent doctrine.
That in turn depends on knowing its practices.
Therefore, I will explain the practices of Bodhisattvas.

1 It is a practice of Bodhisattvas –
For the sake of freeing themselves and others from the ocean of cyclic existence –
To hear, think, and meditate day and night without deviation
Here at this time of having attained the great ship of leisure and fortune hard to gain.

2 It is a practice of Bodhisattvas to give up their fatherland
That has, like water, the fluctuations of desire for the class of friends,

That, like fire, has burning hatred for the class of enemies,
And that has the darkness of obscuration forgetting to adopt and discard.

3 It is a practice of Bodhisattvas to resort to isolation –
Through abandoning bad objects the afflictive emotions gradually diminish,
Through the absence of distraction application to virtue naturally increases,
Through clarity of mind ascertainment of doctrine is generated.

4 It is a practice of Bodhisattvas to renounce this life –
Close friends who companied together for a long time separate,
The wealth and articles achieved with striving are left behind,
And the guest-house of the body is left by the guest of consciousness.

5 It is a practice of Bodhisattvas to abandon bad friends
Who, when accompanied, increase the three poisons [of desire, hatred, and ignorance],
Cause the activities of hearing, thinking, and meditating to deteriorate,
And make love and compassion non-existent.

6 It is a practice of Bodhisattvas to hold more dearly
Than their own body the excellent spiritual guide
Who when relied upon causes faults to be removed
And good qualities to increase like a waxing moon.

7 Who could be protected by a worldly deity
Himself also bound in the prison of cyclic existence?
Therefore, it is a practice of Bodhisattvas to go for refuge
To the Three Jewels which are undeceiving when refuge is sought.

8 The Subduer said that the sufferings of bad transmigrations
Very difficult to bear are the fruits of ill-deeds.
Therefore, it is a practice of Bodhisattvas never to do
Ill-deeds though it comes down to their life.

9 The happiness of the three realms of cyclic existence,
Like dew on the tip of a blade of grass, disintegrates after a brief time.
[Therefore] it is a practice of Bodhisattvas to seek
The supreme state of immutable liberation.

10 What is the use of one's own happiness if mothers
Who were kind to oneself since beginningless time suffer?
Therefore, it is a practice of Bodhisattvas to generate the altruistic intention to become enlightened
In order to free limitless sentient beings.

11 All suffering arises from wanting happiness for oneself
Whereas the perfect Buddhas are born from altruism.
Therefore, it is a practice of Bodhisattvas to switch completely
Their own happiness for others' suffering.

12 Even if someone out of great desire steals all their wealth
Or sends another to steal it away,
It is a practice of Bodhisattvas to dedicate to that person
Their body, resources, and virtues of the three times.

13 Even if someone hacks away at their head
When they do not have the slightest fault
It is a practice of Bodhisattvas out of compassion
To take to themselves the ill-deeds of that person.

14 Even if someone proclaims throughout the billion worlds
Various types of ill-repute about them,
It is a practice of Bodhisattvas to speak with a mind of love
Of the good qualities of that person.

15 Even if someone crowds into the middle of a gathering of many beings
And accusingly speaks bad words about them,
It is a practice of Bodhisattvas to bow respectfully
With a discrimination of that person as a spiritual guide.

16 Even if a person sustained dearly like their own child
Views them as an enemy,
It is a practice of Bodhisattvas to be greatly merciful
Like a mother to her child stricken with illness.

17 Even if a being equal with or below them
Derides them out of pride,
It is a practice of Bodhisattvas respectfully to take
That person to the crown of their head like a guru.

18 Though they are bereft of livelihood, always despised by people,
And afflicted by awful illness and demons,
It is a practice of Bodhisattvas without discouragement
To take all beings' ill-deeds and sufferings to themselves.

19 Though they are famous, respected by many beings,
And have attained the likes of the wealth of Vaishravana,
It is a practice of Bodhisattvas to be uninflated,
Seeing the essencelessness of the glory and wealth of cyclic existence.

20 If the internal enemy of hatred is not tamed,
When one tries to tame external enemies they increase.
Therefore, it is a practice of Bodhisattvas to tame their own continuum
By means of the soldiers of love and compassion.

21 The attributes of the Desire Realm, like salt water,
Increase attachment no matter how much they are used.
Therefore, it is a practice of Bodhisattvas to abandon immediately
Things generating attachment and desire.

22 Whatever appears is one's own mind; the mind itself
Is free from the start from the extremes of elaborations.
It is a practice of Bodhisattvas through knowing just that
Not to take to mind the signs of object and subject.

23 When they meet with attractive objects,
It is a practice of Bodhisattvas to view them as untrue –
Even though appearing to be beautiful like a summer rainbow –
And to abandon attachment and desire.

24 Like the death of a child in a dream, through holding the erroneous appearances

Of the varieties of suffering to be true one makes oneself so tired.
Therefore, it is a practice of Bodhisattvas when meeting
With unfavorable conditions to view them as erroneous.

25 If it is necessary for those who want enlightenment to give up even their body,
What need to say anything about external things?
Therefore, it is a practice of Bodhisattvas to give gifts
Without hope for reward or fruition for themselves.

26 If without proper ethics one's own welfare cannot be achieved,
To assert that others' welfare could be achieved is a source of laughter.
Therefore, it is a practice of Bodhisattvas to keep ethics
Without aspirations involved in cyclic existence.

27 For a Bodhisattva wanting the resources [arising] from virtues
All harmers are like a treasure of jewels.
Therefore, it is a practice of Bodhisattvas to cultivate patience
Without anger or resentment for anyone.

28 In that even Hearers and Solitary Realizers achieving only their own welfare
Are seen to make effort as one would to stop a fire on one's own head,
It is a practice of Bodhisattvas to make effort,
A source of good qualities for the sake of all transmigrators.

29 Understanding that the afflictive emotions are completely conquered
Through special insight thoroughly endowed with calm abiding,
It is a practice of Bodhisattvas to cultivate concentration
That exceeds even the four formless absorptions.

30 Since one cannot attain perfect enlightenment
Through the [other] five perfections without wisdom,

It is a practice of Bodhisattvas to cultivate the wisdom
Possessing method and not conceptualizing the spheres [of object, agent, and action as inherently existent].

31 If one does not analyze one's own mistakes,
One can perform non-practices with the form of a practitioner.
Therefore, it is a practice of Bodhisattvas continually to examine
Their own mistakes and abandon them.

32 If due to afflictive emotions Bodhisattvas speak fault
Of another Bodhisattva, they themselves degenerate.
Therefore, it is a practice of Bodhisattvas not to speak of the faults
Of persons who have entered into the Great Vehicle.

33 To dispute back and forth out of [wanting] goods and services
Causes the activities of hearing, thinking, and meditating to deteriorate.
Therefore, it is a practice of Bodhisattvas to abandon attachment
To the households of friends and patrons.

34 Harsh words disturb others' minds and cause the mode
Of a Bodhisattva's behavior to deteriorate.
Therefore, it is a practice of Bodhisattvas to abandon
Harsh words about the unpleasantness of others.

35 If one becomes accustomed to the afflictive emotions,
They are hard to overcome through their antidotes.
Therefore, it is a practice of Bodhisattvas to overcome
The afflictive emotions of desire and so forth immediately upon their first being produced.

36 In brief, it is the practice of Bodhisattvas to achieve
Others' welfare through continually possessing mindfulness and introspection,
[Knowing] the state of their mind
In each and every form of behavior.

37 It is a practice of Bodhisattvas to dedicate to enlightenment
With the wisdom of the purity of the three spheres [of object, agent, and action]
The virtues achieved with effort in this way
In order to remove the suffering of limitless transmigrators.

For the sake of those wishing to train in the Bodhisattva path
I have written down these thirty-seven practices of Bodhisattvas,
Meanings related in the sūtras, tantras, and treatises,
Drawing on the speech of the excellent.

Because my intelligence is low and training slight,
This is not poetry to delight scholars.
However, because it relies on sūtras and the words of the excellent,
I think it is the unmistaken practice of Bodhisattvas.

Still, it is difficult for one with a low mind such as mine
To penetrate the depths of the great waves of the Bodhisattva deeds.
Therefore, the excellent are asked to bear with
The groups of faults – contradictions, unrelatedness, and so forth.

Through the virtue arising from this may all transmigrators
Become the same as the protector Avalokiteshvara,
Not abiding in the extremes of cyclic existence and [solitary] peace
Through the supreme minds of enlightenment, ultimate and conventional.

4 *Emptiness Yoga*

With compassion and an altruistic intention to become enlightened as their bases, practitioners must also probe the nature of phenomena, generating wisdom realizing the emptiness of inherent existence. Otherwise, innate false superimpositions on phenomena of a goodness or badness beyond that which they actually have will lead to the biased and distorted states of desire and hatred. The process of cultivating such wisdom involves meditating on the selflessness of persons and on the selflessness of other phenomena. The following description of these practices is based, for the most part, on the concise and lucid explanation of the perfection of wisdom in the Fifth Dalai Lama's *Sacred Word of Mañjushrī ('jam dpal zhal lung)*.[54]

Meditation on both the selflessness of persons and of phenomena is framed around four essential steps:

1 ascertaining what is being negated
2 ascertaining entailment
3 ascertaining that the object designated and its basis of designation are not inherently one
4 ascertaining that the object designated and its basis of designation are not inherently different.

FIRST ESSENTIAL: ASCERTAINING WHAT IS BEING NEGATED

With respect to the selflessness of a person, specifically of yourself, the first step is to identify the way we innately misconceive the I to exist inherently. If you do not have a fairly clear sense of an inherently existent I, you will mistake the refutation as negating the I itself rather than a specific reification of the I. Shāntideva's *Engaging in the Bodhisattva Deeds (byang chub sems dpa'i spyod pa la 'jug pa, bodhisattvacharyā-vatāra*, IX.140) says:

> Without contacting the superimposed existent,
> Its non-existence cannot be apprehended.

If an image of the object of negation does not appear well to the mind, the meaning of the selflessness that negates it cannot be ascertained.

The Ge-luk-b̄a order of Tibetan Buddhism makes a clear differentiation between the existent self and the non-existent self as it is posited in each of the four major Buddhist schools of tenets – Great Exposition School, Sūtra School, Mind Only School, and Middle Way School. This assumes a dual meaning to the term "self" – the first, existent one as the person or I and the second, non-existent one as a reification of the status of any object, the reification here being inherent existence *(rang bzhin gyis grub pa, svabhāvasiddhi).*

This distinction is upheld through the observation that when the I is apprehended, there are basically three possibilities with respect to how it is being conceived in relation to the other meaning of "self", inherent existence:

1 You may be conceiving the I to be inherently existent.
2 Or, if you have understood the view of the Middle Way School, you may conceive the I as only being nominally existent.
3 Or, whether you have understood the view of the Middle Way School or not, you may conceive the I without qualifying it with either inherent existence or an absence of inherent existence.

Though uneducated common beings do not *propound* either inherent existence or nominal imputation, the I does appear to them to be inherently existent, and because they sometimes assent to that appearance – though without reasoning – they also have a conception of an inherently existent I. Also, they, like all other beings, even including those who have been educated in wrong systems of tenets, have consciousnesses that do not engage in conceptions of inherent existence, such as when just conceiving of themselves without any particular attention. Therefore, it is not that all consciousnesses conceiving I in the continuum of a falsely educated person are wrong or that all consciousnesses conceiving I in the continuum of uneducated persons are right. Rather, both the uneducated and the falsely educated have the misconception of an inherently existent I as well as consciousnesses conceiving an I that is not qualified by being either nominally imputed or inherently existent.

Still, neither the falsely educated nor the uneducated can distinguish between an imputedly existent I and an inherently existent I. Both must become educated in the Middle Way view of non-inherent existence and imputed existence in order to overcome their innate tendency to assent to the false appearance of the I as if inherently existent, existing from its own side, or existing under its own power. This is the immediate purpose of meditation on selflessness.

The first step in this meditation is to gain a clear sense of the reified status of the I as inherently existent. Even though such a misconception of I is subliminally always present, a condition of its obvious manifestation is required. Therefore, the meditator remembers a situation of false accusation that elicited a strong response or remembers a situation of happiness that did the same, trying to watch the type of I that manifested and how the mind assented to its ever so concrete appearance. Since watchfulness itself tends to cause this gross level of misconception of the I as inherently existent to disappear, the first essential is recognized as very difficult to achieve. One has to learn how to let the mind operate in its usual egoistic way and at the same time watch it, keeping watchfulness at a minimum such that the usual conception of a very concrete and pointable I is generated. The demand for watchfulness is mitigated by the need to allow what is usually unanalyzed to operate of its own accord.

When success is gained, the meditator has found a sense of

an inherently existent I that is totally convincing. As the Dalai Lama said while lecturing to Tibetan scholars in Dharamsala, India, in 1972, one has such strong belief in this reified I that upon identifying it, one has the feeling that if it is not true, nothing is. It would seem, therefore, that the first step in developing the view of the Middle Way is the stark and intimate recognition that for the meditator the opposite of that view seems to be true.

In the face of this particular consciousness, mind and body are not differentiated, and the I is not differentiated from mind and body. However, the I is seen to be self-established, self-instituting, under its own power, existing in its own right. It is not that you have the sense that mind, body, and I *cannot* be differentiated; rather, for *that* consciousness, mind, body, and I simply are not differentiated. For instance, for a consciousness merely apprehending a particular city, say, Chicago, the ground, buildings, and people of that city are not differentiated. These are the bases of designation of Chicago, which seems inextricably blended with them and yet has its own thing.

Recognition of such an appearance with respect to the I and recognition of your assent to this appearance constitute the first essential step in realizing selflessness, emptiness. With this identification, analysis can work on that object; without it, analysis is undirected. From the viewpoint of the Ge-luk-b̄a tradition of Tibetan Buddhism it would seem that most Western attempts to penetrate emptiness fail at this initial step, tending either to assume that the phenomenon itself is being refuted or that a superficial, philosophically constructed quality of the phenomenon, rather than one innately misconceived, is being refuted.

SECOND ESSENTIAL: ASCERTAINING ENTAILMENT

Whereas in the first step the meditator allows an ordinary attitude to operate and attempts to watch it without interfering, in the second step the meditator makes a non-ordinary, intellectual decision that must be brought gradually to the level of feeling. Here, you consider the number of possible relationships between a phenomenon designated and its basis of designation.

Phenomena designated are things such as a table, a body, a person, and a house. Their respective bases of designation are four legs and a top, five limbs (two arms, two legs, and a head) and a trunk, or mind and body, and a number of rooms arranged in a certain shape. The meditator considers whether within the framework of inherent existence these two – phenomenon designated and basis of designation – must be either inherently the same or inherently different or whether there are other possibilities. If there seem to be other possibilities, can these be collapsed into the original two – being inherently the same or being inherently different?

Nāgārjuna is interpreted as listing five possibilities and Chandrakīrti two more beyond the five:

1 inherently the same
2 inherently different
3 the object designated inherently depends on the basis of designation
4 the basis of designation inherently depends on the object designated
5 the object designated possesses the basis of designation either as a different entity in the way a person owns a cow or as one entity in the way a tree possesses its core
6 the object designated is the special shape of the basis of designation
7 the object designated is the collection of the bases of designation.

The last five can be collapsed into the first two as refinements of them: The third and fourth are forms of difference; the first aspect of the fifth is a form of difference; the second, a form of sameness of entity; the sixth and seventh are variations of sameness. Hence, it is claimed that all possibilities of inherent existence can be collapsed into the original two.

Conventionally, however, it is said that the I and its basis of designation, mind and body, are different, but not different entities, and the same entity but not the same. This is technically called being one entity and different isolates[55] – essentially meaning that conceptuality can isolate the two. Why not consider this an eighth possibility?

If the relationship of being one entity and different isolates is within the context of inherent existence, then this possibility is internally contradictory since within the context of inherent existence whatever is inherently the same is the same in all respects, making different isolates impossible. However, if the relationship of being one entity and different isolates is within the context of conventional existence, then there is no need to include it here in this list of possibilities within inherent existence.

The list of possibilities, therefore, does not include all possibilities of the existence of a phenomenon designated – such as the I – and its bases of designation – such as mind and body – because the examination here is concerned only with whether the I exists in the *concrete* manner it was seen to have during the first essential. If it does exist so concretely, you should be able to point concretely to it when examining it with respect to its basis of designation.

Since this decision – that inherent existence involves the necessity of the phenomenon designated being either one with or different from the basis of designation – is the anvil on which the sense of an inherently existent I will be pounded by the hammer of the subsequent reasoning, the second essential is not an intellectually airy decision to be taken lightly. It must be brought to the level of feeling, this being done through considering that anything existent is either one or different, as the great eighteenth century Mongolian scholar J̄ang-ḡya *(lcang skya rol pa'i rdo rje*, 1717-86) says in his *Presentation of Tenets (grub mtha'i rnam bzhag.)*[56] A chair is one; a chair and a table are different; a chair and its parts are different; tables are different, etc. The yogi must heroically set standards that intelligently limit the possibilities so that the subsequent analysis can work, causing disbelief in such an inherently existent I.

Upon coming to this decision, you begin to doubt the existence of the self-instituting I identified in the first essential. Geshe Rabten, a contemporary Ge-luk-b̄a scholar living in Switzerland,[57] compared the effect of this step to having doubts about an old friend for the first time. The emotionally harrowing experience of challenging your own long believed status has begun.

THIRD ESSENTIAL: ASCERTAINING THAT THE I AND THE AGGREGATES ARE NOT ONE

The next step is to use reasoning to determine whether the I and the mental and physical aggregates could be inherently the same or inherently different. Reasoning, here, is a matter not of cold deliberation or superficial summation but of using various approaches to find one that can shake yourself to your being. Since this is the case, the seeming simple-mindedness and rigidity of the reasonings suggested must be transcended.

A *series* of approaches, rather than just one reasoning, is used on the assumption that certain of the reasonings would not work for some people. The first is a challenge from common experience: If the I were one with the body, how could we speak of "my body"? If the I were inherently one with the mind, how could we speak of "my mind"? Should we also speak of the body's body? Or my I?

Still, the Fifth Dalai Lama does not seem to expect that this will be sufficient; he continues with a citation from Nāgārjuna on the same reasoning:

> If, upon thinking thus, [your attempt at understanding] is merely verbal and you do not gain strong conviction, contemplate the following. Nāgārjuna's *Treatise on the Middle Way (rtsa shes/ dbu ma'i bstan bcos, madhyamakashāstra*, XXVII.27) says:
>
> When it is taken that there is no self
> Except the appropriated [aggregates],
> The appropriated [aggregates] themselves are the self.
> If so, your self is non-existent.

The interpretation among Ge-luk-ba scholars is not that Nāgārjuna thought that beings commonly conceive the I to be one with body or one with mind. Rather, his thought is that *if* the I inherently exists, then oneness with its basis of designation would be one of only two exhaustive possibilities. Nāgārjuna's reference is not to ordinary misconception but to a *consequence* of inherent existence, such concreteness requiring a pointable identification under analysis.

The rules for inherent existence, therefore, are not the rules for mere existence. Within the context of concrete existence, sameness of entity requires utter oneness in all respects. Thus, the question is not whether beings ordinarily conceive of such oneness, since it is not claimed that we do, but whether the rules of concrete, pointable existence – the way we experience the I as was discovered in the first essential – are appropriate.

More Reasonings

Permutations of the same reasoning need to be considered; the mere presence of the reasoning is clearly not expected to be convincing. For these permutations to work, the meditator must have gained belief in rebirth. If the I and the body are one, after death when the body is burned, the I also would be burned. Or, just as the I transmigrates to the next life, so the body also would have to transmigrate. Or, just as the body does not transmigrate, so the I also would not transmigrate.

If due to having meditated on such reasonings, you come to think that the I is probably not the same as the body but is probably one with the mind, you are instructed to consider the following fallacies. Since it is obvious that the suffering of cold arises when the I is without clothes and that the sufferings of hunger and thirst arise when the I lacks food and drink, these would – if the I were merely mental – be mental in origin, in which case you could not posit a reason why the same suffering would not be experienced in a life in a Formless Realm. Since the mind would be one with the I, it would still have to make use of gross forms such as food and clothing.

The above permutations of oneness will have prepared the mind for reaching a conclusion upon reflecting on a few more reasonings. First, the selves would have to be as many as mind and body, that is to say, two; or, put another way, the selves would have to be as many as the five aggregates, five. This may seem extraordinarily simple-minded, but the requirements of such pointable, analytically findable existence – not the requirements of mere existence – are the anvil. The meditator is attempting through this analysis, not to describe how he or she ordinarily conceives such an inherently existent I, but to subject such an I to the hammering of probing reasoning based on *consequences* of such inherent existence.

The second additional reasoning revolves around the entailment that the I would have inherently existent production and disintegration, in which case it would be discontinuous. The third depends upon a belief in rebirth and thus reflects the type of reasoning, in reverse, that many use against rebirth. Its concern is not explicitly with the I and the mental and physical aggregates that are its bases of designation but the relationship between the I of this life and the I of the last life. It is: If they were one, then the sufferings of the former life would absurdly have to be present in this life.

If they were different, which by the rules of inherent existence would make them totally, unrelatedly different, remembrance of former lives would become impossible. Moral retribution would be impossible. Undeserved suffering would be experienced. Such difference would make a mere-I, the agent that travels from lifetime to lifetime, engaging in actions and experiencing their effects, impossible.

Oneness of the I and its bases of designation – the mental and physical aggregates – is impossible.

FOURTH ESSENTIAL: ASCERTAINING THAT THE I AND THE AGGREGATES ARE NOT INHERENTLY DIFFERENT

The meditator has been so disturbed by the analysis of oneness that he or she is ready to assume difference. However, the rules of inherent existence call for the different to be unrelatedly different, again the assumption being not that persons ordinarily consider the I and its bases of designation to be unrelatedly different but that within the context of inherent existence, that is, of such pointable, solid existence, difference necessitates unrelatedness. The Fifth Dalai Lama says:

> Now, you might think that the I and the five aggregates cannot be anything but different. Chandrakīrti's *Supplement* (VI.120ab) says:
>
> > There is no self other than the aggregates because,
> > Apart from the aggregates, its conception does not
> > exist.
>
> The inherently different must be unrelated. Therefore, just as within the aggregates you can identify each individually, "This is the aggregate of form," and so forth, so after clearing away the five aggregates you would have to be able to identify the I, "This is the I." However, no matter how finely you analyze, such an I is not at all to be found.

The I, self, or ultimate reality that is left over when all else is removed is exactly what many Hindus are seeking to find; therefore, they would loudly exclaim the contrary: Something *is* found separate from mind and body. But would this be the I that goes to the store? Would this be the I that desires? Hates?

Still, the question is not easy to settle, and it does not appear that easy answers are wanted. Rather, deeply felt conviction is needed.

REALIZATION OF SELFLESSNESS AND DEITY YOGA

With such conviction, the decision reached is that the I cannot be found under such analysis; this shows, not that the I does not exist, but that it does not inherently exist as it was identified as seeming to in the first essential. This unfindability is emptiness itself, and realization of it is realization of emptiness, selflessness.

Incontrovertible inferential realization, though not of the level of direct perception or even of special insight *(lhag mthong, vipashyanā)*, has great impact. For a beginner it generates a sense of deprivation, but for an experienced meditator it generates a sense of discovery or recovery of what was lost. The perception of this vacuousness – the absence of inherent existence – carries emotional overtones, first of loss since our emotions are built on a false sense of concreteness and then of discovery of a lost treasure that makes everything possible. From a similar point of view, the emptiness of the mind is called the Buddha nature, or Buddha lineage, since it is what allows for development of the marvelous qualities of Buddhahood.

In tantric deity yoga, the mind realizing emptiness and motivated by compassion is used as the basis of emanation of a deity such as Kālachakra. The compassionately motivated wisdom consciousness itself provides the stuff of the deity. At the same time as it is appearing as a deity – an ideal person altruistically helping beings – it maintains ascertainment of the absence of inherent existence of the deity. Thereby, the two collections of merit (altuistic deeds) and wisdom (realization of emptiness) are accumulated simultaneously, the two aspects of compassion and wisdom being contained within the entity of one consciousness. Thus, deity yoga is founded on the very heart of the sūtra path of the Great Vehicle, compassion and realization of emptiness. Tantric initiation authorizes those who have some experience of compassion and a degree of understanding of emptiness to practice deity yoga.

5 *History of the Kālachakra Tantra*

According to traditional, sacred history, on the fifteenth day of the third month, a year after his enlightenment, Shākyamuni Buddha appeared at Vulture Peak in the attire of a monk, setting forth the *Perfection of Wisdom Sūtra in One Hundred Thousand Stanzas*, and simultaneously he appeared at Dhānyakaṭaka in South India as Kālachakra, setting forth the *Kālachakra Tantra*.[58] The tantra was preached inside a huge, many levelled monument *(mchod rten, chaitya)*; the location, Dhānyakaṭaka, is identified by George Roerich as Amarāvati in the Sattenpalle Tāluka of Guṇṭūr District, Madras, South India.[59]

The tantra was expounded at the request of King Suchandra,[60] an emanation of Vajrapāṇi, who thereupon compiled the tantra in its long form, said to be twelve thousand stanzas. King Suchandra was from Shambhala, which G. Tucci[61] says "tradition places near the river Sītā (viz. Tarim)," East Turkestan.[62] After hearing the tantra, the King returned to Shambhala, wrote a long exposition of it, and propagated Kālachakra Buddhism as the state religion.

The next six kings of Shambhala maintained the tradition, and the eighth king, Mañjushrīkīrti *('jam dpal grags pa)* initiated so many persons (reportedly thirty-five million seers)[63] into the Kālachakra mandala that he, and subsequent kings, were called *kulika (rigs ldan)*, "one who bears the lineage". Based on the long root tantra, Kulika Mañjushrīkīrti composed a shorter tantra of five chapters, which has one thousand forty-seven stanzas.[64] Named the *Condensed Kālachakra Tantra (bsdus rgyud, laghutantra)*, it is what is currently called the *Kālachakra Tantra*, the longer version not being extant.

Kulika Mañjushrīkīrti was followed by Kulika Puṇḍarīka who composed the currently most famous exposition of the tantra, commonly called the *Great Commentary on the "Kālachakra Tantra", the Stainless Light ('grel chen dri med 'od, vimālaprabhā)*. It is still extant and most likely served as the basis for the subsequent literature.

Another eight hundred years after Kulika Puṇḍarīka, a Moslem invasion weakened the kingdom, this being in 624 A.D.[65] Nevertheless, the lineage of Kulika Kings continued such that the Indian master Chilupā[66] from Orissa travelled to Shambhala and became an expert in the tantra and in Kulika Puṇḍarīka's *Great Commentary*. He returned to India in 966 A.D., and disseminated the teaching, bringing it to prominence there. The author of *The Blue Annals*, the Translator from Gö, Shön-nu-bel (*'gos lo tsā ba bzhon nu dpal*, 1392-1481) argues cogently that the *Kālachakra Tantra* had reappeared in India long before that time, since, among other reasons, Chilupā:[67]

> . . . had read (it) in the vihāra of Ratnagiri (Rin-čhen ri-bo) which had been left undamaged by the Turuṣkhas, and was of the opinion that, in general, for the (attainment) of Enlightenment the Mahāyāna Guhyamantra (gsaṅ-sṅags) was necessary, and that the text had to be studied with the help of the commentary by the Bodhisattvas. Accordingly he proceeded in search of the Kālacakra (so the Kālacakra must have been in existence at that time). Thus it has to be admitted that the system of Kālacakra seems to have reached Āryadeśa [India] at an early date and that (the system) became known to many people in the time of Kālacakrapāda, father and son.

It is likely that Kālachakrapāda the greater ("Kālacakrapāda, father" in the above reference) is Chilupā himself.[68] Helmut Hoffman reports that Chilupā defeated in debate "Pandit Nādapāda, called Nā-ro-pa by the Tibetans" who was then abbot of Nālandā, "which was, together with Vikramashīlā, the most important centre of Buddhism in those days."[69] Chilupā initiated Nāḍapāda, who became known as the Lesser Kālachakrapāda.[70] Hoffman concludes:[71]

> It would seem that the whole further tradition of Kālacakra derived from these two, not only in India but also in Tibet.

Nāḍapāda, in turn, initiated Atīsha into the Kālachakra system, and among Atīsha's students was the famous Kālachakra master Pi-to-pa, also called Pindo Āchārya.[72]

In the histories, there is agreement that the *Kālachakra Tantra* came to be widely known in India from 966 A.D. with Chilupā's return and "became effective in India under King Mahīpāla of Bengal (*c*.974-1026.)"[73]

That even according to the traditional, sacred history the *Kālachakra Tantra* was absent in India for such a long period of time has led to the suspicion that it was written in a Central Asian country. Lokesh Chandra says:[74]

> The Kālacakra is one of the last Sanskrit works to have been written in a Central Asian land whence it is said to have travelled into India.

With Chilupā's efforts, the system was developed in India,[75] spawning numerous compositions on various aspects of the tantra; beyond Kulika Puṇḍarīka's *Great Commentary*, Lokesh Chandra lists forty-seven works by twenty-two authors (including six anonymous works).[76] Sixty years after Chilupā's return, the *Kālachakra Tantra* was introduced into Tibet, this being in 1026,[77] and quickly gave rise to a flourishing tradition.

The first translation was by Gyi-jo, who studied under Bhadrabodhi, a pupil of Chilupā,[78] but "he had only four pupils, and even they did not maintain the tradition after him."[79] A student of Nāḍapāda, the Kashmiri Somanātha, went to Tibet and, after Ye-s̄hay-chok *(ye shes mchog)* of N̄yö *(gnyos)* did not live up to a promise to present him with one hundred ounces of gold, travelled to a region just north of Hla-s̄a, called Pen-b̄o *('phan po)* where with the Translator of Dro, Shay-rap-drak *('bro lo tsā ba shes rab grags)* he completed a translation of Kulika Puṇḍarīka's *Great Commentary on the "Kālachakra Tantra", the Stainless Light*, and a transmission known as the school of Dro was begun.

The other important tradition was the school of the Translator of Ra, Dor-jay-drak-b̄a *(rva lo tsā ba rdo rje grags pa)* who studied the *Kālachakra Tantra* for almost six years in Kashmir with Samantashrī, another former student of Nādapāda. He persuaded his teacher to return with him to Tibet, three hundred ounces of gold being the offering, and the Ra school thereupon became particularly important in the S̄a-ḡya order of Tibetan Buddhism. Through S̄a-ḡya Paṇḍiṭa (1182-1251) and then Pak-b̄a *('phags pa)* the Ra tradition came to have important influence in the period of heavy Mongolian involvement in Tibet. Bu-d̄ön Rin-chen-drup *(bu ston rin chen grub*, 1290-1364) and Dol-b̄a-b̄a S̄hay-rap-gyel-tsen *(dol pa pa shes rab rgyal mtshan*, 1292-1361) of the S̄a-ḡya order who are called "the two great expounders of the Kālachakra in the Land of Snows",[80] received teachings from transmissions stemming from both the Translator Ra and the Translator Dro.

Bu-d̄ön Rin-chen-drup, in particular, wrote prolifically on the *Kālachakra Tantra;* the first five volumes of his Collected Works are devoted solely to these expositions, ranging from an annotated version of the tantra called *Easily Understandable Annotations For the Condensed Glorious Kālachakra Tantra, Great King of Tantras Arisen from the Supreme Original Buddha (mchog gi dang po'i sangs rgyas las phyungs ba rgyud kyi rgyal po chen po dpal dus kyi 'khor lo'i bsdus pa'i rgyud kyi go sla'i mchan)*, to *Annotations to (Kulika Puṇḍarīka's) "Stainless Light" (dri med 'od kyi mchan)*, to numerous texts on topics ranging from the six-branched yoga to astrology to initiation, and so forth.[81]

Bu-d̄ön's disciple, Chö-ḡyi-b̄el *(chos kyi dpal)*, conferred the Kālachakra initiation on D̄zong-ka-b̄a *(tsong kha pa*, 1357-1419), the founder of the Ge-luk-b̄a order of Tibetan Buddhism, who himself wrote several short works on aspects of the tantra.[82] D̄zong-ka-b̄a's disciple, Kay-drup-ge-lek-b̄el-sang *(mkhas grub dge legs dpal bzang,* 1385-1438) composed a gigantic work of four volumes in commentary on the *Condensed Kālachakra Tantra* and Kulika Puṇḍarīka's *Stainless Light,* some of it attributed to his students but included in his Collected Works. Kay-drup also composed shorter works on many aspects of the tantra[83] among which is the mandala ritual translated in this book, the *Mandala Rite of the Glorious Kālachakra: Illumination of the Thought (dpal dus kyi 'khor lo'i dkyil chog dgongs pa rab gsal).*

D̄zong-ka-b̄a's other main disciple, Gyel-tsap-dar-ma-rin-chen *(rgyal tshab dar ma rin chen,* 1364-1432) wrote a highly cogent and readable exposition of the stage of generation and stage of completion called *How To Practice the Two Stages of the Path of the Glorious Kālachakra: Quick Entry to the Path of Great Bliss (dpal dus kyi 'khor lo'i lam rim pa gnyis ji ltar nyams su len pa'i tshul bde ba chen po'i lam du myur du 'jug pa).*[84] The First Paṇchen Lama, L̄o-sang-chö-ḡyi-gyel-tsen *(blo bzang chos kyi rgyal mtshan,* 1567?-1662) wrote a condensation (one hundred eighty-four folios) of Kay-drup's huge work,[85] and many Ge-luk-b̄a lamas have written on various aspects of the tantra.

Thus, in the Ge-luk-b̄a order the *Kālachakra Tantra* has received considerable attention despite its not being their central tantra. In the Ge-luk-b̄a order, the focal Highest Yoga Tantra is the *Guhyasamāja Tantra,* the tantric colleges of upper and lower Hla-s̄a having as their foremost purpose its exposition and practice. In Ge-luk-b̄a, Highest Yoga Tantra is studied mainly in the context of the Guhyasamāja system, which is considered the "general system" of Highest Yoga Tantra through which most other tantras of that class are understood. The *Kālachakra Tantra* is an exception, as it presents a somewhat parallel but interestingly different system for transforming mind and body into purity.

With respect to other Tibetan works on Kālachakra, the S̄a-ḡya author, the Translator D̄ak-tsang-s̄hay-rap-rin-chen *(stag tshang lo tsā ba shes rab rin chen,* born 1405) wrote a famous commentary on the *Kālachakra Tantra* called *The General Meaning of Kālachakra: Ocean of the Teaching (dus 'khor spyi don bstan pa'i rgya mtsho),* and the later eighteenth and early nineteenth Nying-ma scholar Mi-pam-gya-tso *(mi pham rgya mtsho,* 1846-1912) wrote a two volume work, including an edition of the tantra itself and a commentary on the entire text called *Clarifying the Meaning of the Words of the Glorious Kāla-chakra Tantra, Illumination of the Vajra Sun (dpal dus kyi 'khor lo'i rgyud kyi tshig don rab tu gsal byed rdo rje nyi ma'i snang ba).* A select bibliography of a hundred works on the Kālachakra is offered by A-ku Shay-rap-gya-tso *(a khu shes rab rgya mtsho,* 1803-1875).[86]

This huge number of indigenous Tibetan works indicates the importance that the *Kālachakra Tantra* assumed in Tibet and its cultural region, which includes the Himalayan regions of Nepal, Sikkim, and Bhutan as well as the Mongolian areas – Outer Mongolia, Inner Mongolia, the Kalmuck lands, and areas of Siberia. Aside from these areas, however, it appears not to have spread to China, Korea, Japan, or Southeast Asia, and thus the only practitioners today with a full transmission of initiation are in the Tibetan cultural region. Within that, due to Communist takeovers, the only lamas giving initiation are among the Tibetan refugees or in Bhutan and Sikkim.

The tantra has become particularly associated with the Dalai Lamas, some of whom have given the initiation to huge masses of people. The present Dalai Lama has given the initiation eleven times in large public gatherings. For many Tibetans, receiving the Kālachakra initiation from the Dalai Lama or another lama is a major event in their lives. The present Dalai Lama gave the Kālachakra initiation twice in Tibet at his summer palace, the Nor-bu-ling-ḡa, in 1954 and 1956, each time to approximately one hundred thousand persons. He has given it seven times in India – at Thekchen Choeling, Dharamsala, in 1970 to thirty thousand; in Bylakuppe, Karnataka State, in 1971 to ten thousand; in Bodh Gaya, Bihar State, in 1974 to one hundred thousand; in Leh, Ladakh, in 1976 to forty thousand; in Derang, Bomdila, Arunachal Pradesh, in 1983 to ten thousand; and again in Bodh Gaya, Bihar State, in 1985 to two hundred thousand persons. The Dalai Lama also gave the Kālachakra initiation twice in the West, near Madison, Wisconsin, in 1981 to fifteen hundred persons; and in Rikon,

Switzerland in 1985 to three thousand. The commentary that accompanies the translation of the initiation ritual in this work is largely taken from the event in Madison. It indispensably serves to bring the initiation to life so that the audience can visualize, feel, and reflect on the principles of the process.

SHAMBHALA IN THE FUTURE

The current, twenty-first, Kulika is said to have ascended to the throne in 1927, and the reign of the twenty-fifth and last Kulika, called "Rudra With A Wheel", will begin in 2327 – the reign of each Kulika being one hundred years.[87] In the ninety-eighth year of his rule, the year 2425, which according to the Kālachakra calendar is 3304 years after Shākyamuni Buddha's passing away, a great war will be waged from Shambhala during which the barbarians will be defeated.[88] After that, Buddhism will again flourish for eighteen hundred years; thus, in the 5104th year after Shākyamuni Buddha's passing away the period of his teaching will finish, the length of time being 104 years longer than in the Sūtra system.

Although Chilupā travelled to Shambhala, it is sometimes described as like a pure land, a place beyond the reach of ordinary travel, a land that appears only to those of great merit. Through making prayer-wishes persons can be reborn in Shambhala whereby they can enjoy the Kulikas' continual preaching of doctrine. Also, initiation is said to establish predispositions for rebirth in Shambhala not only for the sake of maintaining practice of the Kālachakra system but also for being under the care and protection of the Kulika Rudra With A Wheel when the great war comes. Thus, Shambhala is a beacon of hope in a world of tragedy for many Tibetans, Mongolians, Bhutanese, Sikkimese, Nepalese, and Ladakhis.

6 *Initiations and Mandalas*

Having practiced the paths of recognizing the suffering condition of ordinary life, of developing great compassion and an altruistic intention to become enlightened, and of engendering the view realizing the emptiness of inherent existence, a practitioner is ready to receive initiation. Initiation is a multifaceted process, the meanings of which are explained in great detail and even read into the term for initiation *(abhiṣheka)*. Through imaginatively treating the term "*abhiṣheka*" in many different ways by erasing letters, adding letters, and substituting others, it comes to have the meanings of cleansing, purifying, authorizing, empowering, gaining lordship, depositing potencies, sprinkling, pouring, casting, bestowing behavior and release, and causing possession of a blissful mind.

Through considerable alteration, *ṣheka* becomes *snāyi*, which means cleansing. Just as dirt is cleaned away, so defilements of the mental and physical aggregates, constituents, and senses and sense fields are *cleansed*. Or, *ṣheka* can become *shuddhe*, which means pure. Just as a king is ritually bathed on assuming rule in a Vedic rite called *abhiṣheka*, so the mental continuum is *purified* through cleansing defilements.

Similarly, *abhiṣheka* can become *adhikāra*, which means authority. Just as a king is authorized to engage in royal activities through an inaugural ceremony called *abhiṣheka*, so one is *authorized* to hear the tantras, cultivate the tantric paths, teach the tantras, and to engage in activities to accomplish feats *(dngos grub, siddhi)*. Or, it can become *vasha* or *vashini* (i.e., *vashin*), which mean power. The initiate is *empowered* with respect to all feats and activities according to wish.

Or, it can become *īshvara,* lord. Just as through being inaugurated as a king one gains dominion as lord of the kingdom, so *abhiṣheka* has the sense of attaining a rank of *control* over everything and gaining a *lordship* of good qualities.

Or, *abhiṣhikta* can become *shakti,* which means potency, and *apakṣhepana,* which means to posit or deposit. Initiation *deposits potencies* for attaining all the good qualities of the grounds, paths, and fruits. Or, *abhiṣhiṃcha,* which means to cast or sprinkle; through being *sprinkled* with water, the initiate is cleansed. Or, *abhiṣhikta* becomes *niṣhikta,* which means "poured"; through initiation the potency for exalted wisdom is *poured* into the clean vessel of a mental continuum purified through the Bodhisattva vows. Or, with initiation, one gains the seed producing the fruit through the seed's being *cast* in the basis-of-all (the very subtle mind of clear light). Or, *ṣhiṃcha* can turn into *chārya,* which means deeds or behavior, and *ṣhekta* can become *mukti,* which means release. In this sense, initiation bestows the Secret Mantra style of *behavior* and the *release* that is its fruit. Or, it can become *sukha,* which means bliss, and *yukta,* which means to possess. In this sense, initiation causes the initiate to *possess a blissful mind.*

Clearly, esthetic delight is taken in constructing creative etymologies that accord with important meanings of the initiation process. However, it is not that the term for initiation determines what initiation means but that the various facets of initiation themselves are used to create meanings of the term. Thus, these etymologies give considerable insight into the actual meanings and purposes of initiation. Initiation means to cleanse and purify defilements; to authorize students to hear about and cultivate the tantric paths and to achieve special feats; to empower the attainment of beneficial qualities; to set potencies for attaining levels of the path and the fruits of those paths; to sprinkle water; to pour potencies and cast seeds into the mental continuum of the initiate; to convey a new style of behavior and its attendant releases from distorted states; and to cause initiates to be endowed with a blissful mind. As will be seen in the next two chapters, all of these activities are central to the initiations of the Kālachakra system.[89]

NUMBER AND PURPOSE OF INITIATIONS

For practicing the *Kālachakra Tantra* there are basically fifteen initiations that fall into three groups:

Seven initiations in the pattern of childhood

1 water initiation
2 crown initiation
3 silk ribbon initiation
4 vajra and bell initiation
5 conduct initiation
6 name initiation
7 permission initiation.

Four high initiations

8 vase initiation
9 secret initiation
10 knowledge-wisdom initiation
11 provisional word initiation.

Four greatly high initiations

12 vase initiation
13 secret initiation
14 knowledge-wisdom initiation
15 definitive word initiation.

These same fifteen initiations are also treated as eleven. This is done through taking the seven initiations in the pattern of childhood as seven and then treating the vase, secret, and knowledge-wisdom initiations in the high and greatly high initiations as merely three, as well as including the provisional word initiation from among the high initiations in the knowledge-wisdom initiation in that same group. This, added to the seven initiations in the pattern of childhood, makes ten, and the definitive word initiation is the eleventh. Done this way, the eleven initiations are:

Seven initiations in the pattern of childhood

1 water initiation
2 crown initiation
3 silk ribbon initiation
4 vajra and bell initiation
5 conduct initiation
6 name initiation
7 permission initiation.

Four high initiations

8 two vase initiations (8 and 12 from above)
9 two secret initiations (9 and 13 from above)
10 two knowledge-wisdom initiations and the provisional word initiation (10, 14, and 11 from above)
11 definitive word initiation (15 from above).

In addition, there is a final initiation of a vajra master lord.

From among the fifteen initiations, the first seven authorize students to practice the stage of generation of the Kālachakra system, and the remaining eight authorize practice of the stage of completion. Just as in order to practice the stage of completion it is necessary first to practice the stage of generation, so in order to receive the last eight initiations, it is necessary first to receive the seven initiations in the pattern of childhood.

The first seven initiations establish potencies in practitioners' mental continuums for purifying impure appearances and impure conceptions. Impure appearances are appearances, to the mental consciousness, of ordinary phenomena such as a body made of flesh, blood, and bone; impure conceptions are conceptions of oneself, based on ordinary appearance, to be ordinary. During the stage of generation, practitioners develop clear appearance of themselves as the deity, or ideal being, Kālachakra together with a consort and other deities. When such meditation is successful, all ordinary appearances of bodies made of flesh, blood, and bone and houses made of wood and so forth vanish from the mental consciousness (not the sense consciousnesses) such that all that appears is divine – god and goddess, called a resident mandala, living in an environment and abode called a residence mandala. These mandalas are depicted in pictures that serve as blueprints for imagination; the pictures show the landscape, the house (palace), companions, and yourself as Kālachakra, for instance, in the manner of union with your mate. It is understood that you are engaged in altruistic activities, emitting helpful light rays and emanations into the environment, teaching, and so forth. In this way, you have the abode, body, resources, and activities of a deity, an ideal being whose very substance, as explained earlier, is the wisdom consciousness continuously realizing the emptiness of inherent existence, motivated by great compassion.

Through developing, in the stage of generation, clear appearance of pure body and pure mind, ordinary appearances are stopped for the mental consciousness. Also, based on clear appearance of pure mind and body, the meditator has a sense of divine personhood or selfhood; the person that is designated in dependence upon such vividly appearing pure mind and body is an ideal person, a deity. Thus, successful meditators have a conception of themselves as ideal beings, not inherently existent but merely designated in dependence upon pure mind and body.

For deity yoga to succeed, two prime factors are needed: clear appearance of a divine body and pride in being that deity. With success in visualizing the deity, both mind and body appear to be pure; hence, the sense of self that the meditator has in dependence upon purely appearing mind and body is of a *pure* self, a *divine* self. Divine pride itself is said to harm or weaken the conception of inherent existence which is at the root of all other afflictions in cyclic existence including afflicted pride. About divine pride, the Fourteenth Dalai Lama says in his introduction to *Tantra in Tibet:*[90]

> ... initially one meditates on an emptiness, and then, within the context of the mind's continuous ascertainment of emptiness, the meditator believes that he is using this mind as the basis [or source] of appearance. At that time, the sense of a mere I designated in dependence on the pure resident – the deity – and residence – the palace and sur-

> roundings – is a fully qualified divine pride. As much as one can cultivate such pride, so much does one harm the conception of inherent existence that is the root of cyclic existence.

Due to the initial and then continuous practice of realizing the emptiness of inherent existence, the meditator realizes that the person is merely designated in dependence upon pure mind and body and is not analytically findable among or separate from those bases of designation. Thereby, divine "pride" or sense of self itself serves as a means for eliminating exaggerated conceptions of the status of phenomena including the person. Because identification of oneself as a divine being is within the context of the emptiness of inherent existence – of oneself not being analytically findable among or separate from pure mind and body and of only being designated in dependence upon pure mind and body – afflictive pride, which would be ruinous, is not just not produced, it is counteracted. Identity takes on a new meaning.

MULTIPLE DEITY MEDITATION

During the stage of generation, meditators achieve clear appearance of themselves as deities. However, they do not just imagine themselves to be one deity but individually imagine the different components of their psycho-physical continuum to be deities residing within a mandala, all a manifestation of their own compassionately motivated wisdom consciousness. They imagine their five constituents – earth (hard things such as bone), water (fluids), fire (heat), wind (inner currents), and space (hollow places) – to be deities. They imagine their five aggregates – forms, feelings, discriminations, compositional factors, and consciousnesses – to be deities. They imagine their ten winds (inner currents) as well as their left and right channels to be deities. They imagine their six sense powers – eye, ear, nose, tongue, body, and mental sense powers – as well as their respective objects – visible forms, sounds, odors, tastes, tangible objects, and other phenomena – to be deities. They imagine their six action faculties – mouth, arms, legs, anus, urinary faculty, and regenerative faculty – and their respective activities – discharging urine, speaking, taking, going, discharging feces, and emitting regenerative fluid – to be deities.[90a] They imagine their pristine consciousness aggregate and pristine consciousness constituent, both understood in this context to refer to the bliss especially of sexual pleasure and non-conceptuality, to be deities.

These thirty-six phenomena in seven categories are grouped under four headings – body, speech, mind, and pristine consciousness or bliss.

BODY

five constituents
1 earth
2 water
3 fire
4 wind
5 space
five aggregates
6 forms
7 feelings
8 discriminations
9 compositional factors
10 consciousnesses

SPEECH

ten winds
11 fire-accompanying wind
12 upward-moving wind
13 pervasive wind
14 vitalizing wind
15 downward-voiding wind
16 serpent wind
17 turtle wind
18 chameleon wind
19 devadatta wind
20 dhaṃnajaya wind
two channels
21 left channel
22 right channel

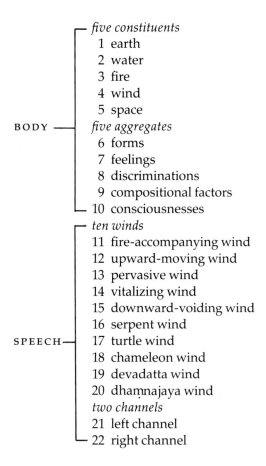

MIND

six sense powers and objects
23 eye sense power and visible forms
24 ear sense power and sounds
25 nose sense power and odors
26 tongue sense power and tastes
27 body sense power and tangible objects
28 mental sense power and other phenomena

six action faculties and activities
29 mouth and speaking
30 arms and taking
31 legs and going
32 anus and discharging feces
33 urinary faculty and discharging urine
34 regenerative faculty and emitting regenerative fluid

BLISS

two factors of pristine consciousness
35 pristine consciousness aggregate
36 pristine consciousness constituent

The seven initiations in the pattern of childhood, those authorizing practice of the stage of generation, are concerned with establishing special potencies in the student's continuum for purifying these seven groups of phenomena:

1 the water initiation purifies the five constituents – earth, water, fire, wind, and space
2 the crown initiation purifies the five aggregates – forms, feelings, discriminations, compositional factors, and consciousnesses
3 the silk ribbon initiation purifies the ten winds (inner currents)
4 the vajra and bell initiation purifies the left and right channels
5 the conduct initiation purifies the six sense powers – eye, ear, nose, tongue, body, and mental sense powers – as well as their respective objects – visible forms, sounds, odors, tastes, tangible objects, and other phenomena
6 the name initiation purifies the six action faculties – mouth, arms, legs, anus, urinary faculty, and regenerative faculty –

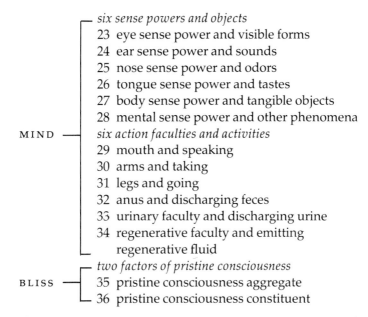

and their respective activities – speaking, taking, going, discharging feces, discharging urine, and emitting regenerative fluid

7 the permission initiation purifies the pristine consciousness aggregate and pristine consciousness constituent.

The four groups of phenomena – body, speech, mind, and pristine consciousness (bliss) – are related respectively with the four faces of Kālachakra – white, red, black (or dark blue), and yellow. Therefore, the students receive the first two initiations concerned with body, the water and crown initiations, from the white face; the next two concerned with speech, the silk ribbon and vajra and bell initiations, from the red face; the next two concerned with mind, the conduct and name initiations, from the black face; and the final permission initiation concerned with pristine mind or bliss, from the yellow face.

Kālachakra's body with black face faces east; thus in pictures of the mandala or of the deity the bottom of the picture is the east, the top is the west, the right side from the main deity's viewpoint is the south, and the left side is the north (thus from the viewpoint of someone looking at the picture, the right side is north and the left side is south). The white face is to the north, the main deity's left; the red face, to the south or right; and the yellow face, to the west or back. As the pictures, called tang-ḡas *(thang ka),* depict Kālachakra, his black, or blue, face is facing forward; white, to his left; yellow to the back; and red to the right. The mandala has four sets of doors on its four sides which serve as approaches to the four faces of Kālachakra.

Given that the students receive the seven initiations from these faces and that the mandala has four doors corresponding to them, the students move from door to door of the mandala to receive the respective initiations. First, at the eastern door, the students request all seven initiations. They then proceed to the northern door for the water and crown initiations, next to the southern door for the silk ribbon and vajra and bell initiations, next to the eastern door for the conduct and name initiations, and finally to the western door for the permission initiation.

THE RESIDENCE AND RESIDENT MANDALAS

The term "mandala" *(dkyil 'khor, maṇḍala)* has many meanings.[91] Our world is conceived as residing on mandalas or spheres of wind, water, and so forth; here "mandala" refers to the four elements that are the *foundation*. In a context such as "being directed toward entry to a path of the mandalas (or spheres) of the bad transmigrations," "mandala" refers to *birth-places*. In "the mandala of the retinue of Bodhisattvas", "mandala" means the *circle* of a retinue. A *drop* of perfumed water can be called a "mandala" of perfumed water. A *garland* or *series* of light rays is called a mandala of light. The earth, or foundation, under a fence is called a mandala, as in "Construct the mandala." "Sun mandala" or "moon mandala" just mean sun and moon but can refer to their *round shape*. In "Bow down with (the body) having five mandalas, " "mandalas" refer to the five *limbs* – two arms, two legs, and head. "Mandala" also refers to an *inestimable mansion that is the residence* of deities, as well as to the *resident deities*. In addition, it can refer to the *combination of divine residence and residents*.

In the initiation ritual for Kālachakra, "mandala" mainly refers to a divine residence as well as to the circle of deities. Still, it is also used frequently to refer to the world system in glorified aspect, as in the offering of "mandala" to the lama. In the context of offering, the term does not refer to the divine residence or to the resident deities, but to the offering that one is making to the lama, the offering being the entire world system visualized in complete purity. Occasionally, the term refers to symbolic representations of the elements, as in mandalas (or spheres) of earth, water, fire, and wind, and the term is also used to refer to the square board on which the students drop a stick in order to indicate their lineage and the type of feat they should work at achieving. In the usage "Kālachakra mandala", however, the reference is only to the divine residence and the resident deities.

RESIDENCE MANDALA

The principal residence mandala is a large building that sits on a raised foundation. The building, a palace, has four walls with double doors in the center of each. The outer walls, which are those of the body mandala, are transparent and in five layers, like five layers of colored glass; the colors, from outside to inside, are yellow, white, red, black, and green.

You are outside, coming up the stairs to the platform or foundation on which the entire building sits. You proceed to the eastern doorway, the one depicted at the bottom of the picture. The doors open to the first level, and you step inside into the body mandala, seeing that half-way in is another set of similar, five layered walls, these being those of the speech mandala. This building within the building again has four double doors, and since it is raised above the body mandala, there are stairs leading up to the doors. It is about four feet above the body mandala level.

You proceed up the stairs; the doors open, and you enter the speech mandala, seeing that halfway inside it is another set of walls, which this time are in three layers – black, red, and white. These are the outer walls of the mind mandala. This third building within the larger building again has four double doors, and since it is raised above the speech mandala, there are stairs leading up to the doors. Again, it is about four feet above the speech mandala level.

You proceed up the stairs; the doors open, and you enter the mind mandala, seeing that halfway inside it is a square platform but with no walls, this being the pristine consciousness mandala. You notice that halfway inside it is another square platform, this being the great bliss mandala.

The building thus has five levels – the body, speech, mind, pristine consciousness, and great bliss mandalas – with three sets of walls, these being for the first three levels. (The walls all reach the same height with a single roof over the entire building.)

Each of the four walls of the body, speech, and mind mandalas has an elaborate doorway. Let's go back down and outside to look at the eastern doorway of the bottom level, the body mandala. First, notice the ground; it is black, corresponding to the black face of Kālachakra that faces the east. Similarly, in the south the ground is red since Kālachakra's red face faces south; in the west the ground is yellow in correspondence to the yellow face, and in the north the ground is white corresponding with the white face.

Notice the entryway at the eastern door, wider than the doorway, with a three storied portico above the entryway. Each of the stories of the portico above the entryway has four pillars across the front, thereby creating three room-like alcoves on each story. In eight of these nine alcoves are goddesses of offering; the middle alcove in the first story on the eastern side has a black wheel of doctrine with a buck and doe to the right and left. The first story sits on the roof of the entryway, smaller than the entryway itself, leaving space on the two ends for someone to stand. In that space on the floor of the first level, on each end, is a lion standing on an elephant and pressing down on its head. The lions appear to be helping to hold up the next floor. On the next floor as well as the top floor, in the equivalent space are male figures called *shāla-bhañjika*.[92] Those at the ends of the second floor of the portico appear to be helping to hold up the next floor, and those on the third floor appear to be helping to hold up the roof. The three levels each have victory banners, and there are tail-hair fans, mirrors, bells, and hanging emblems. On top of the roof, in the middle, is a vase, and on the ends are victory banners.

The same type of entryway, with three story portico, is at each doorway of the body mandala. The only difference is that in the south the middle alcove of the first story has a wonderful red vase in the center with a conch and a lotus to the right and the left. In the north the middle alcove of the first story has a large white drum in the center with a staff and a mallet to the right and the left. In the west is a yellow bodhi tree in the center with a male semi-human to the right and a female semi-human[93] to the left. Notice that the colors of the things in the middle alcoves of the first stories of the four porticos correspond to the basic colors of the four quadrants of the mandala, which as you will remember, correspond to the respective faces of Kālachakra, who stands up on the fifth level of the mandala.

Look up at the top of the wall; see the red jewel-studded frieze; the jewels are triangular, square, and so forth. Above the frieze is an open area, depicted as blue in the picture, with a ledge above it. There, sea monsters spew strings and half-strings of pearls from their mouths. The area is adorned with mirrors, tail-fans, bells, half moons, garlands of flowers, and so forth. Above, on the outside is an ornamental ledge from which an ornamental jeweled design hangs. On it, is another ledge in the shape of half lotus petals. On it, are victory banners and emblems. That is the outside wall of the body mandala; the walls of the speech and mind mandalas are the same.

Now, look down at the base of the outside wall. A white apron surrounds the entire building; it is where goddesses of offering reside. On the white apron, at the corners made by the entryway stand half-moon vajras, and at the four corners, again outside, stand crossed vajras of variegated color.

Let's go back inside the body mandala. Notice that next to the outside wall there is a corridor the color of the ground, being black in the east. Next to it, is a raised white area where gods and goddesses reside; it has a small roof above it. On the other side of it, next to the wall of the speech mandala, is another area the color of the ground in that quadrant. This pattern of a corridor, a white area for gods and goddesses, and an area again the color of the ground of that quadrant is the same in the body, speech, and mind mandalas.

Now let's go on up to the mind mandala. Halfway inside the mind mandala is the square, pristine mind mandala; again, notice that it does not have its own walls and is raised up above the mind mandala, about four feet. It is within the mind mandala, so to speak. It is surrounded by a balustrade of green vajras, on which are four black pillars on each side, making sixteen. The four in the east are marked with black swords representing Amoghasiddhi; the four in the south are marked with red jewels representing Ratnasambhava; the four in the north are marked with white lotuses representing Amitābha; the four in the west are marked with yellow wheels representing Vairochana.

Again, halfway inside the pristine consciousness mandala is the raised, square mandala of great bliss, surrounded by a balustrade of black vajras. In its center is a green lotus with eight petals. In its center is a white moon disc, on which is a red sun disc, a black *rāhu* disc, and a yellow *kālāgni* disc (*rāhu* is a planet, and *kālāgni,* literally, fire at the end of an eon, may be the fiery tail of that planet); these form the seat or basis on which Kālachakra and his consort Vishvamātā stand.

In total, there are seven hundred twenty-two deities situated throughout this five tiered mandala.[94] When the stage of generation is cultivated in its most expansive manner – and this is preferable – the entire residence and resident mandalas are imagined in meditation, first gradually, one by one, and then when the meditator is accustomed to it, all at once. The process is much like moving into a complicated apartment complex or moving to a house in the suburbs in a complex development and eventually coming to know the entire area through gradually taking the lay of the land, so to speak, to mind.

Next we should go through the entire building, identifying everyone inside. However, first, let's go back outside and get familiar with the area outside the building. Remember that the ground, as well as the roof of the resident mandala, is black in the east, red in the south, white in the north, yellow in the west, and blue in the center. Notice that the area outside the body mandala right over to the four tiered perimeter is filled with articles of offering – lotuses, vases, and so forth. The four tiered perimeter itself is composed of earth, water, fire, and wind – yellow, white, red and gray-blue; these are discs that underlie the mandala. A full moon is rising from the southeast, depicted in the picture in the southeast corner on the earth perimeter. The sun is setting in the southwest, depicted in the picture in the southwest corner on the earth perimeter. Also, notice that between the fire and wind perimeters there are eight great cemeteries, depicted in the picture as four red wheels in the principal directions and four white wheels in the intermediate directions. There is also a cemetery above, depicted as an additional wheel in the east (the bottom of the picture), and a cemetery below depicted as an additional wheel in the west (the top of the picture).

Again, outside the space perimeter is a vajra fence, and outside it, blazing light. That is the entire residence mandala.

RESIDENT MANDALA

Let's go back inside the eastern door, up the stairs to the speech mandala, and again up the stairs to the mind mandala. Looking straight ahead and up, between the pillars of the pristine consciousness mandala, we see the centermost, great bliss mandala.

Mandala of Great Bliss

Seeing the mandala of great bliss, you recall the earlier description of the seat as a green lotus with eight petals and that in its center is a white moon disc, on which is a red sun disc, a black *rāhu* disc, and a yellow *kālāgni* planet – these being the seat, or basis, on which Kālachakra and his consort Vishvamātā stand.

Kālachakra. Take a good look at Kālachakra, the central deity. It is important to keep in mind that Kālachakra, no matter what aspect is displayed, is a compassionate appearance of a wisdom consciousness realizing the emptiness of inherent existence. The nature of the glorious Kālachakra is, therefore, great bliss since a supramundane deity is someone who has brought to full development the capacity of the most subtle, innate, blissful consciousness to realize emptiness. Kālachakra's body is fully aspected,[95] emitting pure light rays of five colors – blue, red, white, yellow, and green.[96] His body is blue in color. He has three necks – black in the center, red to his right, and white to his left – and four faces. The black face in the center, facing east, is fierce, with exposed fangs. Let's walk around the corridor of the mind mandala so that we can see the other three faces clearly. Going to the left, we come near the southern door of the mind mandala; from there we see that his right face is red and exhibiting desire. Proceeding on, we see that his back face is yellow and dwelling in meditative stabilization. Proceeding on, we see that his left face is white and very peaceful. All of the faces have three eyes.

Now, returning to the front of the eastern door of the mind mandala, notice that his hair is bound on top of his head and that his crown is adorned with a vajra, a half moon, and

Details of the Kalachakra mandala taken from a painting hanging at Thekchen Choeling, residence of His Holiness the Dalai Lama, Dharamsala, India.

Photographs: pp. 1–3 and 5–8 © John Leidenfrost 1985; p. 4 © Ellen Pearlman 1985.

Vajrasattva (not depicted in the painting). His body is adorned with various adornments – vajra jewels, vajra earrings, vajra necklace, vajra bracelets, vajra belt, vajra ankle bracelets, vajra silk ribbons hanging from his crown, and vajra garlands. His lower robe is a tiger skin.

The first set of shoulders is blue, the second red, the third white; thus there are six shoulders. He has twelve upper arms; the first two upper arms on each side are blue, the second red, and the third white. He has twenty-four lower arms; the first four on each side (starting from the bottom) are black, the second red, the third white. The outsides of the thumbs of the hands are yellow, the index fingers white, the middle fingers red, nameless fingers (ring fingers) black, and the little fingers green. The insides of the first joints of the fingers are black, the second red, and the third white. They are adorned with rings and emit light.

Look at his hands. Starting from the bottom, the first of the four black hands on his right side holds a vajra; the second, a sword; the third, a trident; the fourth, a curved knife. The first of the four red hands on his right side holds a triple arrow;[97] the second, a vajra hook; the third, a resounding drum; the fourth, a mallet. The first of the four white hands on his right side holds a wheel; the second, a spear; the third, a staff; the fourth, an axe.

The first of the four black hands on his left side holds a vajra bell; the second, a shield; the third, a khaṭvāṅga (a three pointed instrument); the fourth, a skull filled with blood. The first of the four red hands on the left side holds a bow; the second, a noose; the third, a jewel; the fourth, a white lotus. The first of the four white hands on his left side holds a conch; the second, a mirror; the third, an iron chain; the fourth, a four faced head of Brahmā.

Look at his legs in the posture of sport. The red right leg is outstretched; the left leg is slightly bent. Under the right foot is a red God of Desire (Cupid), with one face and four hands, holding five flower-like arrows, a bow, a noose, and an iron hook. Under the bent white left leg is white Rudra with one face, three eyes, and four hands, holding a trident, ḍamaru drum, skull, and khaṭvāṅga. Rati, the goddess of the demonic God of Desire, and Uma, the goddess of Rudra, with lowered heads hold onto Kālachakra's heels.

Vishvamātā. Kālachakra's consort, Vishvamātā, embraces him from the front.[98] Her central face is yellow; her right face, white; her back face, blue, and her left face, red. Each face has three eyes. She has four arms on each side. Starting from the top, her right hands hold a curved knife, iron hook, resounding ḍamaru drum, and rosary; her left hands hold a skull, noose, white lotus with a hundred petals, and a jewel. She wears a crown with a Vajrasattva (not depicted in the painting). She is adorned with five types of adornments. With her left leg bent she resides in absorption with the Supramundane Victor Kālachakra.

Both Kālachakra and Vishvamātā are three deities in one. Fused with Kālachakra are Akṣhobhya and Vajrasattva, and fused with Vishvamātā are Vajradhatvīshvarī and Prajñāpāramitā. Let us describe the latter deities as they are when separate from Kālachakra and Vishvamātā. Akṣhobhya is green with three faces – green, red, and white – and six hands, holding in his three right hands a vajra, curved knife, and axe and in his three left hands a vajra bell, skull, and head of Brahmā. He is embraced by Prajñāpāramitā. Vajrasattva is blue with three faces – blue, red, and white – and six hands, holding in his three right hands a vajra, curved knife, and axe and in his three left hands a vajra bell, skull, and head of Brahmā. He is embraced by Dharmadhātvīshvarī. Vajradhatvīshvarī is green with three faces – green, red, and white – and six hands, holding in her three right hands a vajra, curved knife, and axe and in her three left hands a vajra bell, skull, and head of Brahmā; she is embraced by Vajrasattva. Prajñāpāramitā is blue with three faces – blue, red, and white – and six hands, holding in her three right hands a vajra, curved knife, and axe and in her three left hands a vajra bell, skull, and head of Brahmā; she is embraced by Akṣhobhya.

The Ten Shaktis. Kālachakra and Vishvamātā are standing on a yellow *kālāgni* disc, which is over a black *rāhu* disc, which is over a red sun disc, which is over a white moon disc, which is in the center of an eight petalled green lotus. Let's look at the petals where goddesses, called Shaktis *(nus ma)*, stand.[99] On the eastern petal is black Kṛṣhṇadīptā with four faces – black, red, yellow, and white – and eight hands, holding in her right hands vessels of incense, sandalwood, saffron, and a mixture of camphor and musk and in her left hands a bell, lotus, flower of the *deva* tree, and a string of various flowers. On the southern petal is red Raktadīptā, having red, yellow, white, and blue faces and eight hands, holding in her right hands a butter lamp, string of pearls, crown, and bracelet and in her left hands a garment, belt, earring, and anklet.

On the northern petal is white Shretadīptā, with white, black, red, and yellow faces and eight hands, holding in her right hands vessels of milk, water, the supreme of medicines, and beer and in her left hands vessels of ambrosia, accomplished taste,[100] ambrosia-fruit, and food. On the western petal is yellow Pītadīptā, having yellow, white, blue, and red faces and eight hands, holding in her right hands a conch, flute, jewel, and ḍāmaru drum and in her left hands a guitar, drum, resounding gong, and copper conch.

On the southeast petal is black Dhūmā with four faces – black, red, yellow, and white – and eight hands, holding eight black yak-tail fans. On the southwest petal is red Mārīchī, with red, yellow, white, and blue faces and eight hands, holding eight red yak-tail fans. On the northeast petal is white Khadyotā with white, black, red, and yellow faces and with eight hands, holding eight white yak-tail fans. On the northwest petal is yellow Pradīpā, with yellow, white, blue, and red faces and eight hands, holding eight yellow yak-tail fans.

All eight Shaktis have three eyes on all faces, are adorned with the five adornments, have crowns with a Vajrasattva, and reside in the posture of equality.

In the northeast corner of the great bliss mandala is a white conch; in the southwest, a red gong *(gaṇḍi)*; in the southeast, a black wish-granting jewel; and in the northwest, a yellow wish-granting tree.

Ten Shaktis confer the silk ribbon initiation. As described

in L̄o-sang-tsul-trim-d̄en-b̄ay-gyel-tsen's *Initiation Rite of Kālachakra, Stated in an Easy Way* (see pp.292-3 of the translation), the remaining two Shaktis are green Vajradhatvīshvarī with three faces – green, red, and white – and six hands, holding in her right hands a vajra, curved knife, and axe and in her left hands a vajra bell, skull, and head of Brahmā and blue Vishvamātā with three faces – blue, white, and red – and six hands, holding in her three right hands vajra, bell, and axe and in her three left hands a bell, skull, and head of Brahmā.

You have seen all of the deities in the great bliss mandala – Kālachakra, Vishvamātā, the two deities residing with each of them, and the ten Shaktis.[101]

Pristine Consciousness Mandala

Sixteen Ones Gone Thus. In the pristine consciousness mandala are four male Ones Gone Thus (Buddhas) embraced by four female Ones Gone Thus and four female Ones Gone Thus embraced by four male Ones Gone Thus. As you look at the pristine consciousness mandala, you will remember that it is surrounded by a balustrade of green vajras, on which are four black pillars on each side, making sixteen places for eight deities with consorts and eight objects to reside.[102] In the east is black Amoghasiddhi with three faces – black, red, and white – and six hands, holding in his three right hands a sword, curved knife, and trident and in his three left hands a shield, skull, and white khaṭvāṅga; he is embraced by Lochanā. In the southeast is black Tārā with three faces – black, red, and white – and six hands, holding in her three right hands a sword, curved knife, and trident and in her three left hands a shield, skull, and white khaṭvāṅga; she is embraced by Vairochana.

In the south is red Ratnasambhava with three faces – red, white, and black – and six hands, holding in his three right hands a triple arrow, vajra hook, and resounding ḍāmaru drum and in his three left hands a bow, vajra noose, and nine-faceted jewel; he is embraced by Māmakī. In the southwest is red Pāṇḍarā, with three faces – red, white, and black –

and six hands, holding in the three right hands a triple arrow, vajra hook, and resounding ḍāmaru drum and in the three left hands a bow, vajra noose, and nine-faceted jewel; she is embraced by Amitābha.

In the north is white Amitābha with three faces – white, black, and red – and six hands, holding in his three right hands a mallet, spear, and trident and in his three left hands a white lotus with a hundred petals, a mirror, and rosary; he is embraced by Pāṇḍarā. In the northeast is white Māmakī, with three faces – white, black, and red – and six hands, holding in her three right hands a mallet, spear, and trident and in her three left hands white lotuses with a hundred petals, mirror, and rosary; she is embraced by Ratnasambhava.

In the west is yellow Vairochana, with three faces – yellow, white, and black – and six hands, holding in his three right hands a wheel, staff, and frightening vajra and in his three left hands a conch, vajra iron chain, and a ringing bell; he is embraced by Tārā. In the northwest is yellow Lochanā, with three faces – yellow, white, and black – and six hands, holding in her three right hands a wheel, staff, and frightening vajra and in her three left hands a conch, vajra iron chain, and a ringing bell; she is embraced by Amoghasiddhi.

All of the Ones Gone Thus each have three eyes on all of their faces. They are in sitting posture, embracing their respective consorts.

Of the sixteen places in the pristine consciousness mandala, only eight are occupied by the four male Ones Gone Thus and the four female Ones Gone Thus; in the remaining eight are vases. The two vases in the east are filled with purified marrow; those in the south, with purified blood; those in the north, with purified urine; those in the west with purified excrement. Above and below, there are also vases filled with purified semen and menses respectively. They are on lotuses and are covered with lotuses.

The water initiation is conferred by the five female Ones Gone Thus – the four just listed, along with Vajradhatvīshvarī who resides undifferentiably with Vishvamātā but separates out to bestow the initiation. The crown initiation is conferred by the five male Ones Gone Thus – the four just listed, along with Akṣhobhya who resides undifferentiably with Kālachakra but separates out to bestow the initiation.

The Deities of the Mind Mandala

Five Guardians With Consorts. Now, look at the mind mandala itself; it has four doors with guardians at each.[103] At the eastern door is black Vighnāntaka (Atibala), with three faces – black, red, and white – and six hands, holding in his three right hands a sword, curved knife, and trident and in his three left hands a shield, skull, and white khaṭvāṅga. He is embraced by yellow Stambhakī, with three faces – yellow, white, and black – and six hands, holding in her three right hands a wheel, staff, and frightful vajra and in her three left hands a conch, vajra chain, and resounding bell.

At the southern door is red Prajñāntaka (Jambhaka), with three faces – red, white, and black – and six hands, holding in his three right hands a triple arrow, vajra hook, and resounding ḍāmaru drum and in his three left hands a bow, vajra noose, and nine-faceted jewel. He is embraced by white Mānakī, with three faces – white, black, and red – and six hands, holding in her three right hands a mallet, spear, and trident and in her three left hands a white lotus with a hundred petals, a mirror, and a rosary.

At the northern door is white Padmāntaka, with three faces – white, black, and red – and six hands, holding in his three right hands a mallet, spear, and trident and in his three left hands a white lotus with a hundred petals, a mirror, and a rosary. He is embraced by red Jambhakī, with three faces – red, white, and black – and six hands, holding in her three right hands a triple arrow, vajra hook, and resounding ḍāmaru drum and in her three left hands a bow, vajra noose, and nine-faceted jewel.

At the western door is yellow Yamāntaka, with three faces – yellow, white, and black – and six hands, holding in his three right hands a wheel, staff, and frightful vajra and in his three left hands a conch, vajra chain, and resounding bell. He is embraced by black Atibalā, with three faces – black, red, and white – and six hands, holding in her three right hands a sword, curved knife, and trident and in her three left hands a shield, skull, and white khaṭvāṅga.

On a seat above the mind mandala (depicted in the eastern door). is Uṣhṇīṣhachakravartī, with three faces – green, red, and white – and six hands, holding in his three right hands a vajra, curved knife, and axe and in his three left hands a vajra bell, skull, and head of Brahmā. He is embraced by blue Atinīlā, with three faces – blue, red, and white – and six hands, holding in her right a vajra, curved knife, and axe and in her left a vajra bell, skull, and a head of Brahmā.[104]

All of the male and female Wrathful Deities have reddish yellow hair standing on end, are adorned with snakes and the six adornments, and have three eyes on each face. The males stand with right leg outstretched, and the females, with the left leg outstretched.

These ten Wrathful Deities together with Sumbharāja and Raudrākṣhī from the body mandala confer the name initiation.

Twenty-Four Male and Female Bodhisattvas. Look to the left and right of each door and in the four corners of the mind mandala; there you see the twelve male and twelve female Bodhisattvas.[105] To the right of the eastern door is black Khagarbha, with three faces – black, red, and white – and six hands, holding in his right hands a sword, curved knife, and trident and in his left hands a shield, skull, and white khaṭvāṅga. He is embraced by yellow Gandhavajrā, with three faces – yellow, white, and black – and with six hands, holding in her right hands a wheel, staff, and frightful vajra and in her left hands a conch, vajra iron chain, and a resounding bell.

In the southeast corner is black Sparshavajrā, with three faces – black, red, and white – and six hands, holding in her right hands a sword, curved knife, and trident and in her left hands a shield, skull, and white khaṭvāṅga. She is embraced by yellow Sarvanivaraṇaviṣhkambhi, with three faces – yellow, white, and black – and with six hands, holding in his right hands a wheel, staff, and frightful vajra and in his left hands a conch, vajra iron chain, and a resounding bell.

To the right of the southern door is red Kṣhitigarbha, with

three faces – red, white, and black – and six hands, holding in his right hands a triple arrow, vajra hook, and a resounding ḍāmaru drum and in his left hands a bow, vajra noose, and nine-faceted jewel. He is embraced by white Rūpavajrā, with three faces – white, black, and red – and six hands, holding in her right hands a mallet, spear, and trident and in her left hands a white lotus with a hundred petals, a mirror, and rosary.

In the southwest corner is red Rasavajrā, with three faces – red, white, and black – and six hands, holding in her right hands a triple arrow, vajra hook, and a resounding ḍāmaru drum and in her left hands a bow, vajra noose, and nine-faceted jewel. She is embraced by white Lokeshvara with three faces – white, black, and red – and six hands, holding in his right hands a mallet, spear, and trident and in his left hands a white lotus with a hundred petals, a mirror, and rosary.

To the right of the northern door is white Lokeshvara with three faces – white, black, and red – and six hands, holding in his right hands a mallet, spear, and trident and in his left hands a white lotus with a hundred petals, a mirror, and rosary. He is embraced by red Rasavajrā, with three faces – red, white, and black – and six hands, holding in her right hands a triple arrow, vajra hook, and a resounding ḍāmaru drum and in her left hands a bow, vajra noose, and nine-faceted jewel.

In the northeast corner is white Rūpavajrā, with three faces – white, black, and red – and six hands, holding in her right hands a mallet, spear, and trident and in her left hands a white lotus with a hundred petals, a mirror, and rosary. She is embraced by red Kṣhitigarbha, with three faces – red, white, and black – and six hands, holding in his right hands a triple arrow, vajra hook, and a resounding ḍāmaru drum and in his left hands a bow, vajra noose, and nine-faceted jewel.

To the right of the western door is yellow Sarvanivara-ṇaviṣhkambhi, with three faces – yellow, white, and black – and six hands, holding in his right hands a wheel, staff, and frightful vajra and in his left hands a conch, vajra iron chain, and a resounding bell. He is embraced by black Sparshavajrā, with three faces – black, red, and white – and six hands, holding in her right hands a sword, curved knife, and trident and in her left hands a shield, skull, and white khaṭvāṅga.

In the northwest corner is yellow Gandhavajrā, with three faces – yellow, white, and black – and six hands, holding in her right hands a wheel, staff, and frightful vajra and in her left hands a conch, vajra iron chain, and a resounding bell. She is embraced by black Khagarbha, with three faces – black, red, and white – and six hands, holding in his right hands a sword, curved knife, and trident and in his left hands a shield, skull, and white khaṭvāṅga.

To the left of the southern door is green Vajrapāṇi, with three faces – green, red, and white – and six hands, holding in his right hands a vajra, curved knife, and axe and in his left hands a vajra-bell, skull, and head of Brahmā. He is embraced by blue Shabdavajrā, with three faces – blue, red, and white – and six hands, holding in her right hands a vajra, curved knife, and axe and in her left hands a vajra-bell, skull, and head of Brahmā.

To the left of the western door is green Dharmadhātuvajrā, with three faces – green, red, and white – and six hands, holding in her right hands a vajra, curved knife, and axe and in her left hands a vajra-bell, skull, and head of Brahmā. She is embraced by blue Samantabhadra, with three faces – blue, red, and white – and six hands, holding in his right hands a vajra, curved knife, and axe and in his left hands a vajra-bell, skull, and head of Brahmā.

To the left of the eastern door is blue Samantabhadra, with three faces – blue, red, and white – and six hands, holding in his right hands a vajra, curved knife, and axe and in his left hands a vajra-bell, skull, and head of Brahmā. He is embraced by green Dharmadhātuvajrā, with three faces – green, red, and white – and six hands, holding in her right hands a vajra, curved knife, and axe and in her left hands a vajra-bell, skull, and head of Brahmā.

To the left of the northern door is blue Shabdavajrā, with three faces – blue, red, and white – and six hands, holding in her right hands a vajra, curved knife, and axe and in her left hands a vajra-bell, skull, and head of Brahmā. She is embraced by green Vajrapāni, with three faces – green, red, and white – and six hands, holding in his right hands a vajra, curved knife, and axe and in his left hands a vajra-bell, skull, and head of Brahmā.

Twelve Goddesses of Offering. Goddesses of offering reside on the white apron surrounding the mind mandala. On each side of the four doors is a goddess, and there are two above and two below, making twelve.

The Deities of the Speech Mandala

Let's go down the stairs of the mind mandala to the speech mandala. Immediately we see that there are eight large eight-petalled lotuses in the four directions and four intermediate directions. The eight lotuses are each on seats of living beings. In the center of each of the lotuses is a goddess embraced by a god and surrounded by eight goddesses, one on each petal. Thus, there are ten deities on each of the eight lotuses, making eighty deities. The Seventh Dalai Lama's *Means of Achievement of the Complete Mandala of Exalted Body, Speech, and Mind of the Supramundane Victor, the Glorious Kālachakra: the Sacred Word of Scholars and Adepts* identifies each of these eighty (as well as those mentioned below) for the sake of complete meditation. We will not identify in detail the remaining deities, however, as they are not involved in the seven initiations authorizing practice of the stage of generation.

Outside the speech mandala on the apron surrounding it are thirty-six goddesses of desire – four on one side of each of the four doors and five on the other.

The Deities of the Body Mandala

Three Hundred Sixty Deities of the Days. Let's leave the speech mandala, going down the stairs to the body mandala. We see that there are twelve large lotuses with twenty-eight petals each, the petals being in three rows – four in the first row nearest the center, eight in the second, then sixteen in the third. In the center of each lotus is a god embraced by a goddess and surrounded by twenty-eight goddesses, one on each petal. Thus, each of the twelve lotuses has thirty deities, making a total of three hundred sixty, representing the twelve months and three hundred sixty days of a year.[106]

Twelve Wrathful Deities. In each of the four doors and above and below there is a Male Wrathful Deity embraced by a Female Wrathful Deity, making twelve. They are in chariots drawn by boars, horses, elephants, lions, garuḍas, and tigers.

Goddesses of Offering. Let's go outside the body mandala and look at the apron surrounding it. There are thirty-six goddesses of desire – four on one side of the doors and five on the other.

Ten Serpent Kings. Also, on each side of the doors outside the body mandala are seats representing the four elements – earth, water, fire, and wind – making eight, as well as symbols of space and pristine consciousness above and below, respectively. On these are Serpent Kings and their consorts.

Ten Wrathful Goddesses of the Cremation Grounds. Looking out to the cemeteries, or cremation grounds, that are between the fire and wind perimeters, we see the eight cremation grounds of the four directions, four intermediate directions, and above and below. At each of these is a wheel with a lotus in the center on which stands a goddess – making ten goddesses. They are embraced by male deities and surrounded by various deities.

In other Highest Yoga Tantras, the deities in the mandala create an intention to confer initiation which is actually conferred by separate initiation deities who come from the outside. In the *Kālachakra Tantra,* however, the deities in the mandala actually confer the initiations, though there is help from external initiation deities. We have identified where these central deities are in the mandala; in the next chapter, we shall discuss how initiation is conferred.

7 *Procedure of the Enhancement*

Before the actual initiation, first the students who are to receive initiation are enhanced in a separate ritual. This is a preparatory phase, but it is not just a preparation; the status of the students is *elevated, enhanced,* through a twelve step process:

1 readjusting motivation in a more altruistic way
2 being born as a child of the lama
3 making a formal request for the requisites for Mantra practice
4 becoming more firmly interested in Mantra
5 taking the Bodhisattva and Mantra vows
6 being blessed
7 determining lineage
8 taking purifying water, receiving kusha grass to go under mattress and pillow for the sake of protection, and receiving a protective thread
9 imagining six syllables at important places in the body
10 invoking Vajrasattva's blessing
11 becoming more enthusiastic about practicing the Buddhist doctrine and, especially, the tantric doctrine
12 hearing advice on analyzing dreams.

(In Kay-drup's *Mandala Rite,* translated in this book, these twelve are presented in six sections with two parts each.)

First, the students, who are outside the closed doors on the eastern side of the mandala, that is to say, at the doors facing

Kālachakra's front, black face, offer to the lama, who is undifferentiable from Kālachakra, everything that is worthwhile. This is called a mandala offering, the word "mandala" referring not to the resident and residence mandalas of Kālachakra but to a *whole sphere* of offerings. In this offering, which is repeated many times during the course of the initiation ritual, everything of value is offered to the lama in glorified form in order to indicate the value that the students place on receiving the doctrine and to indicate that the teaching which has techniques helpful throughout the course of lives is far more important than any material object, the benefit of which is limited, at maximum, to one short life. Also, by giving to the lama/Kālachakra everything to which the students are attached, they relieve their minds of excessive energy investment in superficial material goods and temporary attachments, allowing their minds to focus, with great power, on the teachings received. How could someone who is not willing to give everything away enter into meditative equipoise on the emptiness of inherent existence in which nothing except the vacuity that is the absence of inherent existence appears, not even one's own body?

Then, the students readjust their motivation so that they do not enter into the practice of Mantra for superficial purposes, such as merely for better health in this lifetime, or even for deeper but still self-centered purposes such as liberation from cyclic existence for themselves. Rather, the motivation is to bring about the welfare of other beings (although once altruism is the motivation, one's own welfare is achieved as it could not be otherwise).

The fact that the ritual begins with a reformation of motivation towards altruism suggests the central and fundamental importance of love and compassion. Also, that this readjustment is actually done in the ritual and not just assumed indicates a stark appraisal of the need continually to redirect the mind away from ingrained selfishness; it suggests that the mind, unless trained, reverts to selfishness and self-centeredness.

With motivation altruistically formed, the students are ready to take birth as a child of the lama, who is viewed as being Kālachakra. This process is called an "internal initiation" and is performed once during the enhancement ritual and four times during the actual rite of the seven initiations authorizing practice of the stage of generation. Much of tantric practice is structured around mimicking ordinary, uncontrolled processes in a manner that serves to purify those processes and bring them under control. In this case, the process of taking rebirth is being mimicked, purified, and brought under control.

In ordinary rebirth,[107] a being in the intermediate state between the last life and the new life sees its father and mother lying together. If the being is to be reborn as a male, he desires the mother and wants to separate from (get rid of) the father. If the being is to be reborn as a female, she desires the father and wants to separate from (get rid of) the mother. When the being, out of wanting to copulate, begins to embrace the one that is desired, he or she perceives only the partner's sexual organ, due to which he/she becomes frustrated and angry. In the midst of desire and anger, the being of the intermediate state dies and thereupon enters the womb, and is reborn in the sense that conception takes place.

Entry into the womb is by way of passing through the father's body. First the being of the intermediate state enters, according to one tantric explanation, through the father's mouth or, according to another tantric explanation, through the top of the father's head. Having entered into the father's body, the being of the intermediate state passes through the body and emerges by way of his penis in the mother's vagina. With the four factors necessary for rebirth – presence of the consciousness of an intermediate state being, presence of semen, presence of ovum (called "blood"), and a karmic connection between father, mother, and intermediate state being – complete, rebirth is taken.

Here in the internal initiation (probably called "internal" because it takes place in the womb of the consort who is called "mother", *yum*), the students imagine that they take rebirth in the pattern just described. They are drawn into the mouth of the lama (who is always understood to be Kālachakra) by light that radiates out from the seed syllable *hūṃ* at the heart of the lama, and having entered his mouth, they pass through his body into the mother's vagina and dissolve in her womb. The dissolution in the mother's womb specifically refers to meditating on the emptiness of inherent existence; not only are all the old coarse appearances of a body made of flesh, blood, and bone withdrawn, but also the vacuity that is the absence of their inherent existence is actualized in vivid realization. Previously, the motivation of great compassion was established; now, the wisdom realizing emptiness is also present.

This wisdom consciousness realizing emptiness and impelled by compassion now becomes the "substance" of the students' reappearance in divine, or ideal, form. Rather than being subjected to rebirth impelled by the afflictive emotions of desire and hatred that are based on the ignorance conceiving of oneself and other phenomena as inherently existent, as is the case in ordinary rebirth, in this repetition of the birth process the students are impelled by great compassion and founded on the wisdom realizing reality. In the womb, the wisdom consciousness first appears as a seed syllable, *hūṃ,* that turns into a vajra. The vajra then transforms into a Kālachakra, an ideal being with a face, arms, legs, and so forth.

The visualization as an ideal being is then further enhanced, or fortified, by imagining that light rays from the seed syllable at the lama's heart draw all enlightened beings into his mouth, who, in passing through his body, melt into an ambrosia that is a light-like fluid called the "mind of enlightenment" *(byang chub kyi sems, bodhichitta)* at his heart, and then emerge as this ambrosia-light into the womb of the mother, anointing the students. Since enlightened beings are manifestations of a non-dual bliss consciousness – the most subtle consciousness that is by nature blissful – realizing the emptiness of inherent existence, when the students in the mother's womb are anointed with the ambrosia-light that the enlightened beings have become, they are fortified with this very nature. The students now have not only a wisdom consciousness realizing emptiness but also a blissful consciousness realizing emptiness. This exalted wisdom of undifferentiable bliss and emptiness that has been generated is the internal initiation.

The steps leading up to this are causal factors of the initiation; the actual initiation is the exalted wisdom of undifferentiable bliss and emptiness that is generated.

The term "mind of enlightenment" has as its broadest referents the conventional mind of enlightenment, which is the altruistic intention to become enlightened, and the ultimate mind of enlightenment, which is a wisdom consciousness in the continuum of a Bodhisattva directly realizing emptiness. However, the term "mind of enlightenment" is also used, as it is here, to refer to semen or, more accurately, to the white and red essential fluids that both males and females have. This usage of the term "mind of enlightenment" in tantric discourse to refer to the essential fluid does not cancel out its meanings as the altruistic intention to become enlightened or the wisdom directly realizing emptiness, for altruism and realization of emptiness are the very basis of the basic tantric meditation of deity yoga, as is obvious from the course of this ritual.[108] Rather, the term is used, additionally, *in specific circumstances,* to refer to the essential white and red fluids. In this case, the reference is to a purified form of semen – ambrosia-light that contains the very essence of all enlightened beings. For psychological reinforcement to occur, the ambrosia-light is imagined as a composite of the qualities of enlightened beings. Being anointed with it and absorbing it into oneself thereby serve not only to reinforce and enhance the wisdom and compassion that have already been meditated but also to engender a bliss consciousness like that which fully enlightened beings have.

Whereas Sigmund Freud was primarily concerned with exposing sexual attractions and so forth masked in other forms, this system self-consciously reenacts those ordinary impulses in order not just to sublimate but to transform them by removing the ignorance conceiving inherent existence that is their basis. That the internal initiation is performed not just once but five times during this series of initiations and that initiation is taken again and again during a practitioner's lifetime indicate that such transformation is not considered to be an easy matter. For, what are involved are the very impulses that have bound beings in cyclic existence since beginningless time. Any system that boasted of easy transformation would be foolhardy.

Thus, a key to understanding tantric initiation and practice is *repetition*. Repetition is not merely to repeat what one did before, but a chance to make progress through deeper realization or movement to a subtler level of consciousness. Repetition is another opportunity and also an acculturation of mind and body to a way of life founded on valid principles rather than impelled by afflictive emotions.

Having received the internal initiation, the students emerge from the mother's womb and are set back on the seat by a pillar outside the eastern door of the mandala. Presumably, the doors of the mandala have remained closed, the nature of the mandala being such that the students were drawn into Kālachakra's mouth by passing through the wall of the eastern side and have returned in the same way. Also, the students are yet to *see* the inside of the mandala, and thus while passing to and from the lama/Kālachakra, did not get a chance to look at the inside of the building. Despite their not yet having put on the blindfold and despite the fact that the walls are transparent, the inside of the mandala is not seen.

In the next step of the enhancement ritual, the students make a supplication, or request, for the rituals of (1) taking refuge in the Three Jewels – Buddha, doctrine, and spiritual community, (2) taking the Bodhisattva vows, and (3) taking the Mantra vows and pledges. The lama responds by speaking to one of the students – every student imagining himself or herself to be that person. Implicitly accepting the request, the lama speaks of the greatness of the Mantra path, thereby causing the student to become more firmly interested in Mantra.

Then, the rituals of taking refuge, the Bodhisattva vows, and the Mantra vows are conducted. It is important to note that although the basic procedure of the entire initiation has already been enacted – the student has imagined generating a blissful consciousness realizing emptiness and has used it as the "substance" for reappearing in ideal form – this very same procedure will be repeated again and again. At this point, it is almost as if the students, having already become a Buddha with all the enlightened beings of all time having dissolved into them, then reenact the first step of the path, taking refuge in Buddha, his doctrine (specifically true cessations of suffering and paths to those cessations), and the spiritual community that helps practitioners to such refuge. If the students had actually become Buddhas during the internal initiation, this, of course, would be sufficient, but since such has been done only through imagination, the process can be repeated with many permutations pertaining to the over-all pattern of the path.

Having taken refuge and the vows, the students are blessed into a magnificent or heightened state through the visualized setting of radiant syllables in their bodies, which are still visualized as Kālachakra. The visualization is further enhanced by the lama's touching a vajra to the student's heart, throat, and top of the head. From the outside, the lama is touching the student with a substance – here, a vajra – and the students *imagine* being heightened into greater radiance; a combination of factors from without and from within is required. The students imagine that all ill-deeds and unfavorable factors of body, speech, and mind are thereby purified as are all predispositions that would cause such in the future. Again, if the mere ritual were considered to be totally efficacious, there would be no need for the rest of the ritual, but this is not the case. Rather, the students are becoming acculturated to a process, a pattern, of purification.

Then, a tooth-stick – an old fashioned toothbrush – is dropped onto a square board called a mandala to determine what type of feat *(dngos grub, siddhi)* the students should work at achieving. When the stick is dropped upright on the board, it falls onto one of four quadrants, in the middle, or off the board. Where it falls (as long as it falls on the board – three times off the board disqualifies a person for initiation for the time being) determines the class of feats that the students can work at most successfully. Just as a toothbrush is used for cleaning the teeth, so the mantra that is used in connection with the toothbrush speaks of cleansing body, speech, and mind through ideal body, speech, and mind that are identified, in entity, with the four doors of liberation – signlessness, wishlessness, emptiness, and non-activity.

In brief, signlessness refers to objects' not being established by way of their own character as produced by causes and conditions. Wishlessness refers to objects' not being established by way of their own character as producing effects. Emptiness is the fact that the entities of objects are not established by way of their own character. Non-activity refers to the fact that the activity of objects' performing functions is not established by way of its own character. In this way, all four doors of liberation refer to the emptiness of inherent existence of any particular object from four different points of view – their causation, their producing effects, their entities, and their performing functions. It is indeed validly established that impermanent objects are caused, produce effects, exist, and perform functions; however, none of these is inherently established. The four doors of liberation are to realize this absence of inherent establishment.

Further purification of body, speech, and mind is imagined through taking three handfuls of water. Then, since the students' dreams during the evening of the enhancement and before the actual initiation ritual are important, protective kusha grass is given for mattress and pillow, as is also a protective thread. These are to defend the mind against interfering influences. The assumption seems to be that our minds are subject to the influence of autonomous forces (autonomous complexes in Carl Jung's vocabulary) and that their power must be thwarted. That the greatest protection is said to be love suggests that an angry defensive posture gives these autonomous forces more power, whereas sympathetic love serves to de-autonomize such forces. Sympathetic love even toward what actually are internal forces reduces the distance between that part of one's mind conceived to be oneself and those parts that have been separated off as autonomous complexes; it also could ameliorate outside forces.

Again, syllables are imagined at important places in the body, this time in connection with the principal male deities of the six lineages whereas earlier it was in connection with six goddesses. Vajrasattva is then invoked to bless the students' body, speech, and mind into magnificence.

This is followed by the students' becoming more enthusiastic for the Mantra doctrine by hearing about its rarity, its power to cleanse bad karma, and its efficacy in bringing about full enlightenment as a Buddha. The enhancement ritual concludes with advice from the lama on analyzing the dreams that occur in the last part of the night around dawn. Dreams at this time are considered to have more meaning than those earlier in the night, which are often too greatly influenced by the previous day's activities to indicate deep predilections. The concern with dreams is here specifically for indications of the students' relationship to the lama and to the initiation. Omens of a good relationship and success with the practice are valued; ill omens are to be dissolved through meditation on emptiness, cultivating love, repeating mantra, and so forth. Still, whether the dreams are good or bad, the students are advised not to over-reify their status and thereby become inflated or deflated. Even good omens do not exist by way of their own nature and should not become objects of attachment by assenting to their seeming inherent existence. Bad omens, being without inherent existence, are subject to transformation and thus should not be considered as sources for discouragement.

The concept of the Buddha nature – the luminous and knowing nature of the mind and the emptiness of inherent existence of the mind – underlies all these transformative processes. The students' status is enhanced, elevated, and glorified through making conscious use of their everpresent basically pure nature, not through mere recognition of this underlying mode of being but through also actively reshaping their manifestation from it.

8 *Procedure of the Initiations*

ENTERING AND SEEING THE MANDALA

The students are outside the closed doors on the eastern side of the mandala – the doors in front of the main, black face of Kālachakra. Wanting to go inside, they request admission and ask again to take refuge, the Bodhisattva vows, and the Mantra vows. The lama (Kālachakra) responds by first giving the students articles of clothing and a head-piece that symbolizes the crown protrusion. These are given to make the students feel more like a deity.

As was discussed earlier, in the practice of the stage of generation, the appearance to the mental consciousness of an ordinary body composed of flesh, blood, and bone is to be stopped and replaced with an appearance of pure mind and body. Designated in dependence upon such pure mind and body is a deity, an ideal person. To increase this sense of a not inherently existent but designatedly existent, ideal, altruistic person, the students, even externally, are made to look like a deity by putting on a deity's clothing. It is said that many persons fear imagining themselves in divine form;[109] thus, playfully putting on a deity's attire must help participants not only in identifying the attire of a deity but also in getting over the sense of oddness.

Since the students are to be let into the mandala but are not yet ready to see it, blindfolds are distributed by the lama's assistants. Then the students re-imagine themselves as Kālachakras, and the lama addresses them, asking them who they are and what they want. The students answer by declaring their altruistic nature as Bodhisattvas or those aspiring to become Bodhisattvas and by declaring their interest in using in the path of Secret Mantra the bliss that arises from desire.

The students supplicate the lama/Kālachakra as a great being who can show the path out of suffering; the lama responds by conducting the ceremonies of going for refuge, taking the Bodhisattva vows, and taking the Mantra vows in the same way as these were done during the enhancement ritual. The altruistic nature of the endeavor is illustrated by the students' repeating:

> I will liberate those not liberated [from the obstructions to omniscience].
> I will release those not released [from cyclic existence].
> I will relieve those unrelieved [in bad transmigrations]
> And set sentient beings in nirvana.

Consonant with this altruism, the students declare their intention to practice the all-encompassing yoga, which has two aspects: (1) the conventional altruistic intention to become enlightened, which is all-encompassing in that it is concerned with establishing an altruistic relationship with *all* sentient beings, and (2) the realization of the ultimate nature of *all* persons and phenomena, their absence of inherent existence. In this practice, the conventional mind of enlightenment – the aspirational intention to become enlightened, which is the thought, "I will attain Buddhahood for the sake of all sentient beings," substantializes in the form of a white, round, flat moon disc at the heart. Similarly, the ultimate mind of enlightenment, in which the emptiness of inherent existence of all phenomena and one's own mind are of one taste, that is to say, of one undifferentiable entity, substantializes as a five-pointed vajra standing on the moon.

As we will see, the students are led again and again through exercises in which the deepest affective attitude, compassion, and the deepest intellectual realization, the wisdom of emptiness, are used as the basis of appearance in form. The suggestion is that in ordinary life attitudes of selfishness, jealousy, enmity, desire, and so forth are the stuff of our appearance. To get control over this process of appearance and to reform it in the healthiest possible way, students are again and again instructed to generate compassion and to reflect on the nature of phenomena and then reappear with those attitudes – consciousnesses, in Buddhist vocabulary – as the bases out of which they or, as in this case, pure objects appear. The objects are then symbols, not in the sense of referring to something else, but in the sense of manifesting what they symbolize within constant exhibition of what they symbolize. Compassion and wisdom do not disappear with their appearance as moon and vajra; rather, they continue within appearance in form. This is the extraordinary feature of tantra.

In the ritual text, these activities are said to be done "outside the curtain". Since the mandala has no curtain, the reference here is to the curtain that surrounds the model of the mandala drawn with colored sands. The drawn mandala is kept inside a curtain out of sight of the students just as, in imagination, the students are outside the closed doors of the mandala.

The doors now open, this being illustrated by the assistants' opening the curtain around the sand mandala. Since the students are still blindfolded, they are led inside by the lama who has come down from the fifth level of the mandala and is holding a vajra in his hand. Each student imagines that he or she takes hold of the vajra and is led into the mandala.

Still blindfolded, the students circumambulate the mandala three times and then go back outside through the eastern door. Obeisance is paid in series to Akṣhobhya, Amoghasiddhi, Ratnasambhava, Amitābha, and Vairochana. For Akṣhobhya, who is fused with Kālachakra, the student turns into Akṣhobhya and makes a supplication; the same is done for Amoghasiddhi, again at the eastern door. Upon going to the corresponding doors by entering the mandala and then going back out at the proper door, obeisance is paid to the other three. Having become similar to the principal deities of the five lineages, the students are sworn to secrecy, sworn to keeping the vows, and to keeping the word of the lama as long as it accords with the doctrine (see p. 242).

By this time, the students have imagined themselves in divine form several times. A different version of this practice is now done. The students imagine themselves in the fierce form of Kālachakra, called Vajravega, and then imagine syllables at important places in their bodies that are stirred into greater radiance and activity by light rays from the lama. Light rays from the heart of the lama also extend out to all the Buddhas in all world-systems who appear, filling all of space, as Kālachakras and Vajravegas. These, in turn, all enter into the student – each student imagining that all dissolve into himself or herself.

Such imaginations suggest that ordinary consciousness is split into a thousand parts that need to be drawn together. Even imagination of fully enlightened beings elsewhere is to be drawn into oneself; energy is to return to its source. Tantra is described as using imagination as the path, and the tremendous reinforcement of personality traits that is accomplished through imagining and identifying with an ideal being and then drawing all such ideal beings in all world-systems into oneself is obviously built on a very active and creative use of imagination. One cannot half-heartedly imagine oneself as composed of compassion and wisdom, thinking that there are real incarnations of compassion and wisdom elsewhere, for those very beings are drawn into oneself. One has to face up to the identification. The power of positive thinking, of imagining situations of supreme success, is basic to the process. It is obvious that Buddhahood, the goal corresponding to this process, is not withdrawal into nothingness, as it often is described in the West, but is a dynamic expression of knowledge, compassion, and power.

Such intense combination into oneself of all ideal beings can be too exciting; thus, it is followed with a calming. This is accomplished by putting a flower, mantrafied with *oṃ āḥ hūṃ* on the student's head. Then, a protective ritual of syllable imagination at important points in the body is done; again, the need for protection suggests that the heightened state is subject to interference from autonomous complexes that have to be thwarted.

Then, in what could only seem to be anti-climactic if it was not kept in mind that deity imagination is to be performed in a multitude of ways in connection with permutations of the path structure, the students lift their blindfolds to see if any particular color appears in the line of sight the first moment after lifting the blindfold. Through the association of activities of pacification, increase, subjugation, and so forth with certain colors, the lama is able to read the type of activity that the student should work at achieving.

Then, the lama, ringing the bell that is in his hand, speaks from within the power of the truth, calling on the students' lineages to be shown when they drop a flower on the mandala board, through which the lineage of the student is known.

The students take off the blindfold and manifestly see the mandala, described in chapter six of the Introduction. The students celebrate what they have seen in song, "*Samaya hoḥ hoḥ hoḥ hoḥ.*"

INITIATION

Now the students are ready for initiation. First, they make a request for all seven initiations, after which the lama clears away interferences (as was just said, the frequency of this activity suggests the perniciousness of the autonomous complexes that undo attempts to live within a heightened psychological state). Then, the lama performs an ablution, cleansing the students' ears, nose, mouth, and body, makes an offering to the now cleansed students, and fumigates the area with incense.

As explained earlier (see pp. 72-73), the seven initiations authorizing practice of the stage of generation are in four groups, corresponding to the four faces of Kālachakra and the four groups of factors to be purified. The structure of all the initiations is the same, with the exception that the second initiation at each face does not require an internal initiation. Roughly there are nineteen steps:

1 the student, at the appropriate door, faces the appropriate face of Kālachakra and makes offering, called "offering mandala".
2 a request for the initiation is made.
3 internal initiation (required for the first, third, fifth, and seventh initiations):
a) the student is drawn into the mouth of the lama, passes through his body into the womb of the Mother, and melts into a drop that dissolves into emptiness.
b) a seed syllable appears and transforms into a symbol, which transforms into a deity corresponding to the face of Kālachakra toward which the student is facing – the deity being embraced by the appropriate consort.
c) the actual deity is drawn by the lama into the body of the student imagined to be that deity, who thereby becomes the actual deity. (The actual deity is called a "wisdom-being" and the imagined deity is called a "pledge being".)
d) Light from the heart of the lama/Kālachakra draws in all of the male and female Buddhas and Bodhisattvas of the ten directions.
e) The lama makes offering to all the Buddhas and Bodhisattvas who are now nearby.
f) The lama asks them to bestow initiation, and the male and female Buddhas and Bodhisattvas respond by entering into absorption with their respective mates, whereupon they melt into ambrosia-light that enters the lama through his crown protrusion.
g) The ambrosia-light passes through his body and emerges into the womb of the consort, the Mother Vishvamātā, anointing the student, thereby conferring initiation.
h) The student emerges from the womb and is set back on the initiation seat at the respective door.
4 Obstructors are cleared away from both the students and the initiation substance – the water, crowns, etc. – with a mantra, *oṃ āḥ hūṃ hoḥ haṃ kṣhaḥ* and by scattering water from a conch.
5 The appropriate factors of the students – the five constituents, five aggregates, and so forth (see chapter six of the Introduction) – as well as the initiation substance are

purified in emptiness by way of reciting and reflecting on the meaning of the mantra oṃ shūnyatā-jñāna-vajra-svabhāvātmako 'ham, "I have the essential nature of indivisible emptiness and wisdom."

6 The corresponding factors of the students and the initiation substances each appear from within the emptiness of inherent existence as syllables, which transform into symbols, such as vajras, which transform into deities, usually embraced by their respective mates.

7 The actual deities are drawn into these imagined beings, whereby the latter become the actual deities.

8 The deities into which the initiation substances have transformed are conferred initiation by the five Mothers from within the mandala. This is done by pouring water from vases into their bodies through the top of their heads; when their bodies are filled, a little water at the crown of their heads transforms into a deity – the latter process being called "seal-impression".

9 Offering is made to the deities which were the initiation substances, whereupon they become absorbed with their partners, due to which they melt, turning again into the initiation substances – the fluid of the vases, the crowns, and so forth. What started out as the initiation substance and turned into a deity now turns back into the initiation substance but in a heightened, glorified form.

10 Light rays from the heart of the lama draw into the surrounding area the initiation deities – the male and female Buddhas and Bodhisattvas; he makes offering to them.

11 The lama requests the initiation deities in space to confer initiation on the students.

12 The initiation deities in space thereby develop an intention to confer initiation, but the actual conferral in the Kālachakra system will be done by deities from the mandala itself – the five female Buddhas, the five male Buddhas, and so forth. Each initiation will be conferred in its respective way – by touching the student with water, by putting on a crown, and so forth.

13 Since initiation is about to be conferred, a poetically thrilling expression of the auspiciousness of the occasion is

made.

14 A rain of flowers falls on the students.

15 The lama/Kālachakra declares that initiation will be conferred and does so through appropriate deities from within the mandala by touching the students' crown protrusion, right and left shoulders, upper arms, thighs, and hips with the respective initiation substance – water, crown, and so forth. Through the touch of these special initiation substances, a special bliss consciousness realizing the emptiness of inherent existence is generated in the student; this exalted wisdom of undifferentiable bliss and emptiness is the entity of each initiation.

16 A water initiation is conferred as an appendage to each initiation (except the first, which is, itself, a water initiation). The same declaration of conferring initiation is made, and the same five places are touched with water, thereby generating an exalted wisdom of undifferentiable bliss and emptiness.

17 The initiation is completed by the respective factors of the students – constituents, mental and physical aggregates, and so forth – actually turning into the corresponding deities. Doubles from the same deities in the mandala separate from them and dissolve into those deities, and all of the initiation deities assembled in space dissolve into those same deities which are purified appearances of the students' constituents, aggregates, and so forth.

18 Offering is made to the students in their divine state.

19 The meaning of the initiation and the purification that the initiation has either effected or established predispositions for effecting in the future are announced.

Basically, each initiation has three phases: (1) the cleansing and purifying of the students and initiation substances by clearing away obstructors and dissolving them into emptiness, (2) the heightening of the initiation substance through its re-appearance as a deity who melts and then transforms back into the initiation substance, and (3) the heightening of the students through their re-appearance as deities who then, by being touched with the initiation substance, engender a special bliss consciousness realizing the emptiness of inherent existence, after which doubles of the corresponding deities dissolve into the students to whom offerings are made. (The offerings have a *nature* of bliss and emptiness; they appear in the *aspect* of offering; and their *function* is as objects of use of the six sense powers in order to generate special uncontaminated bliss.[110] The bliss, in turn, is used to realize the emptiness of inherent existence. Rather than being suppressed, the senses are fulfilled with pleasant objects so that a blissful consciousness realizing emptiness can be produced. Not only is a blissful consciousness stronger, but also a ripening of the mental continuum has undoubtedly occurred through allowing the power latent in sensuous desire to become manifest.)

Through imagination, body, speech, and mind are acculturated to a process of purification that centers around generation of a blissful, and thus powerfully withdrawn, consciousness that is used to realize the nature of phenomena. The students begin from their position in cyclic existence with abject supplications to the supramundane Kālachakra and in the end become Buddhas themselves. The lama/Kālachakra even makes offerings to the students. The process is reminiscent of a Tibetan scholar's description of why Shākyamuni Buddha's teachings are called "wheels of teaching": "Shākyamuni turned down to students just those teachings of practices by which they could revolve upward to his state."

CORRESPONDENCES AND ALIGNMENTS OF THE SEVEN INITIATIONS

Each of the seven initiations is compared to a specific activity or stage in childhood.

Water Initiation

The first two initiations purify body; the water initiation, conferred by the five Mothers (also called the five female Ones Gone Thus or five female Buddhas) purifies the five constituents – earth, water, fire, wind, and space – and is compared a mother's washing her just born child. The correspondences are easy to see: the five constituents are compared to a just born child; the five Mothers are compared to a mother, and the activity of the water initiation is compared to washing a baby.

For the sake of clarity, let us list for the water initiation the five seed syllables, the symbols which those syllables become, the five Mothers with their consorts, the deities that are on their crowns as "seal-impressions", and the constituents that they cleanse:

ā	vajra	green Vajradhātvīshvarī with Vajrasattva	Akṣhobhya	space
ī	sword	black Tārā with Vairochana	Amoghasiddhi	wind
ṝ	jewel	red Pāṇḍarā with Amitābha	Ratnasambhava	fire
ū	lotus	white Māmakī with Ratnasambhava	Amitābha	water
ḹ	wheel	yellow Lochanā with Amoghasiddhi	Vairochana	earth

Of the five Mothers, four – Tārā, Pāṇḍarā, Māmakī, and Lochanā – reside on the fourth level of the mandala, the pristine consciousness mandala, in the intermediary directions. The fifth, Vajradhātvīshvarī, is fused with Kālachakra's consort, Vishvamātā.

Crown Initiation

The crown initiation, conferred by the five male Ones Gone Thus, also called the five male Buddhas, purifies the five aggregates – forms, feelings, discriminations, compositional factors, and consciousnesses – and is compared to fixing up the hair on the top of a child's head. Just as the crown that is used in the initiation is put on the head, so a child's hair is bound on top of the head. Though in the water initiation, the five Mothers are comparable to the mother who first washes her baby, here a correspondence with the five male Buddhas is unclear unless the father traditionally first ties the hair of a male child on top of his head.

For the crown initiation, the five seed syllables, the symbols which those syllables become, the five Buddhas with their consorts, the deities that are on their crown as "seal-impressions", and the aggregates that they cleanse are:

a	vajra	green Akṣhobhya with Prajñāpāramitā	Vajrasattva	consciousness
i	sword	black Amoghasiddhi with Lochanā	Amoghasiddhi	compositional factors
ṛ	jewel	red Ratnasambhava with Māmaki	Ratnasambhava	feelings
u	lotus	red Amitābha with Pāṇḍarā	Amitābha	discriminations
ḷ	wheel	yellow Vairochana with Tārā	Vairochana	forms

Of the five Buddhas, four – Amoghasiddhi, Ratnasambhava, Amitābha, and Vairochana – reside on the fourth level of the mandala, the pristine consciousness mandala, in the four primary directions. The fifth, Akṣhobhya, is fused with Kālachakra.

Silk Ribbon Initiation

The third and fourth initiations purify speech, the basis of which is wind, or inner currents. The silk ribbon initiation, conferred by the ten Shaktis, purifies the ten winds (inner currents) and is compared to piercing the ears of a child and hanging on adornments. The silk ribbons are long adornments hung from the crown that was put on during the second initiation; thus they are somewhat similar to ear-rings that hang from the ears. There seems to be nothing in the initiation similar to piercing the ears, and there seems to be no particular correspondence with the Shaktis unless a female servant pierces the ears of a child.

The ten seed syllables, the symbols which those syllables become, the ten Shaktis (who are all seal-impressed with Vajrasattva), and the winds that they cleanse are:

a	censor	black Kṛṣhṇadīptā	fire-accompanying wind
ha	black yak-tail fan	black Dhūmā	turtle wind
aḥ	butter lamp	red Raktadīptā	upward-moving wind
haḥ	red yak-tail fan	red Mārīchī	chameleon wind
aṃ	divine food	white Shretadīptā	pervasive wind
haṃ	white yak-tail fan	white Khadyotā	devadatta wind
ā	religious conch	yellow Pītadīptā	serpent wind
hā	yellow yak-tail fan	yellow Pradīpā	dhaṃnajaya wind
ho	vajra	green Vajradhatvīshvarī	vitalizing wind
phreṃ	curved knife	blue Vishvamāta	downward-voiding-wind

Of the ten Shaktis, eight reside on the fifth, or top, level of the mandala, the mandala of great bliss, on the eight lotus petals surrounding Kālachakra and Vishvamātā. Presumably, of the two Shaktis remaining, Vajradhatvīshvarī and Vishvamātā, the former is fused with Kālachakra's consort, Vishvamātā, and is the same as the fifth female One Gone Thus mentioned above with respect to the water initiation, and the latter is Vishvamātā herself.

The ten Shaktis are also called by the names of the ten perfections: Dānapāramitā, Shīlapāramitā, Kṣhāntipāramitā, Vīryapāramitā, Dhyānapāramitā, Prajñāpāramitā, Upāyapāramitā, Praṇidhānapāramitā, Balapāramitā, and Jñānapāramitā. They represent the perfections of giving, ethics, patience, effort, concentration, wisdom, method, prayer-wishes, power, and exalted wisdom.

Vajra and Bell Initiation

There are three main channels in the body; the central channel runs from the forehead to the top of the head, down the body near the backbone, and ends in the sexual organ. Above the navel, mainly wind flows in the central channel, and below the navel, mainly semen. The right and left channels are on the two sides of the central channel; above the navel, mainly blood and semen flow in the right and left channels respectively; below the navel, mainly feces and urine.[111] The wind that flows through all three channels is the basis of speech, and thus the vajra and bell initiation, conferred by Kālachakra and his consort Vishvamātā, which purifies the left and right channels, is associated with purifying speech. This initiation cleansing the avenues through which the wind that is the basis of speech moves is compared to a child's laughing and talking. Perhaps, Kālachakra and Vishvamātā can also be compared with the parents with whom the child first talks.

For the vajra and bell initiation, the two seed syllables, the symbols which those syllables become, the two principal deities and their consorts, the deities that are on their crowns as "seal-impressions", channels that they cleanse are:

hūṃ	vajra	blue Kālachakra with Vishvamātā	Akṣhobhya	right channel
phreṃ	curved knife	yellow Vishvamātā with Kālachakra	Vajrasattva	left channel

Conduct Initiation

The fifth and sixth initiations purify mind. The conduct initiation, conferred by the twelve male and twelve female Bodhisattvas, purifies the six sense powers – eye, ear, nose, tongue, body, and mental sense powers – as well as their respective objects – visible forms, sounds, odors, tastes, tangible objects, and other phenomena.[111a] It is compared to a child's enjoying the five attributes of the Desire Realm – pleasant visible forms, sounds, odors, tastes, and tangible objects.

For the conduct initiation, the twelve seed syllables, the symbols which those syllables become, the twelve Bodhisattvas and their consorts, the deities that are on their crowns as "seal-impressions", and the sense powers and objects that they cleanse are:

a	vajra	green Vajrapāṇi with blue Shabdavajrā	Vajrasattva	ear sense
ā	vajra	green Dharmadhātuvajrā with blue Samantabhadra	Vajrasattva	phenomena-constituent
e	sword	black Khagarbha with yellow Gandhavajrā	Amoghasiddhi	nose sense
ai	sword	black Sparshavajrā with yellow Sarvanivaraṇa-viṣhkambhi	Amoghasiddhi	tangible objects
ar	jewel	red Kṣhitigarbha with white Rūpavajrā	Ratnasaṃbhava	eye sense
ār	jewel	red Rasavajrā with white Lokeshvara	Ratnasaṃbhava	tastes
o	lotus	white Lokeshvara with red Rasavajrā	Amitābha	tongue sense
au	lotus	white Rūpavajrā with red Kṣhitigarbha	Amitābha	forms
al	wheel	yellow Sarvanivaraṇa-viṣhkambhi with black Sparshavajrā	Vairochana	body sense
āl	wheel	yellow Gandhavajrā with black Khagarbha	Vairochana	odors

aṃ	vajra	blue Samantabhadra with green Dharmąḍhātuvajrā	Akṣhobhya	mental sense
aḥ	vajra	blue Shabdavajrā with green Vajrapāṇi	Akṣhobhya	sounds

The twenty-four Bodhisattvas reside on the third level of the mandala, the mind mandala, to the right and left of the four doors and in the corners.

Name Initiation

The name initiation, conferred by the twelve male and twelve female Wrathful Deities, purifies the six action faculties – mouth, arms, legs, anus, urinary faculty, and regenerative faculty – and their respective activities – speaking, taking, going, defecating, urinating, and emitting regenerative fluid. It is compared with naming a child. Since, at the end of the initiation, the lama gives names to the students in accordance with their lineage, the initiation is like naming a child; the giver of the name, being the lama, might also be compared with a parent who names a child.

For the name initiation, the twelve seed syllables, the symbols which those syllables become, the twelve Wrathful Deities and their consorts, the deities that are on their crowns as "seal-impressions", and the sense powers and objects that they cleanse are:

ha	vajra	green Uṣhṇīṣha-chakravartī with blue Atinīlā	Vajrasattva	faculty of urination
hā	vajra	green Raudrākshī with blue Sumbharāja	Vajrasattva	emitting semen

ya	sword	black Vighnāntaka with yellow Stambhakī	Amoghasiddhi	mouth faculty
yā	sword	black Atibalā with yellow Yamāntaka	Amoghasiddhi	defecating
ra	jewel	red Prajñāntaka with white Māmaki	Ratnasambhava	arm faculty
rā	jewel	red Jambhakī with white Padmāntaka	Ratnasambhava	going
va	lotus	white Padmāntaka with red Jambhakī	Amitābha	leg faculty
vā	lotus	white Mānakī with red Prajñāntaka	Amitābha	taking
la	wheel	yellow Yamāntaka with black Atibalā	Vairochana	faculty of defecation
lā	wheel	yellow Stambhakī with black Vighnāntaka	Vairochana	speaking
haṃ	vajra	blue Sumbharāja with green Raudrākṣhī	Akṣhobhya	supreme faculty
haḥ	vajra	blue Atinīlā with green Uṣhṇiṣha chakra vartī	Akṣhobhya	urinating

The twenty-four Wrathful Deities are (1) the four male Wrathful Deities with their four consorts residing in the doorways of the third level of the mandala, the mind mandala, (2) Uṣhṇī-shachakravartī with Atinīla who are above the mind mandala, (3) Sumbharāja with Raudrākṣhī who reside in the body mandala, and (4) all of these same deities but with the females predominant.

Permission Initiation

The seventh, and last, initiation purifies bliss. The permission initiation, conferred by Vajrasattva and Prajñāpāramitā, purifies the pristine consciousness aggregate and pristine consciousness constituent, both of which refer to blissful and non-conceptual states. The initiation, in which the students are told to teach doctrine to the various types of sentient beings, is compared to a father's telling a child what to read and so forth. Just as a father gives reading to a child, so the lama gives the *Kālachakra Tantra* to students but for them to teach others.

For the permission initiation, the two seed syllables, the symbols that those syllables become, the two deities, the deities that are on their crowns as "seal-impressions", and the factors that they cleanse are:

haṃ	vajra	blue Vajrasattva with Dharmadhātvīshvarī	Akṣhobhya	pristine consciousness aggregate
kṣhaḥ	vajra	blue Prajñāpāramitā with Akṣhobhya	Akṣhobhya	pristine consciousness constituent

In the mandala, Vajrasattva resides on Kālachakra's head, and Prajñāpāramitā is fused with Kālachakra's consort, Vishvamātā.

TRANSFORMATION

With each internal initiation, the students are reborn in an ideal fashion. The internal initiations purify stages of development in the womb.[111b] The first internal initiation, received from the northern, white, very peaceful, body face of Kālachakra, corresponds to the development of the students' physical constituents and aggregates in the womb. These are the bases of purification to be purified by three activities of the lama (who is in the Vajra Body aspect of Kālachakra):

1 generating the students as Vajra Body deities
2 making them indivisible from the actual Vajra Body Deity, called a Wisdom-Being
3 conferring initiation with the mind of enlightenment which is the melted form of all the Buddhas of the ten directions.

In this way, the first internal initiation purifies the process of the initial development of the students' physical constituents and aggregates in the womb and establishes seeds that serve as antidotes to such uncontrolled development.

In the same pattern, the second internal initiation, received from the southern, red, desirous, speech face of Kālachakra, corresponds to the development of the students' winds and channels in the womb – the winds and channels being the foundation of speech. The third internal initiation, received from the eastern, black, fierce, mind face of Kālachakra, corresponds to the development of the students' sense powers and action faculties in the womb. The fourth internal initiation, received from the western, yellow, meditatively stabilized, pristine consciousness (bliss) face of Kālachakra, corresponds to the development of the students' aggregate of pristine consciousness and constituent of pristine consciousness in the womb. (A wind of pristine consciousness is said to circulate in the womb immediately after conception). These four internal initiations purify, or establish potencies for purifying, the respective development of the students' body, speech, mind, and bliss in the womb-state.

The seven initiations themselves are modelled on important events in childhood, after emergence from the womb. The water initiation corresponds to a mother's washing her newborn child; the crown initiation corresponds to fixing up the hair on the top of a child's head; the silk ribbon initiation corresponds to piercing the ears of a child and hanging on adornments; the vajra and bell initiation corresponds to a child's laughing and talking; the conduct initiation corresponds to a child's enjoying the five sense objects of the Desire Realm; the name initiation corresponds to naming a child; the permission initiation corresponds to a father's giving reading and so forth to a child.

Just as conception and birth are re-lived in each internal initiation, so in the seven initiations significant or even peak childhood events are re-enacted. Of the seven comparisons, at least four – washing the newborn child, fixing up the hair on the top of a child's head, piercing the ears of a child and hanging on adornments, and naming – are so important in the development of a child as to be marked by rites of passage.[112] The other three events are also transitional; a child's first laughing and first talking (which do not occur at the same time) are pivotal events in the development of a child *as experienced by the child,* for the gaining of sufficient control to laugh autonomously and then to utter words under one's own control are events of enormous proportions for a child. With the initial experience of such control is a sense of wonder, of completely being involved in these activities. Also, a child's enjoying the five sense objects of the Desire Realm, whether it be the first occasion (which then would be five occasions corresponding with the five objects) or whenever such enjoyment occurs, is a time of interested fascination and non-conceptual enjoyment. A father's giving reading to a child also marks an introduction to the activities of one's lineage; a child approaches the first enactment of the family duties with the wonder of entering a new world.[113]

These events are cited as comparisons for the seven initiations so that, in reinvoking and reenacting them, the wonder, non-conceptuality, and absorption integral to them can be reexperienced. Then, the wondrous, non-conceptual, absorbed consciousness is to be experienced in a new context of using it to realize the emptiness of inherent existence. The power and focus of such a consciousness is put to use in penetrating the nature of persons and other phenomena. Also, these childhood experiences, still pivotal in our adult experience of ourselves and the world around us, are reframed away from unclear non-conceptuality to clear non-conceptuality that understands, realizes, and comprehends the nature of objects. When a practitioner can use such happily non-conceptual consciousnesses in the path, the consciousnesses become exalted wisdoms of undifferentiable bliss and emptiness. This means that a blissful consciousness and a consciousness realizing the emptiness of inherent existence, which are usually separate, come together in one consciousness; the bliss consciousness (not consciousness *of* bliss but bliss itself) realizes emptiness.

From the viewpoint of the substances used in the seven initiations, the freshness and enjoyment of being touched with water, a crown, a silk ribbon, vajra and bell, a thumb ring, a bracelet, and the five hand-symbols are used to develop a powerful consciousness realizing the nature of phenomena. The comparison with important events in childhood and the usage of a happy, enjoying consciousness in the path suggest that peak experiences of childhood need to be re-evoked and that such happy, fresh minds need to be reframed so that they are endowed with a capacity to realize the nature of phenomena, the emptiness of inherent existence, rather than just being caught up in unclear non-conceptual happiness.

The Four Drops

Basic to this process of utilizing pivotal states and cleansing transformation of them into path-consciousnesses is a presentation, in the Kālachakra system, of four drops that are bases of potential and of defilement, and hence bases to be utilized and purified. There are two sets of four drops; the first set is located at (1) the forehead (or crown), (2) throat, (3) heart, and (4) navel; the second set is located at (1) the navel, (2) secret place (the base of the spine), (3) center of the sexual organ, and (4) tip of the sexual organ.[114] The drops themselves are material, the size of a mustard seed and composed of the basic white and red constituents.

The two sets of drops are coordinated in that (1) the drops at the forehead and the navel produce the state of wakefulness, (2) the drops at the throat and the base of the spine produce the state of dreaming, (3) the drops at the heart and the center of the sexual organ produce the state of deep sleep, and (4) the drops at the navel and the tip of the sexual organ produce the state of absorption (bliss). One drop at the navel contains within it two different predispositions producing the waking state as the fourth of the upper set of drops and producing the state of absorption as the first of the lower set of drops.

At the time of wakefulness, the winds – upon which consciousness is mounted as on a horse – of the upper part of the body collect at the forehead, and the winds of the lower part of the body collect at the navel. Due to the collection of the winds in those places and due to each drop's containing pure and impure potencies, mere appearances of objects and appearances of impure objects are respectively produced.

At the time of dreams, the upper winds collect at the throat and the lower winds collect in the secret region, whereby mere sounds and mistaken speech are produced. At the time of deep sleep, the upper winds collect at the heart and the lower winds collect at the center of the head of the sexual organ, whereby non-conceptuality and unclarity are produced. At the time of absorption of male and female, the upper winds collect at the navel and the lower winds collect at the tip of the sexual organ, whereby bliss and emission (of semen for men and "arousal fluid" for women) are produced.

As is evident, the drops produce effects respectively with regard to body, speech, mind, and pristine consciousness (non-conceptuality and bliss) and hence are called drops of *exalted* body, speech, mind, and pristine consciousness and drops of body, speech, mind, and pristine consciousness, respectively. The organization of the seven initiations into the four groups of body, speech, mind, and pristine consciousness or bliss is, therefore, done in terms of cleansing the impure factors of these four.

Through cleansing, that is, removing, the capacity in the drops at the forehead and the navel to produce the appearance of impure objects, the mere appearance of objects can be utilized in the path, whereby there come to be appearances of empty forms. Through cleansing the capacity in the drops at the throat and the base of the spine to produce mistaken speech, mere sounds can be utilized in the path, whereby they become invincible sound. Through cleansing the capacity in the drops at the heart and the middle of the head of the sexual organ to produce unclarity, non-conceptuality can be utilized in the path, whereby it becomes non-conceptual exalted wisdom. Through cleansing the capacity in the drops at the navel and the tip of the sexual organ to produce emission, bliss can be utilized in the path, whereby it becomes immutable great bliss. Through developing these in higher and higher forms, they become the exalted vajra body, speech, mind, and pristine consciousness (bliss) of a Buddha.

In the Kālachakra system, all obstructions are included in the obstructions of these four types in the sense that the very subtle wind and mind that abide in these drops are bases of infusion of the predispositions for the respective obstructions. In other words, the material of the drops does not constitute the obstructions and does not serve as the basis for the karmic infusion of the obstructions. Rather, the very subtle wind and mind that are located in these two sets of four places are the bases infused by our deeds with karmic potencies.

In Highest Yoga Tantra, the potencies that produce impure environments and beings by way of the very subtle wind and mind that exist in the basic or ordinary state are purified by paths of skill in means, whereby they are transformed into the Form Body and the Truth Body of Buddha. In particular, in the Kālachakra system, the potencies producing impure states through the four types of drops serve as causes for the vajra body, speech, mind, and bliss of a Buddha through being purified by the path. Initiation is an introduction to this process of purification of defilement and utilization of what is basically present.

OTHER CORRELATIONS

Entities Of The Initiation

In the water initiation, the students' crown, right and left shoulders, upper arms, thighs, and hips are touched with water, and the students drink the water.[114a] Thereby, physical defilements of their five impure constituents are cleansed, and great bliss is generated in mind and body. The bliss consciousness ascertains emptiness such that a special exalted wisdom of undifferentiable bliss and realization of emptiness is generated in the students' continuums. That exalted wisdom of bliss and emptiness is the entity of the water initiation; all of the other steps are causal factors producing it, not the actual water initiation.

In the crown initiation, the students' five places are touched with the crown which is also worn, whereby all defilements of the appearance and conception of the five mental and physical aggregates as being ordinary are cleansed, and great bliss is generated in mind and body. The bliss consciousness ascertains emptiness such that a special exalted wisdom of bliss and emptiness is generated in the students' continuums. That exalted wisdom of bliss and emptiness is the entity of the crown initiation. It can be imagined that when the crown is put on the head, ambrosia streams forth from it filling the body, cleansing it and generating the exalted wisdom of bliss and emptiness.

In the silk ribbon initiation, the students' five places are touched with silk ribbons which are also tied on their forehead. From them, ambrosia streams forth, filling the body, cleansing defilements of the ten winds and generating the exalted wisdom of bliss and emptiness that is the entity of the silk ribbon initiation.

In the vajra and bell initiation, the students' five places are touched with vajra and bell which are also set on their head and then given into their hands. From vajra and bell, ambrosia streams forth, filling the body, cleansing defilements of the two channels and generating the exalted wisdom of bliss and emptiness that is the entity of the vajra and bell initiation.

In the conduct initiation, the students' five places are touched with a thumb ring which is also worn on the thumb. From it, ambrosia streams forth, filling the body, cleansing defilements of the sense powers and their objects and generating the exalted wisdom of bliss and emptiness that is the entity of the conduct initiation.

In the name initiation, the students' five places are touched with bracelets which are also worn on the arms. From them, ambrosia streams forth, filling the body, cleansing defilements of the action faculties and their activities and generating the exalted wisdom of bliss and emptiness that is the entity of the name initiation. It is called a "name initiation" because through the purification of the action faculties and their activities, one becomes suitable to be a basis for the name Akṣhobhya, Ratnasambhava, Amoghasiddhi, Amitābha, or Vairochana.

In the permission initiation, the students' five places are touched with five hand-symbols – vajra, sword, jewel, lotus, and wheel – which are also given into their hands. From them, ambrosia streams forth, filling the body, cleansing defilements of pristine mind (bliss) and generating the exalted wisdom of bliss and emptiness that is the entity of the permission initiation.

Then, just as a universal monarch controls all four continents through a jewelled wheel, a wheel is given to the student as a causal factor for turning the wheel of doctrine. A conch is given for the sake of proclaiming the sound of doctrine. Also, a book of the *Kālachakra Tantra* is given so that the students can fill themselves with its meaning and thereupon turn the wheel of Kālachakra doctrine for others. Then, a bell representing the emptiness of inherent existence is given as a reminder of the realization of the status of all persons and all phenomena within which the teaching of doctrine is to be done. Just as a father gives reading and so forth in accordance with the family lineage, so the lama/Kālachakra calls on the students to teach the Buddhist doctrine. That this is to be done in accordance with the dispositions and interests of trainees is indicated by giving the five hand symbols representing the five lineages.

Just as the four internal initiations are concerned with purifying the process of development of body, speech, mind, and bliss in the womb, so the corresponding four groups into which the seven initiations are divided are concerned with purifying the process of development of body, speech, mind, and bliss in childhood after leaving the womb. Since it is explained that the bliss constituent is completed at age sixteen,[114b] the period of childhood development that is the focus of these seven initiations presumably is to age sixteen.

The seven initiations also are correlated with the first seven Bodhisattva grounds, each one establishing potencies for achieving the respective level. Just as each of the seven initiations is an entity of the exalted wisdom of undifferentiable bliss and emptiness, so each Bodhisattva ground is a higher and higher level of meditative equipoise directly realizing emptiness, the wisdom consciousness serving as a basis, or ground, for the flowering of numerous, beneficial qualities. Nevertheless, to achieve any of the seven Bodhisattva grounds, practitioners must receive the higher initiations and practice the stage of completion.

The first six initiations also authorize practitioners to work at achieving feats respectively by way of the five Mothers, the five Buddhas, ten Shaktis, the principal Father Deity and Mother Deity, the male and female Bodhisattvas, and the male and female Wrathful Deities. They also establish potencies in the mental continuum for achieving the five Mothers, the five Buddhas, and the ten perfections, as well as for binding the wind from the right and left channels in the central channel, achieving vajra sense powers and sense fields, and overcoming the four demons through the four immeasurables.

The first two initiations establish potencies for vajra body; the next two, for vajra speech; the next two, for vajra mind; and the last (although unmentioned) for vajra bliss. All seven initiations together *cleanse* defilements of ill-deeds, *authorize* cultivating the stage of generation and the achievement of the final worldly feats of the Highest Pure Land, *set* potencies in the continuum for the collection of merit, and *bestow* practices and releases related with the stage of generation.

Practitioners who have received the seven initiations in the pattern of childhood cultivate a stage of generation that is able to purify both the external and internal bases of purification. The bases of purification are the external worldly environment and the channels, winds, and drops of a person; these are called, respectively, the *external Kālachakra* and the *internal Kālachakra*. For this, meditative cultivation of either a complete mandala of body, speech, and mind, or of just the mind mandala (which here means the top three levels of the mandala), or of a mandala of five or more deities is needed. A simple meditation of just Kālachakra or of just Kālachakra with consort is not sufficient to fulfill the stage of generation. This meditative cultivation of the path, the means of purification, is called the *alternative Kālachakra* as is initiation also. Such a stage of generation is said to serve as a means of ripening roots of virtue for fully generating the stage of completion.

ALTRUISTIC TRANSMUTATION

Through being introduced, during the initiation, to utilizing the Buddha nature – the luminous and knowing nature of the mind and the emptiness of inherent existence of the mind – as a basis of physical, verbal, and mental manifestation, practitioners make a transition to a new mode of life, away from being driven by afflictive emotions and to a state of validly founded freedom that is in the service of altruistic expression. Practitioners have been authorized to practice and have been introduced to the practice of deity yoga, the very appearance of altruistically motivated wisdom in physical form, mimicking a Buddha's manifestation in numerous Form Bodies from within the Truth Body.

Tantric practice, although using the model of the goal – Buddhahood with Truth and Form Bodies – in the path, is still in process toward the goal of altruistic perfection. In other words, that the model of the final state is used in the path does not mean that the goal is conceived as actually being fully manifest in the present state. Rather, the process of the path is *modelled* after the goal-state. Also, despite using desire in the path, it is clear from the numerous cleansings that have occurred in this ritual that tantric practice is still aimed at cleansing the afflictive emotions of desire, hatred, and so forth as well as the entire process of cyclic existence through mimicking its processes in a profoundly different context. There are "upward mimickings" of Buddhahood and "downward mimickings" of the uncontrolled processes of cyclic existence. A prime technique in both of these is to evoke blissful, non-conceptual experiences that are usually associated with unclarity and to utilize those powerful consciousnesses in a clear, insightful way penetrating the nature of phenomena so that afflictive emotions are impossible. Also, that altruism is at the very heart of the process is clear from the fact that the initiation begins with an adjustment of motivation toward altruism and ends with authorization to teach by way of the wise altruism that takes account of individual predispositions and interests.

APPENDAGES

Of the two appendages to the permission initiation, the main is the second, the vajra master initiation. It is preceded by four branches – giving mantra, eye medicine, mirror, and bow and arrow; let us discuss these first.

Mantra is given because both common feats and the uncommon feat of Buddhahood depend upon mantra practice. Common feats of pacification of illness, etc., increase of intelligence, lifespan, etc., subjugation, and ferocity are accomplished based on the usage of mantras during the stage of generation. These are called provisional mantras in relation to the definitive mantra, an actual exalted wisdom of bliss and emptiness, through which the supreme feat of Buddhahood is accomplished.

Then, since the view of the emptiness of inherent existence is essential to mantra practice, both provisional and definitive, eye medicine, mirror, and bow and arrow are given to establish predispositions in the mind, respectively, for realizing emptiness conceptually, for realizing that all appearing and occurring phenomena are like illusions in that they appear to exist inherently but do not, and for realizing emptiness directly. The dramatic experience of realizing emptiness through the medium of an internal image (not just discursively putting together words about emptiness but incontrovertibly realizing it) is like the experience of seeing after having cataracts removed. The experience of phenomena as like illusions is like seeing objects in a mirror. The totally non-dual experience of emptiness in which the emptiness of inherent existence and the wisdom consciousness realizing it are fused is like an arrow piercing its target deeply. These analogs are given so that students will imaginatively enact states that are similar to the wisdom experiences being sought, thereby conditioning the mind in those directions. The metaphors bring home some sense of what it would be like to see without a film of ignorance, what it would be like to see everything as discordant with its appearance, and what it would be like for the mind to pierce into emptiness. The students are directed to imagine that they have attained the "eye" seeing the reality of the emptiness of inherent existence, that they have attained realization – subsequent to meditative equipoise on emptiness – of phenomena as like reflections, and that they have attained direct realization of emptiness. Imagining such establishes potencies for actually doing so.

In the vajra master initiation, the main appendage, the initiation substances are a vajra and a bell. These, along with the students, dissolve into emptiness. The students and the vajra reappear as Vajrasattvas, and the bell reappears as the goddess Prajñāpāramitā ("Perfection of Wisdom"). All of them become the actual deities by drawing the Wisdom Beings (the actual deities) into themselves. The deities are conferred initiation, whereupon those that are the new appearances of the initiation substances melt and turn into vajra and bell.

The vajra is first given to the student as a symbol of the exalted wisdom of great bliss, and then the bell is given as a symbol of the wisdom realizing emptiness. These two – great bliss and the wisdom realizing emptiness – are to be generated as one consciousness, the great bliss consciousness itself realizing emptiness.

That great bliss wisdom consciousness itself appears as a divine body, called a great seal divine body. Technically speaking, the "apprehension aspect" *(bzung rnam)* of the great bliss consciousness appears as a body, but this is explained as meaning that the consciousness itself appears as a deity. The appearance factor of the great bliss consciousness appears as a divine body, and the ascertainment factor continues to realize the emptiness of inherent existence. In this way, the factors of altruistic method and wisdom of the final nature of phenomena are contained in one consciousness. This is the one undifferentiable entity of method and wisdom in tantra – deity yoga. The entity of the vajra master initiation is just this appearance of the blissful wisdom consciousness realizing emptiness in divine form. As a master initiation at this point, it authorizes students to teach Action, Performance, and Yoga Tantra. (The initiation authorizing students to teach Highest Yoga Tantra comes after the four high and four greatly high initiations).

The vajra, representing bliss, is associated with mind. The bell, although representing the wisdom realizing emptiness, is associated with speech in that the wisdom realizing emptiness is the dominant condition giving rise to a Buddha's effortlessly and spontaneously teaching whatever is appropriate to whatsoever trainees. Also, the emptiness of inherent existence is the main topic taught through the speech of all Buddhas since it must be realized (and that realization must be enhanced with altruistic method) to bring about the state of perpetual help and happiness of Buddhahood. The sound of the bell is considered to proclaim the meaning of the emptiness of inherent existence. The great seal, representing a divine body, is associated with body. Thus, the three pledges of vajra, bell, and seal are concerned with body, speech, and mind. By taking the initiation, the students pledge to be mindful of such great bliss, realization of emptiness, and its appearance in divine form through holding vajra and bell and crossing them at the heart.

In this context, "great bliss" does not refer to the bliss arising from embracing a consort, etc., for those bliss consciousnesses realizing emptiness are the entities of the four high and four greatly high initiations that authorize practice of the stage of completion. The harmony between the stage of generation and the stage of completion is that in both blissful consciousnesses are utilized to realize the mode of being of phenomena and to become the stuff of new appearance. However, in the stage of completion more intensely blissful, and thus more withdrawn and more subtle levels of consciousness, are manifested, whereby, eventually, reappearance as a deity can be done in actuality.

That the seven initiations introducing the basic tantric procedure and authorizing their practice end with emphasis on deity yoga and on teaching others illustrates the distinctive feature of tantra – the composite in one consciousness of compassion and wisdom embodied in pure altruistic activity. The seven initiations show that tantra, far from being a divergence from the basic principles of sūtra practice, is a reformulation of those very principles within utilizing many subtle techniques to enhance their incorporation in the body, speech, and mind of practitioners.

9 *The Texts*

INITIATION RITE

The ritual text of initiation that is translated in this book is the *Mandala Rite of the Glorious Kālachakra: Illumination of the Thought (dpal dus kyi 'khor lo'i dkyil chog dgongs pa rab gsal)* by Kay-drup-ge-lek-b̄el-sang *(mkhas grub dge legs dpal bzang,* 1385-1438).[115] Translated from that text are the sections on enhancement of the students and on the seven initiations authorizing practice of the stage of generation, the latter being written mainly for those doing self-entry into the Kālachakra mandala. Self-entry is performed by practitioners who have already received initiation, for the sake of purifying infractions of vows and so forth; practitioners themselves imagine all of the lama's activities involved in entering into the mandala and receiving initiation.

Because the section on the seven initiations authorizing practice of the stage of generation was written mainly in terms of practitioners performing self-entry, it has been supplemented with material from the *Initiation Rite of Kālachakra, Stated in an Easy Way (dus 'khor dbang chog nag 'gros su bkod pa)* by L̄o-sang-tsul-trim-d̄en-b̄ay-gyel-tsen *(blo bzang tshul khrims bstan pa'i rgyal mtshan),* a late nineteenth and early twentieth century scholar from Kam Province *(khams)* known also as D̄re-wo Kang-s̄ar-Ḡyap-gön Rin-b̄o-chay *(tre bo skyabs mgon khang gsar rin po che).*[116] This latter text was written solely for the sake of adapting the former text to conducting an initiation ceremony. The latter text does not contain the prior ritual of enhancement of the student and hence is not complete even in terms of what the initiator must perform for students. However, Kay-drup's text covers all of the stages involved in an initiation ritual, ranging from the rite for taking over the land where the ritual is conducted to the greatly high initiations. Other aspects of the ritual are not complete in Kay-drup's text but can be found in L̄o-sang-tsul-trim-d̄en-b̄ay-gyel-tsen's. For instance, Kay-drup's *Mandala Rite* seldom gives full descriptions of deities, indicating these with ellipses; these, therefore, have been supplemented from L̄o-sang-tsul-trim-d̄en-b̄ay-gyel-tsen's *Initiation Rite.* Thus, the two texts together contain the entire rite.

However, since there are seven initiations with a great deal of repetition, both texts tend to cite in full only once material requiring repetition. To give a more complete picture of the process of initiation, in the translation here, all of these repetitions have been stated in full rather than merely indicated by ellipses.

The portion of Kay-drup's *Mandala Rite* translated in this book concerns the initiations for the stage of generation and, specifically, those parts involving the student, not the preceding sections during which the lama is making preparations. Kay-drup's text is divided into six parts, of which the sections in the sixth part concerned with authorizing students to practice the stage of generation are translated here. The six parts of the text are:

1 the qualifications of a master who confers initiation, 261.2
2 the qualifications of a student on whom initiation is conferred, 262.1
3 divisions of types of mandalas in which initiation is conferred, 262.7
4 the number and order of the initiations that are conferred, 264.2
5 the time of conferral, 265.7
6 the actual rite for conferring initiation, 266.1.

The first five topics are treated only very briefly in five pages.

The sixth topic is subdivided into two sections:

1 the student's first making a supplication and [the master's] taking him/her under his protection, 266.1
2 the stages of how a lama engages in the mandala rite, 266.3.

The first topic is handled in a single line of text. The second topic is again subdivided into four parts:

1 rite for the place, 266.3
2 rite of enhancement, 282.5
3 actual rite, 305.6
4 rite of conclusion.

Among many subdivisions of the rite of enhancement, the second topic, is the rite of enhancing, or preparing, the student (Kay 295.1/Bu 184.1).[117] It is the first activity performed with the students who are to receive initiation, and thus the translation in this book begins here.

The enhancement of the student has six parts:

1 adjusting the motivation and conferring the internal initiation, Kay 295.1/Bu 184.1
2 making a supplication and causing [the student] to apprehend the doctrine, Kay 296.1/Bu 185.1
3 assuming the vows and blessing, Kay 296.6/Bu 185.6
4 casting the tooth stick and giving handfuls of water and so forth, Kay 298.4/Bu 186.7
5 setting the six lineages and evoking Vajrasattva, Kay 299.2/Bu187.5
6 generating enthusiasm through explaining doctrine and giving advice on analyzing dreams, Kay 299.4/Bu 187.7.

Although in Kay-drup's text there are other steps following the enhancement of the students, in practice those are done prior to the enhancement of the student so that the actual initiation ritual can be conducted immediately after the enhancement, on the next day.

The actual rite of conferring the seven initiations has many sub-topics:

A. Entering the mandala, Kay 317.5

1. Entering blindfolded, Kay 317.7
   a. Entering outside the curtain, Kay 318.1/Bu 206.6
   b. Entering inside, Kay 320.4/Bu 210.2
      1) Entering inside and paying obeisance while circling it, Kay 320.4/Bu 210.3
      2) Setting [the student] in the pledges, Kay 322.5/Bu 210.7
      3) Speaking the truth upon the descent of the wisdom being, Kay 323.5/Bu 211.6
2. Entering such that one comes to have the nature of seeing the mandala, Kay 325.5/Bu 213.4

B. Conferring initiation on one who has entered, Kay 326.6/Bu 214.4

1. Conferring the seven initiations in the manner of childhood, Kay 326.6/Bu 214.4
   a. The rites of the seven initations, Kay 326.6/Bu 214.4
      1) Making a supplication in common and purifying inauspiciousness, Kay 326.7/Bu 214.5
      2) Bestowing the seven initiations individually, Kay 327.4/Bu 215.3
      a) Water initiation, Kay 327.4/Bu 215.3
      b) Crown initiation, Kay 332.2/Bu 217.6
      c) Silk ribbon initiation, Kay 333.7/Bu 218.4
      d) Vajra and bell initiation, Kay 336.1/Bu 219.3
      e) Conduct initiation, Kay 337.3/Bu 220.1
      f) Name initiation, Kay 339.4/Bu 220.6
      g) Permission initiation, Kay 341.7/Bu 221.7
         1* Actual permission initiation, Kay 342.1/Bu 221.7
         2* Appendages, Kay 343.7/Bu 223.3
         a* Four branches appended – giving mantra and so forth, Kay 343.7/Bu 223.3
         b* Giving the master's initiation, the main appendage, Kay 345.3/Bu 225.1
   b. Understanding the time of attainment, Kay 348.6/Bu 230.7
   c. Advice to abandon root infractions, Kay 349.2/Bu 231.4

RITES FOR DAILY PRACTICE

The first practice text is *The Guru Yoga of Kālachakra In Connection With the Six Sessions In Completely Facilitating Form (thun drug dang 'brel ba'i·dus 'khor bla ma'i rnal 'byor nag 'gros su mdzad pa)*, (Madison: Deer Park, 1981). At the behest of His Holiness the Dalai Lama, the basic six session yoga was adapted to the practice of Kālachakra by his Senior Tutor, the ninety-seventh occupant of the throne of Gan-den, Tup-d̄en-luṇg-d̄ok-n̄am-gyel-trin-lay *(thub bstan lung rtogs rnam rgyal 'phrin las)* known as L̄ing Rin-b̄o-chay *(gling rin po che,* 1903-1983). Since, as L̄ing Rin-b̄o-chay says, the Dalai Lama indicated "the nature of the contents and how to arrange the order" (see p.424), the authorship seems to be shared between them. (For a discussion of their borrowings from other works, see pp.381-2 and the notes to that section).

The second practice text is the basic six session yoga that was written by the First Paṇ-chen Lama L̄o-sang-chö-ḡyi-gyel-tsen *(blo bzang chos kyi rgyal mtshan,* 1567?-1662). Untitled, it is found in the first volume of his Collected Works.[118] Nowadays it is sometimes mistakenly ascribed to Pa-bong-ka *(pha bong-kha,* 1878-1941) who cites it in its entirety in his *Extensive And Abbreviated Modes of Practicing the Six Session Yoga, Adorned with Quintessential Instructions For Easy Implementation (thun drug gi rnal 'byor rgyas bsdus nyams su len tshul 'khyer bde man ngag gis brgyan pa)*, (Kalimpong: Mani Printing Works, no date). Pa-bong-ka's text has an additional review of the individual vows and three stanzas of prayer-wishes at the end, which are included here.

The final practice text is an untitled abbreviated six session yoga, formulated by L̄o-sang-d̄en-dzin *(blo bzang bstan 'dzin)*, found in the back of the work by Pa-bong-ka just mentioned.[119]

TRANSLATION

During a one month research visit to India in the spring of 1980 sponsored by the American Institute of Indian Studies, I met with His Holiness the Dalai Lama to receive teachings on the Kālachakra system. He gave commentary on (1) the sections on initiation and the stage of generation in Gyel-tsap's *How To Practice the Two Stages of the Path of the Glorious Kālachakra: Quick Entry to the Path of Great Bliss,* (2) the section on the enhancement of the student and the seven initiations authorizing practice of the stage of generation in Kay-drup's *Mandala Rite,* and (3) the Kālachakra practice rite.

In the spring of 1981, Jam-b̄el-shen-pen Rin-b̄o-chay, who was visiting the Center For South Asian Studies at the University of Virginia, taught me the same sections of Kay-drup's *Mandala Rite,* while I was translating it in preparation for the Kālachakra initiation in Madison in July, 1981. Also, his commentary on the section on the Kālachakra system in Nga-w̄ang-b̄el-den's *(ngag dbang dpal ldan,* born 1797) *Illumination of the Texts of Tantra, Presentation of the Grounds and Paths of the Four Great Secret Tantra Sets (gsang chen rgyud sde bzhi'i sa lam gyi rnam bzhag rgyud gzhung gsal byed)* was particularly helpful.

Jam-b̄el-shen-pen Rin-b̄o-chay was born in Ba in the Kam Provinċe of Tibet; he is a Ge-luk-b̄a ge-s̄hay from Gan-den Monastic University who became abbot of the Tantric College of Lower Hla-s̄a during the difficult period of its resettlement in Hunsar in South India. In 1984 he was appointed head of the Ge-luk-b̄a order. Though his speciality is the *Guhyasamāja Tantra,* he prepared for our work by reading a great deal of Kay-drup's four volume commentary on the *Kālachakra Tantra* and on Kulika Puṇḍarīka's *Great Commentary on the "Kālachakra Tantra", the Stainless Light.* Not only were his explanations of the Kālachakra helpful, but also the general background that I gained from his wide experience with tantric ritual was especially helpful.

Just before the initiation in Madison, the Dalai Lama answered a number of questions about the ritual and then during it gave extensive commentary on the initiation process. Afterwards, during 1984 and 1985, I checked the translation of Kay-drup's *Mandala Rite* against the Tibetan while listening to the tapes of the Dalai Lama's and Jam-b̄el-shen-pen Rin-b̄o-chay's explanations, inserting into Kay-drup's text the Dalai Lama's commentaries from the Madison initiation and from our private meetings. The combination of text and commentary (clearly differentiated with the former indented and the latter at the margin) removes much of the obscurity that surrounds tantra by showing how the ritual is actually used and interpreted.

The same process of translation, re-checking against the Tibetan, and insertion of commentary was followed with respect to the Kālachakra daily practice rite. The commentary, mainly from the Dalai Lama but also from Jam-b̄el-shen-pen Rin-b̄o-chay, is in notes at the bottom of the page.

The translations have benefitted greatly from the contextualization and explanation received from these two very distinguished and learned lamas. Frankly, the task could not have been attempted without their help; though not guaranteeing that the translations are error-free, the process of consultation has greatly reduced the number of gross errors.

Also, since Kay-drup relied heavily on the works of Bu-d̄ön Rin-chen-drup, I have made liberal reference to Bu-d̄ön's:

1 *Mandala Rite of the Glorious Kālachakra: Source of Good Qualities (dpal dus kyi 'khor lo'i dkyil chog yon tan kun 'byung)*
2 *Easily Understandable Annotations For the Condensed Glorious Kālachakra Tantra, Great King of Tantras Arisen from the Supreme Original Buddha (mchog gi dang po'i sangs rgyas las phyungs ba rgyud kyi rgyal po chen po dpal dus kyi 'khor lo'i bsdus pa'i rgyud kyi go sla'i mchan)*
3 *Commentarial Explanation of the "Initiation Chapter"* [*of the Kālachakra Tantra*], *Annotations to (Kulika Puṇḍarīka's) "Stainless Light" (dbang gi le'u 'grel bshad dri med 'od kyi mchan)*
4 *Means of Achievement of the Supramundane Victor, the Glorious Kālachakra: Fruit Cluster of the Wish-Granting* [*Tree*] *(dpal dus kyi 'khor lo'i sgrub thabs dpag bsam snye ma)*.

Frequent reference is also made to the Seventh Dalai Lama's *Means of Achievement of the Complete Mandala of Exalted Body, Speech, and Mind of the Supramundane Victor, the Glorious Kālachakra: the Sacred Word of Scholars and Adepts (bcom ldan 'das dus kyi 'khor lo'i sku gsung thugs yongs su rdzogs pa'i dkyil 'khor gyi sgrub thabs mkhas grub zhal lung)* and to a particularly helpful explanation of the initiations by L̄o-sang-tsul-trim-d̄en-b̄ay-gyel-tsen (see Bibliography).

Very helpful also was Dr. Edward W. Bastian's sixteen and a half hour archival video series on the Madison initiation.

10 *The Author of the Mandala Rite*

Kay-drup-ge-lek-b̄el-sang-b̄o *(mkhas grub dge legs dpal bzang po,* 1385-1438), the author of the Kālachakra initiation rite translated in this book, was one of the two chief disciples of D̄zong-ka-b̄a *(tsong kha pa,* 1357-1419), the founder of the Ge-luk-b̄a order of Tibetan Buddhism.[120] Kay-drup was born in Upper D̄zang Province *(tsang stod)* to D̄ra-s̄hi-b̄el-sang *(bkra shis dpal bzang)* and Bu-dren-gyel-mo *(bu 'dren rgyal mo),* as the eldest of three sons. His next younger brother, Ba-s̄o-chö-ḡyi-gyel-tsen *(ba so chos kyi rgyal mtshan,* 1402-1473) became a famous adept in the Ge-luk-b̄a order.[121]

Kay-drup, before becoming D̄zong-ka-b̄a's disciple, was a learned scholar of the S̄a-ḡya-b̄a order of Tibetan Buddhism. Ge-luk-b̄as look on Kay-drup's conversion as an important indication of the strength, cogency, and persuasiveness of D̄zong-ka-b̄a's intellectual prowess and personality. Kay-drup wrote important works on logic and epistemology, on the views on emptiness in the Mind Only School, Autonomy School, and Middle Way School, and so forth as well as on the tantric systems of Hevajra and Guhyasamāja, and wrote prolifically on the Kālachakra system (see p.63).

Kay-drup's *Secret Biography (gsang ba'i rnam thar)* written by Jay-d̄zun Chö-ḡyi-gyel-tsen *(rje btsun chos kyi rgyal mtshan,* 1469-1546) treats his life from a triple perspective:

1 Kay-drup actually had already attained Buddhahood, and since readers know that D̄zong-ka-b̄a was an incarnation of

Mañjushrī, the god of wisdom, the whole drama of conversion is merely a divine display.

2 Kay-drup was a rebirth of Kulika Mañjushrīkīrti, the compiler of the *Condensed Kālachakra Tantra* who was the first ruler of Shambhala to be called "Kulika", as well as of the famous Indian scholars Abhayākara, Rik-b̄ay-ku-chuk the Greater *(rig pa'i khu phyug che ba)*, and so forth. Kay-drup is thereby seen as carrying out, over a continuum of lives, an intense and altruistically motivated dedication to the furtherance of Buddha's doctrine, especially that of Kālachakra, his very life being an exemplification of the giving of doctrine, the supreme form of giving. Kay-drup is thereby a model of altruistic and scholarly endeavor for ordinary religious practitioners.

3 Kay-drup, as a deeply saddened and distressed student after his teacher's death, was a person subject to emotions that make him like the readers of the biography.

That Kay-drup was already a Buddha and thereby beyond actual development, nevermind conversion, does not lessen the impact of the human story; the biography functions on all three levels without one cancelling out another.

Let us cite important events in Kay-drup's life story, as condensed from his *Secret Biography* by Ge-s̄hay Thupten Gyatso, a scholar from the Go-mang College of Dre-b̄ung Monastic University.[122]

A SHORT BIOGRAPHY OF KAY-DRUP-GE-LEK-B̄EL-SANG

By Ge-s̄hay Thupten Gyatso

Our glorious, excellent lama the Omniscient Kay-drup, renowned in the three levels – above, on, and below the ground – had been under the tutelage of the venerable Mañjushrī during many previous lifetimes over a great number of eons. Through Mañjushrī's advice on the modes of the doctrine of the profound emptiness and the vast stages of clear realization – the latter being the hidden meaning of the Perfection of Wisdom Sūtras – Kay-drup traversed the five paths and ten

Bodhisattva grounds and actualized the rank of Vajradhara [a Buddha]. That this is so is established by scripture and reasoning and is clear, in implicit form, in his biography. However, let us speak a little here about his biography in accordance with the perspective of how common trainees perceive it.

Past Lives

While the Teacher Shākyamuni Buddha was dwelling in the world, this foremost lama was born as a novice, called Kamalashīla *(padma'i ngang tshul),* under the Superior Kāshyapa. He came to be familiar with all three scriptural collections – discipline, sets of discourses, and manifest knowledge – and was endowed with the courage of knowledge and release. For this reason, even in his life as Kay-drup, the foremost D̄zong-ka-b̄a appeared in a dream, speaking the *Kāshyapa Chapter Sūtra ('os srung gi le'u, kāshyapaparivarta),* whereupon Kay-drup generated special realization. The dream-appearance rekindled predispositions established from his earlier hearing the same teaching while a student of Kāshyapa.

Furthermore, the foremost Kay-drup earlier took rebirth as Mañjushrīkīrti, the compiler of the *Condensed Kālachakra Tantra,*[123] and also as famous scholars and upholders of the three scriptural collections in India. When he took rebirth as the Indian scholar Abhayākara, he composed the *Ocean of Means of Achievement (sgrub thabs rgya mtsho),* and so forth, as directed by Mañjushrī. Among those many books was a work entitled *Ornament to the Subduer's Thought (thub pa'i dgongs rgyan, munimatālaṃkāra),*[124] which is one of the twenty-one commentaries on Maitreya's *Ornament for Clear Realization (mngon par rtogs pa'i rgyan, abhisamayālaṃkāra)* but also is a commentary on Buddha's thought in general.

Morever, when this foremost lama took rebirth as the paṇḍiṭa Rik-b̄ay-ku-chuk the Greater, he was under the care of the glorious Chandrakīrti, thereby coming to eradicate the bonds of extreme views. At a certain point, Chandrakīrti said, "In the future, the venerable Mañjushrī will take birth as a monk in an outlying area. You also should take birth there, achieve his word, and spread the teaching." The outlying area is Tibet, and Mañjushrī took birth as D̄zong-ka-b̄a.[125]

Scholarship

Through the force of his having trained in the topics of knowledge over many lives and through the force of his being under the care of the venerable Mañjushrī, in this life also, even in his youth, his analytical intelligence was unimpeded with respect to the meaning of the three scriptural collections and the four tantra sets. Due to this, he became a great opener of a chariot-way at the head of all scholars. How was this manifested? When this foremost lama was sixteen years old, the great scholar Bo-dong-chok-lay-ñam-gyel *(bo dong phyogs las rnam rgyal,* 1376-1451) announced that he would refute the *Treasury of Reasoning (rigs gter)* of S̄a-ḡya Paṇḍiṭa Ḡun-ga-gyel-tsen *(sa skya paṇḍiṭa kun dga' rgyal mtshan,* 1182-1251),[126] and asked what S̄a-ḡya-b̄a could answer him. Everyone was discouraged and did not dare answer. At that point, the patron of the Jang-ngam-ring-b̄a Monastery *(byang ngam ring pa)* called together all the scholars, saying, "Bo-dong-wa is refuting the venerable S̄a-ḡya Paṇḍiṭa; therefore, who among you can pluck out the feathers of this bad bird? To whoever can I will give a great reward."

All of the scholars gathered at Jang-ngam-ring-b̄a Monastery. In the middle of their assembly a seat was made for Bo-dong-chok-lay-ñam-gyel, and the patron himself sat on the throne. With all of the scholars in front of him, Bo-dong systematically refuted S̄a-ḡya Paṇḍiṭa's *Treasury of Reasoning;* since none of the scholars could respond, it was decided after the first day that the text was fraught with self-contradiction. The patron then quizzed them on who could put up a defense, and the next day this great being Kay-drup, who was only sixteen years old, dispelled all of the faults imputed to S̄a-ḡya Paṇḍiṭa and with stainless reasoning thoroughly refuted the tenets that Bo-dong-chok-lay-ñam-gyel himself posited. When Kay-drup made it so that he could not even answer, Bo-dong could only say that these were inner contradictions of the tenets of the Sūtra School *(mdo sde pa, sautrāntika)* that S̄a-ḡya Paṇḍiṭa was explicating.

Kay-drup accomplished other such feats of scholarship in

debate, defeating, for instance, the scholar Ȳak-b̄a *(g.yag pa)* in the assembly hall. Through having trained in the fields of knowledge over many lives, no scholar could compete with him.

Encountering D̄zong-ka-b̄a

When Kay-drup first met the foremost D̄zong-ka-b̄a, like the Bodhisattva Always-Crying *(rtag tu ngu, sadāprarudita)* when he saw Dharmodgata, from merely seeing D̄zong-ka-b̄a's glorious form the hairs of his body powerlessly rose, tears of faith streamed from his eyes, and he spontaneously uttered words of praise. Due to former connection, as soon as they met, unparalleled firm faith was engendered.

That night while dreaming, he became sunk and confused in an omnipresent thick darkness for a long time; then from the east appeared a great wheel with hundreds of swords standing on end and with their handles turned to the center. At the tips of the swords were many hundred of suns, and in the center of the wheel in the midst of a rainbow was the venerable Mañjushrī, with orange body, holding a sword and a book, adorned with jewelled adornments, so youthful that looking knew no satisfaction. Happily, Mañjushrī came to Kay-drup and dissolved into him, whereupon a great sun dawned, immediately clearing away all darkness. The latticework of its radiance filled the entire world. That was his dream.

The next day when he met D̄zong-ka-b̄a, he reported his dream and asked what it meant. The foremost D̄zong-ka-b̄a answered, "You saw your lama and tutelary deity as undifferentiable. You are a jewel-like person who is a special, intended trainee of Mantra. Just as you saw me as the venerable Mañjushrī, so I am in fact, but persons of low intelligence see me as ordinary. You will bring great help to many trainees."

Then, the foremost D̄zong-ka-b̄a asked, "Who is your tutelary deity?" Kay-drup replied, "Orange Mañjushrī and Raktayamāri."

D̄zong-ka-b̄a continued, "In general whether you take Raktayamāri, Kṛṣhṇayamāri, or Bhairava as your tutelary deity, Mañjushrī looks after you since these three are increasing degrees of ferocity of Mañjushrī; however, since my transmission is looked after and blessed by Mañjushrī, you should take Bhairava as your tutelary deity [since the fiercest form is most effacacious]... There are many special purposes; others do not understand the importance of these." Then, without having to be asked, D̄zong-ka-b̄a immediately conferred the initiation of Vajrabhairava. From that point on, Kay-drup performed the daily rite without break.

This lama in time became a foremost spiritual son of the venerable D̄zong-ka-b̄a.[127] Through the force of his partaking continually of the ambrosia of D̄zong-ka-b̄a's speech, he attained the rank of a great opener of a chariot-way, endowed with non-erroneous knowledge of the three scriptural collections and the four tantra sets. Through the force of his great compassion such that he had affection for all beings the way a mother does for her sole child, many fortunate trainees were filled with the ambrosia of his good explanations.

Also, in order that future trainees might understand that the body of the path leading to liberation and omniscience – the tracks of passage by the previous Conquerors – is as the foremost D̄zong-ka-b̄a indicated it, in general he made many commentaries on Buddha's word and their commentaries and in particular wrote many treatises clarifying extremely dense diamond-like phraseology and very profound topics of expression in the word of D̄zong-ka-b̄a. He made these as plain as an olive set in your hand. His writings comprise the nine volumes of his Collected Works [that contain fifty-eight separate treatises].

In brief, without consideration for goods, service, or style, he, out of consideration solely for the teaching and sentient beings' welfare, performed countless acts of explanation, debate, and composition concerning the Conqueror Buddha's teachings. That is the main thrust of the biography of this great being; details can be known from his lengthy biography.

ADDENDUM

Ge-s̄hay Thupten Gyatso's condensation of Kay-drup's *Secret Biography* goes on to describe in detail the five visions of

Dzong-ka-ba that appeared to Kay-drup after his teacher's death, during periods of (1) tearful sadness about the level of trainees he was encountering, (2) tearful sadness from his inability to penetrate the meaning of difficult points in texts, (3) tearful mindfulness of the greatness of his teacher's service to the world, (4) tearful wishfulness to be in his teacher's presence given the fragility of Dzong-ka-ba's teaching remaining in the world, and (5) intense longing to rejoin his teacher. In these visions, Kay-drup continued to receive teachings from Dzong-ka-ba, who appeared first in his own form riding an elephant, then on a golden throne, then in youthful form on a frightful white lion, then as a yogi on a frightful male tiger, and finally as a monk in the middle of white clouds. Jay-dzun Chö-gyi-gyel-tsen reports that later, at Kay-drup's own death, certain of his disciples with pure karma had visions of his going to Shambhala.[128]

11 *The Author of the Commentary*

The lama who is conferring a tantric initiation explains the ritual step by step as it progresses, informing the students about required attitudes, visualizations, and reflections on meaning, for actual conferral of initiation is not simply a matter of being present at a ceremony and hearing the sounds. The officiating lama gives commentary on the ritual so that the combination of the lama's and the student's visualizations and ritual performance can be effective. In this case, the commentator is His Holiness Tenzin Gyatso, the Fourteenth Dalai Lama.

The Dalai Lama has published his autobiography[129] and John F. Avedon has written a brilliant book detailing his activities since the Communist takeover.[130] Thus, there is no need to attempt to repeat those here. Very telling, however, is the following account, by a high official of the Tibetan government, Liushar Thupten Tharpa, of the finding of this Dalai Lama after the death of the Thirteenth Dalai Lama. It gives a glimpse of the importance of this prominent world religious figure throughout the Tibetan cultural region.

Liushar Thupten Tharpa was a member of the Tibetan cabinet at the time of the escape to India in 1959, often called "Foreign Minister" in a cabinet that did not assign particular portfolios. He was a monk from a Hla-ša noble family who was deeply devoted to Buddhist practice. While he was serving as the Dalai Lama's representative in New York in the mid-1960s, we began a long friendship that continued through his retirement to the Buddhist monastery in New Jersey where I was studying and finally through his return, at His Holiness's request, to Dharamsala, India. He gave this account at the University of Virginia in 1975 and carefully made corrections later after his return to India.

He had been known in the west as Thupten Tharpa Liushar but directed me to put the family name, Liushar, first. Although he had lived according to the Westernized version of his name in New York, now, in retirement, he had decided to do it his way as a Tibetan. His presence naturally commanded respect, one of his compatriots in the Tibetan government telling me that he derived his power from mantra; indeed his lips were in slight, almost constant motion even as he listened to others talk.

My fondest memory of my old friend, who passed away in 1984, involves a discussion I had with several Tibetan scholars at the monastery in New Jersey. I had expressed the opinion that the view of the absence of inherent existence did indeed seem to be supreme, but that a combination of it with a view that conventionally subject and object are of the same entity was very attractive to me. The scholars were silent at my suggestion of a combination of the views of the Consequence and the Mind Only Schools, but later in the temple Liushar Thupten Tharpa motioned to me to come look at a page of one of D̄zong-ka-b̄a's texts. The line was a direction to practitioners to view themselves and all the other deities of the mandala, as well as the residence mandala, as one entity, manifestations of the same compassionately motivated wisdom consciousness. I started to take the text to the scholars, but he took my arm with one hand and put a finger of his other hand to his lips.

FINDING THE FOURTEENTH DALAI LAMA

By Liushar Thupten Tharpa

In 1932 the Thirteenth Dalai Lama wrote a letter of advice to the government officials. He warned that if they were not extremely careful, the "red view" would take over in Tibet, whereupon not only the monks but also the government workers would be put into a situation where night and day all they could do would be to carry out the Communist views. Therefore, he said, "From now on, you must take great care, great caution . . . I am almost fifty-eight years old and will not be able to do the work of politics much longer." People did not pay much attention at the time, but during the next year when he actually became fifty-eight, he died. That was in 1933.

The night of his death, word went out that he had died, and the government workers as well as a great mass of other people gathered at his summer palace. The very next morning, the clouds in the sky were arranged like a rainbow pointing east; everyone thought, "He must be taking rebirth in the east."

For about two years we engaged in vast offerings, prayer making, and so forth for the sake of his taking speedy reincarnation. According to custom, we took the remains of the body of the Dalai Lama to the Potala, the big palace just on the edge of Hla-ṡa, and put them in a large golden stupa in a huge chapel. There are many such reliquaries there, the largest of which are those of the Fifth and Thirteenth Dalai Lamas, about fifty feet high and gilded with gold. It took us two or three years to make the reliquary for the Thirteenth Dalai Lama's remains and to build a little temple for it on the west side of the Potala next to his main chapel.

We spread word throughout the country for parents of new-born babies to notice whether the child had any special features, whether prior to its birth the parents had any unusual dreams, whether there were special signs associated with the birth, or whether the child had special knowledge, and to inform the government when such occurred. Since, for the identification of the Thirteenth Dalai Lama, the oracle had advised consulting a lake southeast of Hla-ṡa in which the details of his birthplace appeared clearly, we did the same this time. We say that this lake, situated up in a mountain range, is the place of residence of the Glorious Goddess *(dpal ldan lha mo)*. Ra-dreng Rin-ḃo-chay *(ra sgreng rin po che)*, who was the regent, headed a party that went to see what would appear. The regent performed various rites, at the conclusion of which those in the party saw many buildings in the lake. It was like watching a movie; they could see everything. They saw a three-tiered, blue-roofed temple, like a pagoda. There was a roadway, a small villager's house, and then another small house. This turned out to be an exact picture of the place where the Dalai Lama was born.

Having seen this, the regent held a meeting and explained what he had seen, including three big letters which had appeared in the lake – "A," "Ka", "Ma". Everyone wondered and compared thoughts about what this could mean. Subsequently, the government sent lamas to the four directions of Tibet to investigate and see what they could find. People came to these lamas and government officials with special children who had been born in that period.

The actual Dalai Lama was born in Am-do province in an area we call Si-ling which on Western maps is listed as Kokonor, "Blue Lake." Though in Tibet, Kum-bum, the birthplace of D̄zong-ka-b̄a, founder of the Ge-luk-b̄a order, was controlled by China. It took about two hours by horse to go from Kum-bum monastery to the Dalai Lama's birthplace.

Because a Chinese type building had appeared in the lake and they figured that such a scene could only be found in an area controlled by China, a lama called Ḡe-tsang *(ke'u tshang)* had gone to Kum-bum with five or six government officials. His party pretended to be on pilgrimage, not openly seeking the Dalai Lama's reincarnation. Asking here and there if any special children had been born recently in the area, they heard from several people that there was one born to parents who had had many special dreams prior to the birth of the child and around whose house rainbows had appeared at the time of birth.

Continuing their pretense of being on pilgrimage, the party went to this house and asked, "Will you please give us a place to stay for a few days?" The Dalai Lama at that time was about three years old and, as soon as he saw them, came running up as if he knew them, but they just pretended that it did not mean anything and were only friendly in a normal way to him. A monk official who was pretending to head the party, Lama Ḡe-tsang who was pretending to be the official's servant, and a monk from S̄e-ra monastery in Hla-s̄a were talking back and forth, and suddenly the lama asked the boy, "Do you know who this is?" He answered, "This is a monk official." "Who is that over there?" In the Am-do section of Tibet, they call monks "A-ga", and so the boy said, "This is a Ṣe-ra A-ga." Since he had identified the monk's monastery in Hla-ṣa, they thought, "Ah, now we do have something special here."

They sent word back to Hla-ṣa that they had a child who was showing such signs and that the boy, instead of going back to his parents, wanted to stay with the lama, the monk, and the official. The letter was sent to the central government, which asked them to investigate again. They did and answered back, "There is no mistake."

The body of the Thirteenth Dalai Lama had been put in a reliquary in the new temple in the Potala Palace beside which were two wooden columns. Two objects like elephant tusks about a foot high grew out of the floor by the eastern pillars; pictures were taken, and I presume they still can be seen nowadays. These were interpreted as signs that he had been born in the east. Also, despite the fact that it was winter, flowers grew forth on the Dalai Lama's platform-like throne in an outdoor amphitheatre where lectures are given. It was winter, no one was planting seeds or bringing water, but flowers grew forth. People were amazed and wondered why this was. We understood only later that as they were "dragon flowers," it was a sign that in the year of the Dragon, which was 1940, the Dalai Lama would ascend the throne.

At this time, the people of Hla-ṣa started singing, apparently without any reason, something like, "To long-life lake lady, beautiful flower." "Long-life" (Tse-ring, spelled *tshe ring)* indicated the father's name, which was Tse-ring, and the "Lake Lady" (Tso-mo, spelled *mtsho mo)* is the name of his mother, Tso-mo. There were many such signs, but we did not pay any attention at the time.

Upon receiving direction from Hla-ṣa, the party continued their investigation. With them, the investigators had brought two rosaries, a small drum, and a walking stick that had belonged to the previous Dalai Lama and also similar items that had not. The child was first shown two identical black rosaries, and he picked up the right one. Then he was shown two identical yellow rosaries, and once again his preference fell on the right rosary. After this, the child was shown two small drums, of which the actual drum was far poorer than the second drum, which was beautifully carved and had dazzling flappers attached to it. The investigators thought that the child would choose the more attractive and larger drum, but he chose the correct one and started playing it. He picked up one walking stick and looked at it but put that one down and picked up the other one, the right one. So he picked out exactly the right ones. They were amazed and believed that he was the Dalai Lama. They sent word back to Hla-s̄a describing all that had occurred.

The decision about the reincarnation of the Dalai Lama has to be correct, so the government wanted to analyze even more. In front of a very important and valuable image from the time of King S̄ong-d̄zen-gam-b̄o *(srong btsan sgam po,* 569-650) the regent spun two balls in a cup; the balls were made of moistened ground parched barley, little dough balls wrapped around paper that had the names of the two principal candidates written on them. That which spun out of the cup first was broken open, revealing the name Hla-mo-don-drup *(lha mo don grub),* the name given to the Fourteenth Dalai Lama by his parents. The other ball of dough contained the name of the second candidate. This mode of prophecy confirmed that they were unmistaken, and thus it was finally decided that he was the incarnation.

At that time in Si-ling, the main city of the Blue Lake area, there was a terrible governor, Ma-bu-fang, who happened to be not a Buddhist but a Moslem. Thus, the party had to be secretive, not letting on that they thought that this was the actual Dalai Lama. They told the governor, "We are looking for the incarnation of the Dalai Lama and have a child here who, like several others, is unusual. To analyze this, we wish to invite him to Hla-s̄a. After further analysis, we will identify from among them the correct one, but we have not been able to come to any decision." However, the governor thought, "This just might be the Dalai Lama," so he answered, "If you think that he is the Dalai Lama, you had better decide right now." The governor sent word to the parents to come with their child. He picked up the child, put him on his lap, and asked, "Are you the Dalai Lama?" The Dalai Lama said, "Yes, I am."

The governor sought some means to prevent the search party from taking him; so he passed word to Kum-bum monastery that he would send the child there for them to decide whether he was in fact the Dalai Lama. They spent two years deciding, and in the end we had to pay Ma-bu-fang a huge sum of money. He was first presented with a hundred thousand Chinese silver dollars and was later given three hundred thousand Chinese silver dollars along with one whole set of the canon, both the teachings of Buddha and their Indian commentaries – printed in letters of gold.

In 1940 we were finally able to invite the new Dalai Lama to Hla-sa. The trip was over the plains, and as we did not have any roads or cars and so forth, all had to be on horse. We had a chariot, carried by mules, made for him. It took two months on the road. There were escorts sent out from Hla-sa to meet him at various places, and I was sent out as the escort for the third in the escort series.

I met him one pass beyond Nak-chu, about seven or eight days from Hla-sa by horse. As the meeting place was just over a pass, we crossed it and waited. We prepared offerings, tents, and a throne, making a place for the party to stay for that and the next night.

First we welcomed him in a tent. He was presented with a letter stating that it had been formally decided that he was the Dalai Lama. He was only five years old at that time but was not like other children at all; it was very amazing.

Then in Nak-chu itself the central government had made extensive preparations for welcoming the Dalai Lama at the big monastery. There were two or three thousand people, and he was put on a very high throne with his father and mother off to the side on a much lower platform. Other children would not be able to stay in such a place for a long time; they would want to go to their mother and so forth, but people were coming to see him, and he had to spend two hours there. He just sat still for two hours. Other children at least would have looked around, watching what was going on very carefully. However, it was as if he had seen it all before, not paying any attention. I was amazed, very much amazed. Every day we spent two or three hours on the road, only a little time each day travelling.

Two or three days from Hla-s̄a, a great tent community was set up for the government officials, the noble families, and so forth to meet him. Three monks who had been his servants also met him. One is something like a butler, taking care of his food, seeing that it is prepared, and presenting it to him. Another solely takes care of his clothing, seeing that it is clean, taken out, prepared, put away. The third prepares all of the religious articles that are necessary for rites and rituals. These are the three main servants; their positions are very high.

The religious servant had brought with him a tang-ḡa, a painting of the Glorious Goddess, which is kept in a red case with a cap on it. From the time of the Fifth Dalai Lama, the tang-ḡa itself has been considered to be the same as the Glorious Goddess herself. Never opened, it is always left rolled up. It is kept with the Dalai Lama wherever he goes – he is never separate from it. The servant had placed it near the opening of the tent, and as the Dalai Lama passed by, he grabbed it, took it inside the tent, and immediately opened it up. It is usually never seen but they saw it at that time. Then he rolled it back up and put it back in its case. Everyone was amazed at what he had done.

He was brought into Hla-s̄a itself to the main temple to pay respect to the images and then was immediately taken to the summer palace, not the Potala, which is the winter one, but the Nor-bu-ling-ḡa. During the first month of the Tibetan year in 1941, which would be in the second month of the Western calendar, he was invited to his main residence, the Potala, and the actual investiture was done at that time.

On the day he was installed, the two tutors were there, one being the regent Ra-dreng and the other Dak-tra Rin-b̄o-chay. The regent gave the Dalai Lama the name Jay-d̄zun-jam-b̄el-nga-w̄ang-l̄o-sang-ye-s̄hay-d̄en-dzin-gya-tso-s̄i-s̄um-w̄ang-gyur-tsung-b̄a-may-b̄ay-day-b̄el-sang-b̄o[131] that day when he was installed. From that time he has been called Tenzin

Gyatso, a shorter form of the long name.

His head was shaved like a monk, with a little longer hair on top; then this was cut as the sign of his having become a novice monk. The abbot asked at that time, "Do you go homeless?" "Yes, I go homeless."

He assumed residence in the Potala and began studying. Even though he was very young, it was almost as if he did not have to be taught the alphabet and so forth. Other children would need a place to go, others to play with, and so forth, but all that he had were these three old servants – any other child would stay a while and then find it very difficult, saying, "I want to go to my mother." He did none of this. Sometimes his mother did visit, but otherwise, he was alone, reading books in his room. Occasionally they would send in his brother who was just a little older than he.

When the Dalai Lama was thirteen years old, it was time for him to go to visit the monastic colleges at Dre-b̄ung and S̄e-ra. This was like entering into the monastic college and becoming a more studious monk. Each of the colleges made great preparations for him. He spent three weeks in Dre-b̄ung and two in S̄e-ra to mark his entry into formal study of philosophy. He had two main tutors and eight excellent ge-s̄hays, Doctors of Philosophy, to discuss the topics back and forth. All of these remained with him wherever he stayed, in the winter or the summer palace.

At age sixteen, the Chinese first invaded eastern Tibet in Kam Province. Although the Dalai Lamas are usually installed as the head of the government at the age of eighteen, everyone thought that the Dalai Lama should take over the government immediately because it was such a dangerous time. Thus, at a very young age, he took responsibility for the government, a tremendous burden since this was the period that the Chinese came into Tibet. Throughout, he continued his studies and at twenty-five, in 1958, became a ge-s̄hay. In order to do so, he had to debate in front of the other ge-s̄hays at Dre-b̄ung monastery. There were probably several thousand monks, a host of government officials, and many others; he was in the middle of all this. Then he did the same at S̄e-ra and Gan-den. At a final debate which takes place at the New Year's celebration when all of the monasteries gather in Hla-ṡa he had to debate three times. This was in 1959, and subsequent to it he was given the title of a highest rank ge-s̄hay.

It was just a month after becoming a ge-s̄hay that he had to escape to India, where he has stayed until now. There are about eighty thousand refugees in India, and their place of hope is the Dalai Lama; there is no one else. In conversations with the Indian government we, as his representatives, have arranged for settlements for Tibetans. Thus, even though we are refugees, we are in quite a good situation. We have independence to engage in our own religion and do what we want as if it were our own country.

Those left in Tibet are in a very bad situation of suffering. There is nothing that we can do for them now, but the Dalai Lama has assumed the burden of freeing them from misery. He has been able to make visits to Japan, Thailand, and Europe, not as a head of government, but as a private citizen. His idea of visiting, especially the West, is to exchange ideas, to find out what Western ideas are and for him to present some Eastern ideas. Therefore, perhaps there is hope that when he comes to America, you can ask him about the Buddhist doctrine.

By the way, of the three letters in the lake, "A" stood for Am-do, which is the province where the Dalai Lama was born. "Ka" stood for Kum-bum monastery, which was nearby. Most people felt "Ma" referred to his mother, but I asked the Dalai Lama in 1974 what he thought it meant, and he said that as a child he was called Hla-mo-don-drup, an unusual name for a male child because it means "*Goddess* Siddhārtha". "Ma," a feminine ending in Tibetan, referred to that name.

The above is a record of what I have heard and the little that I actually experienced in the search for the fourteenth Dalai Lama. Those interested in more information can consult two reliable sources: one, His Holiness the Dalai Lama's memoirs, *My Land and My People,* and the other, a book by Sonam Wangdu, a member of the search party led by Ḡe-tsang Rin-b̄o-chay, entitled *The Discovery of the 14th Dalai Lama.*[132]

The Dalai Lama's Commentary on the Kālachakra Initiation Rite: Stage of Generation

Note

This is a commentary by His Holiness the Dalai Lama on Kay-drup's *Mandala Rite of the Glorious Kālachakra: Illumination of the Thought (dpal dus kyi 'khor lo'i dkyil chog dgongs pa rab gsal)*. The translation of the mandala rite is supplemented with material from L̄o-sang-tsul-trim-d̄en-b̄ay-gyel-tsen's *Initiation Rite of Kālachakra, Stated in an Easy Way (dus 'khor dbang chog nag 'gros su bkod pa)*.

Commentary by His Holiness the Dalai Lama is at the margin. The indented material is the initiation ritual text itself. Within the text, to differentiate between instructions to the person performing the ritual and what is actually said in the course of conducting the ritual, the former is in italics.

Part One
Enhancing the Students

Background

THE PLACEMENT OF THE *KĀLACHAKRA TANTRA* IN THE BUDDHIST VEHICLES

Buddha, a teacher skilled in method, taught eighty-four thousand bundles of doctrine in accordance with the dispositions and interests of trainees. As Maitreya's *Ornament for the Great Vehicle Sūtras (theg pa chen po'i mdo sde rgyan, mahāyāna-sūtrālaṃkāra,* XI.a)[1] says, "The scriptural collections are either three or two." Buddha's many scriptures can be included into the three scriptural collections – sets of discourses, discipline, and manifest knowledge – or into the scriptures of the two vehicles – the Lesser Vehicle of Hearers and Solitary Realizers and the Great Vehicle of Bodhisattvas. The differentiation between these two vehicles is by way of vastness of thought, that is, of motivation; due to it there is a difference also in path, or method; due to that there is, in turn, a difference in the fruit that is attained. This is how the two vehicles are distinguished.

Concerning the Great Vehicle or Vehicle of Bodhisattvas itself, its sub-divisions – the Perfection Vehicle and the Mantra Vehicle – both require the motivational attitude of altruism and the practice of the six perfections, and both lead to the attainment of the fruit, which is unsurpassed enlightenment. Nevertheless, the two sub-divisions of the Great Vehicle – Sūtra and Mantra – are posited as separate vehicles by way of the profundity of the means for attaining unsurpassed enlightenment; the two thereby differ in the body of the path for attaining the omniscience of Buddhahood. From between these two vehicles, what is being explained here is the Mantra Vehicle.

With regard to mantra, according to the *Vajrapañjara Tantra,* an explanatory tantra, there are four sets of tantras, although other texts speak of various divisions of the tantras into six sets, five sets, and so forth. When four are described, they are Action, Performance, Yoga and Highest Yoga Tantra. Among the four tantra sets, Action Tantra is so called because in its practice of yoga there is more emphasis, relative to the other tantra sets, on external activities of ritual bathing and maintaining cleanliness even though internal meditative stabilization is indeed cultivated. Performance Tantra is so called because of there being equal performance of external activities and internal yoga. Yoga Tantra is so called because between external activities and internal yoga, the latter is principally emphasized. Highest Yoga Tantra [literally, Unsurpassed Yoga Tantra] is so called in that since it exceeds even Yoga Tantra in terms of principally emphasizing internal yoga, there is nothing superior to it. What is being explained here in this initiation is Highest Yoga Tantra.

In general, all the tantra systems have as their basis the attitude of altruistic mind generation and the deeds of the six perfections, which are described in the Perfection Vehicle. The distinctive feature of the Secret Mantra Vehicle comes in terms of additional techniques for quickly developing the meditative stabilization that is a union of calm abiding and special insight – one-pointed meditative stabilization realizing emptiness. This mainly is achieved through deity yoga.

From one point of view, tantra is more powerful than sutra in terms of collecting merit in that yoga is sustained within visualizing one's body as divine. From another point of view, there also is a difference between the Perfection and Mantra Vehicles in terms of the subject, or substratum, the selflessness of which one is realizing in meditation. For, here in Mantra, one realizes the emptiness not of a gross phenomenon such as an ordinary body but rather of a subtle phenomenon that is appearing to one's internal mind – a divine body. This mode of procedure of the path in which there is a yoga of non-duality of the profound and the manifest – the manifest being imaginative observation of a circle, or mandala, of deities and the profound being the wisdom realizing suchness – is the general path in the three lower tantras – Action, Performance, and Yoga Tantras.

Highest Yoga Tantra, in addition to all these features of the Perfection Vehicle and the three lower tantras, has special techniques for concentrated focusing on important points of the body, through which more subtle levels of mind are manifested and transformed into entities of the path. The uncommon profound distinction of all types of Highest Yoga Tantra texts – the distinctive feature in terms of which the uncommon potency of the Highest Yoga Tantra path is developed – is in the explanation of practices for generating the fundamental innate mind of clear light as an entity of the path.

As techniques for manifesting the fundamental innate mind of clear light, some Highest Yoga Tantra texts speak of concentrated focusing on the winds [or internal currents] of the body; some put emphasis on the four joys; and others speak of merely sustaining non-conceptual meditation. The *Guhyasamāja Tantra,* for instance, speaks mainly of putting concentrated focusing on the winds; the *Chakrasaṃvara Tantra* and the *Hevajra Tantra* speak mainly of the four joys; and the technique of manifesting the clear light by way of non-conceptual meditation is mainly found in the great completeness *(rdzogs chen)* of the N̄ying-ma Order and the great seal *(phyag rgya chen po, mahāmudrā)* tradition of the Ḡa-gyu-b̄a Order. All of these are modes of practice described in valid and reliable source-texts within Highest Yoga Tantra.

To become fully enlightened as a Buddha, it is necessary to practice Mantra and, within Mantra, Highest Yoga Mantra; otherwise, it is not possible to attain Buddhahood. The reason for this is that to actualize the effect state of the two bodies of a Buddha – Form Body and Truth Body – it is necessary meditatively to cultivate a path that accords in aspect with those two bodies. Even in the Perfection Vehicle, it is necessary to achieve a cause that is concordant with the effect. The main point is that in order to attain the Form Body of a Buddha it is necessary to have a substantial cause of similar type for a Form Body; also, for the Truth Body it is necessary to have a substantial cause of similar type. Since this is the case, our coarse body, which is a fruition [of past karma], cannot serve as a substantial cause of similar type for a Buddha's Form Body. Also, the mentally imagined divine body that appears to a yogi practicing Yoga Tantra, Performance Tantra, or Action Tantra cannot serve as a substantial cause of similar type for a Buddha's Form Body, nor can even an actual body achieved, for instance, through the practice of Yoga Tantra.

What can serve as such a substantial cause of a Form Body? A Buddha's body is one undifferentiable entity with that Buddha's mind; the form [or body] that is of one undifferentiable entity with a Buddha's *subtle* mind cannot be a *coarse* form. The Form Body that is of one undifferentiable entity with a Buddha's subtle mind is itself a very subtle entity, and thus as its substantial cause of similar type a body that has a very subtle nature must be achieved at the time of the path. In Highest Yoga Tantra, this is achieved (1) in the Guhyasamāja system by way of an illusory body, (2) in the Kālachakra system by way of empty form, or (3) in mother tantras by way of a rainbow body of light. Without such a mode of achieving a subtle body at the time of the path, a Buddha's Form Body cannot be achieved.

Hence, a mode of achieving even the substantial cause of a Buddha's Form Body is not set forth in the three lower tantras or in the Perfection Vehicle, and a mode of achieving the *uncommon* substantial cause of a Buddha's mind is also not set forth in the three lower tantras or in the Perfection Vehicle. The reason for specifying "*uncommon* substantial cause" for the latter is that a common substantial cause of a Buddha's mind, a coarse wisdom consciousness realizing emptiness, is set forth in the three lower tantras and in the Perfection Vehicle. Thus, it can be said that they have a *mere* cause of a Buddha's omniscient consciousness; however, the *uncommon* substantial cause must be the mind of clear light, and the three lower tantras and the Perfection Vehicle do not set forth a means of achieving the fundamental innate mind of clear light.

Therefore, without depending in general on Mantra and in particular on Highest Yoga Mantra, Buddhahood cannot be attained. Similarly, the nirvana that is the extinguishment forever of all adventitious defilements in the sphere of reality through the power of their antidotes is the Buddhist interpretation of liberation, of peace, and those defilements must be extinguished in the sphere of reality only through the technique of ascertaining emptiness and meditating on it. Therefore, the liberation explained in Buddhist texts can be attained only through a Buddhist path. Moreover, among the Buddhist systems, the actual Buddhist liberation can be attained only through relying on the view as explained in the Consequence School.

As Nāgārjuna's *Fundamental Text Called "Wisdom" (dbu ma rtsa ba'i tshig le'ur byas pas shes rab bya ba, prajñānāmamūla-madhyamakakārikā,* XVIII.5a) says, "Through extinguishing [contaminated] actions and afflictions, there is liberation." Through meditating on the reality of the emptiness of inherent existence, actualizing it, and again and again familiarizing with the meaning of reality that has been directly perceived, the adventitious defilements are extinguished forever in the sphere of reality. That sphere of reality – into which the adventitious defilements are extinguished forever – is itself liberation, nirvana. This can be achieved only by one who has perceived the meaning of the reality of the emptiness of inherent existence. Even within Buddhist schools, those of the Great Exposition School, the Sūtra School, the Mind Only School, or the Autonomy School cannot actualize this. In this light, it is said that a Foe Destroyer as explained in the systems of manifest knowledge *(chos mngon pa, abhidharma)* is not a Foe Destroyer. Therefore, just as to attain Buddhahood Highest Yoga Tantra is needed, so to attain liberation from cyclic existence the view of the Consequence School is needed.

Highest Yoga Tantra itself is divided into father and mother tantras, and certain scholars also speak of non-dual tantras, citing the *Kālachakra Tantra* as an illustration. However, according to others who do not assert non-dual tantras that are not included among father and mother tantras, the *Kālachakra Tantra* is a mother tantra, the reason for this being as follows. The *Kālachakra Tantra* has as its main object of discussion the six branched yoga [individual withdrawal, concentration, stopping vitality, retention, subsequent mindfulness, and meditative stabilization], among which the immutable bliss of the sixth branch, meditative stabilization, is the final object of achievement. Because the *Kālachakra Tantra* emphasizes just this immutable bliss, it is called a mother tantra.

Again, the reason why the first group calls the *Kālachakra Tantra* a non-dual tantra is that they identify as its main object of discourse the state of *union* – a combination of empty form and immutable great bliss, immutable great bliss being induced by way of an empty form of the Great Seal. This state of union, or non-dual body and mind, is described in a very clear way in the *Kālachakra Tantra,* unlike its hidden description in the *Guhyasamāja Tantra,* and thus they say that the *Kālachakra Tantra* is a non-dual tantra.

The *Kālachakra Tantra* has many such unique profound distinctive features. In general, Highest Yoga Tantras speak of a stage of generation and a stage of completion, of which the latter is primary. Within the stage of completion itself, there are two levels – one involved with withdrawing the winds or inner energies into the central channel and the other occurring in dependence upon having accomplished that withdrawal. In the Kālachakra system, the initial branches of the six branched yoga are mostly means of withdrawing the winds inside the central channel, and thus, given this emphasis on the phase of withdrawing the winds, the *Kālachakra Tantra* provides profound techniques for the preliminary levels.

Moreover, the *Kālachakra Tantra* has a special connection with a country, Shambhala, as its general religion and thus from this viewpoint also is unique. For, other Highest Yoga Tantras have their origin in relation to individual persons or adepts, as was the case with the *Guhyasamāja Tantra* and the King Indrabhuti. The *Kālachakra Tantra,* however, has been intimately connected with the country of Shambhala – its ninety-six districts, its kings, and retinue. Still, if you lay out a map and search for Shambhala, it is not findable; rather, it seems to be a pure land which, except for those whose karma and merit have ripened, cannot be immediately seen or visited. As is the case, for example, with the Joyous Pure Land *(dga' ldan, tuṣhita)*, Sky Territories *(mkha' spyod)*, the Blissful Pure Land *(bde ba can, sukhāvatī)*, Mount Ḏa-la, and so forth, even though Shambhala is an actual land – an actual pure land – it is not immediately approachable by ordinary persons such as by buying an airplane ticket. Perhaps, if, in the future, spacecrafts improve to the point where they can proceed faster than light, it might be possible to arrive there, but the tickets might be expensive! In fact, we can consider the tickets to be meritorious actions, and thus it takes someone rich in merit to arrive there.

PREPARATION FOR INITIATION

Although conferral of blessings does not necessarily require a mandala, an initiation must be conferred in dependence upon a mandala. The Kālachakra initiation for the stage of generation must be given in connection with a mandala of colored particles, and since this is the case, the area where the mandala is to be constructed must initially be made serviceable. To do this, the area first is analyzed; then, if it is suitable, it is set off, cleansed, and taken over. Such steps are included in the rite of taking over the area, after which come the stages of preparation.

During the preparation, vases are needed; thus, there is a preparation or enhancement of the vases. Similarly, since there are the mandalas of the residence and the resident deities, a preparation or enhancement of the deities is done. After that, there is a preparation or enhancement of the students, making the continuums of the students fit to be vessels for the conferral of initiation. All of these constitute the topics of the stages of preparation. In practice, the enhancement of the students is, for convenience, put just before the actual conferral of initiation. The past few days [here in Madison, Wisconsin] I have been performing the stages of establishing and activating the mandala and making offerings to the deities. Thus we are now ready for the stages of enhancement of the students.

RITE FOR ENHANCING THE STUDENTS

The presentaton of the third topic, the rite for enhancing [or preparing] the student, has six parts: adjusting motivation and conferring the internal initiation; making a supplication and causing [the student] to take up the doctrine; assuming the vows and being blessed into magnificence; casting the tooth-stick and giving handfuls of water and so forth; setting the six lineages [in the student] and invoking Vajrasattva; and generating enthusiasm through explaining [the greatness of] doctrine and giving advice on analyzing dreams.

1 *Motivation and Internal Initiation*

ADJUSTING MOTIVATION AND CONFERRING THE INTERNAL INITIATION

The substances for the preparation [that is, the articles to be used] are kept away from [the student's] sight by a curtain. Outside of that, analyze well [the students]; the qualified[2] *students – twenty-five or less, not an even number – having washed, offer mandala.*

Secret Mantra is a case of using imagination as the path; thus, one imagines that the entire world system appears in glorified aspect as the sport of the exalted wisdom of undifferentiable bliss and emptiness – a union of method (immutable great bliss) and wisdom (realization of emptiness). These appearances having the nature of being the sport of undifferentiable bliss and emptiness are the offerings.

Also, the area should be considered not just to be this beautiful place in Wisconsin but to be the complete inestimable mansion and environment of the Supramundane Victor, Kālachakra, having the very nature of exalted wisdom. Imagine that it is present in just the way that I am meditating on it and that you are in front of it. Imagine that the doors of the inestimable mansion are closed and that you are outside the doors, making offering to the glorious Kālachakra:

To the lama, personal deity, and Three Jewels I offer in visualization
The body, speech, mind, and resources of myself and others,
Our collections of virtue in the past, present, and future,
And the wonderful precious mandala with the masses of Samantabhadra's offerings.
Accepting them through your compassion, please bless me into magnificence.
Idaṃ guru-ratna maṇḍalakaṃ niryātayāmi. [I offer this jewelled mandala to the guru.]

The first step in the preparation, or enhancement, of the students is for the students to adjust their motivation so that it is properly qualified. Most of you know the importance of kindness – the special kind of altruism, called *bodhichitta* in Sanskrit – and of wisdom, called *prajñā*. These two mental developments are the ground or foundation without which we cannot perform any tantric practice. Therefore, both myself as well as you listeners must develop at least some experience of these two minds.

With regard to wisdom, things appear as if independently existent but in reality do not exist that way; we should understand that things do not exist in accordance with their solid mode of appearance. Then, with regard to altruism, human society could not survive, could not exist, without kindness. If we think properly, the entire human society is based on kindness; all human relations are essentially centered in kindness. In the field of religious practice, the feeling of kindness is the key point.

Also, it is very important to realize the nature of suffering. As long as we have this type of physical body under the influence of contaminated actions (*las, karma*) and afflictive emotions (*nyon mongs, klesha*), something will be wrong – this will be wrong or that will be wrong. It is important to realize that the phenomena of cyclic existence have a nature of suffering.

Another important realization is that of impermanence. Things are always changing. You should understand that this is their nature. With these thoughts in mind, we will proceed with the initiation.

The most important factor is good motivation. We have already attained a good, useful human body; we have an opportunity to accomplish something of great impact. You should think that you will do something meaningful with this human body already attained. To do something meaningful with it, you should not be selfish but should generate as much as possible an altruistic attitude. Altruism is most important.

Now, the next question is how to serve other people, how to help other beings – not just humans but all sentient beings. According to Buddhist teaching, events depend upon our own karmic force; for the wanted happiness to occur and the unwanted suffering not to occur, persons need an unmistaken mode of accumulating karma. Therefore, helping others is mainly in terms of explaining to others what is to be adopted in practice and what is to be discarded from our behaviour. As a sūtra says:

The Subduer [Buddhas] neither wash ill-deeds away with water,
Nor remove beings' sufferings with their hands,
Nor transfer their realizations to others.
Beings are released through the teachings of the truth, the final reality.

Furthermore, to be able to teach unmistakenly what is to be adopted in practice and what is to be discarded, these topics cannot be obscure to oneself. As Dharmakīrti's *Commentary on (Dignāga's) "Compendium of Valid Cognition" (tshad ma rnam 'grel, pramāṇavarttika)* says:[3]

In order to overcome suffering [in others]
The merciful manifestly engage in methods.
When the causes of what arise from those methods are obscure [to oneself],
It is difficult to explain them [to others].

If what is to be taught is beyond your ken, you cannot possibly teach it. All possible techniques of practice must be known.

In addition, you need to know, exactly as they are, the various dispositions and interests of those whom you would teach. If you do not know their dispositions and interests, even though your attitude is good, it is nonetheless possible to do harm due to the teaching's not being appropriate. Therefore, as long as your mind is polluted by the obstructions to omniscience such that you are prevented from knowing all objects of knowledge, you cannot fully bring about others' welfare.

This being the case, Bodhisattvas consider their real enemy to be the obstructions to omniscience. If Bodhisattvas had a choice either to get rid of the afflictive obstructions preventing liberation from cyclic existence or to get rid of the obstructions to omniscience, they would choose the latter. However, since the fact is that the obstructions to omniscience are predispositions left by the afflictive obstructions, without removing that which deposits these predispositions there is no way to remove the predispositions; thus, it is necessary to remove first the afflictive obstructions and then the obstructions to omniscience. Hence, to bring about others' welfare, it is necessary to remove entirely both obstructions – to liberation and to omniscience. That level, or ground, at which the afflictive emotions as well as their predispositions have been removed forever is called Buddhahood, a state endowed with the exalted wisdom knowing all aspects of objects of knowledge.

The purpose is to bring about sentient beings' welfare; the means to accomplish this is your own Buddhahood. This sequence of thought is how you come to determine that you must attain Buddhahood for the sake of others. The attitude generated is called *bodhichitta,* the altruistic intention to become enlightened, and it must be cultivated continually, at least in a fabricated way. You should think, "I will rely upon the path of unified Sūtra and Mantra and, within that, on Highest Yoga Tantra – specifically the path of the *Kālachakra Tantra* – as a technique for easily achieving such Buddhahood. Thereby I will achieve highest enlightenment for the sake of others, and for this reason I am requesting initiation."

In the ritual, the words in the rite that represent the adjustment of motivation are taken from the *General Secret Tantra (dkyil 'khor thams cad kyi spyi'i cho ga gsang ba'i rgyud, sarvamaṇḍalasāmānyavidhiguhyatantra),* which is a *general* Action Tantra in that it applies to all lineages of practitioners. The quotation is used in many initiations, not just Kālachakra.

> [*The students*] *place their knees* [*on the ground*] *and bring their palms, with flowers, together at the heart. With them sitting in front* [*of the lama, the lama*] *says:*

> Some seeking to achieve Secret Mantra
> For this [life] enter the mandala.

This describes the mistaken motivation of seeking the happiness of this life, such as entering a mandala in order to prevent disease or to achieve success in a certain venture. A request for initiation with this motivation is mistaken.

> Those wishing for merit are other than them.

There are those who, seeking a future lifetime of high status within cyclic existence, want merit and therefore seek to enter a mandala. This, too, is mistaken. The line also can be interpreted as referring to those who, seeking liberation from cyclic existence for themselves, want merit and therefore enter a mandala; this also is mistaken.

> Others seek the welfare of others in the world.
> The intelligent should enter the mandala
> With many acts of faith
> Seeking the aim of what transcends the world.

Those altruistic persons who have the faith seeking that which transcends the world, the state of the Three Buddha Bodies, are fit to enter a mandala and should be allowed to do so.

The reason why you should seek Buddhahood for the sake of sentient beings is indicated by the remainder of the passage:

> They should not wish for effects in this life.
> Those wanting this life
> Do not accrue the aim of what transcends the world.

Those generating a seeking for what transcends the world
[Gain] expansive fruits [even] in this world.

Having ascertained the meaning of these words, consider as I recite the passage that the principal deity, Kālachakra, is telling you from inside the mandala that you should think this way.

At this time consider in meditation that the lama and the principal deity of the mandala are not different. I am not saying that you should consider me to be God. When doing Mantra practice, one meditates on oneself as a deity and on one's lama also as a deity.

Identify well the meaning of those words so that the students generate awareness of the need to enter the mandala with a thought seeking the non-abiding nirvana [not abiding in the extremes of either cyclic existence or solitary peace] – that which transcends the world – the best of the three motivations.

In accordance with these precepts for motivation, all of us should not be primarily concerned with our own welfare but should mainly become concerned with others' welfare.

[CONFERRING THE INTERNAL INITIATION]

Then [the lama says]:

It is meditated that:
Rays of light from my heart, clarified as Kālachakra – Father and Mother – draw in the students individually; they enter my mouth and dissolve in the Mother's lotus.

This is like taking birth as a child of one's special deity, Kālachakra.

In imagination, visualize the lama as Kālachakra in Father and Mother aspect, that is to say, in union with his consort. Rays of light, spreading out from the *hūṃ* at the heart of the lama who appears as Kālachakra, draw each of the students into the mouth of the lama, passing down through his body into the womb of the Mother. There, the students turn into emptiness.

Do not just withdraw all appearances; also become mindful of the emptiness of inherent existence of all appearing and occurring objects of knowledge, as illustrated by yourself. The altruistic intention to become enlightened, which was earlier cultivated, still remains, and now, in addition, you are thinking, "All phenomena, as illustrated by myself, are empty of inherent existence." This mind itself serves as the "substance" of your appearance as Kālachakra with one face and two arms. The mind, impelled by compassion and realizing the emptiness of inherent existence, transforms into a *hūṃ* that itself transforms into a vajra that in turn transforms into a Kālachakra, not with all the faces and arms of the principal deity of the mandala but with just one face and two arms.

> From hūm and a vajra they are generated as Kālachakras with one face and two hands.

Then, light rays at the heart of the lama as Kālachakra draw in all the Ones Gone Thus – Buddhas – who have the nature of the exalted wisdom of non-dual bliss and emptiness. They enter the lama's mouth, dissolve into light at the heart of the lama, called the mind of enlightenment; that descends into the Mother's womb, conferring initiation on the students who are visualizing themselves as Kālachakras in the Mother's womb. The students, in addition to their wisdom realizing emptiness appearing as Kālachakra, also are experiencing the special exalted wisdom of great bliss. Think that such bliss is generated through the internal initiation.

> The light from the seed syllable at my heart invites in all Ones Gone Thus; they enter my mouth, and at my heart the fire of attraction [i.e., their mutual joy in each other] melts [their bodies into light called] the mind of enlightenment, which emerges through the vajra path. [296] Through this, the students dwelling in the Wisdom Woman's lotus are conferred initiation [whereupon the exalted wisdom of

> emptiness and bliss, the entity of the internal initiation, is generated].

Then, you emerge from the Mother's womb and are again set by the pillar outside the eastern door of the mandala, all the while maintaining visualization of yourself as a Kālachakra with one face and two arms.

> They emerge from the Mother's lotus and are set on their individual places.

There are three levels of doors within the mandala, corresponding to the three levels related with exalted body, speech, and mind. At this point, you are outside the outermost set of doors at the level of the exalted body mandala. Earlier it was explained that prior to initiation you are not allowed to meditate on yourself as a deity, but now that you have received the internal initiation, the process of meditating on yourself as a deity has begun.

The procedure of this imaginative meditation accords with the type of social structure in earlier India so that it easily could appear to their minds. It has connection with the later initiation of a vajra master, in which the student becomes like a representative or royal replacement of the lama.

That concludes adjustment of the motivation and conferral of the internal initiation.

2 *Supplication and Faith*

MAKING A SUPPLICATION AND CAUSING [THE STUDENTS] TO APPREHEND THE DOCTRINE

Cyclic existence is like an ocean with frightful sea monsters of birth, aging, sickness, and death. At the beginning of life is birth, at the end is death, and in between we are pressed with the sufferings of sickness and aging. Throughout our lives, there are a great many things going wrong. Once this is the nature of cyclic existence, it is something that we do not want. The student is asking the lama as Kālachakra, the teacher of the means of release from such fright, to pay heed to himself or herself.

The means, as explained earlier, is to purify utterly the two obstructions – those to liberation and to omniscience – in dependence upon the Vajra Vehicle, the path of Secret Mantra. You are saying that you want this. Since, for that, it is necessary to keep properly the pledges and vows, you are also asking the lama to bestow the pledges and vows. Again, for that, you are also asking for the Bodhisattva vows, and for that, you are requesting the rite for assuming the aspirational altruistic intention to become enlightened, for which you are asking to go to refuge to the Buddha, Doctrine, and Spiritual Community. You are asking for help in entering into the city of great liberation in dependence upon such methods. As you repeat the words, keep their meaning in mind.

The essence of the meaning, in brief, is: "For the sake of all sentient beings – the objects of intent – I want to attain unsurpassed complete perfect enlightenment quickly, and to accomplish that I will practice the path of Mantra. Please bestow on me all that I need to do this."

The students make supplication three times with:

The sole liberator from the ocean of cyclic existence,
Which is frightful with sea monsters and so forth,
The crocodiles of birth, aging, and death
Is you, O Great Joyous Teacher of mine.

O great protector, I am seeking
The firm mode of great enlightenment.
Bestow on me the pledges.
Bestow on me also the mind of enlightenment.

Also bestow on me the three refuges –
Buddha, Doctrine, and Spiritual Community.
O Protector, please let me enter
Into the supreme city of the great liberation.

Having made supplication three times, you are to think that the lama, as Kālachakra, has accepted you, though not in words.

[CAUSING THE STUDENTS TO APPREHEND THE DOCTRINE]

Next is to cause the student to take up the doctrine, that is to say, to generate faith in the Great Vehicle.

The lama, taking one student as the chief,[4] *says:*

Child, come here.
I will thoroughly teach to you
The rites of the mode of practice of Great Vehicle
  Secret Mantra.
You are a vessel of the great way.

The lama calls the student "child", a term of closeness, saying that the student should not be under the influence of conceptuality, conceiving what is not in reality happiness to be happiness and becoming attached to the prosperity of cyclic existence. Not desiring the prosperity of cyclic existence, the student should "come here" without being distracted by the wonderful things of cyclic existence.

Having come here, what activity should the student do? Since you are vessels of and have the lot of practicing the Secret Mantra Vajra Vehicle, I will teach the mode of practice of Great Vehicle Secret Mantra.

> Through the power of Vajra Mantra
> The Buddhas arising in the three times –
> Those having the vajras of exalted body, speech, and mind –
> Thoroughly gain the peerless exalted wisdom.

Those with the vajras of exalted body, speech, and mind are Buddhas since the level of undifferentiable body, speech, and mind is Buddhahood. Thus, the Buddhas of the past, present, and future having an essence of undifferentiable body, speech, and mind have gained, gain, and will gain the thoroughly pure, peerless, exalted wisdom of Buddhahood in dependence upon the power of the path of Secret Mantra.

In brief, the Buddhas of all times – those with an essence of exalted vajra body, speech, and mind – gain, in dependence upon the path of Secret Mantra, an exalted wisdom of fundamental innate clear light, free from all obstructions, the exalted wisdom of the final sphere of reality possessing the two purities – natural purity and purity from adventitious defilements. Since this wisdom has no equal among the exalted wisdom of those still learning, it is "peerless". Through the power of Secret Mantra, they have gained, gain, and will gain such an omniscient Wisdom Truth Body of a Buddha.

Buddhahood – the undifferentiability of exalted body, speech, and mind – is attained in dependence upon the path of Mantra. How is this done? Our present coarse consciousnesses are not suitable to be the substantial cause of a Buddha's omniscient consciousness. That which can serve as such a cause is the most subtle fundamental innate mind of clear light. Nothing else can serve as the direct substantial cause of an omniscient consciousness. Since this is the case, the most subtle fundamental innate mind of clear light must be generated as an entity of the path, as an entity of virtue. This can only be done through a technique of Highest Yoga Mantra in which concentrated emphasis is put on focal points of the body. Without such a technique, there is no way to generate the fundamental innate mind of clear light as an entity of the path, and the three lower tantra sets – Action, Performance, and Yoga Tantras – as well as the Perfection Vehicle do not identify the fundamental innate mind of clear light and do not speak of techniques for generating it into an entity of the path. They only speak of accumulating the collections of merit and exalted wisdom in the context of coarser levels of consciousness.

As long as one cannot generate the subtlest level of consciousness as an entity of the path, the omniscience of a Buddha cannot be achieved. Furthermore, one is seeking such omniscience mainly for the sake of other sentient beings. As Maitreya's *Ornament For Clear Realization (mngon rtogs rgyan, abhisamayālaṃkāra)* says:[5] "[Altruistic] mind generation is the wish for complete perfect enlightenment for the sake of others." Thus the object of intent of one seeking the omniscience of Buddhahood is the welfare of other beings. Now, between a Buddha's Wisdom Truth Body and Form Bodies, it is Form Bodies that actually appear to trainees and thereby bring about their welfare; there is no way for the Wisdom Truth Body to help others through actually appearing to them. Hence, what is mainly being sought are the Form Bodies of a Buddha.

The substantial cause of such Form Bodies cannot be our present body composed of flesh, blood, bone, and so forth. The Perfection Vehicle speaks of achieving a mental body that arises in dependence upon factors called the level of the predispositions of ignorance and uncontaminated karma and that has similitudes of a Buddha's major and minor marks. The Perfection Vehicle says that this special mental body serves as the substantial cause of a Buddha's Form Bodies, but when examined closely, the "level of predispositions of ignorance" refers to the obstructions to omniscience, and thus this mental body is achieved from impure causes. Therefore, being itself produced from impure causes, it cannot serve as the substantial cause of a Form Body that is of the same entity as a Buddha's omniscient consciousness.

The substantial cause of a Buddha's Form Body that is of the same entity as an omniscient consciousness must be achieved in an uncommon way in dependence upon Highest Yoga Mantra. In the *Kālachakra Tantra* this is a great seal empty form; in the *Guhyasamāja Tantra,* an illusory body; or, in another way, it is a rainbow body. Without such a technique, there is no way that our coarse body can serve as the substantial cause of a Buddha's Form Bodies.

Our own *coarse* body, speech, and mind are very different from each other; still, even now we have *subtle* body, speech, and mind that are undifferentiable. Highest Yoga Mantra, with great emphasis, speaks of taking the subtle body, speech, and mind – that in our ordinary state are undifferentiable in terms of their entity and that occur together with defilement – as the basis of practice and transforming these into the exalted body, speech, and mind of the effect stage, Buddhahood. Without the path of Highest Yoga Mantra, there is no way to manifest clearly our subtle body, speech, and mind such that they can perform activities. For instance, to generate our present, subtle mind which has the *capacity* to comprehend objects such that it manifestly performs the function of comprehending objects, the practice of Highest Yoga Mantra is needed, and similarly to develop fully the capacity of our present subtle body – that is to say, our very subtle winds or inner energies – to appear in whatever form one wants, the path of Highest Yoga Mantra is required.

To use well the very subtle wind and mind, it is necessary to stop coarse levels of wind and mind. "Wind" is most likely a special type of energy. In this subtle presentation, mind and wind are one undifferentiable entity; mind, or consciousness, is so named from the viewpoint of knowing objects, and wind, or energy, is so named from the viewpoint of engaging or moving toward objects. In the Kālachakra system, there are descriptions of ten or twelve types of winds – the greater number being due to sub-dividing the downward-voiding wind into three types. The wind called *dhanaṃjaya (nor las rgyal)* causes the body to change from one moment to the next and thus is said to be present even in a corpse.

The coarser levels of wind and mind are forcibly stopped whereby the subtle levels can be used. For stopping the coarser winds and minds, there are no operations or drugs; it is to be done through the power of meditative stabilization or through special physical exercises. Further, it is said that if one is having difficulty in accomplishing this, the channel at the wheel of enjoyment in the throat can be pressed such that the clear light manifests; however, there is the danger that instead of merely manifesting the clear light, one will die! Thus, some of the techniques are very dangerous; similarly, if wind yoga is not cultivated well, there is danger of illnesses. Even for usual meditators, if wind or breath yoga is not done well, you can develop headaches or eye pain. Since this is the case, it is important to train gradually under the guidance of an experienced, qualified teacher.

By way of using such techniques of Highest Yoga Mantra, the coarser levels of wind can be restrained and stopped – not just stopped by the force of karma as at the time of death, but through the power of yoga, through the power of techniques. When coarse wind and mind become inactive, the subtler wind and mind become active. Since this cessation of coarse levels is not by the power of karma but through the power of their being deliberately restrained in dependence upon a new technique, then when a subtler consciousness manifests, it is not unclear but clear, aware. A prime technique is *kuṇḍalini,* utilizing of the refined essence of the body. To do this, it is necessary to ignite the inner heat called the Fierce Female *(gtum mo, chaṇḍāli).* For this, a consort – a Great Seal Woman *(phyag rgya ma, mahāmudrā)* – is used.

The final purpose is to generate, as an entity of the path, the very subtle mind of clear light which can serve as the substantial cause of an omniscient consciousness, an exalted knower of all aspects. This is why the technique of forcibly eliminating the coarser levels of wind and mind is taught, for which one needs to gain control over the spreading out and gathering in of the red and white constituents, for which, in turn, the technique of using a consort is taught.

In brief, the direct substantial cause for achieving a Wisdom Truth Body and the direct substantial cause for achieving a Form Body can be achieved only in dependence upon Secret Mantra. Thus, the Buddhas of the past necessarily became fully enlightened in dependence upon Highest Yoga Mantra, and the Buddhas of the future also must become fully enlightened in dependence upon Highest Yoga Mantra.

> With the peerless[6] Secret mantra yoga
> The supreme ones[7] such as the Lion of Shākyas
> And so forth overcame the very awful
> And very powerful hosts of demons.
>
> Realizing that the world would follow,
> He turned the wheel of doctrine and then passed away.

In dependence upon such marvelous techniques of Secret Mantra, those who attained the supreme state – such as the Teacher Shākyamuni – overcame the hosts of demons, became fully enlightened, thereupon turned the wheel of doctrine, and finally showed the manner of passing away. All of these deeds were just achieved in dependence upon the power of Secret Mantra. Since this is the case, you – vajra students – should have firm, unchangeable interest and faith in Mantra.

> Therefore, in order to attain omniscience,
> O child, do this [with all] your intelligence.
>
> *Explaining the meaning of that, cause the* [*student's*] *prior generation of interest in Mantra to become unchangeably firm.*

3 *Vows and Blessing*

ASSUMING THE VOWS AND BEING BLESSED INTO MAGNIFICENCE

Identify well for the students and cause them to understand in detail[8] *the thought of how to assume, in stages, the common and uncommon Great Vehicle vows and the meaning of keeping the vows.*

In the texts of Indian scholars, various modes of taking the Mantra vows are presented – just during the preparatory phase, just during the actual initiation, and both. Since today we seem to be taking a long time, the Mantra vows will be given tomorrow during the actual initiation. Hence, the Bodhisattva vows will be sufficient today.

To take the Bodhisattva vows, imagine that those objects from whom you are taking the vows, the Buddhas and their "Children" – the Bodhisattvas – are present. We are making a great determination: "I will try to achieve Buddhahood for the sake of other beings. Without actual practice, there is no possibility to achieve Buddhahood; therefore, I will not only create the determination to attain Buddhahood but will also implement all the Bodhisattva practices. In order to do this, I will take the Bodhisattva vows, promising with strong will to train in the trainings of Bodhisattvas. Therefore, I am requesting the Bodhisattva vows." Repetition of the words of the following passage should be done within mindfulness of such meaning.

> *Then, the students repeat [after the lama] three times:* [297]
>
> I go for refuge to the Three Jewels,
> Individually disclose all ill-deeds,
> Admire the virtues of beings,
> And mentally take up the enlightenment of a Buddha.
>
> *Through that, the [Bodhisattva] vow common [to the Sūtra and Mantra Great Vehicles] is taken.*

When, during the third repetition, you say the last line, "And mentally take up the enlightenment of a Buddha," think that you have gained the complete, pure Bodhisattva vows in your continuum. At the least, think that you have gained special merit. However, those who feel that they are incapable of training in the Bodhisattva precepts or who are not interested need not think that they have made a promise to engage in the Bodhisattva practices.

[The rite for taking the Mantra vows is included here for the sake of completeness. For commentary see Part Two, Chapter Two.]

> *Then, the student makes supplication for the sake of the uncommon [Mantric] vow by repeating three times:*
>
> Bestowing on me the excellent
> Irreversible initiation of the [mandala] circle,
> O Protector, please explain
> The principles of the mandala, the deities,
> The activities of a master,
> The pledges of all Buddhas,
> And the supremely secret vows.
> In order to achieve the welfare of all sentient beings
> I will forever act as a master.
>
> *Then, the uncommon Mantric[9] vows are taken by repeating three times:*

O, all Buddhas and Bodhisattvas, please take heed of me.
I (your name) from this time henceforth
Until arriving in the essence of enlightenment
Will generate the excellent unsurpassed
Intention to become enlightened
In just the way that the protectors of the three times
Become definite toward enlightenment.
I will firmly keep individually
The three forms of ethics – the ethical precepts,
The composite of virtuous practices,
And bringing about the welfare of sentient beings.
For the five-pointed vajra [lineage of Akṣhobhya] I will sustain with the crown of my head vajra, bell, seal, and lama.
For the jewel [lineage of Ratnasambhava] I will give gifts; for the wheel [lineage of Vairochana] I will keep the pledges of the supreme Conquerors.
For the sword [lineage of Amoghasiddhi] I will make offerings; for the bright lotus [lineage of Amitābha] I will maintain restraint.
So that sentient beings may be liberated, I will, for the [Vajrasattva] lineage of the progenitor of Conquerors, generate enlightenment.
I will liberate those not liberated [from the obstructions to omniscience].
I will release those not released [from cyclic existence].
I will relieve those unrelieved [in bad transmigrations]
And set sentient beings in nirvana. [298]

[BLESSING (THE STUDENTS) INTO MAGNIFICENCE]

Next is a blessing into magnificence. This is done through imagining the six constituents of the student – earth, water, fire, wind, space, and consciousness – as of the nature of the six Wisdom Women. The students visualize themselves as

Kālachakra and at six places in their body visualize what, in entity, are these six constituents but which appear in the aspect of six syllables. The water constituent of the student is imagined as the syllable *ū*, the nature of Māmakī, on a moon at the forehead; the wind constituent is imagined as the syllable *ī*, the nature of Tārā, on a green *rāhu* disc at the heart; the space constituent is imagined as the syllable *ā*, the nature of Vajradhātvīshvarī, on a drop at the crown protrusion; the earth constituent is imagined as the syllable *ḹ*, the nature of Lochanā, on a yellow *kālāgni* disc at the navel; the fire constituent is imagined as the syllable *ṝ*, the nature of Pāṇḍarā, on a sun at the neck; and the consciousness constituent is imagined as the syllable *āḥ*, the nature of Prajñāpāramitā, in the wheel of exalted wisdom at the secret region.

Then, [the lama] contemplates:

> Setting an ū on a moon at the forehead of the student, an ī on a [green] rāhu disc at the heart, an ā on a drop at the crown protrusion, an ḹ on a [yellow] kālāgni disc at the navel, an ṝ on a sun at the neck, and an āḥ in the wheel of exalted wisdom at the secret region, they are protected by these, which are the entities of the goddesses of the six lineages, the exalted body, speech, and mind of Method and Wisdom.

Then, within visualizing yourself as Kālachakra, visualize a black *hūm* on a green *rāhu* disc at your heart, a red *āḥ* on a sun at the neck, and a white *oṃ* on a moon at the forehead. The nature of your own subtle mind, speech, and body appear in the aspect of these three syllables; imagine that the three syllables are the entities of exalted body, speech, and mind. When I repeat the three syllables – *hūṃ, āḥ, oṃ* – imagine that as I make the gesture of touching your heart, throat, and forehead, I touch you with drops of water from the conch-vase at the heart, neck, and forehead and that light radiates out from the three syllables. Think that all the Buddhas' and Bodhisattvas' magnificent blessings of exalted mind, speech, and body dissolve into those places, thereby purifying ill-deeds and obstructions of mind, speech, and body together with their predispositions accumulated from beginningless time.

> *Then, the lama contemplates:*
>
> A black hūṃ[10] on a [green] rāhu disc at the student's heart, a red āḥ on a sun at the neck, and a white oṃ on a moon at the forehead.
>
> *The master utters the three syllables* [*hūm, āḥ, oṃ*] *in speech, and through touching the three places* [*heart, throat, and top of the head*], *starting with the bottom, with perfumed water taken up with the fingers of the hand, which has a vajra, he blessed* [*the students*] *into magnificence and makes offering* [*to the students*] *with the five enjoyments* [*flowers, incense, lamp, perfumed water, and food*].

Thereby, the three doors of body, speech, and mind are blessed into magnificence. The Tibetan word for "blessing into magnificence" is *jin-lap (byin rlabs); jin* means "magnificence" *(gzi byin),* and *lap* means "transform" *(sgyur ba).* Hence, a blessing into magnificence means to transform what is ordinary and impure into a pure entity.

To be blessed into magnificence, it is necessary from our own side to make exertion. When encountering various good and bad objects, you should not be attached to their appearance as such but see them as like illusions, thereby not coming under the influence of afflictive emotions when encountering those objects. Through viewing them as like illusions appearing to exist inherently but not actually existing inherently, you bring them within the scope of the practice of understanding dependent-arising and emptiness. Another practice is, when encountering objects, to bring them within the scope of factors that assist in igniting bliss. Thus, this blessing into magnificence is a technique for transforming the body, speech, and mind of oneself – the experiencer of various good and bad objects – into pure entities.

Imagine that a garland of flowers is offered for wearing on

your head; this has two purposes, for understanding that phenomena are like illusions and for generating bliss. From conceiving these flowers to exist inherently, obscuration increases; similarly, through the power of conceiving these flowers to exist inherently, attachment is produced thinking, "These flowers are really wonderful," whereupon desire increases. In dependence upon that, anger against whoever or whatever might interfere with your enjoying them occurs. However, if you view the flowers as like a magician's illusions in that, although they appear to exist inherently, they do not exist inherently and use this to assist in igniting bliss, then instead of the perception of the flowers harming your practice, it helps. This is why a garland is offered to you.

Offerings of pleasant scent for your nose, lamps for the eyes for removing darkness and dullness, perfumed water for the body, and food for the tongue are also made. The purpose is the same.

4 *Tooth-Stick, Water, Kusha Grass, and Thread*

CASTING THE TOOTH-STICK AND GIVING HANDFULS OF WATER AND SO FORTH

A tooth-stick [an old-fashioned tooth brush] is cast [or dropped onto a square board drawn in four sections and a central portion] for the sake of analyzing what type of feat *(dngos grub, siddhi)* the student is to work at achieving. For this, the student has to repeat a Sanskrit mantra in which the seed syllables of the six lineages are first recited and then there is mention of the four doors of liberation. The three doors of liberation are signlessness, wishlessness, and emptiness, and in addition here there is a fourth, non-activity – referring to the fact that although causes produce effects, they do not do so inherently. The meaning of the mantra is that body, speech, and mind are cleansed by way of exalted body, speech, and mind that are undifferentiable in entity from the reality of the four doors of liberation.

> *Then, wash with fragrantly perfumed water a twelve finger-width tooth-stick, grown from a milk-fruit tree such as Ficus Glomearata (udumvāra),*[11] *that is without*

any living beings, straight and not split, with non-deteriorated and unscarred skin and bark. At the head [of the tooth-stick] hold a garland of flowers, and having made offerings with scents and so forth say [and have the students repeat]:

Oṃ āḥ hūṃ hoḥ haṃ kṣhaḥ vajra-danta-kāṣhṭha-chatur-vimokṣha-mukha-vishuddha-svabhāvaṃ kāya-vāk-chitta-jñāna-mukha-dantādi-malaṃ vishodhaya svāhā. [May the seed syllables of the six lineages – oṃ āḥ hūṃ hoḥ haṃ kṣhaḥ – and the vajra tooth-stick having the nature of the purity of the four doors of liberation purify the defilements of the teeth and so forth of the faces of exalted body, speech, mind, and pristine consciousness svāhā.]

Give it to the student who is facing east. Having uttered:

Oṃ āḥ hūṃ

seven times, [the student] casts [that is, drops the tooth-stick] onto the mandala – which has a cubit on each side, four corners, and is annointed with the five cow-products.[12] *Through this, one knows that [the student] will achieve the manifold activities concordant with the direction of the head of the tooth-stick.*

[GIVING HANDFULS OF WATER]

Next is the giving of handfuls of water as a means of purifying the three doors of body, speech, and mind.

Then, having uttered:

Oṃ hrīḥ suvishuddha-dharma-sarva-pāpaṃ nichāmasya shodhaya sarva-vikalpanā-apanaya hūṃ. [Oṃ hrīḥ purify all ill-deeds of this aggregation by way of the thorough purity of phenomena, remove all conceptuality hūṃ.]

> *pour three handfuls of fragrant water along with the five ambrosias [into the student's] hand.*

First, take a little of the water poured into your hand and use it to rinse out your mouth. Then, take the remaining water in three sips, considering them as means of purifying respectively body, speech, and mind.

GIVING KUSHA GRASS

In connection with advice, given later, for analyzing tonight's dreams, kusha grass is given for the sake of having unmistaken, clear dreams. It is also for the sake of clearing away pollutants and uncleanliness so that your mind will be clear.

> *Then, clear away [obstructors from] kusha grass, the tips of which are not deteriorated and are large, and having said:*
>
> Generated from hūṃ.
>
> *repeat hūṃ and the six syllables [oṃ āḥ hūṃ hoḥ haṃ kṣhaḥ]. It is for the mattress, whereas the smaller one, having said:*
>
> Arisen from dhīḥ.
>
> *and repeated dhīḥ and the six syllables [oṃ āḥ hūṃ hoḥ haṃ kṣhaḥ], is for the pillow. These are given between the pressed palms of the two hands of the student,* [299] *uttering:*
>
> Oṃ vajra-tīkṣhṇa baṃ. [Oṃ vajra sharpness baṃ.]

The larger one is to put under your mattress, and the smaller, under your pillow.

GIVING A PROTECTIVE THREAD

> *Then, cleanse and purify a red thread the length of the student's body, wound three times:*

Arisen from hūṃ.

Having repeated hūṃ and the six syllables [oṃ āḥ hūṃ hoḥ haṃ kṣhaḥ] seven times, tie three knots in it. Uttering:

Oṃ buddha-maitri rakṣha rakṣha sarvān svāhā. [Oṃ protect, protect against all (the unfavorable) with buddha-love svāhā.]

tie it on the student's shoulder. The purpose of these is like that explained elsewhere.

The mantra uses the word for love, *"maitri"*, because love is the real protection. As much as love increases in your mind, so much do harmful forces not affect you. Since this is the case, the actual method for protecting against harm is the cultivation of love.

5 *Six Lineages and Vajrasattva*

SETTING THE SIX LINEAGES AND INVOKING VAJRASATTVA

The seed syllables of the six lineages – the usual five lineages of Akṣhobhya, Amoghasiddhi, Ratnasambhava, Amitābha, and Vairochana and a sixth lineage of Vajrasattva – are set in six places in the student's body. Whether you are male or female makes no difference; imagine yourself mentally as having the body of Kālachakra. Imagine that your forehead is marked with a white *oṃ,* that your neck is marked with a red *āḥ*, that your heart is marked with a black *hūṃ,* that your navel area is marked with a yellow *hoḥ*, that your crown protrusion is marked with a green *haṃ,* and that your secret region is marked with a blue *kṣhaḥ*.

> A [white] oṃ is set at the student's forehead, a [red] āḥ at the neck, a [black] hūṃ at the heart, a [yellow] hoḥ at the navel, a [green] haṃ at the crown protrusion, and a [blue] kṣhaḥ at the secret region.

[INVOKING VAJRASATTVA]

Next, the students repeat after the lama the mantra invoking Vajrasattva. The essential meaning of the mantra is: May

Vajrasattva, the pure exalted wisdom, bestow the supreme [feat of Buddhahood on me] through the magnificent blessings of Kālachakra's exalted body, speech, and mind entering into my continuum.

Through uttering:

Oṃ ā ā aṃ aḥ vajrasatva-mahāsukha-vajra-kāla-chakra shiṣhyasya abhimukho bhava saṃtuṣhṭo bhava varado bhava, kaya-vāk-chittādhiṣhṭhānaṃ kuru svāhā. [Vajrasattva, Vajra Kālachakra of great bliss, approach the student, thoroughly please (the student), bestow the supreme, bless into magnificence exalted body, speech, and mind.]

invoke Vajrasattva, through which the student's exalted body, speech, and mind are blessed into magnificence. Thereupon think that the supreme [feat of Buddhahood] has been bestowed.

6 *Enthusiasm and Dreams*

GENERATING ENTHUSIASM THROUGH EXPLAINING DOCTRINE AND GIVING ADVICE ON ANALYZING DREAMS

The passage used for developing appreciation of the doctrine is taken from the *Condensed Kālachakra Tantra.*

> *Then:*[13]
>
> In the womb there is the suffering of dwelling in the womb; at birth and while a child there is also suffering.
>
> Youth and adulthood are filled with the great sufferings of losing one's mate,[14] wealth, and fortune, as well as the great suffering of the afflictive emotions.
>
> The old have the suffering of death and again the fright of the six transmigrations such as the Crying and so forth.[15]

This speaks of the sufferings of humans as well as the indefiniteness of the type of suffering to be experienced after death in any of the six transmigrations, as a hell-being, hungry ghost, animal, human, demi-god, or god. From the time of dwelling in the womb, there are many sufferings just as there are after birth and then as a child. Even as an adult one loses one's mate, wealth, and so forth. Even in countries of great material progress there is much pain; in countries of little material development there are many varieties of pain. Then, in old age there is the suffering of more illnesses and, as death approaches, the suffering of death. After death, there again is the suffering of definitely having to wander in any of the six transmigrations.

That we undergo such suffering is not without causes and conditions. What causes it?

> All these transmigrating beings, deluded by illusion, grasp suffering from suffering.

What actually is suffering is not understood to be suffering but, out of obscuration, is mis-identified as happiness and clung to. Similarly, what is not an inherently existent self appears to be an inherently existent self and is, out of obscuration, conceived to be so. Through this ignorance misconceiving the nature of persons and of other phenomena, actions are done through which good and bad karma that propels lifetimes in cyclic existence is accumulated, and the round of suffering continues. Similarly, although one wants happiness, out of ignorance one does not know how to achieve it, and even though one does not want suffering, due to being obscured with respect to the causes of suffering one engages, as if intentionally, in achieving the very causes of suffering. In this way, what are to be adopted and to be discarded are reversed, one suffering leading to another.

The eyes of those attending a magical show are affected by the magician's mantra, and, due to this obscuration, generate attachment when they see illusory horses, elephants, and so forth that appear. In a similar way, due to the obscuration of the conception of inherent existence, beings exaggerate the status of good and bad phenomena and are thereby led into desire and hatred and thereby into accumulating actions *(las, karma)*.

Is it possible for such a situation of suffering to be removed? If it is, what is the method? As explained earlier, all of us have the Buddha nature, and when one becomes capable of transforming subtle body, speech, and mind into pure body, speech, and mind, suffering as well as its predispositions is purified forever.

Still, the mere existence of such a method does not bring about release from suffering; the method must be generated in your continuum – it must be implemented through effort. At this juncture, we have a good opportunity which therefore must not be wasted.

> Though some become humans in cyclic existence,
> few have a spiritual attitude.
> Fewer, through the force of the virtue of being
> attracted to Buddha, enter into the prime vehicle.
> Still fewer engage their entire intelligence in cultivating the glorious Vajra Vehicle.
> Even more, those wishing Buddhahood who enter
> into the states of the supreme bliss are, alas,
> extremely rare. [300]

Within cyclic existence, those who have a human life-support are few since a life of high status as a human is achieved only from having created good causes. From among those few, those who have encountered a spiritual system and whose minds have turned toward it are even fewer. Again, among them, those who have entered into the Great Vehicle teaching and are seeking the enlightenment of a Buddha are even fewer. Among them, those who have faithful interest in the Secret Mantra Vehicle are even more rare; such beings hardly occur. Then, those who not only have faithful interest in the Secret Mantra Vehicle but who practice its path properly to achieve Buddhahood are even more rare.

Hence, at this point we have gained a human body, encountered Buddha's teaching and, within it, the Great Vehicle teaching, and furthermore have faithful interest in the Secret Mantra Vehicle. That we have a wish to practice this profound doctrine is indeed very fortunate.

Next, enthusiasm for taking up the doctrine is generated through reflecting on words from the *General Secret Tantra*.

Also:

The Omniscient Ones arise
In the world rarely,
Only sometimes, like an udumvāra flower,[16]
And then do not appear.

The arising of the mode of Secret Mantra practice
Is even rarer than that.

In general, the appearance of a Buddha is rare; even rarer is the appearance of Mantra. Why is the appearance of Mantra so rare? It is because beings who have the capacity to achieve its powerful practices are so rare. The remainder of the passage sets forth the great power of Mantra in that through it one can achieve Buddhahood in this very lifetime, and so forth.

Through it, the unequalled welfare of sentient beings
Can be accomplished without passing away.

Even ill-deeds done earlier
Over many ten millions of eons
Are all entirely removed
Immediately upon seeing such a mandala.

Thus what need is there to mention about dwelling
In the mode of Mantra practice endlessly renowned!

It is possible, immediately upon seeing a mandala that has been properly achieved and is blessed into magnificence, to cleanse ill-deeds accumulated over many eons. If that is so, there is no need to mention that it is beneficial to practice its path in the proper way.

If one repeats protective secret mantra,
One will achieve the unsurpassed state.

The term "mantra" is etymologized as "mind-protection", specifically protecting the mind from ordinary appearance and conceptions of being ordinary. If such protective secret mantra is repeated properly, highest enlightenment can be attained even in one lifetime.

Whosoever's mind is very non-fluctuating
About this supreme of practices
Will eliminate the bad transmigrations
Which give rise to all suffering.

The compassionate Supramundane Victor, skilled in means, set forth basically three modes of practice: for those interested in the low, he set forth practices free from desire; for those interested in the vast he set forth the practices of the Bodhisattva grounds and perfections, and for those very interested in the profound he set forth practices in which desire for the attributes of the Desire Realm is used in the path. If, from among the three styles of practice, you have a very non-fluctuating, reasoned, firm faith in the supreme mode of Secret Mantra involving usage of the attributes of the Desire Realm in the path, you can easily eliminate rebirth in the bad transmigrations that are sources of great suffering.

You great beings have today[17]
Found the unparalleled finding,
For all of you will be upheld
In this teaching by the Conqueror and his Children,

And you great beings
Are dwelling in being born into it.
Through that, tomorrow you will be born
Thoroughly into the Great Vehicle.

You great beings, that is to say, you students, have attained the lot of entering into the path of Secret Mantra, an unparalleled finding. For, today you are beginning the process of becoming yogis practicing the Secret Mantra Vehicle in that you have asked for initiation. Tomorrow you will enter the mandala and, the next day, will attain the initiations, through which you will become Knowledge-Bearers of the Vajra Vehicle, Māntrikas.

Through proceeding on that glorious supreme path
Greatly giving rise to the Great Vehicle
You will become Ones Gone Thus [Buddhas]

Knowing all the world,
Self-arisen beings of great fortune.

You are coming to have the potential of attaining Buddhahood in this lifetime in dependence upon the path of Highest Yoga Mantra which easily gives rise to the Truth and Form Bodies of a Buddha. This supreme path is glorious in that while on the path a practitioner actualizes a body similar in aspect to a Buddha's Form Body in dependence upon which the body of the effect state as a Buddha is actualized.

Since you vajra students are proceeding on this path, you will, in not long, become "self-arisen beings of great fortune" in that when the Wisdom Truth Body is actualized, the Form Body is simultaneously actualized without depending on any other conditions or agents, independently. In this sense, the Form Body is called "self-arisen". Similarly, the Truth Body is also called "self-arisen" in the sense that the emptiness that is the object of the Wisdom Truth Body has abided beginninglessly whether the Ones Gone Thus arise or not and thus the suchness of phenomena remains of its own accord. Furthermore, the mind of clear light that remains of one undifferentiable entity with that suchness – the exalted wisdom of the fundamental innate mind of clear light – is beginningless in terms of its entity. The undifferentiable entity of the object – suchness – and the subject – the fundamental innate mind of clear light – is the basis of emanation or creator of all Buddhas. Hence, in this sense the Truth Body is self-arisen. Due to possessing such self-arisen Form and Truth Bodies, Buddhas are beings of "great fortune".

Through explaining the meaning of that, generate enthusiasm.

[ANALYZING DREAMS]

Next is advice on how to analyze the dreams that occur tonight. If it is convenient, arrange your bed so that the head of the bed is towards the mandala; if not convenient, imagine it. Put the larger kusha grass under your mattress, and the smaller piece under your pillow. Sleep on your right side in the lion posture. When you first lie down, assume this posture; if during the night your posture changes, it is all right; otherwise, you would have to be bolted down to the mattress!

In your thought, do not allow your mind to be polluted by other conceptions; just be mindful of Kālachakra, and within that, think, as much as you can, of the altruistic intention to become enlightened and the view of emptiness. If you cannot do that, first cultivate faith and compassion, and look straightforwardly at mind itself.

If you usually sleep too heavily, it will lighten your sleep to use a point of imagination higher up in the body. Again, if you sleep too lightly, using a point of imagination lower in the body will make your sleep more heavy.

Engage in techniques so that you fall asleep within a virtuous attitude. Then, it is explained that from among the four periods of the night, there is a possibility of analyzing the dreams around dawn in the fourth period. In general, around us there are many mysteries, many facts, that are not seen with the eye. Because we have a coarse physical body, when it is very active, it is difficult to have direct contact with these mysteries, but when we become semi-conscious – when our consciousness becomes more subtle – there is a diminishment of the coarse consciousnesses that depend on the coarse physical body, and it is easier to make connection with such mysteries.

This is why various portents of future events and so forth appear during dreams. If you have deeper meditation, you can know these things through certain meditative experiences, but for ordinary people the only alternative is through dreams.

I will give you an oral transmission for a mantra to be repeated tonight.

> *Give the six syllables* [*oṃ āḥ hūṃ hoḥ haṃ kṣhaḥ*] *for the sake of repetition. Having told the students to lie down with their heads in the direction of the lama or the mandala and to tell you in the morning about what dreams were seen in the fourth part of the night, near dawn, send the students to their own*[18] *places.*

That concludes the enhancement of the student for the initiation of the Supramundane Victor, Kālachakra. I still have various things to do; thus, after offering mandala, you should leave.

(End of first day at Madison.)

Part Two
Entry into the Mandala

1 *Structure*

ADVICE ON DREAMS

Yesterday, it was explained that you were to analyze the slight signs occurring in your dreams in the fourth portion of the night, around dawn. In general, if, from among the four constituents of earth, water, fire, and wind, the earth constituent is particularly thick in the body, there are cases of not having clear dreams. If a dream did occur, experiencing fright or mental discomfort is considered to be slightly negative. Also, even though finding many flowers in a dream brings pleasure, if the flowers are red, then it is not good; however, there are exceptions, such as when performing rites to achieve certain activities. Also, even though you may have come upon a temple, if it was not brilliant but decayed, dirty, or dilapidated or, even though you may have come upon an image, if it was not magnificent but covered with dust, these are bad.

On the other hand, dreams of things that please the mind are better. Still, it is said that even if you had a good dream, you should not develop pleasure in it that involves attachment. Similarly, even if you had a bad dream, you should not be too concerned about it. If you had no dreams, it is neutral.

There are ways of overcoming bad dreams; the main technique is to meditate on emptiness, but also, in situations of fright and discomfort, it is important to take specific cognizance of the object – the person or being who is the source of the fright or displeasure – and then cultivate compassion and love. This is the best method of overcoming the problem. The being who is trying to harm you is like yourself in wanting happiness and not wanting suffering. Thus, the best protection is to think, "Just as I want happiness, so this being wants happiness. May this being attain happiness, may this being come to possess happiness!"

According to my own experience, reciting mantra and doing visualizations do not have much effect during a nightmare, but as a last resort, remembering compassion and altruism toward that object brings immediate peace. The best protection is to protect ourselves – this means to protect ourselves from anger, hatred, and fear by remaining always with the courage and determination of compassion.

Now as an additional means to overcome bad dreams, I will scatter water, simultaneously reciting the mantra *oṃ āḥ hūṃ hoḥ haṃ kṣhaḥ*. During this, visualize that all bad effects are cast away by the force of the mantra and the wisdom understanding emptiness.

STRUCTURE OF THE INITIATION

For an initiation to occur, there are many things that the lama must perform and many that the student must do. What have I done? First I have cultivated self-generation as Kālachakra using the full mandala rite of exalted body, speech, and mind. Then, the vases were transformed [into deities who then reappeared as vases] after which I did generation of the deity, Kālachakra, in front. There are two varieties of generation or imagination of the deity in front – one with the deity as the same entity as oneself and the other with the deity as a different entity. This being the *Kālachakra Tantra*, the Kālachakra as whom one is imagining oneself and the Kālachakra imagined in front are seen as different entities.

Then, to refurbish vows that have been taken, one performs self-entry into the mandala; if the Dalai Lama had been stupid [and transgressed a vow], he would have restored the vows by performing the rite of self-entry into the mandala. Next are a supplication for the sake of the student and an expression of the power of truth. Then, there is a giving of food-offerings to obstructing spirits who might interrupt the initiation, and there is meditative cultivation of a wheel of protective deities. Those are what the lama must do. I now am maintaining conception of myself as the principal deity of the mandala, Kālachakra; after performing self-entry into the mandala, I have maintained the "pride" of being the principal deity.

The students have to make obeisance, rinse their mouths, and then make mandala-offerings, these having just been done. Now, just as yesterday, imagine that you are outside the three-tiered mandala, outside the level of exalted body. Think that from there you make [another] mandala-offering.[19]

To the lama, personal deity, and Three Jewels I offer in visualization
The body, speech, mind, and resources of myself and others,
Our collections of virtue in the past, present, and future,
And the wonderful precious mandala with the masses of Samantabhadra's offerings.
Accepting them through your compassion, please bless me into magnificence.
Idaṃ guru-ratna-maṇḍalakaṃ niryātayāmi. [I offer this jewelled mandala to the guru.]

To enter the Kālachakra mandala and receive initiation, as mentioned yesterday, it is important to listen within having adjusted well your motivation to be an altruistic intention to become enlightened and within the correct view of the emptiness of inherent existence.

HISTORY OF THE *KĀLACHAKRA TANTRA*

According to one interpretation, the *Kālachakra Tantra* was first spoken by the Teacher, Shākyamuni Buddha, at the time of the full moon in the third month of the year after his having shown the manner of becoming completely and perfectly enlightened.[20] According to another interpretation, Shākyamuni, having showed the manner of becoming completely and perfectly enlightened, turned the three wheels of doctrine, and then one year before his passing away set forth the *Kāla-*

chakra Tantra. About this, the root *Kālachakra Tantra* says:

> Just as the Teacher [set forth] the mode of the Perfection of Wisdom at Vulture Peak
> So at the stūpa of Dhānyakaṭaka *('bras spungs)* he set forth all the modes of [this] Secret Mantra.

A literal reading of this passage indicates that just as, for example, Shākyamuni set forth many styles of teachings such as the Perfection of Wisdom Sūtras at many places – Vulture Peak and so forth – so at Dhānyakaṭaka he turned a wheel of doctrine of Secret Mantra with the *Kālachakra Tantra* as the principal tantra.

In the country of Shambhala, Shākyamuni Buddha set forth specifically this tantra for many trainees – both gods and humans, illustrated by King Suchandra *(rgyal po zla ba bzang po).* The *Kālachakra Tantra* itself has twelve thousand stanzas; King Suchandra composed a commentary sixty thousand stanzas in length.

Occasional citations of the root tantra in Kulika Puṇḍarīka's *Great Commentary on the "Kālachakra Tantra", the Stainless Light (dri med 'od, vimālaprabhā)* and in other commentaries and the *Brief Explication of Initiations (dbang mdor bstan, shekhoddesha)* were translated into Tibetan, but the root tantra itself was not translated. Then, after seven religious kings, King Mañjushrīkīrti *('jam dpal grags pa)* allowed many trainees such as Sūryaratha *(nyi ma'i shing rta)* to enter the mandala and thereby to be ripened, blending all of these persons into one vajra lineage; hence from that point, the religious kings were given the title *kulika (rigs ldan),* "one who bears the lineage". It was indicated in the root tantra itself that in the future someone named "Kīrti" would make a shorter version of the tantra, and, just so, Kulika Mañjushrīkīrti condensed the main points of the tantra into the present one of five chapters having over one thousand stanzas, called the *Condensed Kālachakra Tantra.* Since his doing this was prophesied in the root tantra itself, the *Condensed Kālachakra Tantra* is accepted as an actual tantra.

Later, Kulika Puṇḍarīka composed a commentary on the *Condensed Kālachakra Tantra,* called the *Stainless Light,* which is twelve thousand stanzas long. These two, the *Condensed Kālachakra Tantra* and *Stainless Light,* were translated into Tibetan, and explanations of the *Kālachakra Tantra* are based mainly on these two texts. Among commentaries by Tibetan scholars, the commentaries of annotations on the tantra itself and on Kulika Puṇḍarīka's *Stainless Light* by the S̄a-ḡya scholar Bu-d̄ön Rin-chen-drup *(bu ston rin chen grub,* 1290-1364) are the best.

Two translations of the tantra were made into Tibetan, one by the Translator Ra Dor-jay-drak-b̄a *(rva lo tsā ba rdo rje grags pa)* and one by the Translator Dro Shay-rap-drak *('bro lo tsā ba shes rab grags).* The main transmissions of explanation are from Ra and Dro, these being combined in Bu-d̄ön Rin-b̄o-chay. The oral transmission of the tantra that I have is this one, which was passed down from Bu-d̄ön Rin-b̄o-chay to the present to my kind root lama, L̄ing Rin-b̄o-chay. I received the transmission of the explanation of the tantra from S̄er-ḡong Rin-b̄o-chay, who has two different transmissions of explanation. I am still a student of the *Kālachakra Tantra,* an elder student perhaps.

TOPICS OF THE TANTRA

With respect to the subjects of the five chapters of the *Condensed Kālachakra Tantra,* first, what is Kālachakra – "Wheel of Time"? What is "time"? What is the "wheel"? "Time" refers to immutable bliss, and "wheel" to various empty forms. In the *Kālachakra Tantra,* two types of emptiness are described – aspected and unaspected. The unaspected emptiness is exactly the emptiness described in the treatises of the Middle Way School *(dbu ma pa, mādhyamika)* – the emptiness of inherent existence. The mind of clear light that takes this emptiness as its object probably is also called an unaspected emptiness. This is like, for example, the usage of the term "concordant ultimate" for a wisdom consciousness that realizes emptiness.[21]

"Aspected emptiness", on the other hand, refers to empty forms. Hence, whereas the object of negation of unaspected emptiness is inherent existence, the object of negation of aspected emptiness is material phenomena composed of particles. Therefore, "aspected emptiness" refers to various forms, or physical objects, that are beyond materiality.

On the basis of what are these various empty forms achieved? They are achieved in terms of the mind. In the *Kālachakra Tantra,* wind yoga is described, but there is not an emphasis on wind yoga as there is in the *Guhyasamāja Tantra* and the *Heruka Tantra* [also called the *Chakrasaṃvara Tantra*], for empty forms are not achieved by way of wind.

Thus, taken together, the term "Kālachakra" refers to a *union* in one entity of immutable bliss and empty form. This explanation is primarily in terms of the effect stage of Buddhahood, the time of the final object of attainment. Since, to actualize such an effect through paths of practice, it is necessary to have a basis in dependence upon which the paths are practiced, there come to be external, internal, and alternative Kālachakras.

The external Kālachakra refers to all of the environment – the mountains, fences, homes, planets, constellations of stars, solar systems, and so forth. The internal Kālachakra refers to the person's body having a nature of channels, winds, and drops of essential fluid. The alternative Kālachakra refers to the methods for purifying the impure factors of the external and internal Kālachakras – these being the bases of purification – and thereby bringing about transformation into a Kālachakra of the effect state of Buddhahood. Again, within the alternative Kālachakra – the path – there are the divisions of (1) the stage of completion, which brings the path to completion and is comprised of the six-branched yoga; (2) the stage of generation, which matures one for the practice of the stage of completion, and (3) the initiations authorizing one to listen to, think about, and meditate on such paths of the stages of generation and completion.

These three Kālachakras – external, internal, and alternative – are the subjects discussed in the five chapters of the *Condensed Kālachakra Tantra.* The full meaning of the external, internal, and alternative Kālachakras is contained in the ten letters of the root mantra of Kālachakra, *haṃ kṣhaḥ ma la va ra ya.* The mantra is called the powerful one having ten aspects *(rnam bcu dbang ldan)*. In *haṃ kṣhaḥ ma la va ra ya*, there are the seven letters – *h*, *kṣh*, *m*, *l*, *v*, *r*, and *y* – as well as the *visārga* [in *kṣhaḥ* which appears as a half moon], the *anusvāra* [in *haṃ*], and the vowel *a* which is the "life" [of the consonants], thereby making ten. Also, there is an eleventh symbol, the *nāda* [a wiggly line rising from the dot on top].

The explanations of the formation of the mantra and of its meaning are complicated, but in brief, when these ten letters are associated with the external Kālachakra, they symbolize the four elements, Mt. Meru, sun, moon, and so forth. In the Kālachakra system, there are thirty-one categories of cyclic existence, which, in turn, are condensed here into eleven categories through abridging the levels of gods.

When the ten letters are associated with the internal Kālachakra, they symbolize the practitioner's four internal elements of earth, water, fire, and wind, the spinal column, the channel center at the secret region, the central, right, and left channels, and bliss.

When the ten letters as well as the *nāda* are associated with the alternative Kālachakra and, within that, with the initiations that ripen trainees, they symbolize the eleven initiations. In the more extensive enumeration of the initiations, there are fifteen, but these are included in eleven types. Of these, the first seven initiations are those in the pattern of childhood:

1 water initiation
2 crown initiation
3 silk ribbon initiation
4 vajra and bell initiation
5 conduct initiation
6 name initiation
7 permission initiation.

Then, there are the four high initiations:

8 vase initiation
9 secret initiation
10 knowledge-wisdom initiation
11 provisional word initiation.

And then the four greatly high initiations:

12 vase initiation
13 secret initiation
14 knowledge-wisdom initiation
15 definitive word initiation.

To re-classify these fifteen as eleven, the vase initiation, secret initiation, and knowledge-wisdom initiation from among the greatly high initiations are included in the similar ones in the high initiations, and the provisional word initiation from among the high initiations is included in the knowledge-wisdom initiation in that same group, leaving the definitive word initiation as the eleventh. [Thus the eleven initiations are:

Seven initiations in the pattern of childhood
1 water initiation
2 crown initiation
3 silk ribbon initiation
4 vajra and bell initiation
5 conduct initiation
6 name initiation
7 permission initiation.

Four high initiations
8 two vase initiations (8 and 12 from above)
9 two secret initiations (9 and 13 from above)
10 two knowledge-wisdom initiations and the provisional word initiation (10, 14 and 11 from above)
11 definitive word initiation (15 from above).]

When the ten letters as well as the *nāda* are associated with the alternative Kālachakra and, within that, with the stage of generation, they symbolize the mandalas [i.e., spheres] of the four elements, Mount Meru, the inestimable mansion on top of Mount Meru, the three seats of *rāhu*, sun, and moon as well as the circle of deities – [i.e., the mandala meditated in the stage of generation]. Similarly, when the ten letters as well as the *nāda* are associated with the alternative Kālachakra and, within that, with the stage of completion, they symbolize the channel centers and so forth. In this way, the powerful mantra of ten aspects indicates the bases, paths, and fruits of the Kālachakra system – all of the external, internal, and alternative Kālachakras.

DETAILS OF THE OCCASION

The *mandala in which the initiations will be conferred* is a mandala of colored particles. Except for certain exceptional circumstances, the seven initiations in the pattern of childhood must be conferred in dependence upon a mandala of colored particles.

The *vajra master* who confers initiation in dependence upon such a mandala must, as is said in the *Kālachakra Tantra,* have attained initiation, be maintaining properly the pledges and vows, be skilled in the tantra and activities of the mandala, have done prior approximation [of the state of the deity] and thereupon received permission to confer initiation, and so forth. There are many such qualifications. We will say that I am just in the process of coming to have the minimum qualifications.

The *students,* also, should have faithful interest from the depths of their hearts in the altruistic intention to become enlightened and in the correct view of the emptiness of inherent existence. Even if they do not have experience of these, they should have the thought – from the depths of their being, "These are really needed; these are really good." In addition, the students must have faithful interest in Mantra.

The *place* where initiation is to be conferred is this fully qualified area in Wisconsin – isolated, clean, and quiet. And if you are hungry, you can go over to the corn field and eat some corn!

The *time* is preferably at the full moon of the third month of the Kālachakra system (thus to know this system well, it is necessary to know astrology – the houses, constellations, and so forth); otherwise, it can be the full moon period of any of the twelve months. Tomorrow is the full moon of the fifth month. Usually, in Hla-sa the fifteenth day of the fifth month is a day of celebration of the general prosperity of the world. Although we did not plan it this way, it is a happy coincidence.

The *initiations* being conferred are those ripening the continuum for the stage of generation – the seven initiations in the pattern of childhood. I think that there need be no rush for the high and greatly high initiations. When done properly, the initiations are given in estimation of what is needed at the particular time, whereas when treated just as a public ceremony they are all given at one time. The process of the seven initiations in the pattern of childhood is in two parts; on this particular occasion, the first day is for the topics involved in entering the mandala, with the second day being for conferring initiation upon having entered the mandala.

2 *Outside the Curtain*

The presentation of the rite of conferring initiation has two parts: entering the mandala and conferring initiation on those who have entered.[22]

ENTERING THE MANDALA

This section has two parts: entering blindfolded and entering such that one comes to have the nature of seeing the mandala. [318]

ENTERING BLINDFOLDED

This section has two parts: entering outside the curtain and entering inside.

ENTERING OUTSIDE THE CURTAIN

[*If you are performing self-entry (bdag 'jug) into the mandala*] *you imagine that the principal deity who is not different from the lama performs the activities of the lama and that you do the activities of the student. Having bathed, you dwell at the eastern door of the mandala and having made homage, offer a golden mandala.*

Initially, there are things to be done outside the mandala, the first of which is to generate enthusiasm. The mantra that will be recited means that you are taking pleasure in the fact that you are receiving the initiations giving rise to all feats – supreme and common. Repeat the mantra within mindfulness of its meaning.

> *Pressing your palms together, say:*
>
> Oṃ pravishaya bhagavān mahāsukha-mokṣha-puraṃ sarva-siddhi-sukha-pradaṃ paramasukha-uttamasiddhya jaḥ hūṃ baṃ hoḥ prasiddhyasva.
>
> *Or, translated into Tibetan [now English], say three times:*
>
> Supramundane Victor, let me enter for great bliss
> Into the city of liberation [the mandala],
> The joyous bliss of all feats.
> Through the feat of excellent supreme bliss
> Make it be thoroughly accomplished jàḥ hūṃ baṃ hoḥ.

The supreme feat is Buddhahood itself; middling feats are the eight great feats and so forth; low feats are the accomplishments of activities such as pacifying illness, etc. Through training in the stage of generation, common feats are achieved; through training in the six branched yoga of the stage of completion, the supreme feat of Buddhahood is achieved. All of these feats arise in dependence upon training in the paths of the two stages – the stage of generation and the stage of completion. To achieve any of these, your mental continuum first has to be ripened through initiation; then, it is necessary to train in the stage of generation. To achieve the supreme feat, it is also necessary to train in the stage of completion. Thus, all of these arise in dependence upon the condition of having received initiation; hence, initiation is, so to speak, the source of all feats. You are asking to enter the city of liberation, the mandala that is endowed with such marvelous qualities, and to be blessed – to be transformed into a magnificent state – so that you can achieve the supreme feat of Buddhahood.

Next, there is a supplication, the words of which were explained yesterday. The essence of the meaning is that you are requesting the deity to let you enter the mandala and to bestow the pledges and vows for progressing to the levels of liberation and omniscience.

Then, make supplication three times with:

The sole liberator from the ocean of cyclic existence,
Which is frightful with sea monsters and so forth –
The crocodiles of birth, aging, and death –
Is you, O Great Joyous Teacher of mine.

O great protector, I am seeking
The firm mode of great enlightenment.
Bestow on me the pledges.
Bestow on me also the mind of enlightenment.

Also bestow on me the three refuges,
Buddha, Doctrine, and Spiritual Community.
O protector, please let me enter
Into the supreme city of the great liberation.

When practicing Mantra in a mandala, it is necessary to have clear appearance of yourself as a deity and the pride [or conception] of yourself as a deity. The chief of these two is the pride of being a deity for which it is necessary to have clear appearance of yourself as a deity. In the process of doing so, you are not refuting the ordinary appearances seen by your eyes. Rather, you are not allowing ordinary phenomena to appear to the mental consciousness and, instead, are causing divine appearances to shine forth. When, by stopping ordinary appearances for the mental consciousness and developing clear appearance of yourself as a deity, such clear appearance becomes steady, the appearance of ordinary mental and physical aggregates, ordinary constituents, and ordinary senses and sense fields ceases. Instead, divine mental and physical aggregates, divine constituents, and divine senses and sense fields appear. At this point, an awareness thinking of oneself, "I", as designated in dependence on such pure mental and physical aggregates, pure constituents, and pure senses and sense fields dawns. In this way, these Mantra practices, in addition to the practice of method and wisdom in the Perfection Vehicle, bring together many techniques for quick development.

In order to promote mindfulness of the clear appearance of yourself as a deity and pride in yourself as a deity, you put on various articles of apparel and so forth of a deity.

> *Then respectively with the three* [*parts of the following mantra*]*:*
>
> Oṃ sarva-tathāgata-anuttara-bodhi-alaṃkāra-vastra-pūja-megha-samudra-spharaṇa samaya shrī ye hūṃ, oṃ vajra-rakṣha haṃ, oṃ vajra-uṣhṇīṣha hūṃ phaṭ. [Oṃ the pledge issuing forth an ocean of clouds of offerings of garments as adornments of the highest enlightenment of all Ones Gone Thus shrī ye hūṃ. Oṃ vajra protection haṃ. Oṃ vajra crown protrusion hūṃ phaṭ.]
>
> *give* [*to the student the clothing of a deity*] *the lower robe of the various cloths, the yellow upper robe, and the red crown protrusion which have been mantrified with the six syllables* [*oṃ āḥ hūṃ hoḥ haṃ kṣhaḥ*] *and have* [*the student*] *put them on* [*in order to enhance the sense of being a deity*].

Since, for the time being, it is not suitable for the student to see the secrecies of the mandala, blindfolds are given.

> *Then, with:*
>
> Oṃ dvadasha-aṅga-nirodha-kāriṇi hūṃ phaṭ. [Oṃ making the cessation of the twelve branches hūṃ phaṭ.]
>
> [*have the student*] *tie on a blindfold of orange or laytun (las 'thun) colored cloth.*

So that later when you enter the mandala and meet the deity you will have a present to offer him, you are given a garland of flowers. As I give it to you, imagine that the workers distributing the garlands are vajra-workers appearing as Kālachakras with one face and two arms.

> *[Have the student] hold a garland of flowers with:*
>
> Āḥ khaṃ-vīra hūṃ.

Now, as yesterday, the students drop the tooth-stick for the sake of determining what type of feat they are to work at achieving, and also handfuls of water are given.[23]

> *Wash with fragrantly perfumed water a twelve finger-width tooth-stick, grown from a milk-fruit tree such as udumvāra, that is without any living beings, straight and not split, with non-deteriorated and unscarred skin and bark. At its head hold a garland of flowers, and having made offerings with scents and so forth say:*
>
> Oṃ āḥ hūṃ hoḥ haṃ kṣha vajra-danta-kāṣhṭha-chatur-vimokṣha-mukha-vishuddha-svabhāvaṃ kāya-vāk-chitta-jñāna-mukha-dantādi-malaṃ vishodhaya svāhā. [May the seed syllables of the six lineages, oṃ āḥ hūṃ hoḥ haṃ kṣhaḥ and the vajra tooth-stick having the nature of the purity of the four doors of liberation purify the defilements of the teeth and so forth of the faces of exalted body, speech, mind, and pristine consciousness svāhā.]
>
> *Give it to the student who is facing east. Having uttered:*
>
> Oṃ āḥ hūṃ
>
> *seven times, [the student] casts [that is, drops the tooth-stick] onto the mandala – which has a cubit on each side, four corners, and is anointed with the five cow-products.[24] Through this, one knows that [the student] will achieve the manifold activities concordant with the direction of the head of the tooth-stick. Then, having uttered:*

> Oṃ hrīḥ suvishuddha-dharma-sarva-pāpaṃ-nichā-masya shodhaya sarva-vikalpanā-apanaya hūṃ. [Oṃ hrīḥ purify all ill deeds of this aggregation by way of the thorough purity of phenomena, remove all conceptuality hūṃ.]

> *pour three handfuls of fragrant water along with the five ambrosias* [*into the student's*] *hand.*

Next is to generate yourself as a deity – to imagine that you are a deity. The students, whether male or female, are to imagine themselves as Kālachakra, blue in color.

> *Then clear away* [*obstructors*] *by uttering the six syllables,* [*oṃ āḥ hūṃ hoḥ haṃ kṣhaḥ, and*] *with water from the Mahāvijaya conch.* [*The lama says:*]

> Instantaneously, [you students] as Kālachakra, blue in color and holding vajra and bell, dwell with right leg outstretched, embracing Vishvamātā, blue in color and holding curved knife and skull.

Instantaneously, become mindful of your own final reality – the emptiness of inherent existence of yourself – and then for your own perspective withdraw all ordinary appearance, cleansing it, so to speak, in emptiness. Think that from within this emptiness you are transformed into Kālachakra. Then, think that there is a black *hūṃ* on a rāhu disc at the heart, a red *āḥ* on a sun disc at the throat, and a white *oṃ* on a moon disc at the forehead. Think that rays of light from the three syllables turn your body into clear light.

> A black hūṃ is on a [green] rāhu disc at the heart, a red āḥ on a sun disc at the throat, and a white oṃ on a moon disc at the forehead. Rays of light from the three syllables turn your body into clear light. [319]

Then, the lama-deity asks about the student's lineage with "O, who are you?" Then, with "What do you want?" he enquires about the student's interest. The student answers the first question with, "A Fortunate One am I," meaning that the student does not have an intention to achieve liberation for himself or herself alone, but instead has an altruistic intention wishing to achieve help and happiness for all sentient beings. Such a Fortunate One is one whose predispositions for the Bodhisattva path have been activated, one whose Bodhisattva lineage has been manifested. Still, even if the Bodhisattva lineage has not been manifested in the sense of your having actually generated great compassion, you are in the process of activating that lineage of the Great Vehicle.

With the second answer, "Great bliss," you are indicating that within the Great Vehicle, your interest is in Secret Mantra. When I ask the questions and you answer, if you answer perfunctorily without any feeling, it will be no more than play; instead, you need to generate feeling in your mind and then answer from that feeling.

> [*The lama asks about the student's lineage and interest:*]
>
> O, who are you? What do you want?
>
> *To the lama's question the student answers:*
>
> A Fortunate One am I. Great bliss.
>
> *Through* [*the answer*] *the* [*student's Great Vehicle*] *lineage and interest* [*in Secret Mantra*] *are known.*

Now the students make a supplication in three stanzas, the first two being from Nāropa's commentary [on the *Brief Explication of Initiations*] and the third being from Kulika Puṇḍarīka's *Great Commentary*.

> *Then,* [*the student*] *makes supplication:*
>
> I go for refuge to the feet of you,
> Remover of the frights of cyclic existence,
> Unsullied by the faults of cyclic existence,
> Essence of all excellences.

In this context of Secret Mantra, how are the frights of cyclic existence removed? In the Low Vehicle, a Hearer who engages in practices devoid of desire removes the frights of cyclic existence through viewing the attributes of the Desire Realm one-pointedly as faulty and thereby turning away from them. In Mantra, however, that which removes the frights of cyclic existence is a practice using the attributes of the Desire Realm in the path. Thus, the very entity of the path removing the frights of cyclic existence involves using the attributes of the Desire Realm in the path but in a manner such that one is not sullied by the faults of cyclic existence. Due to assistance from special method and wisdom, even though one makes use of the attributes of the Desire Realm, the faults of those actions' impelling rebirth in cyclic existence are not incurred. Without such method and wisdom, partaking of the attributes of the Desire Realm serves as a cause inducing more suffering of birth, aging, sickness, and death.

> For me there is no other refuge
> From the inexhaustible frights of cyclic existence.
> Therefore, being very compassionate,
> Be kind to me today.

> Frightened by awful cyclic existence, from today I especially go for refuge to the Conquerors,
> With pure body, speech, and mind also to your lotus feet, definitely removing the frights of cyclic existence.

You especially go for refuge to the Buddhas and go for refuge to the lotus feet of the lama. Because the lama, being a composite of all of three refuges, has the capacity, through his or her blessings, of removing the frights of cyclic existence, you go for refuge with pure body, speech, and mind – bowing down with the body, praising through speech, and being respectfully faithful in mind.

> *Having made that supplication, take the two vows as before on the occasion of the student's preparation.*[25]

Next is to take the Bodhisattva vows. Imagining that all the Buddhas and Bodhisattvas are present as witnesses, contemplate: "I will attain unsurpassed perfect enlightenment for the sake of bringing help and happiness to all sentient beings – the objects of intent." Merely making wishes is not sufficient for attaining Buddhahood; also, the Buddhas cannot give it as a present. How is Buddhahood attained? Each individual must make effort at it. Therefore, the earlier Bodhisattvas, as techniques for attaining Buddhahood, initially generated an altruistic intention to become enlightened and then trained in the six perfections whereby they became fully enlightened. Therefore, you should think: "Just as the earlier Bodhisattvas generated an altruistic intention to become enlightened, so I also will generate such an intention. Just as they trained in the Bodhisattva deeds, so I will train in those deeds. Thereby I will attain Buddhahood. That is what I will do." A combination of this aspiration to Buddhahood for the sake of others and training in the Bodhisattva deeds is needed.

It is just as Shāntideva says in his *Engaging in the Bodhisattva Deeds (byang chub sems dpa'i spyod pa la 'jug pa, bodhicaryāvatāra):*[26]

Just as the earlier Ones Gone to Bliss
Generated an altruistic intention to become enlightened
And dwelt by stages in the learnings of Bodhisattvas,
So I also for the sake of helping transmigrators
Will generate an altruistic intention to become enlightened
And train in stages in the learnings of Bodhisattvas.

Create strong determination in your mind to generate an altruistic aspiration for supreme enlightenment – this mind of aspiration serving as the basis for the Bodhisattva deeds – and strong determination to take the Bodhisattva vows as well as to train in all the Bodhisattva deeds.

In the stanza that is recited, the first line, "I go for refuge to the Three Jewels," is the taking of refuge. The second line, "Individually disclose all ill-deeds," is a disclosure, within a sense of contrition, of the ill-deeds that you have done and accumulated since beginningless time. The third line, "Admire the virtues of beings," is a joyous admiration – from the depths of your heart, without any jealousy or competitiveness – of your own and others' roots of virtue that have been accumulated. The fourth line, "And mentally take up the enlightenment of a Buddha," is the statement that you – with refuge, disclosure of ill-deeds, and admiration of virtues as precursors – will, no matter what happens, attain Buddhahood for the sake of all sentient beings and for that purpose will take the Bodhisattva vows and will train properly in them. However, those who do not feel that they can take the Bodhisattva vows should not think that they are taking them; they should merely think to generate this good altruistic intention to become enlightened.

> *Identify well for the students and cause them to understand in detail the thought of how to assume the common and uncommon Great Vehicle vows in stages and the meaning of keeping the vows. Then, the students repeat* [*after the lama*] *three times:*
>
> I go for refuge to the Three Jewels,
> Individually disclose all ill-deeds,
> Admire the virtues of beings,
> And mentally take up the enlightenment of a Buddha.
>
> *Through that the* [*Bodhisattva*] *vows common* [*to the Sūtra Great Vehicle and the Mantra Great Vehicle*] *are taken.*

With the second repetition, generate an even stronger wish to generate an altruistic intention to become enlightened, to take the Bodhisattva vows, and to train in the Bodhisattva deeds. Then, at the end of the third repetition, when you finish saying, "And mentally take up the enlightenment of a Buddha," one-pointedly think that the pure Bodhisattva vows have been generated in your continuum.

As is said in Shāntideva's *Engaging in the Bodhisattva Deeds*[27] there is great benefit in even generating the aspirational form of the altruistic intention to become enlightened; hence, there is no need to say that taking the Bodhisattva vows and thereupon training in the deeds are of inconceivable benefit.

Next is a specific supplication for the Mantra vows.

> *Then, the student makes supplication for the sake of the uncommon* [*Mantra*] *vows by repeating three times:*
>
> Bestowing on me the excellent

Irreversible initiation of the [mandala] circle,
O Protector, please explain
The principles of the mandala, the deities,
The activities of a master,
The pledges of all Buddhas,
And the supremely secret vows.
In order to achieve the welfare of all sentient beings
I will forever act as a master.

The "circle" is the Kālachakra mandala. The "irreversible initiation" is the vajra master initiation so called because it establishes special potencies for irreversibility.

Mantra vows are taken only by those with the vajra master initiation; without it, Mantra vows are not given. You are requesting the vajra master, called "Protector", to explain about the mandala, the deities in it, the activities of a vajra master, the pledges of the five Buddha lineages, and the general Mantra vows. In brief, to achieve the welfare of all sentient beings, you wish to act as a vajra master, and in order to become a vajra master you are requesting the vajra master initiation, and for that you are asking that the Mantra vows be given.

Now, in the words of actually taking the Mantra vows, you state your own name for the sake of making your promises firm, of guaranteeing that you will not deviate from them. The vows are not limited by months, years, or even this lifetime; rather, you are declaring your intention to keep the precepts until Buddhahood, the essence of enlightenments.

What are the vows being taken? First, there is the altruistic intention to become enlightened. You are saying: "Just as the 'Protectors of the three times' – the Buddhas of the past, present, and future – definitely take this altruistic mind as the life of the path for attaining unsurpassed enlightenment, so I will generate this altruistic aspiration to highest enlightenment. Not just generating this attitude, I will firmly – that is to say, again and again – keep the three aspects of ethics – the ethical precepts, the composite of virtuous practices, and bringing about the welfare of sentient beings."

Then, the uncommon Mantra vows are taken by repeating three times:

O, all Buddhas and Bodhisattvas, please take heed of me.
I (your name) from this time henceforth
Until arriving in the essence of enlightenments
Will generate the excellent unsurpassed mind
Of intention to become enlightened
In just the way that the Protectors of the three times
Become definite toward enlightenment.
I will firmly keep individually
The three forms of ethics – the ethical precepts,
The composite of virtuous practices,
And bringing about the welfare of sentient beings.

Then, with respect to the pledges of the five Buddha lineages:[28]

For the five-pointed vajra [lineage of Akṣhobhya] I will maintain vajra, bell, seal, and lama with the crown of my head.

Literally, the text reads, "the desirous vajra" *('dod pa'i rdo rje)*; however, "desire" here is a term for "five", the connection being that there are *five* attributes of the Desire Realm – pleasant visible forms, sounds, odors, tastes, and tangible objects. The lineage of the five-pointed vajra is that of Akṣhobhya, and the pledges that correspond to this lineage are to keep (1) the vajra, which symbolizes the exalted wisdom of great bliss, (2) the bell, which symbolizes the wisdom realizing emptiness, and (3) the great seal, which here refers to a divine body – the appearance of the apprehension factor of such bliss and wisdom realizing emptiness as a deity. You are saying that you always will keep these, without forgetting them, and not only those, but also will maintain (4) proper reliance, with the crown of your head, on the lama who teaches the modes of those three.

For the jewel [lineage of Ratnasambhava] I will give gifts; for the wheel [lineage of Vairochana] I will keep the pledges of the supreme Conquerors.

The uncommon pledges to be kept by a practitioner of the jewel lineage, that of Ratnasambhava, are to train always in the ten aspects of giving – giving to others wealth such as precious substances, iron, copper, cattle, horses, elephants, and so forth as well as one's mate and children, one's own flesh, etc.

The wheel lineage is that of Vairochana. A practitioner of this lineage is especially to maintain the pledges of the supreme Conquerors, the five Ones Gone Thus – that is to say, to use the five fleshes and five ambrosias, which have the nature of the five male and female Ones Gone Thus, and to take care of the body and sense powers. Vairochana is the factor of purification of the form aggregate, and the five fleshes and five ambrosias are used as means of enhancing the body, which is the basis of bliss. Similarly, asceticism that makes the body deteriorate is to be avoided.

> For the sword [lineage of Amoghasiddhi] I will make offerings; for the bright lotus [lineage of Amitābha] I will maintain restraint.

For the sword lineage of Amoghasiddhi, the uncommon or emphasized pledges are to make offerings – external, internal, secret, and of suchness – to high objects such as gurus, Buddhas, Bodhisattvas, and so forth. The lotus lineage is that of Amitābha, practitioners of which especially should keep the pledge of restraining from, or abandoning, the bliss of emission, even though making use of a consort, and thereby maintain pure behavior.

> So that sentient beings may be liberated, I will, for the [Vajrasattva] lineage of the progenitor of Conquerors, generate enlightenment.

The lineage of the progenitor of Conquerors is that of Vajrasattva – also called Vajradhara – the lineage of the one-pointed vajra. A practitioner of this lineage puts particular emphasis on generating enlightenment. That is to say: Unsurpassed enlightenment is a state of the full perfection or development of the capacity of the most subtle wind and mind. As a means for accomplishing this, the most subtle mind that we naturally have is to be generated into the path as an undifferentiable entity of method and wisdom, of compassion and the wisdom realizing emptiness, the feat of the great seal. Since highest enlightenment is to be achieved in this way, one who has the lineage of Vajrasattva puts emphasis on generating the very subtle consciousness itself into an entity of path – undifferentiable method and wisdom – as a technique for attaining such enlightenment.

What is the purpose of keeping these pledges? It is for the sake of (1) liberating from the obstructions to omniscience those beings who, even though they are free from the obstructions to liberation from cyclic existence, are not free from the obstructions to omniscience, (2) liberating those who, nevermind the obstructions to omniscience, are not free from the obstructions to liberation, (3) relieving those who, nevermind removing either the obstructions to omniscience or the obstructions to liberation, are under the influence of afflictive emotions such that they are in a state of deprivation from happiness in bad transmigrations as hell-beings, hungry ghosts, or animals.

In brief, you should think, "I am taking these vows in order to set each and every sentient being in the non-abiding nirvana of Buddhahood. Taking the lama and the deities of the mandala as witnesses, I will train in the path of Highest Yoga Mantra in order to bring help and happiness to all sentient beings, and to do that I am taking the Mantra vows."

> I will liberate those not liberated [from the obstructions to omniscience].
> I will release those not released [from cyclic existence].
> I will relieve those unrelieved [in bad transmigrations]
> And set sentient beings in nirvana.

In brief, Mantra vows are kept in order to be able to set all sentient beings in the non-abiding nirvana of Buddhahood.

These vows and pledges are for those who intend to enter the mandala and receive initiation and who feel that they can keep the pledges and vows. With the third repetition, as before, think strongly and with enthusiasm that you are gaining the Mantra vows, and with the end of the last line, "And set sentient beings in nirvana," think that pure Mantra vows have been generated in your continuum.

Next is the giving of the twenty-five modes of conduct, which are to refrain from the five ill deeds, the five secondary ill deeds, the five murders, the five malices, and the five desires.[29]

> Harmfulness, untruth, and others' mates[30] are to be abandoned; likewise are others' wealth and the drinking of beer.
> These are the five ill deeds,[31] vajra nooses, destroyers of your virtue.
> These are given with the name of [Shākyamuni and so forth] gurus of gods and humans – having arisen at the time [of his teaching].
> You also should keep this word of [Shākyamuni and so forth] chief of [all] the various [beings], destroying the frights of cyclic existence.
>
> You should not play dice, eat unseemly food, read bad words, or perform rites of sacrifice for ancestors or extremist religious practices,
> Or the five killings – of cattle, children, women, men, or the gurus of gods and humans,[32]
> Nor be contentious with friends, leaders, the gurus of gods and humans,[33] the Spiritual Community, or those who trust you,
> Or allow the senses to be attached. Thus are the twenty-five modes of conduct of the lords of existence.

The five ill deeds are to harm others – ranging from small harms up to killing – as well as lying, stealing others' wealth, adultery, and drinking beer; if you cannot give up alcohol completely, then reduce your consumption. The five secondary ill deeds are betting; eating impure or improper flesh; reading about things such as war without any purpose or stories written for the sake of increasing desire, hatred, or wrong views; performing sacrifice of living beings for ancestors, or engaging in rites of animal sacrifice, and extremist religious practices. The five murders are to kill cattle, children, women, and men, and to destroy religious symbols of exalted body, speech, and mind. The five malices are to have malice for friends, leaders, gurus, the Spiritual Community, or those who trust and rely on you. The five desires are to be mentally captivated by pleasant visible forms, sounds, odors, tastes, and tangible objects, viewing them as singly advantageous without being aware of their disadvantages. Practitioners are to refrain from these twenty-five.

> *The student accepts them by saying three times:*
>
> I will forever keep
> These twenty-five modes of conduct,
> Destroying the frights of cyclic existence
> In accordance with the word of [Shākyamuni and
>   so forth] the chief of the various [beings]. [320]

Next is to generate the mind of the all-encompassing yoga; this means to generate the conventional and ultimate minds of enlightenment. This is the most important part. First, we should think about being kind and altruistic, other-oriented, as much as we can, through reasons and through whatever approach is effective. In brief, it is as Shāntideva says in his *Engaging in the Bodhisattva Deeds* about the opposite of altruism:[34]

If one does not switch
One's own happiness for others' suffering,
One will not achieve Buddhahood
And will not have happiness even in cyclic existence.

If we are not able to switch our self-centeredness, in which we think only about our own happiness and neglect others, for an attitude of emphasizing others' happiness, not only will we not be able finally to achieve Buddhahood, but also for the time being we will be uncomfortable and have to undergo many various sufferings even while remaining in cyclic existence.

Obviously, even in our present situation, through anger and hatred we cannot achieve real lasting world peace. Though many talk about good topics such as disarmament and arms control, how can these goals be achieved through hatred? It is impossible. They can be achieved only through a peaceful mind – through love, kindness, and mutual trust. Through hatred we cannot develop mutual trust, and without trust how can such beautiful goals be achieved? You can make a huge document with a huge pen, but nobody will respect it if something is wrong in your heart. So, all of these things can be achieved only through a good heart.

Thus, on the levels of the individual family, the nation, and the world, peace is achieved through good motivation, a warm heart, real human feeling. Even if a couple has promised to live together for the rest of this life, once anger and hatred develop and grow, the result is divorce. These unnecessary things come because of hatred, because of a lack of kindness, lack of love, lack of understanding, lack of mutual respect. This is very clear.

We must develop kindness with strong determination. Then, think that this attitude of kindness – which you have developed such that you are strongly and vividly moved to help all sentient beings – transforms into a moon disc at your heart. Without such feeling, it is nothing just to visualize a moon disc. Therefore, we must develop a determined feeling, which then can be transformed into a moon disc. This is the part of the all-encompassing yoga concerned with the conventional mind of enlightenment.

The other part is concerned with realization of emptiness. How do all occurring objects of knowledge appear to us? When they appear to us, they do not appear to be posited through the power of conceptuality; rather, they appear to exist objectively. That is definite. If they exist the way they appear, then when the objects designated are sought, they should become clearer and clearer. However, the fact is that when the objects designated are sought, they become unclear – they are not found.

However, this does not show that phenomena are non-existent, for they obviously bring help and harm. Since this is the case, they definitely exist, but since when the objects designated are sought, they are not found to exist objectively in their own right, it is ineluctably established that they exist not from their own side but instead through the power of other conditions. Since they exist through the power of other conditions, they are dependently established. Since they are dependently established, they are devoid of independence, of being under their own power – they are empty of independence, of being under their own power.

Think this way about all phenomena; come to a decision that there is no way that any phenomenon could be established from its own side, that all phenomena are not established from their own side. This mind then transforms into a vajra standing on the moon at your heart.

Thus, first meditatively cultivate an altruistic intention to become enlightened; then, transform that mind into a moon disc.

> *Saying the following,* [*cause the students to*] *generate a mind of intention toward the all-encompassing yoga:*

> The conventional aspirational intention to become enlightened, thinking, "I will attain Buddhahood for the sake of all sentient beings," transforms into the aspect of a full moon disc at the heart.

Then seek the understanding that all phenomena do not inherently exist. Think that this mind has transformed into a vajra.

> The ultimate mind of enlightenment, in which the emptiness of inherent existence of all phenomena and your own mind are of one taste, transforms into the aspect of a five-pointed vajra on the moon.

These two minds are the causes of a Buddha's Form Body and Truth Body, respectively. Thinking that you will maintain these minds without ever losing them, repeat:

> Oṃ sarva-yoga-chittaṃ utpadayāmi. [I am causing the mind of all-encompassing yoga to be generated.]

Imagine such a moon and vajra at the heart also of Kālachakra, from which a duplicate separates and dissolves into the same at your heart, thereby making it firm.

> *The lama holds a vajra with a flower at [the student's] heart. With:*
>
> Oṃ surata-samayas tvaṃ hoḥ siddhya-vajra-yathā-sukhaṃ. [May you having the pledge of thorough joy achieve the vajra (of Buddhahood) as wanted.]
>
> *make it firm.*

Think that those minds [attitudes] have become firm. You need continually to be mindful of these two again and again. These are the roots. All the techniques of Mantra – initiations and so forth brought together from so many points of view – are for the sake of enhancing and improving these two minds, altruism and wisdom.

The view realizing emptiness, which presently is a coarse form of the mental consciousness, must eventually be transformed into the subtler consciousness mentioned earlier.

Next is an exhortation to secrecy, not to speak of Mantra practices widely but to keep them secret.

> Today you will be blessed into magnificence by all the Ones Gone Thus. You should not speak about this supremely secret mandala of all the Ones Gone Thus to those who have not entered a mandala, nor to those without faith.

After this, you enter the mandala.

3 *Seeing the Mandala*

The presentation of entering inside the mandala has three parts: (1) entering inside and paying obeisance while circling it, (2) setting [the student] in a pledge [of secrecy], and (3) expressing the truth upon the descent of the wisdom being.

ENTERING INSIDE AND PAYING OBEISANCE WHILE CIRCLING THE MANDALA

Then, you actually take hold of the vajra in the hand of the lama and meditatively imagine that the Wrathful One at the eastern door, says:

Oṃ vighnāntakṛt hūṃ.

while leading you inside. Think that you arrive inside the mandala, [while the lama] says:

Āḥ khaṃ[35]-vīra hūṃ,

and you actually enter inside the curtain.

While I say the mantras, *oṃ vighnāntakṛt hūṃ* **and** *āḥ khaṃ-vīra hūṃ,* imagine that all three levels of doors open and that you enter the eastern door into the level of the exalted body mandala.

After that, while you repeat the following mantra, imagine that you circumambulate the mandala three times to the right [i.e., clockwise] inside the wall of the exalted body mandala but outside the white area where the deities of that level sit.

> *Then, saying:*
>
> Oṃ mahārata, sudriḍḍha sutoṣhyo, susuṣho, vajrasatva ādya-siddhya māṃ. [May great joy, thorough firmness, thorough happiness, thorough bliss, Vajrasattva, be established in me today.]
>
> *you either circumambulate the mandala three times or meditate such.*

After circumambulating three times, you go out through the eastern door and, by the pillar of the eastern door, pay obeisance mainly to Akṣhobhya. You have been visualizing yourself as Kālachakra; now change into a blue Akṣhobhya.

> You instantaneously turn into Akṣhobhya.

Imagining that you are bowing down, repeat this mantra:

> Oṃ sarva-tathāgata-pūja-upasthānāya ātmānaṃ niryātayāmi, sarva-tathāgata-vajrasatva adhitiṣhṭhasva mām hūṃ. "Since I offer myself for the worship and service of all Ones Gone Thus, may Vajrasattva, the entity of all the Ones Gone Thus, please bless me into magnificence." [321]

Think that you have been blessed in accordance with your supplication.

> Through making supplication thus at the eastern door, you are blessed into magnificence such that you have the capacity of worshipping and serving all Ones Gone Thus.

You have been imagining yourself as Akṣhobhya; now turn into a black Amoghasiddhi.

> You turn into Amoghasiddhi.

Imagining that you are bowing down mainly to the Amoghasiddhi lineage, repeat the mantra:

> Oṃ sarva-tathāgata-pūja-karmaṇe ātmānaṃ niryātayāmi, sarva-tathāgata vajra-karma kuru mām. "Since I offer myself for the activity of worshipping all the Ones Gone Thus, may all the Ones Gone Thus please grant me the vajra activities."

Think that you have been blessed in accordance with your supplication.

> Through making supplication thus at the eastern door, you are blessed into magnificence such that you have the capacity of worshipping all the Ones Gone Thus as well as of sublime activities.

Now, enter the mandala through the eastern door; walk to and go back out through the southern door. Imagine that you have turned into a yellow Ratnasambhava. As before, bow down, repeat the mantra and its translation, and think that you have been blessed.

> You turn into Ratnasambhava.
>
> Oṃ sarva-tathāgata-pūja-abhiṣhekāya ātmānaṃ niryātayāmi, sarva-tathāgata vajra-ratna-abhiṣhiṃcha mām. "Since I offer myself for the worship of all Ones Gone Thus and for conferral of initiation, may all the Ones Gone Thus please confer on me the vajra jewel initiation."
>
> Through making supplication thus at the southern door, you are blessed into magnificence such that you have the capacity of worshipping all the Ones Gone Thus and conferring initiation.

Enter the mandala through the southern door; walk to and go out through the northern door. Imagine that you turn into a white Amitābha. As before, bow down, repeat the mantra and its translation, and think that you have been blessed.

> You turn into Amitābha.
>
> Oṃ sarva-tathāgata-pūja-pravaratanāya ātmā-

> naṃ niryātayāmi, sarva-tathāgata vajra-dharma-pravarataya māṃ. "Since I offer myself to all the Ones Gone Thus for the thorough turning [of the wheel of doctrine], may all the Ones Gone Thus please thoroughly turn [the wheel of] vajra doctrine for me."
>
> Through making supplication thus at the northern door, you are blessed into magnificence such that you have the capacity of worshipping all the Ones Gone Thus and turning the wheel of doctrine. [322]

Then, enter the mandala through the northern door, and circumambulating to the right, go outside through the western door. Imagine that you turn into a yellow Vairochana. As before, bow down, repeat the mantra and its translation, and think that you have been blessed.

> You turn into Vairochana.
>
> Oṃ sarva-buddha-pūja-upasthānāya ātmānaṃ niryātayāmi, sarva-tathāgata-vajra-vairochana adhitiṣhṭha māṃ. "Since I offer myself to all the Ones Gone Thus for worship and service, may Vairochana, the entity of all the Ones Gone Thus, bless me into magnificence."
>
> Through making supplication in that way at the western door, you are blessed into magnificence such that you have the capacity of worshipping and serving all the Ones Gone Thus.
>
> *At these times, if initiation is being conferred on a student, at the four doors respectively you [the student] actually should in the east (1) stretch out the vajra palms and perform obeisance such that all the body descends to the ground and (2) joining the vajra palms at the heart, perform obeisance with the top of the head touching the earth; in the south (3) placing the vajra palms at the heart perform obeisance such that the forehead touches the earth; in the north (4) putting the vajra palms together at the forehead perform obeisance*

such that your mouth touches the earth; and in the west (5) stretch out the vajra palms and perform obeisance such that all the body descends to the ground.

Then enter inside the western door, and circumambulating to the right, go out through the eastern door. There, bow down mainly to the lama.

Then, at the eastern door, pay obeisance to the feet of the lama.

Repeat:

> Oṃ guru-charaṇa-pūja-upasthānāya ātmānaṃ niryātayāmi, sarvasatva-paritrāṇāya ātmānaṃ niryātayāmi. [I offer myself for worship and service at the feet of the guru, I offer myself for the help of all beings.]

SETTING [THE STUDENT] IN THE PLEDGES

The student is set in a pledge of secrecy by way of indicating the benefits of maintaining secrecy, the dangers of not doing so, and both the benefits and the dangers. First is by way of the benefits.

> Today you will enter into the lineages of all the Ones Gone Thus. Therefore, I will generate in you the exalted vajra wisdom. Through this exalted wisdom you will attain the feats of all Ones Gone Thus. Thus, what need is there to mention that you will attain other feats! You should not speak about this in front of those who have not seen a mandala; your pledges will deteriorate.

Then, the student is set in a pledge of secrecy by way of speaking of the physical dangers.

Again, setting the vajra on the [*student's*] *head,* [*the lama*] *says:*

> This is your pledge vajra. If you speak about this mode to anyone who is unfit, it will split your head.

Finally, the student is set in a pledge of secrecy by way of speaking of the mental dangers.

> *Placing the vajra at the [student's] heart, [the lama says]:*
>
> Oṃ, today Vajrasattva himself
> Has thoroughly entered into your heart. [323]
> If you speak about this mode,
> Immediately thereafter he will separate and leave.

Here "Vajrasattva" refers to the exalted wisdom of undifferentiable bliss and emptiness.

> *Respectively, with these three [the student] is set in the pledges by way of the benefits, dangers, and both. In particular, [the student] is set in the pledge [to keep from] the root infraction of proclaiming the secret to immature humans.*

This sets you in a pledge particularly not to speak [of the initiation and so forth] to those whose continuums have not matured [through practice of the path, initiation, etc.] Thus, it is particularly related with the seventh infraction of the Mantra vows – to proclaim the secret to the unripened – and is a pledge to keep from that infraction.

Then, the student is set in a pledge to keep from root infractions in general, by way of speaking of both the benefits and dangers.

> *Then, taking up water from the Mahāvijaya religious conch with the thumb and nameless finger, give the water into the student's mouth and say:*
>
> If you transgress the pledges
> This water of hell will burn.
> If the pledges are kept, it will bestow feats.
> Drink the water of vajra-ambrosia.
> Oṃ vajra-udakaṭhaḥ. [Oṃ drink the vajra water.]
>
> *Pour the oath-water, and set [the student] in the pledges by way of the benefits of keeping them, dangers*

of not keeping them, and both. Thereby [the student] is set in the general pledges, root and secondary.

Next the student is set in a pledge to obey the word of the lama. This is related particularly with keeping from the first root infraction of the Mantra vows – to deride the lama.

> *Then, the lama grasps the right hand of the student and sets [the student] particularly in the pledge [to keep from] the first infraction:*
>
> From henceforth, I am your Vajrapāṇi. You must do what I tell you to do. You should not deride me, and if you do, without forsaking fright, the time of death will come, and you will fall into a hell.

Nevertheless, Ashvaghoṣha's *Fifty Stanzas on Guru Devotion (bla ma lnga cu pa, gurupañchāsika),* which speaks on how to acquaint with and rely on a guru – lama – from the viewpoint of Highest Yoga Tantra, says that if from among what the lama says there is something that does not accord with reason or something that you cannot do, you should explain the reasons and not do it.[36] Therefore, it is necessary to discriminate between the general procedure and exceptions to it.[37]

EXPRESSING THE TRUTH UPON THE DESCENT OF THE WISDOM-BEING

The wisdom-being [actual deity] descends, and then there is an expression of the power of the truth [i.e., an oath based on true fact]. First, the student makes a supplication for the sake of the descent of the wisdom-beings:

> [*The student*] *makes a supplication:*
>
> May all the Ones Gone Thus bless me into magnificence.
> May the glorious Kālachakra please descend into me.

Since this is for the sake of blessings into magnificence, it is important to know how blessings are received. First, you generate, or imagine, your body as a divine body, which in this case is that of the fierce deity, Vajravega. Then, in addition to this, you set the seed syllables of the four elements – earth, water, fire, and wind – in your body in a state of fluctuation; this affects your thought such that the exalted wisdom of bliss and emptiness is generated in your continuum. This is what you are to imagine.

First, everything is purified into emptiness. In the last deity generation while paying obeisance at the four doors, you became Vairochana; this dissolves into emptiness, and then from within emptiness a *hūṃ* appears; it turns into a vajra, which then transforms into Vajravega.

> [*The lama*] *clears away* [*obstructors*] *with water from the Mahāvijaya conch and the six syllables* [*oṃ āḥ, hūṃ hoḥ haṃ kṣhaḥ*].

> Oṃ shūnyatā-jñāna-vajra-svabhāvātmako' haṃ. [I have an essential nature of indivisible emptiness and wisdom.]
>
> From within emptiness from hūṃ and [then] a vajra, you are generated as Vajravega,[38] with a blue body, having three necks – black in the center, red to the right, and white to the left – and having four faces – blue in the center, red to the right, white to the left, and yellow to the back. Also, each of the faces has exposed fangs and is frightful. All of the faces have three orange eyes. The orange hair on the head is standing on end. The first set of shoulders is black, the second red, the third white; thus there are six shoulders, with twelve upper arms, and twenty-four lower arms. The first four lower arms [on each side] are black, the second red, the third white, and of the remaining two lower arms the right is black and the left is yellow. [On the outside] the thumbs of the hands are yellow, the index fingers white, the middle fingers red, nameless fingers black, and the little fingers green. [The inside of] the first joints of the fingers are black, the second red, and the third white. They are adorned

> with rings and emit light. The red right leg and white left leg, in a posture with the right one outstretched, press down on the hearts of a demonic god of the Desire Realm and an afflicted Īshvara. You have the snake and bone adornments and the lower robe of a tiger skin as well as a garland of heads and skulls hanging down and the full complement of nāga adornments and hand symbols.
>
> *When conferring initiation on students, identify these individually.*

What is the purpose of meditating on such a deity with all these fantastic features? In general, the Form Body of a Buddha, as is said in Shāntideva's *Engaging in the Bodhisattva Deeds,* appears variously to trainees – through the force of having collected the two accumulations of merit and wisdom – naturally, spontaneously and without striving, in accordance with the dispositions and interests of trainees. It is not that a Buddha has a particular form whether there are trainees or not.

The Form Bodies of a Buddha depend upon the situations and needs of trainees. Some even say that Form Bodies are included in the continuums of trainees; whether this position is literally acceptable or not, it prompts understanding of the nature of Form Bodies. The purpose of the appearance of a Form Body is as an object of observation of meditation by a womb-born being with the six constituents of earth, water, fire, wind, space, and consciousness; thus, the appearance of a particular Form Body is related with a meditator and accords with the situation of that practitioner.

Now, in the case of Kālachakra, the mode of practice of the *Kālachakra Tantra* is related with meditation of the cosmic factors of the external Kālachakra mentioned earlier. Therefore, the particular form of divine body upon which a practitioner meditates is related with such meditation. The number of faces, the number of arms, and so forth – their color and shape – from one point of view are related with the body of the meditator and from another point of view are related with the sun, moon, constellations, and so forth.

Then, with respect to visualizing the four elements:

> At your navel[39] is a laṃ, from which comes a yellow square earth mandala, marked by a wheel and on which, on a [yellow] kālāgni disc, is a yellow ho. [324] At your heart is a yaṃ, from which comes a black bow-shaped mandala of wind, marked by two waving banners and on which, on a [green] rāhu disc, is a black huṃ. At your neck is a raṃ, from which comes a red triangular mandala of earth marked by a jewel and on which, on a sun, is a red āḥ. At your forehead is a baṃ from which comes a round white mandala of water marked by a vase and on which, on a moon disc, is a white oṃ. The rays of light of the four syllables and the light rays of the hūṃ at the heart of the lama, who is not separate from the principal deity, invite the four Vajra Deities [i.e., body, speech, mind, and bliss consciousness], which dissolve into the four syllables. From a yaṃ under the feet comes a wind mandala that ignites a raṃ from which comes a red triangular mandala of fire marked by a raṃ and on which, on the two soles of the feet, red jhai come to emit light rays.

At this point, from outside yourself light rays from the heart of the lama enter inside your body and activate the four elements inside your body. Through these two conditions, an exalted wisdom of great bliss – a meditative stabilization of bliss and emptiness – is generated in your continuum. In this way, think that a special exalted wisdom of undifferentiable bliss and emptiness in which a blissful consciousness ascertains the emptiness of inherent existence is generated in your continuum. In addition, all the Buddhas of the ten directions are drawn in and enter into your body, with all the blessings of the deities of exalted body, speech, mind, and bliss. This is the blessing.

> Through being hit by light rays from the heart of the lama, who is not different from the principal

deity, the wind is stirred up, whereby the fire is ignited, due to which the light rays from the jhai enter holes in the feet – the light rays agitate the four syllables from which light rays are emitted, filling the entire body. Light rays from the huṃ at the heart of the lama, who is not different from the principal deity, invite in all the Buddhas in the form of the Supramundane Victor Kālachakra and the King of Wrathful Ones. All of these, filling the realm of space, enter into your body.

Oṃ āḥ ra ra ra ra, la la la la, vajra-aveshaya hūṃ.[Oṃ āḥ ra ra ra ra, la la la la, may the vajras thoroughly descend hūṃ.]

Saying that with strong intonation, ring the bell. Fumigate with incense of the five fleshes and the five ambrosias and with saffron. If the master has previously done ten million repetitions of this [mantra] and performed burnt offering a tenth as many times, through merely turning the mind [to this, the deities] will descend. Then give a flower that has been mantrified with:

Oṃ āḥ hūṃ

[to be put] on the head. Even uncalm forms of descent are pacified by this. The signs of coming should be known in detail from the commentary on the tantra.[40]

[The descent] is made firm and guarded with the six lineages of method and wisdom.[41]

Then, with [the seed syllables of] the six lineages of method and wisdom make protection:

At the [student's] forehead, a [white] oṃ; at the heart a [black] hūṃ; at the crown protrusion a [yellow] haṃ; at the navel a [yellow] hoḥ; at the throat a [red] āḥ; at the secret region a [blue] kṣhaḥ.

Next, the students are directed to remove the blindfold and look at intermediate space to see what color is appearing. The lama asks what you are seeing.

Then, if initiation is being conferred on students, have them [pull up the blindfold and] look at space above the mandala. Ask:

What appeared in your path of sight?

Through differences of the color of the sky [that appears to the individual students], the specific activities that [they should work at] achieving can be understood.

Sometimes certain colors are seen; other times, no particular color. This is for the sake of determining the type of feat at which you should work. Put the blindfold back on.

Next, as before, imagine that you are circumambulating the mandala three times as you repeat the mantra *oṃ āḥ.hūṃ hoḥ haṃ kṣhaḥ*.

Then, the Vajra Worker grasps the two thumbs of the students with his right hand that also [holds] a vajra; they do the vajra dance, and repeating the six syllables [oṃ āḥ hūṃ hoḥ haṃ kṣhaḥ], they circumambulate the mandala three times.

Then, at the eastern door I make a supplication to the mandala so that when the students drop a flower onto a mandala [here a square board marked in sections], what their lineages are and what feats they will achieve will unmistakenly manifest.

At the eastern door of the mandala the master rings a bell and makes a blessing of truth:

May the level of divine lineage
Of these students whom I enter
Into this excellent mandala
Be shown in accordance with their merit.

May their feats be shown.
May the lineage of which they are vessels be shown.
May the measure of the power of their merit
Be shown as it is in the mandala.

ENTERING SUCH THAT ONE COMES TO HAVE THE NATURE OF SEEING THE MANDALA

Everyone has the Buddha nature and thus is basically fit to become enlightened as a Buddha; however, it is not clear which your lineage is from among the five lineages of Ones Gone Thus. That lineage is identified in dependence on casting a flower onto a mandala.

From the garland of flowers that you were given earlier, take one flower, and imagine that you have arrived inside the mandala. [The students or their representative drop the flower onto this small mandala to see in which section it falls.]

> *From among the garland of flowers given earlier, remove one flower, light and not old, and having mantrified it with trāṃ, imagine it as a jewel flower and give it into the student's cupped palms. Imagining that it hits the head of the central deity of the mandala, have the student actually cast it on five signs on the top of the Vijaya vase. Utter:*

> Oṃ sarva-tathāgata-kula-vishodhani svāhā. [Oṃ the purification of the lineages of all Ones Gone Thus svāhā.]

> *For self-entry [into the mandala] imagining that it is cast while saying the mantra is sufficient; it is not necessary actually to cast it on the signs. Through the flower's hitting a particular sign, the divine lineage of the student is identified.*

Imagine that, when you drop it onto the mandala, you are offering the flower to the deities of the mandala, who bless it into magnificence and then give it back to you. Then, put it on your head; merely through this, the exalted wisdom of bliss and emptiness is generated in your continuum.

> *Then, have the students tie*[42] *that flower into the earlier garland of flowers, and then tie it on their heads, or tie it on your own [if doing self-entry]. Say:*

> Oṃ pratigṛhnas tvaṃ imaṃ satva-mahābala.

[Great Powerful Being, take care of this (student).] [326]

Calling the deity hit by the flower, urge the student on the deity:

Powerful Heroic Being, take care of this student until enlightenment is attained.

When you have identified the lineage of the Conqueror as whom you will be enlightened, you are to take the deity of that lineage as your main deity and are to emphasize keeping mainly the pledges of that particular lineage. The determination of lineage depends upon the relative strength of the afflictive emotions in your mind as well as on many factors structured by your level of merit, which result in differences in sense faculties, disposition, and so forth.

Then, after tying the flowers on the head or simultaneous with casting the flower, [*the lama*] *says:*

Today, Kālachakra is making effort
To open your eyes.
Through being opened, all will be seen.
The vajra eye is unsurpassed.
Oṃ divyendriyānudghataya svāhā. [Oṃ opeṇ the divine sense power svāhā.]

Open the blindfold.

Now, take off the blindfold; think that the darkness of ignorance has been removed.

Having taken off the blindfold, think that you are looking at the mandala.

[*The lama*] *says:*

Now through the power of faith
Look at just this mandala and that [symbolized by it].[43]
You have been born into the Buddha lineage
And blessed into magnificence by seal and mantra.

The fulfilment of all feats

Will accrue to you as the supreme [holder of the] pledges.
Through play at the tips of vajra and lotus
You will achieve the secret mantras.
He vajra-pashya. [O, look at the vajra (mandala).]

"Play at the tips of vajra and lotus" indicates that the Mantra path must be achieved by undifferentiable method and wisdom.

Then, [say]:

You are manifestly seeing the entire mandala.

Thinking that, generate strong faith. When conferring initiation on a student, identify the deities individually in accordance with the Means of Achievement (sgrub thabs, sādhana).

Now, while you look at a drawing of the mandala, I will introduce you to it. As I do this, think that you are seeing the respective parts of the actual mandala. First, on the very outside there is a series of colored lights [representing a mountain of fire surrounding the mandala]. Inside that, is a green section symbolizing space, most likely not uncompounded space but compounded space as found in holes. The vajras in it constitute a protective circle [surrounding the mandala]. Inside that are four layers – gray, red, white, and yellow, with swastikas in the last – representing wind, fire, water, and earth. Thus, the layers from the green to the yellow represent the five elements – space, wind, fire, water, and earth.

Then, inside those, look at the different colors of the underlying ground in the four directions. Since the east [which is the bottom as we look at the painting but is the front from the viewpoint of the deity sitting in the middle] is Amoghasiddhi, it is black. The south, being Ratnasambhava, is red; the north, being Amitābha, is white; and the west, being Vairochana, is yellow. The colors of the four directions are mainly imitating the colors of the four faces of Kālachakra in the middle.

On this ground is the square, fully adorned mandala of three levels with four doors each – the outermost being the exalted body mandala, then the exalted speech mandala, and the innermost being the exalted mind mandala. In the very middle is a green eight petalled lotus, at the center of which is the glorious Kālachakra and his consort, Vishvamāta. Kālachakra has four faces, twenty-four hands, two legs. I will not go into greater detail about Kālachakra now.

You should think that you have encountered and seen the entire mandala just as it appears in the painting – having a nature of light. Think that you are meeting manifestly with Kālachakra and consort.

On the eight petals surrounding Kālachakra and consort are the eight Shaktis. The place where the principal deity, consort, and the eight Shaktis reside is the mandala of great bliss. Just outside it there is a square area with sixteen sections; this is the mandala of pristine consciousness. In the four directions are the four male Ones Gone Thus, and in the intermediary directions are the four female Ones Gone Thus [depicted by lotuses]. The four male Ones Gone Thus embrace four female Ones Gone, and the four female Ones Gone Thus embrace four male Ones Gone Thus.

Now, let us identify all of the segments in one direction, the east. Just outside the mandala of exalted wisdom is a black area which is the floor of the exalted mind mandala. Then, the white area is where the six male and six female Bodhisattvas of the exalted mind mandala reside; it is the equivalent of a seat for these deities. Then, outside that is a very small black strip of the floor of the exalted mind mandala.

Inside each of the four doors are the four fierce deities [depicted by lotuses] that protect the doors. The fierce deity that protects the upper direction is indicated by a second lotus in the east. Then, just outside the black strip of floor is the three layered wall of the exalted mind mandala – white, yellow, and blue. Then, outside the wall is a white area that is the white apron where the goddesses of offering reside. There are also twelve protectors, two in each of the four directions and two above and below. That completes the exalted mind mandala. Think that you are meeting and seeing all seventy deities of the exalted mind mandala.

Then, you come down the stairs to the next level, to the floor of the exalted speech mandala [depicted by a black strip]. Just as in the exalted mind mandala, there is a white area where deities of the exalted speech mandala reside. On it are eight yoginis of exalted speech – one in each of the four directions and the four intermediate directions [depicted by lotuses]. They are embraced by male deities and surrounded by eight goddesses each. Thus, there are eighty deities.

Then, as before, there is a gray or black strip that is the floor of the exalted speech mandala, and next is the five layered wall of the exalted speech mandala. Outside the wall, on the white apron surrounding the speech mandala, are thirty-six goddesses; from the viewpoint of the corresponding face of the principal deity there are five to the right of the door and four to the left of the door. Thus, to this point there have been one hundred eighty-six deities; think that you are meeting and seeing all of them.

Next, coming down the stairs from the exalted speech mandala, you arive at the exalted body mandala. Again, there is the black floor, next to which is the white area where deities of the exalted body mandala reside. In each of the four directions there are two principal great deities of the days, and in each of the four intermediate directions there is one – making twelve [representing the twelve months]. Each of them is embracing a consort and is surrounded by twenty-eight deities [totalling thirty in each group and thus representing the days of the month]. These are the three hundred sixty deities of the days of a year.

Then, in each of the four doors of the exalted body mandala are protectors of the four doors, and there are also protectors above and below, depicted respectively at the top and bottom of the picture on a circle of water. Then, outside of the five layered wall of the exalted body mandala on the white apron, there are thirty-six goddesses, equivalent to those of the exalted speech mandala, five to the right and four to the left from the viewpoint of the corresponding face of the principal deity.

Next are the deities to the right and left of the doorways on the white outer apron: on the eastern side there are bow shaped spheres of wind; on the southern side, triangular shaped spheres of fire; on the northern side, round shaped spheres of water; and on the western side, square shaped earth mandalas. On each of these are eight nāgas, embraced by very fierce female deities. In total, there are ten nāgas – eight having lotus seats.

To the right of the eastern door is a mandala of space, and exactly opposite on the western side is a mandala of exalted wisdom; these two are above and below the mandala respectively. That finishes the exalted body mandala.

Then, on the circles of fire and wind are ten wheels in ten cemeteries – four in the primary directions, four in the intermediate directions, and above and below. On the eight spokes of those wheels are eight very fierce female deities – making ten sets of eight very fierce female deities embraced by nāgas. Then, between each of the eight cemeteries there are eleven principal spirits or elementals, totalling eighty-eight. These are the main among the millions of elementals.

Counting the eighty-eight elementals, the entire mandala has seven hundred twenty-two deities. Think that you actually have seen all of them.

The count of the main deities in the mandala is explained by a correspondence with the number of channel petals that a person has. The channel center at the crown protrusion has four channel petals; the channel center at the throat has thirty-two channel petals; the channel center at the heart has eight channel petals; the channel center at the crown of the head has sixteen channel petals; the channel center at the navel has sixty-four channel petals; the channel center at the secret region has sixty-four channel petals. In addition, there are the six channels of the six lineages as well as the right, left, and central channels above the navel – *lalanā, rasanā* and *avadhūtī* – and the same below the navel, the latter being the channels for urine, feces, and seminal fluid. Altogether, these amount to one hundred sixty-two.

Among the deities mentioned above, seventy-eight who are in union with consorts have lotus seats; counting the consorts separately, there are one hundred fifty-six. When the six deities that perform the seal-implanting are added, there are one hundred sixty-two. Thus, the one hundred sixty-two main deities in the Kālachakra mandala complement the one hundred sixty-two main channels in the body.

Think that you have actually met the full total of seven hundred twenty-two deities of the Kālachakra mandala having such significance in terms of external and internal factors.

Next is to raise up song in joy at manifestly seeing the deities.

> *Then, [the student] utters the pledge:*

> Oṃ I have entered the vajra mandala, the
> great mandala.

The "vajra mandala" is mentioned because in Highest Yoga Tantra, the Akṣhobhya lineage or vajra lineage is supreme among all of the lineages, whereby the vajra mandala is the great mandala.

> I am seeing the yogic mandala, the great mandala.

The harmony of method and wisdom is said to be the meaning of "yoga"; here, method is immutable bliss, and wisdom is realization of the emptiness of inherent existence. The exalted wisdom of undifferentiable bliss and emptiness appears in the aspect of a mandala, and thus this is a yogic mandala. Since it is superior to material mandalas, it is great. You are seeing that.

> I am being conferred initiation in the secret
> mandala, the great mandala.

It is secret because it is hidden from those initiated only into Yoga Tantra and so forth. Thus, this Kālachakra mandala of Highest Yoga Tantra is superior to mandalas of the lower tantras and hence is great. Since you are receiving initiation in such a mandala, you raise up happy song:

> Samaya hoḥ hoḥ hoḥ hoḥ.

That finishes the topics involved in entering the mandala.

(End of the second day in Madison.)

Part Three
Initiations

CONFERRING THE SEVEN INITIATIONS IN THE PATTERN OF CHILDHOOD

This section has three parts: (1) the rites of the seven initiations, (2) understanding the time of attainment, and (3) advice to abandon root infractions.

THE RITES OF THE SEVEN INITIATIONS

This section has two parts: (1) making a supplication in common [for the seven initiations] along with purifying inauspiciousness and (2) bestowing the seven initiations individually.

Orientation

Today you are to enter the mandala, and initiation is to be conferred. In general, there are conferral of the seven initiations in the pattern of childhood, conferral of the higher initiations, and conferral of the vajra master initiation. Among these, those to be conferred here are the seven initiations in the pattern of childhood.

First, the students offer mandala, after which they make a supplication for all seven initiations. Then, the lama clears away any inauspiciousness and confers the seven initiations individually. In offering mandala, imagine that, as before, you are outside the eastern door of the exalted body mandala. Since today is the time of actually receiving initiation, you should be careful to perform the necessary imaginations for each part as I identify them.

To the lama, personal deity, and Three Jewels I offer in visualization
The body, speech, mind, and resources of myself and others,
Our collections of virtue in the past, present, and future,
And the wonderful precious mandala with the masses of Samantabhadra's offerings.
Accepting them through your compassion, please bless me into magnificence.
Idaṃ guru-ratna-maṇḍalakaṃ niryātayāmi. [I offer this jewelled mandala to the guru.]

MAKING A SUPPLICATION FOR ALL [SEVEN INITIATIONS] AND PURIFYING INAUSPICIOUSNESS

Having offered mandala, set the right knee on the ground, [327] *place your cupped palms together at your heart, holding a flower in them, and make supplication three times:*

Just as Bodhivajra bestowed
The great offering [of initiation] on the Buddhas,
Today bestow such on me, O Space Vajra,
So that I may be thoroughly released.

Kālachakra is called "Space Vajra" because Kālachakra is an appearance – in the aspect of a body with a face, arms, and so forth – of the space-like exalted wisdom of clear light, which is of an undifferentiable entity with the space-like reality of the emptiness of inherent existence. Thus Kālachakra is a final Form Body that has the capacity of serving as a means of purifying trainees' suffering as well as its causes. You are asking such a Kālachakra to bestow the seven initiations on you today. The supplication is to be repeated three times within reflecting on such meaning.

[PURIFYING INAUSPICIOUSNESS]

When we wash, we need materials for washing; similarly, here various substances are used in connection with cleansing and purifying obstructors, ill-deeds, and obstructions. As I make the gesture of circling these materials in front of me while reciting the mantra, think that these inauspicious factors are being taken away.

When doing self-entry, [*the following*] *is meditated or actually done by an Action Vajra; when conferring initiation on a student, the lama does it. Grasp with the fists of both hands mustard seed into which the six syllables* [*oṃ āḥ hūṃ hoḥ haṃ kṣhaḥ*] *have been repeated seven times and circle it twice to the left, saying:*

Oṃ sarva-pāpaṃ dahana-vajrāya vajrasatvasya, sarva-pāpaṃ daha svāhā. [Oṃ burn away all ill deeds for the sake of Vajrasattva's vajra burning all ill deeds svāhā.]

Cast the mustard seed forcefully into fire. Likewise, also circle it twice to the right. Then, take up water with the fists, and do likewise. Then, do such four times with white camphor, then four times with extrusions of cow manure together with shoots of sward grass, four times with extrusions of pap, and four times with pieces of white cloth,[44] *circling as before to the left and right. However, the camphor and below are not cast into the fire.*

That is followed by an ablution, a washing of the ears, nose, mouth, and body, this being done through my making a gesture of touching these places with a special fluid thereby symbolizing such cleansing.

Then, do the ablution.

Next an offering, similar to the one during the preparation of the student, is made to the student.

Utter the mantra of the principal deity [Kālachakra], and having made offering [to the student] of perfume at the heart, flowers at the head, and oblation in front, circle [the student] with a butter lamp.

Then, a censer is used for infusing incense.

Infuse with white incense together with butter into which the six syllables [oṃ āḥ hūṃ hoḥ haṃ kṣhaḥ] have been repeated seven times.

BESTOWING THE SEVEN INITIATIONS INDIVIDUALLY

This section has seven parts.

The seven initiations are now conferred in order, beginning with the water initiation. In the general mode of procedure of the path in Highest Yoga Tantra, the way that highest enlightenment is achieved is not through an external substance but through taking as the basis of achievement a phenomenon – subtle consciousness – that we naturally have [but do not utilize] in the ordinary state. With this as the basis, Highest Yoga Tantra sets forth techniques for perfecting the Buddha qualities of exalted body, speech, and mind.

In the Kālachakra system there is reference to four factors – body, speech, mind, and bliss.[45] It also speaks of four drops in a person's body. With respect to the four drops in the upper part of the body, at the crown of the head is the drop that produces the waking state; at the throat is the drop that produces the dream state; at the heart is the drop that produces the deep sleep state; and at the navel is the drop that produces the fourth, or bliss, state.

The drop at the crown of the head that produces the waking state has the capacity of causing various appearances of objects. In our ordinary state as a sentient being, that is to say, as a non-Buddha, it produces appearances of impure objects. Through the process of the path, one makes use of this capacity for the mere appearance of objects by activating it and overcoming the factor that brings about impure appearances; when this is done, various pure forms – subtle and gross – appear by way of the activated capacity of the drop that produces the waking state. Thus, at the time of the path, it is through utilizing the capacity of this drop that various empty forms are achieved, and in dependence upon these, one achieves the Form Bodies of the time of the fruit of Buddhahood.

The drop at the throat that produces the dream state has the capacity of causing various appearances of mere sounds. It is what brings about the various manifestations of impure sounds. At the time of the path, it is utilized to achieve invincible sound, in dependence upon which, at the time of the fruit of Buddhahood, exalted speech in all aspects is achieved.

The drop at the heart that produces the deep sleep state has the capacity of causing non-conceptual consciousness – impure and pure. In the ordinary state, it produces impure or unclear non-conceptuality, whereas at the time of the path its capacity to produce very luminous and clear awareness is utilized. Then, in dependence upon that, at the time of the fruit of Buddhahood, the non-conceptual Truth Body – the factor of complete pacification of the elaborations of conceptuality at Buddhahood – is achieved.

The drop at the navel that produces the fourth state has the capacity of producing mere bliss. At an impure level, it produces the bliss of emission – the predispositions for emission being a cause of travelling in cyclic existence. Through the power of the techniques in the path of Highest Yoga Tantra, the capacity for producing mere bliss is utilized and enhanced, whereby at the time of the path twenty-one thousand six hundred periods of immutable bliss are generated. Then, at the time of the fruit of Buddhahood, the Nature Body *(ngo bo nyid sku, svabhāvikakāya)* of great bliss is achieved; Highest Yoga Tantra speaks of a compounded Nature Body, not just uncompounded.

In this way, the entire structure of the Kālachakra path revolves around the defilements of the four types of drops and the predispositions for emission of the essential constituent. Emission of the essential constituent does not just refer to the emission of coarse semen but refers mainly to predispositions, for even those of the Formless Realm are said to have predispositions for emission. Indeed, this is a type of desire. Through the predispositions for emission one moves in cyclic existence; hence those of the Formless Realm are said to have the predispositions for emission. Those of the Formless Realm are said also to have "semen" [or essential stuff]; the "semen" of those of Desire Realm has five qualities; the "semen" of those of the Form Realm has three qualities; the "semen" of those of the Formless Realm has two qualities. Hence, "emission" and "semen" have a more subtle meaning.

In brief, to achieve a Buddha's exalted body, speech, and mind in terms of subtle consciousness, it is necessary first to purify our gross mental and physical aggregates, constituents, and sources of consciousness [the sense fields and sense organs]. The seven initiations – the water initiation and so forth – are associated in gradual order with purifying these grosser impure factors. The water initiation purifies impure factors of the five constitutents; the crown initiation purifies impure factors of the five mental and physical aggregates, and so on.

1 *Water Initiation*

OFFERING AND SUPPLICATION

The water and crown initiations are means of purifying the body; therefore, during these initiations the students face the northern, white, body-face of the principal deity Kālachakra and generate, that is, imagine, themselves as the white deity called Vajra Body.

> The lama, with his right hand that has a vajra, leads the student by the left hand, and [always] facing the mandala in front, circles it to the right. At the north door the student, facing the [white] body-face [of Kālachakra], sits on the initiation seat. Mandala is offered to the lama, undifferentiable from the Vajra Body of Kālachakra, as a present for giving the initiations that cleanse the body.
>
> *Offer mandala.*[46]
>
> To the lama, personal deity, and Three Jewels I offer in visualization
> The body, speech, mind, and resources of myself and others,
> Our collections of virtue in the past, present, and future,
> And the wonderful precious mandala with the masses of Samantabhadra's offerings.

Accepting them through your compassion, please bless me into magnificence.
Idaṃ guru-ratna-maṇḍalakaṃ niryātayāmi. [I offer this jewelled mandala to the guru.]

Repeat this mantra after me:

Make supplication three times with:

Oṃ haṃ hāṃ hiṃ hīṃ hṛṃ hṝṃ huṃ hūṃ hḷm hḹṃ ā ī ṝ ū ḹ vajra-ḍākiṇyau vajra-amṛta-ghaṭair abhiṣhiñchantu māṃ svāhā. [Oṃ haṃ hāṃ hiṃ hīṃ hṛṃ hṝṃ huṃ hūṃ hḷm hḹṃ ā ī ṝ ū ḹ please may the Vajra Female Sky-Goers confer initiation on me with the vases of vajra ambrosia svāhā.][47]

The ten syllables – *haṃ hāṃ hiṃ hīṃ hṛṃ hṝṃ huṃ hūṃ hḷm hḷm* – are the seed syllables of the ten vases, and the five vowels – *ā ī ṝ ū ḹ* – are the seed syllables of the five Mothers in dependence upon whom the water initiation is being given. The rest of the mantra, roughly speaking, means, "Vajra Sky-Goers, confer initiation on me with the vases of vajra ambrosia." The same type of supplication is made at the beginning of all seven initiations with variations appropriate to the particular initiation.

INTERNAL INITIATION

Next is conferral of the internal initiation. The students are drawn into the body of the lama who is in the form of the principal deity, pass through his body into the womb of the consort, dissolve into emptiness, and then reappear generated as the deity, Vajra Body. The Wisdom Being [the actual deity] is invited, enters inside the student generated as the same deity, is bound together with that imagination, takes pleasure in this, and becomes of one taste with the student. All the male and female Conquerors and Bodhisattvas are invited and offering is made to them. The lama makes a supplication, after which the male and female Conquerors become attracted to each other and, having entered into absorption, melt into an entity of ambrosia called the mind of enlightenment. The ambrosia enters the body of the lama, who is the principal deity and passes through his body, conferring initiation on the students who are, as mentioned just above, in the form of Vajra Body deities in the womb of the consort. Then, the students emerge from the womb of the consort and are set on the initiation seat. This procedure is the same for the remaining initiations.

> *With the six syllables* [*oṃ āḥ hūṃ hoḥ haṃ kṣhaḥ*] *and water from the conch,* [*obstructors*] *are cleared away.*

> Rays of light from huṃ at the heart of the lama who is not different from the principal deity draw you in; [328] you enter his mouth, pass through the center of his body, and through the vajra path enter the Mother's lotus and melt into a drop which turns into emptiness.

You need to reflect on two kinds of emptiness – a combination of (1) an immaculate vacuity that is the withdrawal of all old appearances and (2) the emptiness of inherent existence.

> From within emptiness comes an oṃ [which transforms into] a lotus from which a white Vajra Body Deity is generated, with three faces – white, black and red – and six hands, holding in the three right hands a mallet, a spear, and a trident and in the left hands a white lotus with a hundred petals, a wheel, and a rosary. You are embraced by Pāṇḍarāvāsin.
>
> Rays of light from the heart of the lama who is not different from the principal deity draw in the Wisdom-Beings who are like the meditated ones. Jaḥ hūṃ baṃ hoḥ hi. [Be summoned, enter, become fused with, be pleased, and become of the same taste.] They become of the same taste.
>
> Light rays from the heart of the lama who is not different from the principal deity draw in all the Conquerors of the ten directions – Fathers, Mothers, Sons, and Daughters. Vajra-bhairava ākarṣhaya jaḥ. [Vajra Frightful One, summon jaḥ.]

Make offering with:

Gandhaṃ puṣhpaṃ dhūpaṃ dīpaṃ akṣhate naividye lāsye hāsye vādye nṛtye gītye kāme pūja kuru kuru svāhā.[48] [Make offering with perfume, flowers, incense, lamps, fruit, food, lower robe, smiles, music, dance, singing, and touch svāhā.]

Just as Vajradhara bestowed
Initiations, sources of good qualities,
On the Buddhas for the sake of protecting trans-
migrating beings,
So please also bestow such here.

Through making supplication in that way, all the Conquerors, Fathers and Mothers and so forth, become absorbed, are melted by the fire of great desire [i.e., by great bliss], and enter by way of the crown protrusion of the lama who is not different from the principal deity. Emerging from the vajra-pathway, the mind of enlightenment confers initiation on yourself made into a Vajra Body Deity. You emerge from the Mother's lotus and are set on the initiation seat.

With respect to the deities being "melted by the fire of great desire", it is necessary to understand that bliss in this context is generated from desire but is not polluted with the faults of desire. Just as, for example, a worm generated from wood eats that wood, so the yoga generated from desire destroys desire.

These reflections on emptiness and on the usage of the attributes of the Desire Realm in the path are to be applied also to all the other initiations.

CLEANSING, PURIFICATION, AND DEIFICATION OF THE STUDENTS AND INTITATION SUBSTANCES

Next, the substance of the initiation, the water of the vases, is to be generated into a deity. The Mahāvijaya conch that is in front of me has been generated – from its transformational establishment at the time of the preparation – sometimes as the exalted mind mandala but mostly as the full mandala of exalted body, speech, and mind and thus has been blessed into magnificence. Inside the vases of the ten directions, the five male and five female Ones Gone Thus have been generated, and thus those vases have been blessed into magnificence. Water from each of the vases has been put into the Mahāvijaya conch.

The water initiation is the means of purifying the five constituents. The practitioner's five constituents – not including the sixth constituent, pristine mind [bliss] – are the internal substances that are the bases to be purified, and the external substance is the water of the vases. The respective portions of water and internal constituents are generated as the five female Ones Gone Thus – Vajradhātvīshvarī, and so forth – who themselves are the factors of purification of the five constituents. It is important that you actively imagine what the words of the ritual say.

> *Then, uttering "Oṃ prajñāpāramitā huṃ hūṃ phaṭ" [the lama] takes a little water from the vases above and below, and likewise with "Oṃ lochani huṃ hūṃ phaṭ" from the west and northwest, with "Oṃ māmakī huṃ hūṃ phaṭ" from the north and northeast, with "Oṃ pāṇḍarā huṃ hūṃ phaṭ" from the south and southwest, and with "Oṃ tāra huṃ hūṃ phaṭ" from the east and southeast. These are collected and mixed together in the Mahāvijaya conch which is set in front. The student and the water in the vase are cleansed [of obstructors] with the six syllables [oṃ āḥ hūṃ hoḥ haṃ kṣhaḥ]. With:*

> Oṃ shūnyatā-jñāna-vajra-svabhāvātmako 'haṃ. [I have the essential nature of indivisible emptiness and wisdom,] the five constituents of the student[49] and the water in the vase turn into emptiness. [329] From within emptiness the space constituent of your [the student's] body and the upper and lower portions of water mixed with the water of the religious conch [appear as two] ā [which transform into two] vajras, from which are generated [two] green Vajradhātvīshvarīs, with three faces – green,[50] red, and white – and six hands, holding in

the three right hands a vajra, curved knife, and axe and in the three left hands a vajra bell, a skull, and a head of Brahmā. She is embraced by Vajrasattva.

The wind constituent of your body and the eastern and southeastern portions of water mixed with the water of the religious conch [appear as two] ī [which transform into two] swords from which are generated [two] black Tārās with three faces – black, red, and white – and six hands, holding in the three right hands a sword, curved knife, and trident and in the three left hands a shield, skull, and white khaṭvāṅga. She is embraced by Vairochana.

The body's fire constituent and the southern and southwestern portions of water mixed with the water of the religious conch [appear as two] ṝ [which transform into two] jewels, from which are generated [two] red Pāṇḍarā, with three faces – red, white, and black – and six hands, holding in the three right hands a triple arrow, a vajra hook, and a resounding ḍāmaru drum and in the three left hands a bow, vajra noose, and nine-faceted jewel. She is embraced by Amitābha.

The body's water constituent and the northern and northeastern portions of water mixed with the water of the religious conch [appear as two] ū [which transform into two] lotuses from which are generated [two] white Māmakīs, with three faces – white, black, and red – and six hands, holding in the three right hands a mallet, spear, and trident and in the three left hands white lotuses with a hundred petals, mirror, and rosary. She is embraced by Ratnasambhava.

The body's earth constituent and the western and northwestern portions of water mixed with the water of the religious conch [appear as two] *ḹ* which transform into [two] wheels from which are generated [two] yellow Lochanās, with three faces – yellow, white, and black – and six hands, holding in the three right hands a wheel, staff, and frightening vajra and in the left hands a conch, vajra iron chain, and a ringing bell. She is embraced by Amoghasiddhi.

At their foreheads are oṃ; at their throats āḥ; at their hearts hūṃ; and at their navels hoḥ. Light is emitted from the hūṃ at their hearts, which draws in Wisdom Beings like those meditated. Jaḥ huṃ baṃ hoḥ hi. [Be summoned, enter, become fused with, be pleased, and become of the same taste.] They become of one taste with their respective Pledge Beings.

Oṃ ā ī ṝ ū ḹ pañcha-dhātu-vishodhani svāhā. [Oṃ ā ī ṝ ū ḹ be founded in the purification of the five constituents.] The Mothers confer initiation on the deities of the initiation substance. These, respectively, are seal-impressed by Akṣhobhya, Amoghasiddhi, Ratnasambhava, Amitābha, and Vairochana.

TRANSFORMATION OF THE DEITIES BACK INTO THE INITIATION SUBSTANCE IN HEIGHTENED FORM

Then the lama makes offering to the deities.

Make offering with:

Gandhaṃ puṣhpaṃ dhūpaṃ dīpaṃ akṣhate naividye lāsye hāsye vādye nṛtye gītye kāme pūja kuru kuru svāhā. [Make offering with perfume, flowers, incense, lamps, fruit, food, lower robe, smiles, music, dance, singing, and touch svāhā.] [330]

The Father and Mother Deities become absorbed, through which the fire of great desire melts the mind of enlightenment, which becomes the fluid of the vase.

INITIATION OF THE STUDENTS THROUGH USING THE INITIATION SUBSTANCE

With respect to what deities give the actual initiation, not only are initiation deities invited and drawn in from many other lands, but also the five goddesses [called the five Mothers] who reside in the mandala perform the activities of conferring initiation.

> Light rays from the heart of the lama who is not different from the principal deity draw in the initiation deities – Father and Mother Conquerors, Sons, and Daughters – filling the expanse of space. Vajra-bhairava ākarṣhaya jah. [Vajra Frightful One, summon, jaḥ.]
>
> *Make offering with:*
>
> Gandhaṃ puṣhpaṃ dhūpaṃ dīpaṃ akṣhate naividye lāsye hāsye vādye nṛtye gītye kāme pūja kuru kuru svāhā. [Make offering with perfume, flowers, incense, lamps, fruit, food, lower robe, smiles, music, dance, singing, and touch svāhā.]
>
> *Make a supplication:*
>
> Just as Vajradhara bestowed
> Initiations, sources of good qualities,
> On the Buddhas for the sake of protecting transmigrating beings,
> So please also bestow such here.
>
> *Then:*
>
> The Conquerors in space – Fathers and Mothers – make the intention to confer initiation. The Bodhisattvas make expressions of auspiciousness. Rūpavajrā and so forth make offering, and a rain of flowers and so forth descend. Male and Female Wrathful Ones expel obstructors. The Mothers residing in the mandala that has been achieved [are about to] confer initiation with white vases held slightly slanted with their hands and filled with the ambrosia of the mind of enlightenment.[51]

Then, auspiciousness is expressed with a stanza:

Through an auspiciousness dwelling in the hearts of all the sentient,

The essence of all [Buddhas], the supreme lord of all lineages,
Progenitor of all the sentient [Buddhas], the great bliss,
May you have today auspiciousness at the supreme conferral of initiation.

To understand Mantra well, it is helpful to understand the meaning of this stanza: Something auspicious resides in the essence of all beings. This can be explained in terms of the clear light as object – the emptiness of inherent existence – and in terms of the clear light as subject – consciousness. In terms of the clear light as object, the reality of the mind – its emptiness of inherent existence – which resides in, or pervades, the heart of all consciousness is the nature of all the stable and moving phenomena of cyclic existence and of nirvana, the mode of subsistence of all pure and impure phenomena and thus the essence of all.

The great bliss consciousness that is of the same undifferentiable entity as the reality of emptiness appears as the deity, Akṣhobhya, whose lineage is supreme among the five lineages. Among the five mental and physical aggregates that are the basis being purified, the aggregate of consciousness is the chief, the others being secondary; thus, among the five Conqueror lineages Akṣhobhya is chief since he is associated with purifying the aggregate of consciousness. The exalted wisdom of undifferentiable bliss and the emptiness of inherent existence of the mind – which has become devoid of obstructions – is the definitive Akṣhobhya, the definitive Kālachakra.

Since this great bliss consciousness is that generating all pure sentient beings – Buddhas, Ones Gone to Bliss – it is the progenitor of all the sentient, the basis of emanation or progenitor of all pure sentient beings and their environments. Furthermore, its appearance as a deity with a face, arms, and so forth is Akṣhobhya, or Kālachakra, who is the supreme, the lord, of all of the other Buddha lineages. Today, an auspiciousness has been created through generating such a great bliss consciousness in your continuum.

Then, in terms of the clear light as subject, the essential auspiciousness is the fundamental innate mind of clear light which we have had since beginningless time. It also is called the Buddha nature. The *Kālachakra Tantra* speaks of this essence when it says, "Sentient beings are Buddhas; other great Buddhas do not exist in the worldly realms." Similarly, the *Hevajra Tantra* says:

Sentient beings are just Buddhas,
But they are defiled by adventitious stains.
When those are removed, they are Buddhas.

Likewise, the *Vajrapañjara Tantra,* an explanatory tantra [of the Hevajra cycle], says:

Aside from the precious mind
There are no Buddhas, there are no sentient beings.

Just as the entity of even dirty water is not polluted by filth, so the nature of the fundamental innate mind of clear light is not polluted by defilements. Thus, the mind of clear light of an impure sentient being is not polluted by the afflictions; it is the Buddha nature, which is the "substance" that is transformed into a Buddha's Wisdom Truth Body. Hence, Buddhahood is not to be sought from the outside. Since this is the case, as long as you do not understand that the fundamental innate mind of clear light is your nature, you are a sentient being, and when you have final understanding that it is your nature, you are a Buddha.

Moreover, the *Hevajra Tantra* says:

Buddhas are not to be found elsewhere
In any of the realms of the world.
Just sentient beings are just complete Buddhas.
Buddhas are not demonstrable elsewhere.

This is called "cyclic existence";
This is just nirvana.
Due to obscuration, it has the form of cyclic existence;
Without obscuration, cyclic existence is just pure.

The one fundamental innate mind of clear light is called cyclic existence and is called nirvana. Then, what kind of state is called cyclic existence? What kind of state is called nirvana? The difference depends upon whether you have obscuration about your own nature or not.

The fundamental innate mind of clear light abides in or pervades the heart of all sentient beings. It also is the final essence and creator of all environments and beings, the basis of emanation of all of cyclic existence and nirvana. For, all phenomena – environments and beings – are the sport or artifice of the fundamental innate mind of clear light, called the basis of all. It is the basis of emanation of all five Conqueror lineages and thus "the supreme lord of all lineages" since the fundamental innate mind of clear light is divided into the five exalted wisdoms from which the five Conqueror lineages appear. It also is the "progenitor of all the sentient" in that it is what produces all pure and impure sentience, the final basis of designation of all persons.

"Great bliss" has two connotations. One meaning refers to a blissful consciousness that arises through the force of the melting of the essential constituent at the time of the path, and the other refers, in the basic state, to the mind of clear light which, because it has a nature of non-conceptuality, is free from the pollution of conceptuality.

With this as background, you can put together the particular explanations in the *Kālachakra Tantra,* the *Guhyasamāja Tantra,* the *Hevajra Tantra,* and the *Chakrasaṃvara Tantra* as well as the systems based on these tantras – the great seal *(phyag rgya chen po, mahāmudrā)* as taught in the Ḡa-gyu-b̄a order, the view of the undifferentiability of cyclic existence and nirvana in terms of the causal continuum of the basis-of-all that is a union of manifestation and emptiness as found in the S̄a-ḡya-b̄a order, the Ge-luk-b̄a presentation of the fundamental innate mind of clear light according to the Guhyasamāja system, and the great completeness of the N̄ying-ma order in which all appearances of environments and beings are decisively settled as the artifice, or self-effulgence, of basic mind from within the division of mind *(sems)* and basic mind *(rig pa)* – everything not passing beyond the sport of this basic mind. All of these practices come down to the same final thought. With understanding and analysis of many texts of the Middle Way School and of Highest Yoga Mantra, all of these are seen as coming together in the same basic thought.

However, if you are not familiar with these texts, you might think that these systems are radically different just from seeing and being amazed at their different vocabulary.[52]

The mind of clear light is present right now in our mental continuum. At the point of the conferral of the water initiation, you taste the water, an external substance, and similarly perform the internal imaginations. Through these, for the time being, conceptuality stops, and a non-conceptual awareness is generated. Even if you are not able actually to do this, you should mimic the state in imagination.

Stopping distraction to the outside, develop whatever understanding you can of the mere luminous and knowing nature of the mind and, even more, of subtler consciousness, and then within that state become mindful of the reality of the mind, its emptiness of inherent existence. Still, when we contemplate the reality of the mind, even though it is necessary to induce ascertainment of the emptiness of inherent existence, experience of the mind – the factor of luminosity and knowing – which ascertains the emptiness of inherent existence dawns. Therefore, it probably is the case that in meditative equipoise one is set in equipoise on the mere factor of luminosity and knowing [and not just on the emptiness of inherent existence].

Today you have been initiated into generating this fundamental innate mind of clear light as an entity of immutable bliss of undifferentiable method and wisdom in the sense that this has been generated in your continuum. This is what you are to think; this is the auspiciousness. You should listen to the stanza within reflecting on this meaning.

> *The Vajra Worker raises up the vase. Auspiciousness is expressed with:*

> Through an auspiciousness dwelling in the hearts
> of all the sentient,
> The essence of all, the supreme lord of all lineages,
> Progenitor of all the sentient, the great bliss,
> May you have today auspiciousness at the supreme
> conferral of initiation.

Then, there are three stanzas by Nāgārjuna that express auspiciousness by way of speaking about the qualities of the Three Jewels – Buddha, his doctrine, and the spiritual community.

> Through the Buddha possessing perfection like a gold mountain,
> Protector of the three worlds who has abandoned the three defilements, [331]
> With a face like the broad petals of a lotus,
> May you have today the auspiciousness of pacification.

A Buddha's qualities of exalted body adorned with marks and beauties are like a gold mountain. A Buddha is a protector of the worlds below, above, and on the ground through teaching how beings of the three transient worlds can achieve their temporary and final aims. In terms of mental qualities, a Buddha has abandoned all obstructions – those to liberation, to omniscience, and to meditative equipoise. In terms of verbal qualities, a Buddha's mouth radiates teaching like the petals of a marvelous lotus.

> Through the highest supreme unwavering teaching set forth by him,
> Renowned in the three worlds, worshipped by gods and humans,
> Most excellent of doctrine, pacifying all beings,
> May you have today the auspiciousness of pacification.

The teaching set forth by such a Buddha who has removed all faults and is endowed with all good attributes is comprised of the verbal and realizational excellent doctrine. Since, in dependence upon unerring advice to trainees on what to adopt and what to discard, their temporary and final aims can be achieved, his teaching is supreme. Being without contradiction or taint and not subject to unbiased dispute, his teaching is unwavering.

In another way, "highest supreme" can be taken as true

paths from among the four noble truths – the wisdom directly realizing the meaning of suchness, emptiness, and thereby acting as a direct antidote to the obstructions that are to be abandoned due to which it is "highest" and "supreme". The true cessation that is a state of having separated forever from any level of those objects of abandonment due to its having been extinguished in the sphere of reality is gained at the time of the path of release and is such that it will never be produced again, due to which it is "unwavering". Such doctrine is the excellent means for achieving temporary and final aims; it is renowned and worshipped by gods and humans in that it is put to use by them, bringing them the peace of temporary and final happiness.

> Through the excellent spiritual community, rich with the auspiciousness of having heard the doctrine,
> Place of worship by humans, gods, and demi-gods,
> Highest supreme of assemblies, knowing conscience, and the foundation of glory,
> May you have today the auspiciousness of pacification.

The excellent spiritual community is comprised by those who, practicing such doctrine, have attained realization of true paths and true cessations in their continuums. Since they not only have these qualities of practical realization but also are skilled in developing and increasing such realizations in others, they are said to have heard much doctrine in that they are ready and capable to communicate it. They are able not only to practice the doctrine but also to explain it to others. In that they are the supreme of groups, they are revered by beings; they are the "foundation of glory" in that they are an excellent field for beings to accumulate merit.

> *When doing self-entry, a rain of flowers falls on oneself, and when initiation is conferred on a student, a rain of flowers falls on the student. It is a great mistake [to think that] the flowers fall on the vase.*

When I recite the following stanza and mantra, imagine that as I make the gesture of touching the conch with water in it to your five places – crown protrusion, shoulders, upper arms, thighs, and hips – such is actually done and you attain the water initiation. Think that the entity of the water initiation – a special non-conceptual exalted wisdom of bliss and emptiness – is generated in your continuum. The conferral of initiation is called a "great vajra" because the entity of the initiation that is generated in the student's continuum – the exalted wisdom of undifferentiable bliss and emptiness – is capable, like a vajra or diamond, of overcoming objects of abandonment and is such that those defilements cannot affect or pierce it. It is fit to be revered by beings of the Desire, Form, and Formless Realms.

Then, the master, with right leg outstretched, says:

I will give the great vajra conferral of initiation,
Revered by those of the three realms,
Arisen from the source of the three
Secrecies of all the Buddhas.

Oṃ ā ī ṝ ū ḹ pañcha-dhātu-vishodhani svāhā.
[Oṃ ā ī ṝ ū ḹ be founded in the purification of the five constituents.]

With the water touch the five places – crown protrusion, right and left shoulders, upper arms, thighs, and hips – and having sprinkled a little, [have the student] drink a little and also wash, conferring initiation.

Imagine that, as mentioned earlier, a non-conceptual awareness is generated through the coming together of external and internal conditions, and through this, great bliss is generated in your continuum. The great bliss consciousness ascertains the emptiness of inherent existence, and, thereby, a special exalted wisdom of undifferentiable bliss and emptiness is generated.

According to the uncommon mode of procedure of the *Kālachakra Tantra*, you should imagine that when conceptuality ceases and then there is a thick state of non-conceptuality, appearances of empty forms are naturally generated, the first being an appearance like smoke. Gradually, the empty forms become more and more subtle to the point where finally a Buddha's Complete Enjoyment Body dawns.

Now, except for the constituent of pristine mind [bliss], the remaining five constituents of your own body – earth, water, fire, wind, and space – transform in *aspect* into the five goddesses called the five Mothers while *in entity* being the five constituents. At your crown protrusion is the entity of the space constituent of your body, transformed into the aspect of a green Vajradhātvīshvarī. At your forehead is the entity of the wind constituent, transformed into the aspect of Tārā. At your throat is the entity of the fire constituent, transformed into the aspect of Pāṇḍarā. At your heart is the entity of the water constituent, transformed into the aspect of Māmakī. At your naval is the entity of the earth constituent, transformed into the aspect of Lochanā.

> Through sprinkling and washing in that way, sufferings and defilements are purified; through drinking it, great bliss is experienced. The five constituents of the body become the five Mothers.

Light rays from them draw in doubles from the five Mothers in the mandala; these dissolve into the five Mothers visualized at those respective places in your body. Also, think that the initiation deities are drawn in and dissolve into them.

> Light rays from them draw in the five Mothers of the mandala in the manner of a second butter lamp separating off from the first. The five Mothers dissolve into the five Mothers of your own body. Also, all the deities of initiation are summoned and dissolve into your own five constituents, clarified as the five Mothers.
>
> *Make offering with:*
>
> Gandhaṃ pushpaṃ dhūpaṃ dīpaṃ akṣhate naividye lāsye hāsye vādye nṛtye gītye kāme pūja

kuru kuru svāhā. [Make offering with perfume, flowers, incense, lamps, fruit, food, lower robe, smiles, music, dance, singing, and touch svāhā.]

MEANING OF THE INITIATION

Then, express the meaning of the initiation and its purification: [332]

Corresponding to a mother's washing her just born child, this cleanses defilements of the five constituents. It authorizes you to achieve feats and activities dependent upon the five Mothers. It sets potencies for [achieving] the five Mothers in your continuum and causes you to have the capacity to attain the first ground as its fruit.

The seven initiations in the pattern of childhood, which are means of ripening the mental continuum for the practice of the stage of generation, establish potencies for achieving the first seven Bodhisattva grounds. Nevertheless, a Bodhisattva ground is actually achieved only during the stage of completion.

In the Great Vehicle, the attainment of the first Bodhisattva ground is simultaneous with attaining the path of a Superior (*'phags pa, āryan*). Thus, the correspondence of the stage of generation with the first seven grounds is from the point of view that when the stage of generation is finished, the collection of merit that has been achieved is equal to that of a seventh ground Bodhisattva of the Perfection Vehicle. Since even a first ground Bodhisattva has realized emptiness directly, a practitioner of Highest Yoga Mantra who has finished the stage of generation is lesser in that respect, but from the viewpoint of having accumulated the collections of merit, such a Mantrika is equal to a seventh grounder.

In this way, the seven initiations in the pattern of childhood are teamed with the seven Bodhisattva grounds, the water initiation having established potencies for attaining the first ground.

2 *Crown Initiation*

The basic mode of procedure for the crown initiation is the same as that for the water initiation. The difference is that your five mental and physical aggregates and the five-part crown are generated in series as Akṣhobhya and so forth.

OFFERING AND SUPPLICATION

Mandala is offered to the lama, undifferentiable from the Vajra Body of Kālachakra, as a present for giving the crown initiation that cleanses the defilements of the five aggregates.

Offer mandala:

To the lama, personal deity, and Three Jewels I offer in visualization
The body, speech, mind, and resources of myself and others,
Our collections of virtue in the past, present, and future,
And the wonderful precious mandala with the masses of Samantabhadra's offerings.
Accepting them through your compassion, please bless me into magnificence.
Idaṃ guru-ratna-maṇḍalakaṃ niryātayāmi. [I offer this jewelled mandala to the guru.]

Make this supplication three times with:[53]

Oṃ aṃ iṃ ṛṃ uṃ ḷṃ sarva-buddha-vajra-mukuṭaṃ mama pañcha-buddha-ātmakaṃ bandhayantu huṃ hūṃ phaṭ. [Oṃ aṃ iṃ ṛṃ uṃ ḷṃ please may all the Buddhas bind on me the vajra crowns having the nature of the five Buddhas huṃ hūṃ phaṭ.]

CLEANSING, PURIFICATION AND DEIFICATION OF THE STUDENTS AND INITIATION SUBSTANCES

Since here it is not necessary to perform the internal initiation again, clear away [obstructors from the student] and the crown with the six syllables [oṃ āḥ hūṃ hoḥ haṃ kṣhaḥ] and water from the conch. With:

Oṃ shūnyatā-jñāna-vajra-svabhāvātmako 'haṃ [I have the essential nature of indivisible emptiness and wisdom,] the five aggregates of the [student] and the crown, the substance involved in the initiation, transform into emptiness. From within emptiness, your aggregate of consciousness and the green crown [appear as two] a [which transform into] vajras from which are generated green Akṣhobhyas with three faces – green, red, and white – and six hands, holding in the three right hands a vajra, curved knife, and axe and in the three left hands vajra and bell, skull, and a head of Brahmā. They are embraced by Prajñāpāramitā.

Your aggregate of compositional factors and the black crown [appear as two] i [which transform into] swords, from which are generated black Amoghasiddhis with three faces – black, red, and white – and six hands, holding in the three right hands a sword, curved knife, and trident and in the three left hands a shield, skull, and white khaṭvāṅga. They are embraced by Lochanā.

Your aggregate of feelings and the red crown [appear as two] ṛ [which transform into] jewels, from which are generated red Ratnasambhavas with three faces – red, white, and black – and six hands, holding in the three right hands a triple arrow, vajra hook, and resounding ḍāmaru drum and in the three left hands a bow, vajra noose, and nine-faceted jewel. They are embraced by Māmaki.

Your aggregate of discrimination and the white crown [appear as two] u [which transform into] lotuses, from which are generated white Amitābhas with three faces – white, black, and red – and six hands, holding in the three right hands a mallet, spear, and trident and in the three left hands a white lotus with a hundred petals, a mirror, and rosary. They are embraced by Pāṇḍarā.

Your aggregate of forms and the yellow crown [appear as two] ḷ [which transform into] wheels, from which are generated yellow Vairochanas, with three faces – yellow, white, and black – and six hands, holding in the three right hands a wheel, staff, and frightening vajra and in the three left hands a conch, vajra iron chain, and a ringing bell. They are embraced by Tārā.

At their foreheads is oṃ; at their throats āḥ; at their hearts hūṃ; and at their navels hoḥ. Light is emitted from the hūṃ at their hearts, which draws in Wisdom Beings like those meditated. Jaḥ hūṃ baṃ hoḥ hi. [Be summoned, enter, become fused with, be pleased, and become of the same taste.] They become of one taste with their respective Pledge Beings.

Oṃ ā ī ṝ ū ḷ pañcha-dhātu-vishodhani svāhā. [Oṃ ā ī ṝ ū ḷ be founded in the purification of the five constituents.] The Mothers confer initiation on the deities of the initiation substance. These, respectively, are seal-impressed by Vajrasattva, Amoghasiddhi, Ratnasambhava, Amitābha, and Vairochana.

TRANSFORMATION OF THE DEITIES BACK INTO THE INITIATION SUBSTANCE IN HEIGHTENED FORM

Make offering with:

Gandhaṃ puṣhpaṃ dhūpaṃ dīpaṃ akṣhate naividye lāsye hāsye vādye nṛtye gītye kāme pūja kuru kuru svāhā. [Make offering with perfume, flowers, incense, lamps, fruit, food, lower robe, smiles, music, dance, singing, and touch svāhā.] [333]

The Father and Mother Deities become absorbed; upon being melted by the fire of great desire they become the crown, the initiation substance.

INITIATION OF THE STUDENTS THROUGH USING THE INITIATION SUBSTANCE

Light rays from the heart of the lama who is not different from the principal deity draw in the initiation deities – Father and Mother Conquerors, Sons, and Daughters – filling the expanse of space. Vajra-bhairava ākarṣhays jaḥ. [Vajra Frightful One, summon, jaḥ.]

Make offering with:

Gandhaṃ puṣhpaṃ dhūpaṃ dīpaṃ akṣhate naividye lāsye hāsye vādye nṛtye gītye kāme pūja kuru kuru svāhā. [Make offering with perfume, flowers, incense, lamps, fruit, food, lower robe, smiles, music, dance, singing, and touch svāhā.]

Make a supplication:

Just as Vajradhara bestowed
Initiations, sources of good qualities,
On the Buddhas for the sake of protecting transmigrating beings,
So please also bestow such here.

Then:

The Conquerors in space – Fathers and Mothers – make the intention to confer initiation. The Bodhisattvas make expressions of auspiciousness. Rūpavajrā and so forth make offering, and a rain of flowers and so forth descend. Male and Female Wrathful Ones expel obstructors. The five Buddhas, who reside in the mandala that has been achieved and who hold the crowns, [are about to] confer initiation.

The Vajra Worker raises up the crown. Auspiciousness[54] *is expressed with:*

Through an auspiciousness dwelling in the hearts of all the sentient,
The essence of all, the supreme lord of all lineages,
Progenitor of all the sentient, the great bliss,
May you have today auspiciousness at the supreme conferral of initiation.

Through the Buddha possessing perfection like a gold mountain,
Protector of the three worlds who has abandoned the three defilements,
With a face like the broad petals of a lotus,
May you have today the auspiciousness of pacification.

Through the highest supreme unwavering teaching set forth by him,
Renowned in the three worlds, worshipped by gods and humans,
Most excellent of doctrine, pacifying all beings,
May you have today the auspiciousness of pacification.

Through the excellent Spiritual Community, rich with the auspiciousness of having heard the doctrine,
Place of worship by humans, gods, and demi-gods,

Highest supreme of assemblies, knowing conscience, and the foundation of glory,
May you have today the auspiciousness of pacification.

When doing self-entry, a rain of flowers falls on oneself, and when initiation is conferred on a student, a rain of flowers falls on the student. Then, the master, with the right leg outstretched says:

I will give the great vajra conferral of initiation,
Revered by those of the three realms,
Arisen from the source of the three
Secrecies of all the Buddhas.

As I make the gesture of touching the crown to your head and so forth, imagine that the five Ones Gone Thus who reside in the mandala put the crown, which is the substance of the initiation, on your head. Think that in dependence upon that, a special non-conceptual wisdom consciousness is generated in your continuum and that potencies for achieving the body of a Buddha with the major and minor marks are thereby set in your continuum.

Oṃ a i ṛ u ḷ pañcha-tathāgata-parishuddha svāhā. [Oṃ a i ṛ u ḷ be founded in the thorough purity of the five Ones Gone Thus.]

Touch the crown to the five places [crown protrusion, both shoulders, upper arms, thighs, and hips], and wear it on the head.

Next a water initiation is conferred as an appendage to the crown initiation.

Then,[55] the master, with right leg outstretched, says:

I will give the great vajra conferral of initiation,
Revered by those of the three realms,
Arisen from the source of the three
Secrecies of all the Buddhas.

Oṃ ā ī ṝ ū ḹ pañcha-dhātu-vishodhani svāhā. [Oṃ ā ī ṝ ū ḹ be founded in the purification of the five constituents.]

> *With the water touch the five places – crown protrusion, right and left shoulders, upper arms, thighs, and hips – and having sprinkled a little, drink a little and also wash, conferring initiation.*

That completes the appendage.

> Through being conferred initiation in that way, your five aggregates become the five Buddhas.

At the crown of your head, the entity of your aggregate of consciousness transforms into Akṣhobhya. At your forehead, the entity of your aggregate of compositional factors transforms into Amoghasiddhi. At your throat, the entity of your aggregate of feelings transforms into Ratnasambhava. At your heart, the entity of your aggregate of discriminations transforms into Amitābha. At your navel, the entity of your aggregate of forms transforms into Vairochana.

> Light rays from them draw in the five Buddhas of the mandala in the manner of a second butter lamp separating off from the first. The five Buddhas dissolve into the five Buddhas of your own body. Also, the initiation deities are summoned and dissolve into your five aggregates clarified as the five Buddhas.
>
> *Make offering with:*
>
> Gandhaṃ puṣhpaṃ dhūpaṃ dīpaṃ akṣhate naividye lāsye hāsye vādye nṛtye gītye kāme pūja kuru kuru svāhā. [Make offering with perfume, flowers, incense, lamps, fruit, food, lower robe, smiles, music, dance, singing, and touch svāhā.]

MEANING OF THE INITIATION

> *Then, express the meaning of the initiation and its purification:*
>
> This corresponds to fixing up the hair on the top of a child's head. It cleanses defilements of the five

aggregates. It authorizes you to achieve feats by way of the five Buddhas. It sets potencies for the five Buddhas in your continuum and causes you to have the capacity to attain the second ground as its fruit.

Then, express the purification common to those two initiations:

Just as in the womb the constituents and the aggregates are initially formed, the two initiations in the area of the northern face of exalted body cleanse physical defilements and establish seeds for a vajra body in order to establish potencies such that the impure constituents and aggregates which are factors of your own body are made devoid of defilement as entities of the male and female Ones Gone Thus. [These two initiations] authorize you to achieve the feat of a vajra body.

3 *Silk Ribbon Initiation*

The first two initiations purify body; the next two purify speech. Since the root of speech is wind, or inner energies, which dwell mainly in the two channels, the silk ribbon initiation and the vajra and bell initiation purify the ten winds and the two channels, respectively. For these initiations, the students proceed to the southern door of the mandala so that they can face the exalted speech face of the central deity, Kālachakra.

OFFERING AND SUPPLICATION

Again, circling to the right, the student is led to the southern door. [334] Facing the [red] exalted speech face [of Kālachakra], the student sits on the initiation seat. Mandala is offered to the lama, undifferentiable from the Vajra Speech of Kālachakra, as a present for giving the silk ribbon initiation that cleanses defilements of the ten winds.

Offer mandala.

To the lama, personal deity, and Three Jewels I offer in visualization
The body, speech, mind, and resources of myself and others,

Our collections of virtue in the past, present, and future,
And the wonderful precious mandala with the masses of Samantabhadra's offerings.
Accepting them through your compassion, please bless me into magnificence.
Idaṃ guru-ratna-maṇḍalakaṃ niryātayāmi. [I offer this jewelled mandala to the guru.]

By reciting a mantra, the student requests the initiation. The mantra means, "May the ten Shaktis, having the nature of the ten perfections, confer on me the silk ribbon initiation."

Make supplication three times with:

Oṃ a ā aṃ aḥ ha hā haṃ haḥ phreṃ hoḥ sarva-pāramitā mama vajra-paṭṭam bandhayantu huṃ hūṃ phaṭ. [Oṃ a ā aṃ aḥ ha hā haṃ haḥ phreṃ hoḥ please may all the Perfection Goddesses tie on me the vajra silk ribbon huṃ hūṃ phaṭ.]

INTERNAL INITIATION

Since the silk ribbon initiation and the vajra and bell initiation are means of purifying speech, for these initiations the students have to generate themselves as Vajra Speech Deities. Therefore, you should imagine such in accordance with the rite.

With the six syllables [oṃ āḥ hūṃ hoḥ haṃ kṣhaḥ] and water from the conch, [obstructors] are cleared away.

Rays of light from huṃ at the heart of the lama who is not different from the principal deity draw you in; you enter his mouth, pass through the center of his body, and through the vajra path enter the Mother's lotus and melt into a drop, which turns into emptiness. From within emptiness comes an āḥ [which transforms into] a jewel from which a red Vajra Speech Deity is generated, with three faces – red, white, and black – and six hands holding in the three right hands a triple arrow, a vajra hook, and reverberating drum and in the left hands a bow, vajra noose, and nine-faceted jewel. You are embraced by Māmakı.

Rays of light from the heart of the lama who is not different from the principal deity draw in the Wisdom-Beings like the meditated ones. Jaḥ hūṃ baṃ hoḥ hi. [Be summoned, enter, become fused with, be pleased, and become of the same taste.] They become of the same taste.

Light rays from the heart of the lama who is not different from the principal deity draw in all the Conquerors of the ten directions – Fathers, Mothers, Sons, and Daughters. Vajra-bhairava ākarṣhīyī jaḥ. [Vajra Frightful One, summon jaḥ.]

Make offering with:

Gandhaṃ puṣhpaṃ dhūpaṃ dīpaṃ akṣhate naividye lāsye hāsye vādye nṛtye gītye kāme pūja kuru kuru svāhā. [Make offering with pertume, flowers, incense, lamps, fruit, food, lower robe, smiles, music, dance, singing, and touch svāhā.]

Just as Vajradhara bestowed
Initiations, sources of good qualities,
On the Buddhas for the sake of protecting transmigrating beings,
So please also bestow such here.

Through making supplication in that way, all the Conquerors, Fathers and Mothers and so forth, become absorbed, are melted by the fire of great desire [i.e., by great bliss], and enter by way of the crown protrusion of the lama who is not different from the principal deity. Emerging from the vajra-pathway, the mind of enlightenment confers initiation on yourself made into a Vajra Speech Deity. You emerge from the Mother's lotus and sit on the initiation seat.

CLEANSING PURIFICATION AND DEIFICATION OF THE STUDENTS AND INITIATION SUBSTANCES

The silk ribbons that are the external substances involved in the initiation are to be generated as goddesses called the ten Shaktis *(nus ma)*, and the ten winds of the students are also to be generated as similar deities.

> *Then, clear away* [*obstructors*] *from the student and from the silk ribbon* [*with the six syllables, oṃ āḥ hūṃ hoḥ haṃ kṣhaḥ, and water from the conch*] *and purify them. With:*

> Oṃ shūnyatā-jñāna-vajra-svabhāvātmako 'haṃ [I have the essential nature of indivisible emptiness and wisdom,] your ten winds and the silk ribbons transform into emptiness.

The fire-accompanying wind and turtle wind are winds of the wind constituent. The upward-moving wind and chameleon wind are winds of the fire constituent. The pervasive wind and *devadatta* wind are winds of the water constituent. The serpent wind and *dhaṃnajaya* wind are winds of the earth constituent. The vitalizing wind is a wind of the space constituent. The downward-voiding wind is a wind of the pristine mind [or bliss] constituent.

> From within emptiness, your fire-accompanying wind and turtle wind and two black silk ribbons [appear as two sets of] a and ha [which transform into] censors and black yak tail fans, from which are generated black Kṛṣhṇadīptās with four faces – black, red, yellow, and white – and eight hands, holding in the right hands vessels of incense, sandalwood, saffron, and a mixture of camphor and musk and in the left hands a bell, lotus, flower of the *deva* tree, and a string of various flowers and also black Dhūmās with four faces – black, red, yellow, and white – and eight hands holding eight yak-tail fans.

Your upward-moving wind and chameleon wind and two red silk ribbons [appear as two sets of] aḥ and haḥ [which transform into] butter lamps and red yak-tail fans, [335] from which are generated red Raktadīptās, having red, yellow, white, and blue faces and eight hands, holding in the right hands a butter lamp, string of pearls, crown, and bracelet and in the left hands a garment, belt, earring, and anklette, and also red Mārīchīs, with red, yellow, white, and blue faces and eight hands, holding eight red yak-tail fans.

Your pervasive wind and devadatta wind and two white silk ribbons [appear as two sets of] aṃ and haṃ [which transform into] divine food and white yak-tail fans, from which are generated white Shretadīptās, with white, black, red, and yellow faces and eight hands, holding in the right hands vessels of milk, water, the supreme of medicines, and beer and in the left hands vessels of ambrosia, accomplished taste,[56] ambrosia-fruit, and food, and also white Khadyotās with white, black, red, and yellow faces and with eight hands holding eight white yak-tail fans.

Your serpent wind and dhaṃnajaya wind and two yellow silk ribbons [appear as two sets of] ā and hā [which transform into] religious conches and yellow yak-tail fans, from which are generated yellow Pītadīptās, having yellow, white, blue, and red faces and eight hands, holding in the right hands a conch, flute, jewel, and ḍāmaru and in the left hands a guitar, drum, resounding gong, and copper conch, and also yellow Pradīpās, with yellow, white, blue, and red faces and eight hands, holding eight yellow yak-tail fans.

Your vitalizing wind and the green silk ribbon [appear as two] ho [which transform into] vajras, from which are generated green Vajradhatvīshvarīs with three faces – green, red, and white – and six hands, holding in the right hands a vajra, curved knife, and axe and in the left hands a vajra bell, skull, and head of Brahmā.

Your downward-voiding wind and the blue silk ribbon [appear as two] phreṃ [which transform into] curved knives, from which are generated blue Vishvamātās with three faces – blue, white, and red – and six hands, holding in the three right hands vajra, bell, and axe and in the three left hands a bell, skull, and head of Brahmā.

At their foreheads is oṃ; at their throats āḥ; at their hearts hūṃ; and at their navels hoḥ. Light is emitted from the hūṃ at their hearts, which draws in Wisdom Beings like those meditated. Jaḥ hūṃ baṃ hoḥ hi. [Be summoned, enter, become fused with, be pleased and become of the same taste.] They become of one taste with their respective Pledge Beings.

Oṃ ā ī ṝ ū ḹ pañcha-dhātu-vishodhani svāhā. [Oṃ ā ī ṝ ū ḹ be founded in the purification of the five constituents.] The Mothers confer initiation on the deities of the initiation substances. These are seal-impressed by Vajrasattva.

TRANSFORMATION OF THE DEITIES BACK INTO THE INITIATION SUBSTANCE IN HEIGHTENED FORM

Make offering [*to those deities*] *with:*

Gandhaṃ pushpaṃ dhūpaṃ dīpaṃ akṣhate naividye lāsye hāsye vādye nṛtye gītye kāme pūja kuru kuru svāhā. [Make offering with perfume, flowers, incense, lamps, fruit, food, lower robe, smiles, music, dance, singing, and touch svāhā.]

The ten Shaktis melt, whereupon they become the silk ribbons that are the substances of the initiation.

INITIATION OF THE STUDENTS THROUGH USING THE INITIATION SUBSTANCE

Light rays from the heart of the lama who is not different from the principal deity draw in the initiation deities – Father and Mother Conquerors, Sons, and Daughters – filling the expanse of space. Vajra-bhairava ākarṣhaya jaḥ. [Vajra Frighthul One, summon, jaḥ.]

Make offering with:

Gandhaṃ puṣhpaṃ dhūpaṃ dīpaṃ akṣhate naividye lāsye hāsye vādye nṛtye gītye kāme pūja kuru kuru svāhā. [Make offering with perfume, flowers, incense, lamps, fruit, food, lower robe, smiles, music, dance, singing, and touch svāhā.]

Make a supplication:

Just as Vajradhara bestowed
Initiations, sources of good qualities,
On the Buddhas for the sake of protecting transmigrating beings,
So please also bestow such here.

Then:

The Conquerors in space – Fathers and Mothers – make the intention to confer initiation. The Bodhisattvas make expressions of auspiciousness. Rūpavajrā and so forth make offering, and a rain of flowers and so forth descend. Male and Female Wrathful Ones expel obstructors. The ten Shaktis residing in the mandala that has been achieved, holding the silk ribbons, [are about to] confer initiation.

The Vajra Worker raises up the silk ribbons. Auspiciousness is expressed with:

Through an auspiciousness dwelling in the hearts of all the sentient,
The essence of all, the supreme lord of all lineages,

Progenitor of all the sentient, the great bliss,
May you have today auspiciousness at the supreme conferral of initiation.

Through the Buddha possessing perfection like a gold mountain,
Protector of the three worlds who has abandoned the three defilements,
With a face like the broad petals of a lotus,
May you have today the auspiciousness of pacification.

Through the highest supreme unwavering teaching set forth by him,
Renowned in the three worlds, worshipped by gods and humans,
Most excellent of doctrine, pacifying all beings,
May you have today the auspiciousness of pacification.

Through the excellent spiritual community, rich with the auspiciousness of having heard the doctrine,
Place of worship by humans, gods, and demi-gods,
Highest supreme of assemblies, knowing conscience, and the foundation of glory,
May you have today the auspiciousness of pacification.

When doing self-entry, a rain of flowers falls on oneself, and when initiation is conferred on a student, a rain of flowers falls on the student. Then, the master, with right leg outstretched, says:

I will give the great vajra conferral of initiation,
Revered by those of the three realms,
Arisen from the source of the three
Secrecies of all the Buddhas.

The ten Shaktis are the eight Shaktis actually visible in the mandala as well as two Shaktis, Prajñāpāramitā *(shes rab kyi pha rol tu phyin ma)* and Jñānapāramitā *(ye shes kyi pha rol tu phyin ma)* who are of one undifferentiable entity with Kālachakra's consort, Vishvamātā, and are here to be separated out from her. When I make the gesture of touching the silk ribbons to your five places, imagine that these ten Shaktis who reside in the mandala confer on you the silk ribbon initiation.

The function of the silk ribbon initiation is to bless your ten winds into magnificence, making them serviceable. Think that the fluctuation of impure conceptuality ceases, in dependence upon which a special non-conceptual wisdom is generated, and bliss is generated. Imagine that an exalted wisdom of undifferentiable bliss and emptiness is engendered in your continuum.

> Oṃ a ā aṃ aḥ ha hā haṃ haḥ hoḥ phreṃ dasha-pāramitā pāripūraṇi svāhā. [Oṃ a ā aṃ aḥ ha hā haṃ haḥ hoḥ phreṃ the Female Fulfillers of the ten perfections svāhā.]
>
> *Touch the silk ribbons to the five places* [*crown protrusion, both shoulders, upper arms, thighs, and hips*],[57] *and tie them on the forehead.*

Next is a water initiation as an appendage to the silk ribbon initiation.

> *Then, the master, with right leg outstretched, says:*
>
> I will give the great vajra conferral of initiation,
> Revered by those of the three realms,
> Arisen from the source of the three
> Secrecies of all the Buddhas.
>
> Oṃ ā ī ṛ ū ḷ pañcha-dhātu-vishodhani svāhā. [Oṃ ā ī ṛ ū ḷ be founded in the purification of the five constituents.]
>
> *With the water, touch the five places – crown protrusion, right and left shoulders, upper arms, thighs, and hips – and having sprinkled a little,* [*have the student*] *drink a little and also wash, conferring initiation.*

That completes the appendage.

Through being conferred initiation in that way, your ten winds become the ten Shaktis.

According to the Kālachakra system, the ten winds are associated with the eight channel petals at the heart and the channels above and below the heart. Above the heart is the vitalizing wind, and below the heart is the downward-voiding wind; the remaining eight winds are associated with the eight petals of the heart. Your ten winds are to be generated as the ten Shaktis at those places.

Light rays from them draw in the ten Shaktis of the mandala in the manner of a second butter lamp separating off from the first. The ten Shaktis dissolve into the ten Shaktis of your own body. Also, all the initiation deities are summoned and dissolve into your ten winds clarified as the ten Shaktis.

Make offering with:

Gandhaṃ puṣhpaṃ dhūpaṃ dīpaṃ akṣhate naividye lāsye hāsye vādye nṛtye gītye kāme pūja kuru kuru svāhā. [Make offering with perfume, flowers, incense, lamps, fruit, food, lower robe, smiles, music, dance, singing, and touch svāhā.]

MEANING OF THE INITIATION

Then, express the meaning of the initiation and its purification:

This corresponds to piercing the ears of a child and hanging on adornments. [336] It cleanses defilements of the ten winds and makes them serviceable. It authorizes you to achieve feats by way of the ten Shaktis. It sets potencies for the ten perfections in your continuum and causes you to have the capacity to attain the third ground as its fruit.

4 *Vajra and Bell Initiation*

OFFERING AND SUPPLICATION

Again, mandala is offered to the lama, undifferentiable from the Vajra Speech of Kālachakra, as a present for the vajra and bell initiation that cleanses the two channels.

Offer mandala.

To the lama, personal deity, and Three Jewels I offer in visualization
The body, speech, mind, and resources of myself and others,
Our collections of virtue in the past, present, and future,
And the wonderful precious mandala with the masses of Samantabhadra's offerings.
Accepting them through your compassion, please bless me into magnificence.
Idaṃ guru-ratna-maṇḍalakaṃ niryātayāmi. [I offer this jewelled mandala to the guru.]

The *Sūtra of Teaching to Nanda on Entry to the Womb (tshe dang ldan pa dga' bo mngal du 'jug pa bstan pa, āyuṣhmannanda-garbhābhāvakrāntinirdesha)* says that in our bodies there are eighty thousand channels. In Mantra, the count of the channels is seventy-two thousand. Among these, the main channels are three – the right, left, and central channels. Among these, a practitioner is seeking to make use of the central one.

When the right and left channels – *rasanā* and *lalanā* – are active, conceptions of subject and object are generated. Hence, in order to purify the right and left channels, the students make supplication to receive the vajra and bell initiations.

Make supplication three times with:

Oṃ hūṃ hoḥ vijñāna-jñāna-svabhāve karuṇā-prajñā-ātmake vajra-vajra-ghaṇṭe savyetarakarayor mama vajrasatvaḥ saprajño dadātu huṃ hūṃ phaṭ. [Oṃ hūṃ hoḥ please may Vajrasattva together with (his) Wisdom Woman bestow the vajra and vajrabell that have a nature of consciousness and exalted wisdom (and) an essence of compassion and wisdom in my right hand and other hand huṃ hūṃ phat.]

CLEANSING, PURIFICATION, AND DEIFICATION OF THE STUDENTS AND INITIATION SUBSTANCES

Then, the student's right and left channels and the substances of the initiation, vajra and bell, are generated as [two sets of] Kālachakra and his consort, Vishvamātā. Therefore, listen carefully to the ritual instructions and imagine the process as indicated.

Clear away [obstructors] from the student and from the vajra and bell [with the six syllables, oṃ āḥ hūṃ hoḥ haṃ kṣhaḥ and water from the conch] and purify them. With:

Oṃ shūnyatā-jñāna-vajra-svabhāvātmako 'haṃ [I have the essential nature of indivisible emptiness and wisdom,] you and the vajra bell turn into emptiness. From within emptiness, your right channel and the vajra which is the initiation substance [each appear as] hūṃ [which transform into] vajras, from which are generated blue Kālachakras with one face and two hands holding vajra and bell; they are embraced by Vishvamātās holding a curved knife and a skull. Your left channel and the bell [each appear as] phreṃ [which transform into] curved knives, from which are generated yellow Vishvamātās with one face and two hands holding a curved knife and skull; they are embraced by Kālachakra. At the forehead of these two is oṃ; at the neck āḥ; at the heart hūṃ; and at the navel hoḥ. Light, emitted from the hūṃ at their heart, draws in Wisdom Beings like the meditated ones. Jaḥ hūṃ baṃ hoḥ hi. [Be summoned, enter, become fused with, be pleased, and become of the same taste.] They become of one taste with their respective Pledge Beings.

Oṃ ā ī ṝ ū ḹ pañcha-dhātu-vishodhani svāhā. [Oṃ ā ī ṝ ū ḹ be founded in the purification of the five constituents.] The Mothers confer initiation on the deities of the initiation substances. The Father Deity [Kālachakra] is seal-impressed by Akṣhobhya, and the Mother Deity [Vishvamātā] is seal-impressed by Vajrasattva.

TRANSFORMATION OF THE DEITIES BACK INTO THE INITIATION SUBSTANCE IN HEIGHTENED FORM

Make offering [*to those deities*] *with:*

Gandhaṃ puṣhpaṃ dhūpaṃ dīpaṃ akṣhate naividye lāsye hāsye vādye nṛtye gītye kāme pūja kuru kuru svāhā. [Make offering with perfume, flowers, incense, lamps, fruit, food, lower robe, smiles, music, dance, singing, and touch svāhā.]

The Father Deity and Mother Deity become absorbed; upon being melted by the fire of great desire they become the vajra and bell that are the initiation substances.

INITIATION OF THE STUDENTS THROUGH USING THE INITIATION SUBSTANCE

Light rays from the heart of the lama who is not

different from the principal deity draw in the initiation deities – Father and Mother Conquerors, Sons, and Daughters – filling the expanse of space. Vajra-bhairava ākarṣhaya jaḥ. [Vajra Frightful One, summon, jaḥ.]

Make offering with:

Gandhaṃ puṣhpaṃ dhūpaṃ dīpaṃ akṣhate naividye lāsye hāsye vādye nṛtye gītye kāme pūja kuru kuru svāhā. [Make offering with perfume, flowers, incense, lamps, fruit, food, lower robe, smiles, music, dance, singing, and touch svāhā.]

Make a supplication:

Just as Vajradhara bestowed
Initiations, sources of good qualities,
On the Buddhas for the sake of protecting transmigrating beings,
So please also bestow such here.

Then:

The Conquerors in space – Fathers and Mothers – make the intention to confer initiation. The Bodhisattvas make expressions of auspiciousness. Rūpavajrā and so forth make offering, and a rain of flowers and so forth descend. Male and Female Wrathful Ones expel obstructors. The principal Father Deity and Mother Deity in the mandala that has been achieved, holding vajra and bell, [are about to] confer initiation.

The Vajra Worker raises up the vajra and bell. Auspiciousness is expressed with:

Through aṇ auspiciousness dwelling in the hearts of all the sentient,
The essence of all, the supreme lord of all lineages,
Progenitor of all the sentient, the great bliss,
May you have today auspiciousness at the supreme conferral of initiation.

Through the Buddha possessing perfection like a gold mountain,
Protector of the three worlds who has abandoned the three defilements,
With a face like the broad petals of a lotus,
May you have today the auspiciousness of pacification.

Through the highest supreme unwavering teaching set forth by him,
Renowned in the three worlds, worshipped by gods and humans,
Most excellent of doctrine, pacifying all beings,
May you have today the auspiciousness of pacification.

Through the excellent spiritual community, rich with the auspiciousness of having heard the doctrine,
Place of worship by humans, gods, and demi-gods,
Highest supreme of assemblies, knowing conscience, and the foundation of glory,
May you have today the auspiciousness of pacification.

When doing self-entry, a rain of flowers falls on oneself, and when initiation is conferred on a student, a rain of flowers falls on the student.

When I make the gesture of touching the vajra and bell to your five places, think that your right and left channels become serviceable such that these channels, rather than acting as unfavorable circumstances blocking entry of wind into the central channel, act as favorable circumstances for such. In dependence upon that, from henceforth the winds in the right and left channels are restrained in the sense of being gathered together in the central channel, where the winds remain and dissolve. Through that, the level of subsequent mindfulness, in which the great seal of empty form is actualized, and the level of immovable meditative stabilization are generated. Think that predispositions are being established for the gradual generation of these levels of the path and that a special non-conceptual meditative stabilization is engendered.

Then, the master, with right leg outstretched, says:

I will give the great vajra conferral of initiation,
Revered by those of the three realms,
Arisen from the source of the three
Secrecies of all the Buddhas.
Oṃ huṃ hoḥ sūrya-chandra-vishodhaka svāhā.
[Oṃ huṃ hoḥ thoroughly purifying sun and moon svāhā.]

Touch the vajra and bell to the five places [crown protrusion, both shoulders, upper arms, thighs, and hips], and having placed them to the top of the head, give them into the hands of the student who assumes the manner of embrace.

Next is a water initiation as an appendage to the vajra and bell initiation.

Then, the master, with right leg outstretched, says:

I will give the great vajra conferral of initiation,
Revered by those of the three realms,
Arisen from the source of the three
Secrecies of all the Buddhas.
Oṃ ā ī ṝ ū ḹ pañcha-dhātu-vishodhani svāhā.
[Oṃ ā ī ṝ ū ḹ be founded in the purification of the five constituents.]

With the water, touch the five places – crown protrusion, right and left shoulders, upper arms, thighs, and hips – and having sprinkled a little, [have the student] drink a little and also wash, conferring initiation.

That completes the appendage.

Through being conferred initiation in that way, your left and right channels become the principal Father Deity and Mother Deity. Light rays from them draw in the principal Father Deity and Mother

Deity of the mandala in the manner of a second butter lamp separating off from the first. The principal Father Deity and Mother Deity dissolve into your left and right channels clarified as the principal Father Deity and Mother Deity. Also, all the initiation deities are summoned and dissolve into your right and left channels clarified as the principal Father Deity and Mother Deity.

Make offering with:

Gandhaṃ puṣhpaṃ dhūpaṃ dīpaṃ akṣhate naividye lāsye hāsye vādye nṛtye gītye kāme pūja kuru kuru svāhā. [Make offering with perfume, flowers, incense, lamps, fruit, food, lower robe, smiles, music, dance, singing, and touch svāhā.]

Then, express the meaning of the initiation and its purification:

This corresponds to a child's laughing and talking. It cleanses defilements of the right and left channels. [337] It sets potencies for binding [the winds in] the right and left channels in the central channel and establishes seeds for exalted mind – the immutable great bliss – and exalted speech in all forms. It authorizes you to achieve feats of the principal Father Deity and Mother Deity and causes you to have the capacity to purify [internal] sun and moon[58] together and to attain the fourth ground.

MEANING OF THE INITIATION

Then, express the purification common to those two initiations:

Just as in the womb the winds and channels are formed, the two initiations in the area of the southern face of exalted speech cleanse defilements of the winds, the root of speech. They empower you with respect to the activities of vajra speech; they place seeds of vajra speech [in your continuum] and authorize you to achieve feats of vajra speech.

5 *Conduct Initiation*

The fifth and sixth initiations are means of purifying mind – the first two having purified body and the third and fourth having purified speech. The student proceeds to the eastern door so as to face the mind face of Kālachakra.

OFFERING AND SUPPLICATION

Again, circling to the right, the student is led to the eastern door. Facing the [black] exalted mind face of [Kālachakra], the student sits on the initiation seat. Mandala is offered to the lama, undifferentiable from the Vajra Mind of Kālachakra, as a present for giving the conduct initiation that cleanse defilements of the sense powers and objects.

Offer mandala.

To the lama, personal deity, and Three Jewels I offer in visualization
The body, speech, mind, and resources of myself and others,
Our collections of virtue in the past, present, and future,
And the wonderful precious mandala with the masses of Samantabhadra's offerings.
Accepting them through your compassion, please bless me into magnificence.

Idaṃ guru-ratna-maṇḍalakaṃ niryātayāmi. [I offer this jewelled mandala to the guru.]

Make supplication three times with:

Oṃ a ā e ai ar ār o au al āl aṃ aḥ sarva-bodhisatvāḥ sabhāryāḥ sarvadā-sarvakāma-upabhogaṃ vajra-prataṃ mama dadantu svāhā. [Oṃ a ā e ai ar ār o au al āl aṃ aḥ please may all the Bodhisattvas with their consorts bestow on me the vajra conduct of thoroughly enjoying all desires at all times svāhā.]

INTERNAL INITIATION

The students now generate themselves as Vajra Mind Deities according to the rite.

Clear away [obstructors] as before [with the six syllables, oṃ āḥ hūṃ hoḥ haṃ kṣhaḥ, and water from the conch].

Rays of light from huṃ at the heart of the lama who is not different from the principal deity draw you in; you enter his mouth, pass through the center of his body, and through the vajra path enter the Mother's lotus, melting into a drop that turns into emptiness. From within emptiness comes a hūṃ [which transforms into] a vajra, from which is generated a black Vajra Mind Deity, with three faces – black, red and white – and six hands, holding in the right hands a sword, curved knife, and trident and in the left hands a shield, skull, and white khaṭvaṅga; you are embraced by Lochanā.

Rays of light from the heart of the lama who is not different from the principal deity draw in Wisdom Beings like the meditated ones. Jaḥ hūṃ baṃ hoḥ hi. [Be summoned, enter, become fused with, be pleased, and become of the same taste.] They become of the same taste.

Light rays from the heart of the lama who is not different from the principal deity draw in all the

Conquerors of the ten directions – Fathers, Mothers Sons, and Daughters. Vajra-bhairava ākarṣhaya jaḥ. [Vajra Frightful One, summon, jaḥ.]

Make offering with:

Gandhaṃ puṣhpaṃ dhūpaṃ dīpaṃ akṣhate naividye lāsye hāsye vādye nṛtye gītye kāme pūja kuru kuru svāhā. [Make offering with perfume, flowers, incense, lamps, fruit, food, lower robe, smiles, music, dance, singing, and touch svāhā.]

Just as Vajradhara bestowed
Initiations, sources of good qualities,
On the Buddhas for the sake of protecting transmigrating beings,
So please also bestow such here.

Through making supplication in that way, all the Conquerors, Fathers and Mothers and so forth, become absorbed, are melted by the fire of great desire [i.e., by great bliss], and enter by way of the crown protrusion of the lama who is not different from the principal deity. Emerging from the vajra-pathway, the mind of enlightenment confers initiation on yourself made into a Vajra Mind Deity. You emerge from the Mothers's lotus and sit on the initiation seat.

CLEANSING, PURIFICATION AND DEIFICATION OF THE STUDENTS AND INITIATION SUBSTANCES

In the conduct initiation, the students' sense powers and their respective objects are blessed into magnificence such that they become serviceable. In the twelve links of the dependent-arising of cyclic existence, the coming together of sense power, object, and consciousness produces the mental factor of contact that distinguishes objects as attractive, unattractive, or neutral. Then, in dependence upon such, there are feelings of pleasure, pain, or neutrality. Then, in dependence upon that, desire, hatred, and obscuration increase.

All of these are engendered by way of the coming together of sense powers and objects; hence, here in this initiation the sense powers and their objects are blessed into magnificence such that only virtuous consciousnesses are produced and the continuum of conceptuality is cut. In place of the generation of non-virtuous consciousnesses and conceptuality, the coming together of sense power and object thereby serve as conditions for the generation of non-conceptuality. To accomplish this, in the initiation the sense powers and their objects are generated as deities.

Just as the sense powers are being restrained and their objects are being experienced within the confines of bliss and emptiness, so the external substance given in this initiation is a ring that acts as a restraint on the finger. There could be five rings for all five fingers, which are associated with earth, water, fire, wind, and space, but when done with a single ring, it is to be put on the thumb, which is identified as yellow since this color is associated with earth; the earth-constituent, in turn, is related with the five sense powers. The one ring, called a "thumb-vajra", is generated as a series of deities.

Concerning how the ring is generated as deities, listen to the description of the initiation rite.

> *Then, clear away* [*obstructors*] *from the student and from the thumb vajra* [*with the six syllables, oṃ āḥ hūṃ hoḥ haṃ kṣhaḥ, and water from the conch*] *and purify them. With:*
>
> Oṃ shūnyatā-jñāna-vajra-svabhāvātmako 'haṃ [I have the essential nature of indivisible emptiness and wisdom,] your sense powers and their objects[59] as well as the thumb vajra turn into emptiness.

In what follows, the sense powers are not teamed with their respective objects but with different objects. For instance, the objects of the ear sense power are sounds, but in the first pair the ear sense power is teamed with the phenomena-constituent, which refers to the special objects of the mental consciousness.

From within emptiness, your ear sense power and the objects – the phenomena-constituent – as well as the thumb vajra [appear as two sets of] a and ā [which transform into] vajras, from which are generated green Vajrapāṇi and Dharmadhātuvajrā, with three faces – green, red, and white – and six hands, holding in the right hands a vajra, curved knife, and axe and in the left hands a vajra-bell, skull and head of Brahmā. Respectively, they are embraced by Shabdavajrā and Samantabhadra.

Your nose sense power and the objects – tangible objects – as well as the thumb vajra, [appear as two sets of] e and ai [which transforms into] swords, from which are generated black Khagarbha and Sparshavajrā, with three faces – black, red, and white – and six hands, holding in the right hands a sword, curved knife, and trident and in the left hands a shield, skull, and white khaṭvaṇga. Respectively, they are embraced by Gandhavajrā and Sarvanivaraṇaviṣhkambhi. [338]

Your eye sense power and the objects – tastes – as well as the thumb vajra, [appear as two sets of] ar and ār [which transform into] jewels from which are generated red Kṣhitigarbha and Rasavajrā, with three faces – red, white, and black – and six hands holding in the right hands a triple arrow, vajra hook, and a resounding ḍamaru drum and in the left hands a bow, vajra noose, and nine-faceted jewel. Respectively, they are embraced by Rūpavajrā and Lokeshvara.

Your tongue sense power and the objects – visible forms – as well as the thumb vajra, [appear as two sets of] o and au [which transform into] lotuses, from which are generated white Lokeshvara and Rūpavajrā with three faces – white, black and red – and six hands holding in the right hands a mallet, spear, and trident and in the left hands a white lotus with a hundred petals, a mirror, and rosary.

Respectively, they are embraced by Rasavajrā and Kṣhitigarbha.

Your body sense power and the objects – odors – as well as the thumb vajra, [appear as two sets of] al and āl [which transform into] wheels, from which are generated yellow Sarvanivaraṇaviṣhkambhi and Gandhavajrā, with three faces – yellow, white, and black – and with six hands, holding in the right hands a wheel, staff, and frightful vajra and in the left hands a conch, vajra iron chain, and resounding bell. Respectively, they are embraced by Sparshavajrā and Khagarbha.

Your mental sense power and the objects – sounds – as well as the thumb vajra [appear as two sets of] aṃ and aḥ [which transform into] vajras, from which are generated blue Samantabhadra and Shabdavajrā, with three faces – blue, red, and white – and six hands, holding in the right hands a vajra, curved knife, and axe and in the left hands a vajra-bell, skull, and head of Brahmā. Respectively, they are embraced by Dharmadhātuvajrā and Vajrapāṇi.

At their foreheads is oṃ; at their throats āḥ; at their hearts hūṃ; and at their navels hoḥ. Light is emitted from the hūṃ at their hearts, which draws in Wisdom Beings like those meditated. Jaḥ hūṃ baṃ hoḥ hi. [Be summoned, enter, become fused with, be pleased, and become of the same taste.] They become of one taste with their respective Pledge Beings.

Oṃ ā ī ṝ ū ḹ pañcha-dhātu-vishodhani svāhā. [Oṃ ā ī ṝ ū ḹ be founded in the purification of the five constituents.] The Mothers confer initiation on the deities of the initiation substances. The black deities are seal-impressed by Amoghasiddhi; the red ones, with Ratnasambhava; the white ones, with Amitābha; the yellow ones with Vairochana; the green ones, with Vajrasattva; and the blue ones with Akṣhobhya.

TRANSFORMATION OF THE DEITIES BACK INTO THE INITIATION SUBSTANCE IN HEIGHTENED FORM

Make offering with:

Gandhaṃ pushpaṃ dhūpaṃ dīpaṃ akṣhate naividye lāsye hāsye vādye nṛtye gītye kāme pūja kuru kuru svāhā. [Make offering with perfume, flowers, incense, lamps, fruit, food, lower robes, smiles, music, dance, singing, and touch svāhā.]

The Father and Mother Deities become absorbed, whereby they are melted by the fire of great desire and turn into the thumb vajra, the substance of the initiation.

With respect to the meaning of the meditation, the thumb vajra melts and turns into two letters, from which two deities are generated; it is not that the thumb vajra becomes one deity, which melts and becomes another deity, etc. This should be understood also with respect to the bracelets later.

INITIATION OF THE STUDENTS THROUGH USING THE INITIATION SUBSTANCE

Light rays from the heart of the lama who is not different from the principal deity draw in the initiation deities – Father and Mother Conquerors, Sons, and Daughters – filling the expanse of space. Vajra-bhairava akarṣhaya jaḥ. [Vajra Frightful One, summon, jaḥ.]

Make offering with:

Gandhaṃ pushpaṃ dhūpaṃ dīpaṃ akṣhate naividye lāsye hāsye vādye nṛtye gītye kāme pūja kuru kuru svāhā. [Make offering with perfume, flowers, incense, lamps, fruit, food, lower robe, smiles, music, dance, singing, and touch svāhā.]

Make a supplication:

Just as Vajradhara bestowed

Initiations, sources of good qualities,
On the Buddhas for the sake of protecting transmigrating beings,
So please also bestow such here.

Then:

The Conquerors in space – Fathers and Mothers – make the intention to confer initiation. The Bodhisattvas make expressions of auspiciousness. Rūpavajrā and so forth make offering, and a rain of flowers and so forth descend. Male and Female Wrathful Ones expel obstructors. The male and female Bodhisattvas residing in the achieved mandala, holding thumb vajras, [are about to] confer initiation.

The Vajra Worker raises up the vajra and bell. Auspiciousness is expressed with:

Through an auspiciousness dwelling in the hearts of all the sentient,
The essence of all, the supreme lord of all lineages,
Progenitor of all the sentient, the great bliss,
May you have today auspiciousness at the supreme conferral of initiation.

Through the Buddha possessing perfection like a gold mountain,
Protector of the three worlds who has abandoned the three defilements,
With a face like the broad petal of a lotus,
May you have today the auspiciousness of pacification.

Through the highest supreme unwavering teaching set forth by him,
Renowned in the three worlds, worshipped by gods and humans,
Most excellent of doctrine, pacifying all beings,
May you have today the auspiciousness of pacification.

Through the excellent spiritual community, rich with the auspiciousness of having heard the doctrine,
Place of worship by humans, gods, and demi-gods,
Highest supreme of assemblies, knowing conscience, and the foundation of glory,
May you have today the auspiciousness of pacification.

When doing self-entry, a rain of flowers falls on oneself, and when initiation is conferred on a student, a rain of flowers falls on the student.

When I make the gesture of touching the ring that is the initiation substance to your five places, imagine that the male and female Bodhisattvas who reside in the mandala do this, bestowing the conduct initiation. Think that thereby your internal five sense powers and their respective objects are blessed into magnificence such that they become serviceable, inducing generation of special non-conceptual consciousness, engendering firm meditative stabilization in which the exalted wisdom realizing the emptiness of inherent existence and bliss are of a single undifferentiable entity.

Then, the master, with right leg outstretched, says:

I will give the great vajra conferral of initiation,
Revered by those of the three realms,
Arisen from the source of the three
Secrecies of all the Buddhas.

Oṃ a ā e ai ar ār o au al āl aṃ aḥ viṣhayendriya-vishodhani svāhā. [Oṃ a ā e ai ar ār o au al āl aṃ aḥ purification of the objects and sense powers svāhā.]

Having touched the five places [crown protrusion, both shoulders, upper arms, thighs, and hips], say:

This rests on the hands of all
Buddhas, Vajrasattvas.
You should always hold
The firm conduct of Vajrapāṇi. [339]

Give the thumb vajra. Put flowers on the ears and so forth.

From henceforth no matter what good or bad appearances occur to the sense powers, you should not come under the influence of conceptions of ordinariness but should view whatever appears as the sport of emptiness and as the sport of bliss and, within that perspective, make use of the visible forms, sounds, odors, tastes, and objects of touch of the Desire Realm.

For example, if you look at a green leaf before putting on yellow sun glasses, you see that it is green; then, even though after putting on the sun glasses, it appears to be yellow, right from its appearance as yellow this very appearance serves as a condition for your thinking that the yellowness of the leaf is due to the glasses, that the leaf is not yellow. Seeing the yellow leaf serves as a condition for the ascertainment that the leaf does not exist as it appears. In the same way, once you have developed good understanding in your mind that phenomena are dependent-arisings and thus are empty of inherent existence, then, upon the undeniable appearance of objects as if they inherently exist, that very appearance serves as a condition inducing ascertainment that except for appearing that way, those objects do not inherently exist. From the very appearance of objects as if they exist in their own right, ascertainment of the emptiness of their existing that way is found.

When encountering objects, instead of coming under the influence of their appearance as if they inherently exist, that very appearance serves to assist ascertainment that those objects do not inherently exist. Similarly, during meditative equipoise, the consciousness ascertaining the meaning of emptiness is a blissful one that has arisen upon the melting of internal essential constituents. When that blissful consciousness one-pointedly ascertains emptiness, subsequent to such meditative equipoise whatever appears dawns not only as the sport of emptiness but also as the sport of bliss due to the force of the earlier one-pointed, strong consideration of emptiness and bliss as undifferentiable during meditative equipoise.

When you are used to this practice, it is not necessary to withdraw the senses from their objects in order to control them. Rather, within letting the senses encounter their objects, you do not come under the influence of conceptuality. That is the essential meaning and purpose of the conduct initiation. This is vajra conduct – indivisible, unbreakable conduct; within making use of the attributes of the Desire Realm, one does not come under the influence of bad conceptuality which otherwise is ruinous. Thereby, the visible forms, sounds, odors, tastes, and objects of touch of the Desire Realm cannot overwhelm, pollute, or interrupt you; instead, you have control over them; hence, this is called vajra conduct – a vajra or diamond symbolizing indivisibility, unbreakability.

Next is a water initiation as an appendage to the vajra and bell initiation.

> *Then, the master, with right leg outstretched, says:*
>
> I will give the great vajra conferral of initiation,
> Revered by those of the three realms,
> Arisen from the source of the three
> Secrecies of all the Buddhas.
> Oṃ ā ī ṝ ū ḹ pañcha-dhātu-vishodhani svāhā. [Oṃ ā ī ṝ ū ḹ be founded in the purification of the five constituents.]
>
> *With the water touch the five places – crown protrusion, right and left shoulders, upper arms, thighs, and hips – and having sprinkled a little, [have the student] drink a little and also wash, conferring initiation.*

That completes the appendage.

> Through being conferred initiation in that way, the sense powers and objects in your continuum become the male and female Bodhisattvas. Light rays from them draw in the male and female Bodhisattvas of the mandala in the manner of a second butter lamp separating off from the first. The male and female Bodhisattvas dissolve into the sense

powers and objects in your own continuum clarified as the male and female Bodhisattvas. Also, all the initiation deities are summoned and dissolve into the sense powers and objects of your own continuum clarified as the male and female Bodhisattvas.

Make offering with:

Gandhaṃ puṣhpaṃ dhūpaṃ dīpaṃ akṣhate naividye lāsye hāsye vādye nṛtye gītye kāme pūja kuru kuru svāhā. [Make offering with perfume, flowers, incense, lamps, fruit, food, lower robe, smiles, music, dance, singing, and touch svāhā.]

MEANING OF THE INITIATION

Then, express the meaning of the initiation and its purification:

This corresponds to the child's enjoying the five attributes of the Desire Realm. It cleanses defilements of the sense powers and objects. It authorizes you to achieve feats of the male and female Bodhisattvas and empowers you to enjoy the five attributes of the Desire Realm by way of knowing their nature. It makes you into having the capacity to achieve vajra sense powers and sense fields *(skye mched, āyatana)* and attain the fifth ground as its fruit.

6 *Name Initiation*

To receive the sixth, the name initiation that purifies the action faculties as well as their activities, the students offer mandala and, after that, make a supplication.

OFFERING AND SUPPLICATION

Mandala is offered to the lama, undifferentiable from the Vajra Speech of Kālachakra, as a present for the name initiation that cleanses the action faculties as well as their activities.

Offer mandala.

To the lama, personal deity, and Three Jewels I offer in visualization
The body, speech, mind, and resources of myself and others,
Our collections of virtue in the past, present, and future,
And the wonderful precious mandala with the masses of Samantabhadra's offerings.
Accepting them through your compassion, please bless me into magnificence.
Idaṃ guru-ratna-maṇḍalakaṃ niryātayāmi. [I offer this jewelled mandala to the guru.]

Make supplication three times with:

Oṃ ha hā ya yā ra rā va vā la lā sarva-krodha-rājāḥ sabhāryā maitrī-karuṇā-mudita-upekṣhā-sarva-samatā-svabhāvaṃ vajra-pūrvaṃgamaṃ nāma me dadantu huṃ hūṃ phaṭ. [Oṃ ha hā ya yā ra rā va vā la lā may all the Kings of Wrathful Ones with their consorts bestow on me the name preceding the vajra which has the nature of entirely equal love, compassion, joy, and equanimity huṃ hūṃ phat.]

CLEANSING, PURIFICATION, AND DEIFICATION OF THE STUDENTS AND INITIATION SUBSTANCES

Next, the students' action faculties and their activities are to be generated as deities. In this, Method and Wisdom [Deities] are associated with the elements that oppose each other. The opponent of earth is fire; the opponent of fire is water, etc.

Clear away [obstructors from] the student and the bracelets [with the six syllables, oṃ āḥ hūṃ hoḥ haṃ kṣhaḥ, and water from the conch] and purify them. With:

Oṃ shūnyatā-jñāna-vajra-svabhāvātmako 'ham [I have the essential nature of indivisible emptiness and wisdom,] your action faculties and their activities[60] as well as the bracelets turn into emptiness.

In what follows, the action faculties are not teamed with their respective activities but with the activities of other faculties.

From within emptiness, your faculty of urination and the activity of emitting regenerative fluid as well as the bracelet that is the initiation substance [appear as two sets of] ha and hā [which transform into] vajras, from which are generated Uṣhṇīṣha-chakravartī and Raudrākṣhī, with three faces – green, red, and white – and six hands, holding in the three right hands a vajra, curved knife, and axe and in the left hands a vajra-bell, skull, and head of

Brahmā. Respectively, they are embraced by Atinīlā and Subharāja.

Your mouth faculty and the activity of discharging feces as well as the bracelet that is the initiation substance [appear as two sets of] ya and yā [which transform into] swords, from which are generated black Vighnāntaka [Atibala] and Atibalā, [340] with three faces – black, red, and white – and six hands, holding in the three right hands a sword, curved knife, and trident and in the three left hands a shield, skull, and white khaṭvaṅga. Respectively, they are embraced by Stambhakī and Yamāntaka.

Your arm faculty and the activity of going as well as the bracelet that is the initiation substance [appear as two sets of] ra and rā [which transform into] jewels, from which are generated red Prajñāntaka [Jambhaka] and Jambhakī, with three faces – red, white, and black – and six hands, holding in the three right hands a triple arrow, vajra hook, and resounding ḍāmaru drum and in the left hands a bow, vajra noose, and nine-faceted jewel. Respectively, they are embraced by white Mānakī and Padmāntaka.

Your leg faculty and the activity of taking as well as the bracelet that is the initiation substance [appear as two sets of] va and vā [which transform into] lotuses, from which are generated white Padmāntaka and Mānakī, with three faces – white, black, and red – and six hands, holding in the right hands a mallet, spear, and trident and in the three left hands a white lotus with a hundred petals, a mirror, and a rosary. Respectively, they are embraced by red Jambhakī and Prajñāntaka.

Your anus faculty and activity of speaking as well as the bracelet that is the initiation substance [appear as two sets of] la and lā [which transform into] wheels, from which are generated yellow Yamāntaka and Stambhakī, with three faces – yellow, white, and black – and six hands, holding in the three right hands a wheel, staff, and frightful vajra and in the three left hands a conch, vajra chain, and resounding bell. Respectively, they are embraced by black Atibalā and Vighnāntaka.

Your supreme faculty and the activity of emitting urine as well as the bracelet that is the initiation substance [appear as two sets of] haṃ and haḥ [which transform into] vajras, from which are generated blue Sumbharāja and Atinīlā with three faces – blue, red, and white – and six hands, holding in the right a vajra, curved knife, and axe and in the left a vajra and bell, skull, and a head of Brahmā. Respectively, they are embraced by green Raudrākṣhī and Uṣhṇīṣhachakravarti.

Here, the color, faces, and hands of all the male and female Wrathful Ones, Father and Mother Deities, are done in accordance with the six lineages; thus, they differ from other occasions.

At their foreheads is oṃ; at their throats āḥ; at their hearts hūṃ; and at their navels hoḥ. Light is emitted from the hūṃ at their hearts, which draws in Wisdom Beings like those meditated. Jaḥ huṃ baṃ hoḥ hi. [Be summoned, enter, become fused with, be pleased, and become of the same taste.] They become of one taste with their respective Pledge Beings.

Oṃ ā ī ṝ ū ḹ pañcha-dhātu-vishodhani svāhā. [Oṃ ā ī ṝ ū ḹ be founded in the purification of the five constituents.]

The Mothers confer initiation on the deities of the initiation substances. Respectively, they are seal-impressed with Vajrasattva, Amoghasiddhi, Ratnasambhava, Amitābha, Vairochana, and Akṣhobhya.

TRANSFORMATION OF THE DEITIES BACK INTO THE INITIATION SUBSTANCE IN HEIGHTENED FORM

Make offering with:

Gandhaṃ pushpaṃ dhūpaṃ dīpaṃ akṣhate naividye lāsye hāsye vādye nṛtye gītye kāme pūja kuru kuru svāhā. [Make offering with perfume, flowers, incense, lamps, fruit, food, lower robe, smiles, music, dance, singing, and touch svāhā.]

The male and female deities become absorbed; upon being melted by the fire of great desire, they become the bracelets that are the initiation substances. [341]

INITIATION OF THE STUDENTS THROUGH USING THE INITIATION SUBSTANCE

Light rays from the heart of the lama who is not different from the principal deity draw in the initiation deities – Father and Mother Conquerors, Sons, and Daughters – filling the expanse of space. Vajra-bhairava ākarṣhaya jaḥ. [Vajra Frightful One, summon, jaḥ.]

Make offering with:

Gandhaṃ pushpaṃ dhūpaṃ dīpaṃ akṣhate naividye lāsye hāsye vādye nṛtye gītye kāme pūja kuru kuru svāhā. [Make offering with perfume, flowers, incense, lamps, fruit, food, lower robe, smiles, music, dance, singing, and touch svāhā.]

Make a supplication:

Just as Vajradhara bestowed
Initiations, sources of good qualities,
On the Buddhas for the sake of protecting transmigrating beings,
So please also bestow such here.

Then:

The Conquerors in space – Fathers and Mothers – make the intention to confer initiation. The Bodhisattvas make expressions of auspiciousness. Rūpavajrā and so forth make offering, and a rain of flowers and so forth descend. Male and Female

Wrathful Ones expel obstructors. The Male and Female Wrathful deities in the mandala that has been achieved, holding the bracelets, [are about to] confer initiation.

The Vajra Worker raises up the bracelets. Auspiciousness is expressed with:

Through an auspiciousness dwelling in the hearts of all the sentient,
The essence of all, the supreme lord of all lineages,
Progenitor of all the sentient, the great bliss,
May you have today auspiciousness at the supreme conferral of initiation.

Through the Buddha possessing perfection like a gold mountain,
Protector of the three worlds who has abandoned the three defilements,
With a face like the broad petals of a lotus,
May you have today the auspiciousness of pacification.

Through the highest supreme unwavering teaching set forth by him,
Renowned in the three worlds, worshipped by gods and humans,
Most excellent of doctrine, pacifying all beings,
May you have today the auspiciousness of pacification.

Through the excellent spiritual community, rich with the auspiciousness of having heard the doctrine,
Place of worship by humans, gods, and demi-gods,
Highest supreme of assemblies, knowing conscience, and the foundation of glory,
May you have today the auspiciousness of pacification.

When doing self-entry, a rain of flowers falls on oneself, and when initiation is conferred on a student, a rain of flowers falls on the student.

The male and female Wrathful Deities of the mandala, holding the bracelets that are the substances of the initiation, give these to you. When they touch the bracelets to your five places, your action faculties as well as their activities are blessed into magnificence such that they become serviceable. Think that a special non-conceptual wisdom is thereby generated in your continuum.

Then, the master, with right leg outstretched, says:

I will give the great vajra conferral of initiation,
Revered by those of the three realms,
Arisen from the source of the three
Secrecies of all the Buddhas.

Oṃ ha hā ya yā ra rā va vā la lā chatur-brahma-vihāra-vishuddha svāhā. [Oṃ ha hā ya yā ra rā va vā la lā the thorough purity of the four abodes of purity svāhā.]

Touch bracelets of jewels or flowers etc. to the five places [crown protrusion, both shoulders, upper arms, thighs, and hips] and put them on the arms and legs.

The reason why this is called a name initiation is that when someone is called a teacher or engineer, for instance, the name is designated in dependence upon an activity, and this initiation is primarily concerned with purifying the action faculties and their respective activities, whereupon the students are designated or prophesied as achieving enlightenment.

Next is a water initiation as an appendage to the name initiation.

Then, the master, with right leg outstretched, says:

I will give the great vajra conferral of initiation,
Revered by those of the three realms,
Arisen from the source of the three
Secrecies of all the Buddhas.

Oṃ ā ī ṝ ū ḹ pañcha-dhātu-vishodhani svāhā. [Oṃ ā ī ṝ ū ḹ be founded in the purification of the five constituents.]

With the water touch the five places – crown protrusion, right and left shoulders, upper arms, thighs, and hips – and having sprinkled a little, [have the student] drink a little and also wash, conferring initiation.

That completes the appendage.

Now, with respect to designating you with a name, the lama puts on the outer religious robes in the manner of the guru Shākyamuni Buddha and rises. He holds a corner of the religious robe in the manner of a lion's ear, symbolizing fearlessness. He then designates the student with a name concordant with the lineage determined earlier through the dropping of the flower on the square board, prophesying that with such and such a name you will become a One Gone Thus with Truth and Form Bodies. When the lama speaks the name, imagine that a non-conceptual state is engendered in your mind, great bliss is generated, and a special exalted wisdom of undifferentiable bliss and emptiness in which the bliss consciousness ascertains the absence of inherent existence is generated in your continuum.

The lama assumes the mode of a One Gone Thus; with his left fist he holds [two] corners of his religious robe at his heart and forms the seal of bestowing non-fright with his right hand. Say:

I with [all] Vajrasattvas, Ones Gone Thus,
Prophesy here that you,
Having been relieved[61] from the bad transmigrations
Of cyclic existence, will thoroughly pacify cyclic existence.

You are prophesied as becoming a Buddha through actualizing Form Bodies that have the function of relieving transmigrators from bad rebirths in cyclic existence and actualizing a Truth Body that is an extinguishment of cyclic existence in the sphere of profound peace.

O Vajra (your Mantra name), tathāgata-siddhi-samayas tvaṃ bhūr bhuva[ḥ]svaḥ. [O, since you are able to realize the reality (of the three realms) below the ground, on the ground, and the heavens, you will be established as the One Gone Thus, Vajra (your mantra name).]

Use the name that accords with the lineage that the flower hit [when dropped onto the mandala].

Through being conferred initiation and prophesied in that way, your action faculties and activities become the Male and Female Wrathful Deities. Light rays from them draw in the male and female Wrathful Deities of the mandala in the manner of a second butter lamp separating off from the first. The male and female Wrathful Deities dissolve into your action faculties and their activities clarified as the male and female Wrathful Deities. Also, all the initiation deities are summoned and dissolve into your action faculties and their activities clarified as the male and female Wrathful Deities.

Make offering with:

Gandhaṃ puṣhpaṃ dhūpaṃ dīpaṃ akṣhate naividye lāsye hāsye vādye nṛtye gītye kāme pūja kuru kuru svāhā. [Make offering with perfume, flowers, incense, lamps, fruit, food, lower robe, smiles, music, dance, singing, and touch svāhā.]

MEANING OF THE INITIATION

Then, express the meaning of the initiation and its purification:

This corresponds to naming a child. It cleanses defilements of the action faculties and their activities. It authorizes you to achieve feats of the Male and Female Wrathful Deities. It makes you into having the capacity to overcome the four demons through the four immeasurables and to attain the sixth ground as its fruit.

Then, express the purification common to those two initiations:

Just as the action faculties and their activities are established in the womb, the two initiations in the area of the eastern face of exalted mind cleanse defilements of the mind that cause the senses to engage objects and the action faculties to engage in activities. They set potencies [in your continuum] for exalted vajra mind and authorize you to achieve feats of exalted vajra mind.

7 *Permission Initiation and Appendages*

This section has two parts: the actual permission initiation and its appendages. [342]

PERMISSION INITIATION

The permission initiation is concerned with authorizing the students to teach persons of the various lineages, such as the Vairochana lineage, in accordance with their respective interests and dispositions. For this, initially the students view the lama as undifferentiable from the Vajra Pristine Consciousness Deity, offer mandala, and make a supplication.

OFFERING AND SUPPLICATION

Again, circling to the right, the student is led to the western door. Facing the [yellow] pristine consciousness face [of Kālachakra], the student sits on the initiation seat. Mandala is offered to the lama, undifferentiable from the Vajra Pristine Consciousness of Kālachakra, as a present for giving the permission initiation that cleans pristine consciousness [i.e. bliss].

Offer mandala.

To the lama, personal deity, and Three Jewels I offer in visualization
The body, speech, mind, and resources of myself and others,
Our collections of virtue in the past, present, and future,
And the wonderful precious mandala with the masses of Samantabhadra's offerings.
Accepting them through your compassion, please bless me into magnificence.
Idaṃ guru-ratna-maṇḍalakaṃ niryātayāmi. [I offer this jewelled mandala to the guru.]

Make supplication three times with:

Oṃ evaṃ padma-vajra-chīhnau prajñopāyau maṇḍala-adhipati-vajra-sukha-jñānāṃgaṃ mama dadatāṃ haṃ haḥ hūṃ phaṭ. [Oṃ evaṃ please may wisdom and method symbolized by lotus and vajra be bestowed on me as the branch of exalted wisdom of vajra bliss of a lord of the mandala haṃ haḥ hūṃ phat.]

INTERNAL INITIATION

Then, an internal initiation is conferred during which the students are generated as Vajra Pristine Consciousness Deities.

Clear away [obstructors from the students with the six syllables, oṃ āḥ hūṃ hoḥ haṃ kṣhaḥ, and water from the conch].

Rays of light from huṃ at the heart of the lama who is not different from the principal deity draw you in; you enter his mouth, pass through the center of his body, and through the vajra path enter the Mother's lotus and melt into a drop, which turns into emptiness. From within emptiness comes a ho [which transforms into] a wheel, from which is generated a yellow Vajra Pristine Consciousness

Deity, with three faces – yellow, white and black – and six hands, holding in the right hands a wheel, staff and frightful vajra and in the left a conch, vajra chain, and resounding bell; he is embraced by Tārā.

Rays of light from the heart of the lama who is not different from the principal deity draw in Wisdom Beings like the meditated ones. Jaḥ hūṃ baṃ hoḥ hi. [Be summoned, enter, become fused with, be pleased, and become of the same taste.] They become of the same taste.

Light rays from the heart of the lama who is not different from the principal deity draw in all the Conquerors of the ten directions – Fathers, Mothers, Sons, and Daughters. Vajra-bhairava ākarṣhaya jaḥ [Vajra Frightful One, summon, jaḥ.]

Make offering with:

Gandhaṃ puṣhpaṃ dhūpaṃ dīpaṃ akṣhate naividye lāsye hāsye vādye nṛtye gītye kāme pūja kuru kuru svāhā. [Make offering with perfume, flowers, incense, lamps, fruit, food, lower robe, smiles, music, dance, singing, and touch svāhā.]

Just as Vajradhara bestowed
Initiations, sources of good qualities,
On the Buddhas for the sake of protecting transmigrating beings,
So please also bestow such here.

Through making supplication in that way, all the Conquerors, Fathers and Mothers, and so forth, become absorbed, are melted by the fire of great desire [i.e., by great bliss], and enter by way of the crown protrusion the lama who is not different from the principal deity. Emerging from the vajra pathway, the mind of enlightenment confers initiation on yourself made into a Vajra Pristine Consciousness Deity. You emerge from the Mother's lotus and sit on the initiation seat.

CLEANSING, PURIFICATION, AND DEIFICATION OF THE STUDENTS AND INITIATION SUBSTANCES

The external substances of the initiation are hand-symbols [vajra, sword, jewel, lotus, and wheel], and the internal factor is the student's aggregate of pristine consciousness. From among the thirty-six categories of the mental and physical aggregates and the constituents, the generation of thirty-four as deities has been accomplished. The permission initiation is a means of purifying the aggregate and constituent of pristine consciousness.

"Pristine consciousness" here is related with the drop of the fourth state and thus refers to the factor generating bliss and non-conceptuality. This factor of pristine consciousness as well as the hand-symbols are now generated as the deities, Vajrasattva and Prajñāpāramitā.

> *Then, clear away* [*obstructors*] *from the student and the hand symbols* [*with the six syllables, oṃ āḥ hūṃ hoḥ haṃ kṣhaḥ, and water from the conch*] *and purify them. With:*
>
> Oṃ shūnyatā-jñāna-vajra-svabhāvātmako 'haṃ. [I have the essential nature of indivisible emptiness and wisdom], your aggregate of pristine consciousness and consciousness constituent[62] as well as the hand symbols turn into emptiness. From within emptiness, your aggregate of pristine consciousness [i.e., bliss], your consciousness constituent, and the hand-symbols that are the initiation substances [appear as two sets of] haṃ and kṣhaḥ [which transform into] vajras, from which are generated blue Vajrasattva and Prajñāpāramitā, with three faces – blue, red, and white – and six hands, holding in the three right hands a vajra, curved knife, and axe and in the three left hands a vajra-bell, skull, and head of Brahmā. Respectively, they are embraced by Dharmadhātvīshvarī and Akṣhobhya.
>
> At their foreheads is oṃ; at their throats āḥ; at their hearts hūṃ; and at their navels hoḥ. Light is

emitted from the hūṃ at their hearts, which draws in Wisdom Beings like those meditated. Jaḥ hūṃ baṃ hoḥ hi. [Be summoned, enter, become fused with, be pleased, and become of the same taste.] They become of one taste with their respective Pledge Beings.

Oṃ ā ī ṛ ū ḹ pañcha-dhātu-vishodhani svāhā. [Oṃ ā ī ṛ ū ḹ be founded in the purification of the five constituents.]

The Mothers confer initiation on the deities of the initiation substances. They are seal-impressed by Akṣhobhya.

TRANSFORMATION OF THE DEITIES BACK INTO THE INITIATION SUBSTANCE IN HEIGHTENED FORM

Make offering [to those deities] with:

Gandhaṃ puṣhpaṃ dhūpaṃ dīpaṃ akṣhate naividye lāsye hāsye vādye nṛtye gītye kāme pūja kuru kuru svāhā. [Make offering with perfume, flowers, incense, lamps, fruit, food, lower robe, smiles, music, dance, singing, and touch svāhā.]

The Father and Mother Deities become absorbed, whereby they are melted by the fire of great desire and turn into the hand symbols that are the substances of initiation.

INITIATION OF THE STUDENTS THROUGH USING THE INITIATION SUBSTANCE

Light rays from the heart of the lama who is not different from the principal deity draw in the initiation deities – Father and Mother Conquerors, Sons, and Daughters – filling the expanse of space. Vajra-bhairava ākarṣhaya jaḥ. [Vajra Frightful One, summon, jaḥ.]

Make offering with:

Gandhaṃ puṣhpaṃ dhūpaṃ dīpaṃ akṣhate

naividye lāsye hāsye vādye nṛtye gītye kāme pūja kuru kuru svāhā. [Make offering with perfume, flowers, incense, lamps, fruit, food, lower robe, smiles, music, dance, singing, and touch svāhā.]

Make a supplication:

Just as Vajradhara bestowed
Initiations, sources of good qualities,
On the Buddhas for the sake of protecting transmigrating beings,
So please also bestow such here.

Then:

The Conquerors in space – Fathers and Mothers – make the intention to confer initiation. The Bodhisattvas make expressions of auspiciousness. Rūpavajrā and so forth make offering, and a rain of flowers and so forth descend. Male and Female Wrathful Ones expel obstructors. Vajrasattva and Prajñāpāramitā residing inside the mandala, [are about to] confer initiation while holding the hand symbols.

The Vajra Worker raises up the hand symbols. Auspiciousness is expressed with:

Through an auspiciousness dwelling in the hearts of all the sentient,
The essence of all, the supreme lord of all lineages,
Progenitor of all the sentient, the great bliss,
May you have today auspiciousness at the supreme conferral of initiation.

Through the Buddha possessing perfection like a gold mountain,
Protector of the three worlds who has abandoned the three defilements,
With a face like the broad petals of a lotus,
May you have today the auspiciousness of pacification.

Through the highest supreme unwavering teaching set forth by him,
Renowned in the three worlds, worshipped by gods and humans,
Most excellent of doctrine, pacifying all beings,
May you have today the auspiciousness of pacification.

Through the excellent spiritual community, rich with the auspiciousness of having heard the doctrine,
Place of worship by humans, gods, and demi-gods,
Highest supreme of assemblies, knowing conscience, and the foundation of glory,
May you have today the auspiciousness of pacification.

When doing self-entry, a rain of flowers falls on oneself, and when initiation is conferred on a student, a rain of flowers falls on the student.

Through touching the student's five places with the five hand-symbols together, a permission initiation of the five lineages in general is conferred. Imagine that Vajrasattva and Prajñāpāramitā who reside in the mandala, holding the five hand symbols, touch your five places, whereupon the exalted wisdom of great bliss is generated in your continuum. That is how the initiation is conferred.

In order to help all sentient beings
In all worlds in all ways,
Turn the doctrine-wheel
In accordance with how various beings are tamed.

Since all sentient beings are to be helped and those beings are of various lineages, interests, and dispositions, you should teach doctrine in accordance with their lineage, that is, in accordance with their interests and dispositions. Whatever is suitable for taming those particular lineages – the vajra, sword, lotus, jewel, and wheel lineages – should be taught.

Oṃ haṃ kṣhaḥ dharma-chakra-pravartaka svāhā. [Oṃ haṃ kṣhaḥ turner of the wheel of doctrine svāhā.]

Confer it touching the five places [*crown protrusion, both shoulders, upper arms, thighs, and hips*] *with all five hand symbols together.*

In order to help all sentient beings
In all worlds in all ways,
Turn the vajra-wheel
In accordance with how various beings are tamed.
Oṃ haṃ kṣhaḥ vajra-chakra-pravartaka svāhā.
[Oṃ haṃ kṣhaḥ turner of the vajra-wheel svāhā.]

In order to help all sentient beings
In all worlds in all ways,
Turn the sword-wheel
In accordance with how various beings are tamed.
Oṃ haṃ kṣhaḥ khaḍga-chakra-pravartaka svāhā.
[Oṃ haṃ kṣhaḥ turner of the sword-wheel svāhā.]

In order to help all sentient beings
In all worlds in all ways,
Turn the jewel-wheel
In accordance with how various beings are tamed.
Oṃ haṃ kṣhaḥ ratna-chakra-pravartaka svāhā.
[Oṃ haṃ kṣhaḥ turner of the jewel-wheel svāhā.]

In order to help all sentient beings
In all worlds in all ways,
Turn the lotus-wheel
In accordance with how various beings are tamed.
Oṃ haṃ kṣhaḥ padma-chakra-pravartaka svāhā.
[Oṃ haṃ kṣhaḥ turner of the lotus-wheel svāhā.]

In order to help all sentient beings
In all worlds in all ways,
Turn the wheel-wheel
In accordance with how various beings are tamed.
Oṃ haṃ kṣhaḥ chakra-chakra-pravartaka svāhā.
[Oṃ haṃ kṣhaḥ turner of the wheel-wheel svāhā.]
[343]

Give into the hands of the students the five hand symbols, vajra and so forth [*one by one*].

Students are of various lineages – some being of the Akṣhobhya lineage, some of Vairochana, some of Ratnasambhava, and so forth; thus, you should teach doctrine to the trainees of the various lineages in accordance with their dispositions.

Next is a water initiation as an appendage to the permission initiation.

Then, the master, with right leg outstretched, says:

I will give the great vajra conferral of initiation,
Revered by those of the three realms,
Arisen from the source of the three
Secrecies of all the Buddhas.
Oṃ ā ī ṝ ū ḹ pañcha-dhātu-vishodhani svāhā. [Oṃ ā ī ṝ ū ḹ be founded in the purification of the five constituents.]

With the water touch the five places – crown protrusion, right and left shoulders, upper arms, thighs, and hips – and having sprinkled a little, [*have the student*] *drink a little and also wash, conferring initiation.*

That completes the appendage.

Through being conferred initiation in that way, your aggregate of pristine consciousness [i.e., bliss] and consciousness constituent become Vajrasattva, Father and Mother. Light rays from them draw in Vajrasattva, male and female, of the mandala in the manner of a second butter lamp separating off from the first. Vajrasattva, male and female, dissolve into your aggregate of pristine consciousness and consciousness constituent clarified as Vajrasattva, male and female. Also, all the initiation deities are summoned and dissolve into your aggregate of pristine consciousness and consciousness constituent.

Make offering with:

Gandhaṃ pushpaṃ dhūpaṃ dīpaṃ akṣhate naividye lāsye hāsye vādye nṛtye gītye kāme pūja kuru kuru svāhā. [Make offering with perfume, flowers, incense, lamps, fruit, food, lower robe, smiles, music, dance, singing, and touch svāhā.]

So that the student is moved to bring about the welfare of other beings, a wheel that symbolizes this is given.

Then:

From bhrūṃ arises a wheel.
Oṃ vajra-hetu maṃ. [Oṃ vajra cause maṃ.]

Give it in front or on the seat.

How is the welfare of others to be accomplished? It is mainly through explaining the doctrine. Therefore, you are to bring about others' welfare through proclaiming the sound of the conch of doctrine.

From the final vowel aḥ arises a conch.
Oṃ vajra-bhāṣha raṃ. [Oṃ vajra speech raṃ.]

Give it into the right hand.

What doctrine is to be taught? For the time being you should teach whatever doctrine is appropriate to the interests and dispositions of sentient beings, leading them finally to the path of the *Kālachakra Tantra*.

From the first vowel a arises a book [of the *Kālachakra Tantra*].
A.

From this time today of generating an intention [to turn the wheel of doctrine],
Having been completely and in all ways filled
From the unsurpassed conch of doctrine,
Turn the wheel of doctrine.[63]

Give it in the middle of the two hands.

Also, when teaching doctrine, you should, in all respects, keep knowledge of the emptiness of inherent existence in mind and within that knowledge view everything as like a magician's illusions. Within such knowledge of the mode of subsistence of phenomena and motivated by single-pointed altruism, you should bring about the welfare of sentient beings.

> From the final vowel aḥ arises a bell.
> Aḥ.
>
> *Give it into the left hand and have* [*the student*] *ring it.*

Repeat the following stanzas after me, and at the end of the last line ring the bell. The meaning of the stanzas is: "All phenomena have the nature of space." What is the character of space? "Space" is designated from the viewpoint of a mere negation of obstructive contact. Similarly, all phenomena are empty of inherent existence, and just as space is designated only from the viewpoint of an elimination of obstructive contact and is not designated by way of any positive phenomena, so the final nature of all phenomena is a mere elimination of inherent existence and is merely nominally established. "Through joining your awareness in equality with this nature of phenomena that is like space, the supreme nature of phenomena – their reality – is made clear in all respects." For when the emptiness of inherent existence of one phenomenon is seen, one can, in dependence on just that realization, also understand the emptiness of all other phenomena. Therefore, you should teach doctrine that is derived from the meaning of the emptiness of inherent existence of all phenomena.

> All have the nature of space.
> Space also has no nature [of inherent existence].
> Through the yoga of equality with space,
> The supreṃe of all is clear in equality.
>
> From this time today of generating an intention [to
> turn the wheel of doctrine],
> Having been completely and in all ways filled

From the unsurpassed conch of doctrine,
Turn the wheel of doctrine.

In order to help all sentient beings
In all worlds in all ways,
Turn the wheel of doctrine
In accordance with how various beings are tamed.

Now bring about the welfare of sentient beings
Through [the doctrine] having the essential nature
 of wisdom and method,
High like a wish-granting jewel,
Without discouragement and free from qualms.

In such a way you should bring about the welfare of sentient beings, not allowing method (altruistic motivation) and wisdom to become separated.

Now you declare that you will do just as instructed.

The student, having made homage to the lama, says:

As the Sovereign says, I will do.

APPENDAGES

The section on the appendages to the permission initiation is in two parts: (1) the four branches appended – giving mantra, and so forth – and (2) giving the master's initiation, the main appendage.

THE FOUR BRANCHES APPENDED – GIVING MANTRA, EYE MEDICINE, MIRROR, AND BOW AND ARROW

GIVING MANTRA

The lama petitions:

O Supramundane Victors, I will bestow it.
Please take heed of this. [344]

To receive these blessings into magnificence the students make a supplication.

The student says:

> Supramundane Victor, I will assume it.
> Please take heed of me.

The first appendage is the giving of the mantras of Kālachakra. Activities of pacification and so forth are achieved in dependence upon mantras of provisional meaning during the stage of generation whereas during the stage of completion the supreme feat and common feats are achieved in dependence upon the mantra of definitive meaning – the exalted wisdom of undifferentiable bliss and emptiness. For the success of such practice of mantra, special potency needs to be developed by way of the view realizing emptiness. Hence, in order to establish predispositions for the initial realization of emptiness through the route of conceptual meaning-generalities on the path of accumulation and the path of preparation, eye medicine is given after the giving of mantra. Then, in order to establish predispositions for perceiving all phenomena as like illusions after rising from such meditative equipoise on emptiness, a mirror is given. Then, in order to establish predispositions for directly perceiving emptiness after practicing a union of such meditative equipoise and subsequent attainment, bow and arrow are given. After that, the actual vajra master initiation is conferred.

During the first part, you repeat the mantras upon the lama's saying them. First, instantaneously visualize yourselves as Kālachakras. With the initial repetition of the mantra, a series of mantra letters at the heart of the lama, who is visualized as Kālachakra, emerges from his mouth and enters into your mouth and is set at your heart. With the second repetition it becomes undifferentiable from the mantra series at your heart, and with the third repetition becomes firm, such that you thereby receive all the magnificent blessings of the mantra.

Then:

> From the heart of the lama who is not different from the principal deity a series of mantra emerges, comes out of his mouth, enters your mouth, and remains at your heart surrounding the syllable hūṃ.

Repeat after the lama three times the essence, condensed essence, and root mantras:

> Oṃ āḥ hūṃ hoḥ haṃkṣhaḥmalavaraya hūṃ phaṭ.

The second mantra is the condensed essence mantra.

> Oṃ hrāṃ hṝṃ hrāṃ hṝṃ hruṃ hṛḷ hraḥ svāhā.

The third is the mantra of exalted vajra body.

> Oṃ shrī-kālachakra huṃ hūṃ phaṭ.

> That is the permission for mantra for the sake of eliminating obstructors, achieving feats of pacification and so forth, and purifying the field of feats through the ultimate mantra.

GIVING EYE MEDICINE

The purpose of giving eye medicine is to establish predispositions for engendering special realization of the emptiness of inherent existence, this realization being through the medium of a meaning-generality [i.e., a conceptual image] on the paths of accumulation and preparation. The students imagine that on each of their eyes is the black syllable *praṃ;* these are considered to contain all of the student's ill-deeds and obstructions and, in particular, factors preventing perception of reality. When I make the gesture of opening your eyes with the eye-spoon, imagine that the syllables are suddenly removed.

> *Then, with a gold spoon take eye medicine of butter and honey from a gold or silver vessel and then apply it to the eyes. Think that:*

> On each of your two eyes is a black praṃ.

> *Think that they are removed with the point of the spoon and that your eyes are opened with the golden eye-spoon.*

> Oṃ vajra-naitra-apahara-paṭalaṃ hrīḥ. [Oṃ remove the covering obstructing the vajra eye hrīḥ.]

Just as a king of eye doctors
Removes cataracts in the world,
So, Child, will the Conquerors remove
Your[64] dimness of unknowingness.
Oṃ divya-nayana-mudghātayāmi svāhā, [Oṃ I am opening the divine eye svāhā.]

Freed from the dimness of ignorance, the eye of exalted wisdom has been opened.

GIVING A MIRROR

After perceiving the emptiness of inherent existence during meditative equipoise through the medium of a meaning-generality, during the period subsequent to meditative equipoise all phenomena can be perceived as like illusions or as like reflections in a mirror in that, although they appear to be inherently existent, they are empty of inherent existence. To establish predispositions so that you can actualize such realization, a mirror is given.

Think that:

From āḥ a mirror arises.

Then, show it.

Phenomena are like reflections,
Luminous and clear, without befoulment,
Unapprehendable, and inexpressible,
Arisen from causes and actions *(las, karma).*

Just as those are like a mirror
Luminous, clear, and unsullied,
So I, Kālachakra, the essence of all Buddhas,
Will remain in your heart, O child.

Knowing phenomena in that way
As without inherent existence and without a base,
Bring about the unparalleled welfare of sentient beings. [345]
You are born as a child of the Protectors.

> Know that in general all phenomena are like reflections in a mirror and in particular that the Kālachakra residing in your heart is like a reflection in a mirror.

You should understand that Kālachakra's blessing as well as the very subtle wind and the very subtle mind of clear light – into which the blessings enter and which is the creator of all appearing and occurring phenomena – are without inherent existence like reflections in a mirror.

GIVING BOW AND ARROW

Next a bow and arrow are given. Just as an arrow pierces its target deeply, so when you continually become accustomed to perceiving the emptiness of inherent existence through the medium of a conceptual image, finally all pollutions of dualistic appearance are extinguished such that your consciousness realizing emptiness and emptiness itself are like water put in water – subject and object having become one undifferentiable entity. Yogic direct perception realizing suchness is thereby achieved. Thus, bow and arrow are given as a means of ripening your continuum so that such realization will be generated speedily.

> [*Think that*]:
>
> From hoḥ are generated bow and arrow. Hoḥ.
>
> Oṃ sarva-tathāgatān anurāgayasva. [Oṃ make all the Ones Gone Thus pleased.]
>
> *Saying that, give them to the student.*

As I make the gesture of shooting arrows in the four directions as well as above and below, repeat this mantra after me:

> Oṃ sarva-tathāgatān anurāgayāmi. [Oṃ I make all the Ones Gone Thus pleased.]
>
> *With the thought that the factors of obstruction are being pierced, show the manner of shooting arrows in the four directions as well as above and below.*

GIVING THE MASTER'S INITIATION, THE MAIN APPENDAGE

This section has two parts: the actual master's initiation and indicating the phenomena of purification.

ACTUAL MASTER'S INITIATION

The main appendage is the master's initiation in which the three pledges of vajra, bell, and seal are given, these being pledges of exalted mind, speech, and body. The apprehension aspect[65] of the exalted wisdom of non-dual bliss and emptiness appears in the form of a deity; this itself is the master's initiation at this point in the Kālachakra system. First, the students and vajra and bell are generated as deities.

Clear away [obstructors] from the student and vajra and bell [with the six syllables, oṃ āḥ hūṃ hoḥ haṃ kṣhaḥ, and water from the conch] and purify them. With:

Oṃ shūnyatā-jñāna-vajra-svabhāvātmako 'haṃ [I have the essential nature of indivisible emptiness and wisdom,] you and vajra and bell turn into emptiness. From within emptiness, yourself and the vajra [appear as two] hūṃ [which transform into] vajras, from which are generated [two] Vajrasattvas. The bell [appears as] āḥ [which transforms into] a curved knife, from which is generated Prajñāpāramitā. All three have blue bodies, with three faces – blue, red, and white – and six hands, holding in the three right hands a vajra, curved knife, and axe and in the three left hands a vajra-bell, skull, and head of Brahmā. At their foreheads is oṃ; at the neck āḥ; at their heart hūṃ; and at their navels hoḥ. Light emitted from the hūṃ at their hearts draws in the Wisdom Beings like the meditated ones.

Jaḥ hūṃ baṃ hoḥ hi. [Be summoned, enter,

become fused with, be pleased, and become of the same taste.]

They become of one taste with their respective Pledge Beings.

Oṃ ā ī ṛ ū ḷ pañcha-dhātu-vishodhani svāhā. [Oṃ ā ī ṛ ū ḷ be founded in the purification of the five constituents.]

The Mothers confer initiation on the deities of the initiation substances with the fluid of ambrosia. They are seal impressed by Akṣhobhya. They melt and turn into vajra and bell.

The beginningless and endless heroic mind
Is the greatly joyous Vajrasattva,
The all-good, the essence of all,
The essence that is lord of Vajra Dignity,
Supramundane Victor, glorious supreme primordial being.

The fundamental innate mind of clear light has no beginning or end; when it is generated as an entity of immutable bliss, it is called the "greatly joyous Vajrasattva". Since it is virtuous in the beginning, middle, and end, it is "all-good". As a symbol of the undifferentiability of entity of method and wisdom, Vajrasattva is depicted as in union with the goddess Vajra Dignity.

Oṃ mahā-vajra hūṃ. [Oṃ great vajra hūṃ.] [346]

The non-dualistic exalted wisdom, the Conqueror's mind undifferentiable from emptiness, is the secret vajra. For the sake of remembering this, maintain holding the vajra by way of the vajra principle.

Saying that, give it into the student's right hand.

The vajra symbolizes the exalted wisdom of great bliss; this is the definitive vajra. Since you must always utilize the exalted wisdom of great bliss, you should hold a vajra symbolizing it.

The bell symbolizes the wisdom realizing the emptiness of

inherent existence. Now, the exalted wisdom of great bliss, symbolized by the vajra, and the wisdom realizing emptiness, symbolized by the bell, are to be generated as one entity of establishment and abiding.

> This [bell] and that [symbolized by it] are explained
> as concordant
> With the tone of the wisdom of all Buddhas.
> You also should always hold it.
> The Conquerors assert this as supreme enlightenment.

"This" refers to the symbol, the bell; "that" refers to the symbolized, the definitive bell – the wisdom realizing emptiness, the main object of expression by the exalted qualities of speech of all the Buddhas who, by proclaiming the sound of the emptiness of inherent existence, overcome what is unfavorable and needs to be abandoned in the continuum of trainees. You should hold such a bell.

> Thinking that the bell proclaims the sound of the absence of inherent existence of all phenomena, maintain the ringing of the bell by way of the principle of the bell.
>
> *Give it into the left hand.*

Imagine that, while you repeat this stanza, the sound of the bell proclaims the meaning of the emptiness of inherent existence.

> *Ringing the bell, say:*
>
> Cyclic existence is naturally pure.
> Through this reality, one separates from cyclic existence.
> Through possessing a mind of [such] natural purity
> Excellent existence will be made.

Cyclic existence is naturally pure, due to which it is possible to release oneself from cyclic existence. Through possessing such a naturally pure mind the excellent existence of Buddhahood can be attained.

Say that, and ring the bell.

The student actually or imitatingly generates the exalted wisdom of undifferentiable bliss and emptiness, which are symbolized by vajra and bell. Thereupon, one-pointed belief that the apprehension factor of that exalted wisdom consciousness itself appears as the body of Vajrasattva is the actual vajra master initiation at this point in the *Kālachakra Tantra.* Observing this great seal divine body of Vajrasattva, which is an appearance of the apprehension aspect of the exalted wisdom of undifferentiable bliss and emptiness symbolized by vajra and bell – an innate body of undifferentiable method and wisdom – think that the entity of the vajra master initiation has been generated in your continuum.

Think:

I have become clarified as the great seal divine body, which is the appearance of the apprehension aspect of the exalted wisdom of undifferentiable bliss and emptiness as the exalted body of Vajrasattva.

Mindful of the principles of the vajra and bell, hold these crossed at the heart.

Cause the meaning of great bliss and the meaning of emptiness to appear to your mind, and thinking that just this exalted wisdom realizing emptiness appears as the divine body of Vajrasattva, observe the divine body one-pointedly.

Next, there is a water initiation as an appendage to the master's initiation.

Then, the master, with right leg outstretched, says:

I will give the great vajra conferral of initiation,
Revered by those of the three realms,
Arisen from the source of the three
Secrecies of all the Buddhas.
Oṃ ā ī ṛ ū ḷ pañcha-dhātu-vishodhani svāhā. [Oṃ ā ī ṛ ū ḷ be founded in the purification of the five constituents.]

With the water touch the five places – crown protrusion, right and left shoulders, upper arms, thighs, and hips – and having sprinkled a little, [have the student] drink a little and also wash, conferring initiation.

You are seal-impressed by Akṣhobhya.

Make offering with:

Gandhaṃ puṣhpaṃ dhūpaṃ dīpaṃ akṣhate naividye lāsye hāsye vādye nṛtye gītye kāme pūja kuru kuru svāhā. [Make offering with perfume, flowers, incense, lamps, fruit, food, lower robe, smiles, music, dance, singing, and touch svāhā.]

Concerning this, the main appendage mentioned in the [Kālachakra] Tantra where it says,[66] *"The Lord of Conquerors thoroughly bestows the permission [initiation] as well as the appendages," is the master initiation. Furthermore, the tantra says,*[67] *"Upon having thoroughly bestowed vajra and bell, the doctrine of purification is to be indicated with thoroughly supreme compassion." Through its explicit mention of bestowing the pledges of vajra and bell, it is implicitly understood that it is also necessary to bestow the seal pledge. About how to do this, others [assert that this is to be done] in accordance with [the mode of procedure of the Guhyasamāja Tantra and so forth, which is described in this way]:*

Completely embrace with [your] arms
A Wisdom [Woman] aged sixteen,
Together with vajra and bell.
This is asserted as the master initiation.

They say that upon the students meditating [on themselves] in the aspect of Vajrasattva – Father and Mother – in embrace, the principle of a Seal is to be taught by way of the words: "Having blessed the Wisdom Seal [i.e., imagined consort] into magnificence..." [Their assertion, however,] is not feasible [347] *since in that case one would [absurdly] have to take it that just the exalted wisdom of bliss generated in dependence upon having meditated on embracing an Exalted Wisdom Seal [i.e., a consort] and so forth is the master initiation on this occasion [in the Kālachakra Tantra] and in that case it would not differ from the vase initiation in the conferral of the higher initiations in dependence upon a Wisdom Seal. Therefore, while such is not mentioned in the [Kālachakra] Tantra, they hold it to be the case through faults of their own mind, and although such a master initiation [as described in the Kālachakra Tantra] is attained, since it is said that this just allows one to be a master authorized to explain, etc., Yoga Tantra and below, [they would absurdly have to hold] that although one attained the master initiation indicated [in the system of Guhyasamāja and so forth] through that stanza, one would not be fit as a master authorized to explain, etc., Highest Yoga Tantra. Thereby they would, with great striving, be taking upon themselves the very heavy karmic obstruction of abandoning the doctrine, [holding that] "There is no fully qualified vajra master initiation in other classes of initiations, such as those of Guhyasamaja, Hevajra, and Chakrasaṃvara." Therefore, here [in the Kālachakra Tantra the term] "seal pledge" refers not to a seal that is a Knowledge Woman [a consort] but to the divine body great seal [i.e., imagination of oneself in divine form]. Nevertheless, it differs from the mode of teaching the divine body great seal in Yoga Tantra; this can be understood from what has been explained earlier, and I have explained this extensively elsewhere.*

INDICATING THE PHENOMENA OF PURIFICATION

Those of the vajra lineage definitely should take life; those of the sword [should speak] untrue words.

Those of the jewel should steal others' wealth; those of the lotus lineage should steal others' mates.
Those of the wheel should make use of intoxicants, the Buddha lamps [the five fleshes and the five ambrosias], and all good objects.
Those of the curved knife should not deride the sky-lotus of any woman, those of low type and so forth.
You should give this body as well as wealth for the sake of sentient beings; you should not [selfishly] keep it.
O Child of good lineage, the Conqueror says that [through this] you will become a Buddha and otherwise will not even over limitless eons.[68]

In that way, indicate the pledges in their provisional and definitive senses. The statement in the tantra beginning with "Water (chu)" and ending with "are to be thoroughly bestowed (rab sbyin bya)"[69] is a summarization of the meaning explained earlier: "In that way the master thoroughly bestows on the student the seven – the water initiation and so forth." [348] *The import is not that, when conferring initiation, the master should speak these words to the student.*

Such statements are explained in two ways, provisionally and definitively. For example, in the *Guhyasamāja Tantra* one statement such as, "If [you] kill the groups of Ones Gone Thus, [you] will attain the highly supreme feat," must be explained in many different ways, these being called the six modes and four ways.

Here, in the statement of these pledges, it is said that those of the vajra lineage – that is to say, those of the Akṣhobhya lineage – "definitely should take life". In its provisional sense, this means that those of the Akṣhobhya lineage, motivated by compassion, could – under special circumstances – kill persons who are harmful to the teaching or who hate sentient beings and are about to commit hideous non-virtues but cannot be restrained by other means. In its definitive sense, this means that those of the Akṣhobhya lineage should bind the white mind of enlightenment, which is the basis of bliss, in the crown protrusion and should take the life of the winds that bring about emission.

It is said that those of the Amoghasiddhi lineage symbolized by the sword should speak "untrue words". In its provisional sense, this means that those of the Amoghasiddhi lineage should speak various doctrines – interpretable and definitive – in accordance with sentient beings' interests and predispositions, thus allowing that, for a worthwhile purpose of the teaching or for sentient beings, one could communicate meanings in which the mode of appearance of phenomena and their actual mode of being do not agree. In its definitive sense, this means that those of the Amoghasiddhi lineage should speak the thoroughly non-abiding false word of the unconquerable short *a* at the heart upon withdrawing the winds in the central channel. In the *Guhyasamāja Tantra,* it is said that one should speak false words in the sense that since whereas phenomena do not inherently exist they appear to inherently exist, one should speak of the emptiness of inherent existence which does not accord with the false mode of appearance of phenomena.

It is said that those of jewel lineage of Ratnasambhava "should steal others' wealth". In its provisional sense, this means that those of the Ratnasambhava lineage, whose predominant affliction is great miserliness, under special circumstances could – in order to overcome it – steal others' wealth in order to use it in helping sentient beings. In its definitive sense, this means that those of the Ratnasambhava lineage should steal the wish-granting jewel of the immutable drop at the throat, this being like the statement in the *Guhyasamāja Tantra* that one should take Buddhahood without its being given since it is something that cannot be given but must be achieved oneself.

It is said that those of the lotus lineage of Amitābha "should steal others' mates". In its provisional sense, this means that those of the Amitābha lineage, in order to help a sentient being who is particularly attached to his or her mate and, due to which, is accumulating bad karma, could – under special circumstances and for the sake of helping that person – take his or her mate. In its definitive sense, this means that those of the Amitābha lineage should steal the great seal woman with immutable bliss, possessing all the supreme aspects, at the forehead. In the *Guhyasamāja Tantra*, the emptiness of inherent existence is given the name "mate", and when it is said that one should make use of another's mate, this is taken as meaning that one should always acquaint oneself with the emptiness of inherent existence.

It is said that those of the Vairochana lineage symbolized by the wheel should make use of intoxicants, the Buddha lamps – the five fleshes and the five ambrosias – and all good objects. In its provisional sense, this means that those of the Vairochana lineage could use the substances indicated in the pledges without any attachment. In its definitive sense, this means that those of the Vairochana lineage should, with innate joy, bind at the navel the essence of all the faculties and constituents, the one like ambrosia, without emission.

It is said that those of the Vajrasattva lineage symbolized by a curved knife "should not deride the sky-lotus of any woman", those of low type and so forth. In its provisional sense, this means that those of the Vajrasattva lineage should not deride a woman of any of the five lineages even if she be lowly. In its definitive sense, this means that those of the Vajrasattva lineage should use seals [consorts] but within binding, without emission, the white mind of enlightenment that is the basis of bliss.

That all of these activities are to be done within being motivated by compassion and altruism and for the sake of accumulating merit is indicated by the statement that, "You should give this body as well as wealth for the sake of sentient beings; you should not [selfishly] keep it." Through training in such a unified practice for accumulating the collections of merit and wisdom, one abides in the principles of the Mantra path, whereby Buddhahood can be easily achieved. Without it, through practicing merely the path of the Perfection Vehicle even over an immeasurable period of eons, Buddhahood cannot be attained.

MEANING OF THE INITIATION

Now, listen to the purification brought about by the permission initiation and by all seven initiations.

> *Then, express the meaning of the initiation and its purification:*
>
> The permission initiation in the area of the western, pristine consciousness face corresponds to a father's giving a reading lesson and so forth to a child. Just as the wind of pristine consciousness [bliss] circulates just after a child is conceived, the permission initiation as well as its appendages cleanses defilements of pristine consciousness [bliss]. Through putting the seed of Vajrasattva [in the continuum], it purifies the constituent of pristine consciousness [bliss] and causes you to have the capacity to attain the seventh ground as its fruit.
>
> *Then, express the purification of the seven initiations in common:*
>
> In that way, you have obtained in a mandala of colored particles – from among the four types of mandalas – all seven initiations called "water initiations" in that they are followed by a rite of water. They cleanse defilements of ill-deeds. They authorize cultivating the stage of generation and the achievement of the final worldly feats of the Highest Pure Land. They set potencies in the continuum for the collection of merit and bestow practices and releases related with the stage of generation. Having become an aspirant *(dge bsnyen, upāsaka)* of Secret Mantra, if during this life you actualize the wheel of the mandala, in this life you will become a lord of the seventh ground. If, how-

ever, it does not occur during this life but you remain free from the ten non-virtues, in seven lifetimes you will attain the lordship of the seventh ground.

Then, with the sense of attaining the seventh Bodhisattva ground and with your arms crossed in front of you, repeat this mantra.

Say this mantra and maintain the pride of being the deity:

Oṃ sarva-tathāgata-sapta-abhiṣheka-sapta-bhūmi-prāpto 'haṃ. [Oṃ through all the Ones Gone Thus manifestly bestowing the seven initiations I have attained the seven grounds.]

The petitions for the seven initiations, the mantras for conferring the initiation, and the mantra for assuming the pride [*of being the deity*] *are all set out in the Means of Achievement (sgrub thabs, sādhana).*[70]

Part Four
Conclusion

1 *Understanding the Time of Attainment*

The following is not needed for self-entry but is to be done when conferring initiation on students. Concerning it, [the master] says. "Here at such and such a year at the time when such and such a kulika king is teaching doctrine, on such and such a month in such and such a period with such and such planets and constellations with such and such means, I the vajra master so and so have conferred on such and such students initiation by way of the seven initiations in a mandala of the primordial Buddha. I have prophesied their achieving the worldly feat of their final existence in the Highest [Pure Land] and their attaining the fruit of merit and exalted wisdom, which is the leadership of all sentient beings, and have [bestowed] permission on them." This is for the sake of understanding seniority of initiation.

With regard to the time of thoroughly granting initiation here in the Kālachakra mandala with the seven initiations:[71] According to Kay-drup-jay, Shākyamuni Buddha – the unequalled Teacher – became completely enlightened in the water-male-horse year called "the various"; thus 2857 years have passed whereby this is the 2858th year. Two thousand eight hundred and fifty-six years have passed since Shākyamuni

Buddha set forth the root *Kālachakra Tantra* in the water-female-sheep year at the Dhānyakaṭaka *('bras spungs)* stūpa; thus this is the 2857th year since then. From among the seven Religious Kings and Kulikas [lineage bearers] in Shambhala to the north, from the time that the twenty-first Kulika Aniruddha *(ma 'gags pa, aniruddha)* assumed the throne fifty-three years have passed, and thus this is the fifty-fourth year.

According to the prevalent interpretation of the Thera-vādins, this is the 2525th year since Shākyamuni Buddha passed away.

Within the sixteenth cycle this is the iron-female-bird year.

According to the Kālachakra system, this is the middle month of summer; in coarser terms the month of ñön *(snron, jyeṣṭhā)*, and in finer terms the chu-d̄ö *(chu stod, pūrvāṣhādhā)* month, the fifteenth day. The sun is in the house of conjugality.

According to another system of calculation, this is the month of great earth-male-monkey in the waxing phase.

According to the Kālachakra system, this is the vowel *ḷ* and the consonant *ṭ*; in terms of constituent, it is earth; in terms of the desirous attributes, it is odor; in terms of planet, it is Venus (Friday); at such a time activities of increase and explaining doctrine are favored. The constellation is chu-d̄ö *(chu stod, pūrvāṣhādhā)*; thus, consecrations and initiations are favored. The conjunction is w̄ang-b̄o *(dbang po)*, and thus study is favored. From among the twelve limbs of dependent-arising, it is grasping, and thus going to the South and North is favored. The trö-chung *('phrod chung)* is earth and water, and thus [the occasion] is very happy with physical magnificence and wealth, having festive occasions and installations in higher rank, good for wearing special clothes, adornments, and sporting. The trö-chen *('phrod chen)* is increase, due to which wealth and resources increase.

At this time of such qualities, I as Vajra Master, have conferred initiation on you students by way of the seven initiations, as well as the appendages, in a colored particle mandala of the Glorious Primordial Buddha, Kālachakra. It is explained that if you keep the vows and pledges, in seven lifetimes you will be able to actualize the state of the seventh Bodhisattva ground.

2 *Advice to Abandon the Root Infractions*

The passage detailing the fourteen root infractions is from the *Condensed Kālachakra Tantra:*[72]

> If through the force of being deceived a root infraction occurs, you will go to hell, for these are [conditions for] suffering.

If, having received the vows, you do not keep them properly due to coming under the influence of the afflictive emotions, this will serve as a condition for the onset of suffering. Therefore, you should keep the vows properly.

> There is purification of root infractions for those dwelling with the seven initiations and possessing the qualities [of intention of restraint in the future by way of repeating their deity's mantra thirty-six thousand times].[73]

If a root infraction does occur, it needs to be purified through developing a strong force of regret for having done the infraction as well as a strong intention to restrain from that action in the future. Those who have received just the seven initiations in the pattern of childhood should repeat the mantra of the deity, on which the flower has fallen, thirty-six thousand times, whereby it is said that the infraction will be purified.

> Those having the vase and secret initiations [purify infractions] through the force of assuming a [special] mode of conduct. For those having the higher [initiations] there is no purification [through just those means].

Those who have also received the vase initiations and the secret initiations can purify infractions through engaging in earnest and special accumulation of merit. For them it is not sufficient just to repeat the mantra of their deity; rather, they must make special effort at accumulating collections of merit and earnest training in ethics.

Those who have received initiations higher than the vase and secret initiations – that is to say, the knowledge-wisdom initiation and above – cannot purify infractions merely by repeating mantra or assuming a special mode of conduct, but can do so through also receiving the magnificent blessings of Buddhas and Bodhisattvas after assuming a special ethical mode of conduct. As one's status becomes higher and higher due to receiving higher initiations, the responsibilities become greater and greater such that even small deviations incur great fault. Even though the infraction is the same, greater fault is incurred by those with the higher initiations, and thus there are different means of purification.

> Those for whom a root infraction has occurred should, for the sake of purifying that infraction, enter into this mandala,
> But despite having attained permission [that is, restored the vow] your name becomes lesser in the assembly.

For the sake of purifying a root infraction, one should re-enter the mandala and receive initiation, thereby restoring the vows, but due to having earlier incurred fault one's position in the assembly of yogis becomes lower.

Then, what constitute root infractions?

> From disturbing the mind of the glorious lama, childish beings come to hold the first[74] root infraction.

If you do not follow the word of the lama from whom you receive the glorious Kālachakra initiation – with the priviso that the word of the lama accords with the doctrine – and thereby disturb the lama's mind, this constitutes the first infraction. Kulika Puṇḍarīka's *Great Commentary on the "Kālachakra Tantra", the Stainless Light* says that not following instructions by the lama that do not accord with the doctrine is without fault. As is said, "Act in accordance with virtuous doctrine; act in discordance with non-virtuous doctrine." With apology and explanation of the reasons, you should refrain from doing what does not accord with the doctrine; it is not suitable to take the lama's absence of accordance with the doctrine as a condition generating disrespect and lack of faith.

> Through deviating from his word, there is another; likewise, through anger at brothers [and sisters] there is the third.

If you transgress the precepts set forth by the lama without any regard for them, there is the second infraction, different from the first. The third is, out of anger, to speak fault of or become belligerent toward vajra brothers and sisters – those who have received initiation from the same lama, either before, later, or at the same time.

> Through forsaking love there is the fourth; from losing the mind of enlightenment there is the fifth.

The fourth infraction is to lose your love for sentient beings. With regard to the fifth infraction, the most excellent means for achieving complete perfect enlightenment is the exalted wisdom of immutable bliss, and the essential constituent, which is white like the kunda flower and is called by the name "mind of enlightenment", is the basis of that bliss. Hence, if a practitioner does not keep this white "mind of enlightenment" without emission and instead becomes attached to the bliss of its being emitted outside, thereby allowing its emission, this constitutes an infraction. Similarly, losing the aspirational altruistic intention to become enlightened is also a root infraction.

> The sixth is to deride the tenets [of the Perfection Vehicle]; the seventh is from giving the secrecies to unripened persons.

The sixth infraction is to deride the Perfection Vehicle as useless merely because through its practice *alone* Buddhahood cannot be achieved. The seventh is to give the secrecies to those whose continuums have not been ripened by initiation or who do not have faith.

> From afflicting your [mental and physical] aggregates there is the eighth; again, the ninth is non-faith in the [natural] purity of phenomena.

The mental and physical aggregates of a yogi, which are such that they allow practice of the exalted wisdom of bliss and emptiness, are very valuable. Hence, it is the eighth infraction to afflict your own mental and physical aggregates with the intention of causing your body to deteriorate. The ninth is to not have faith in the natural purity of phenomena, their suchness or mode of subsistence, which is the emptiness of inherent existence. If you do not have faithful interest in the view of emptiness of either the Mind Only School or the Middle Way School and turn away from it, this constitutes an infraction.

> Deceitful love is the tenth, and [having] qualms about the bestowal of the bliss devoid of names and so forth is the eleventh.

"Deceitful love" means that there is a discordance between your mouth and your heart. If in your heart you harbor dislike but, out of a wish to deceive, in your mouth you pretend to be sweet and loving, this is the tenth infraction. "The doctrine devoid of names" is emptiness, and thus to abandon the exalted wisdom of immutable bliss and emptiness, not making effort at the means to realize it, is the eleventh infraction.

From speaking fault about pure sentient beings
there is the twelfth; forsaking pledges that have
been attained is another [the thirteenth].

"Pure sentient beings" here are yogis; to speak fault of them is the twelfth infraction. Neglecting pledges requiring one to make use of seals, vajra, bell, and so forth with the sense that these are not needed in one's training constitutes the thirteenth infraction.

Deriding any woman is the fourteenth. These are
for those abiding in the Vajra Vehicle.

In general, women are very kind and, in particular, assist greatly in the generation of the exalted wisdom of bliss and emptiness. Therefore, all women are to be respected with discrimination of them as like your mother. If, opposite to that, you deride any woman, this is the fourteenth root infraction. These are precepts to be kept by those who have entered a mandala of the Mantra Vehicle and have received the Mantra vows.

When conferring initiation on a student, [the lama] should explain the meaning of those in detail.[75]

Next, the student accepts to do what the lama has advised.

Then, the student says three times:

I will do all
That the principal deity has advised.

Thus the foregoing completes well the conferral of the seven initiations in the manner of taking care of a child, as well as the subsequent water initiations. At the end is a celebration of the virtue of the event, followed by an offering of mandala.

Then:[76]

Now my birth is fruitful.
My being alive is also fruitful.
Today I have been born in the Buddha lineage.
I have today become a Buddha Child.

Offer mandala.

To the lama, personal deity, and Three Jewels I offer in visualization
The body, speech, mind, and resources of myself and others,
Our collections of virtue in the past, present, and future,
And the wonderful precious mandala with the masses of Samantabhadra's offerings.
Accepting them through your compassion, please empower me with blessings.
Idaṃ guru-ratna-maṇḍalakaṃ niryātayāmi. [I offer this jewelled mandala to the guru.][77]

3 *Prayer-Wishes*

All should make good prayer-wishes. Let us recite the wishes found in the daily practice rite (pp.414-423):

Through the power of the great increase of the vast lake
Of the collections of virtue upon the accumulation – again and again
In the lake of my mind – of the stainless stream of meditation,
Repetition, and offering from the snow mountain of such pure special thought

And through the power of mentally gathering together
All the collections of virtues related with the past, present, and future,
May I be taken care of in life after life
By holy protectors, spiritual guides of the supreme vehicle.

From the instructions happily bestowed by them
May I come to know the way of gathering together the doctrines
Of the three vehicles and from practicing their meaning
Ripen my mental continuum with the common paths.

Through attaining the seven pure initiations
May potencies for the seven grounds be well established,
The seven stains of the constituents and so forth be cleansed,

And I be empowered to practice the yoga of the first stage and
achieve the common feats.

Through the four supreme initiations, mundane and supramundane,
May the seeds of the four vajras of the Four Bodies be established
And I be authorized to hear, explain, and cultivate
The four branches of approximation and achievement of the
second stage.

Sitting well on the throne of the four pure initiations
In the supreme inestimable mansion of the Vajra Vehicle
With the foot-stool of non-deteriorated vows and pledges
May I become a universal monarch of the doctrine of the two
stages.

Through exalted body, speech, mind, and wisdom, cleansed
and purified,
Through the yoga of meditating on the six lineages and the six
branches,
And through the light of vajras set in individual places in the
body,
Strongly blazing, may demons and obstructors be burned.

May mandalas of the four elements be generated
In the middle of the expanse of space
And from their combining into one may a five- and three-
staged fence
As well as a palace with a seat be established.

In the center of that may I as the glorious Vajravega
Through the firm meditative stabilization of the King of
Wrathful Ones
Put an end to external and internal demons and obstructors
By emitting a host of sixty guardians of the doors.

Considering that through the exercise of dispersal and gathering

The field of accumulation pervades the full expanse of space,
May the collections, powerful like waves, be thoroughly completed
Through performing the amassing of the accumulations – the preparation – according to the rite.

Through cultivating the pride of the Truth Body at the end
Of the dissolution of the six constituents just as in the stages of death
May I complete the meditative stabilization of the four doors of liberation
Bringing about full enlightenment instantaneously.

Through meditating on space, wind, fire, water, earth, and Mount Meru,
May I realize the status of vajra-body,
With channel wheels and so forth at the crown of the head,
Forehead, neck, heart, navel, and secret region.

Through meditating well on a vajra tent
On top of lotus, moon, sun, rāhu, and kālāgni,
May the collections of winds of the right and left channels be stopped
In the channel-with-conch through the supreme vajra yoga.

Through the power of meditating on an inestimable mansion
With the light of stainless jewels inside the vajra tent
May the land where I will be enlightened as a Buddha
Be purified and my physical support become free from defilement.

Through meditating on the twos – moon and sun, vowels and consonants,
Wind and mind, and the two letters – combining into one, the letter *haṃ*,
May great bliss be generated from the gathering together in the central channel
Of the white and red constituents and the subtle wind and mind.

Then through the power of meditating on the deities of the mandala of great bliss –
The exalted body of Kālachakra, complete in all aspects,
Having the nature of the great bliss possessing the supreme of all aspects
Together with his Knowledge Woman –

May [these meditations] serve as causes of generating
The supreme stages of completion in which the Great Seal
Of empty form is filled with the taste of immutable innate bliss,
Actually embraced respectively by the aspected and unaspected Seals.

Through cultivating manifest enlightenment by way of the five aspects,
The supreme king of mandalas, the branch of approximation,
Generating from the seed of absorption of Father and Mother
The supreme complete circle of the deities in the womb

And setting them well in their respective places,
May I generate the supreme realizations of the path
Through purifying the aggregates, constituents, sense faculties,
Objects, action faculties, and activities.

With the vajric Supramundane Victor as well as a Knowledge Woman
Who abide in the lotus of the wheel of great bliss
And dwell in the form of a drop of great bliss
Through the force of having been melted by the fire of the fierce woman at the navel,

May I meditatively cultivate the branch of near-achievement, the supreme
King of activities, by means of enlightenment in twenty aspects –
The five arousals by the pleasant song of goddesses,

The five constructions, and the five comprised by the five Fierce Ones

Drawing [the wisdom-beings] to the circle of pledge-beings,
Entry, binding, being delighted, and becoming of one taste –
And by means of bestowing initiation, seal-impression, and mindfulness of purity,
And thereby may the meanings of those be actualized.

Through the blazing upward in the central channel
Of the fire of the fierce woman incited by the downward-voiding wind
Upon blessing the secret space into magnificence and becoming absorbed
And, from that, the gradual descent of the mind of enlightenment

Due to the melting of the letter *haṃ* at the crown of the head
And the stopping of the movement of the winds in the right and left channels,
May the yoga of the drops be actualized, the supreme branch of achievement
Causing me to understand well the four joys of the forward process.

Through the four joys of stability from below of the passage
Upward again in the same procedure
May I bring to completion the branch of great achievement,
The subtle yoga, and the manifest enlightenment of the magical net.

In short, may I bring to completion the effort of cultivating in four sessions
The supreme stage of generation purifying the external and internal bases of purification,
Water cleansing ordinary appearance and the conception of ordinariness,
The path ripening for the full generation of the stage of completion.

Also, may I ripen limitless transmigrators through unimpededness
In achieving the feats of final achievement
Of the highest type through striving
At repetition, burnt offering, and giving of offerings.

May I familiarize with the six-branched yoga:
The two virtues at the beginning – individual withdrawal and concentration,
The two virtues in the middle – the paths of vitality-stopping and retention,
And the two virtues at the end – mindfulness and meditative stabilization.

May my mind be set one-pointedly, free from laxity and excitement,
On the place where it is contemplated that a corner of the eyes
Enters inside the upper point of the central channel
Through the gaze of half-closed eyes, turned upward.

Through that may the four night signs – like smoke, mirage,
Fireflies, and butter lamp – be manifested,
Unmistaken signs of the gathering of the collections
Of the winds of the right and left channels in the central channel.

Also, through meditating well as before
In the manner of looking at space free from clouds,
May the six signs – blazing, moon, sun, rāhu,
Lightning, and drop – be completed.

Through the concentration of one-pointed observation of forms
According to my wish, upon the gradual withdrawal
Of the empty forms in the area of the body-drop,
May the bliss of physical and mental pliancy be induced.

Through the power of one-pointed familiarization with the two yogas
Of achieving empty forms in that way
And of making steady those achieved,
May I achieve the word of truth and the five clairvoyances.

Through familiarizing with the vitality-stopping of spontaneous vajra repetition
In which the wind and mantra are inseparable in the path of rāhu
And the vitality-stopping of pot [-like wind control]
In which the upper and lower winds cease at the navel,

May the special signs of the collections of the winds
Entirely entering and remaining for a while
In the center of the wheel of emanation dawn
And the melodiousness praised by Bodhisattvas be actualized.

Through the yoga of holding my mind steadily at the end of generating
The four joys of descent from above and stability from below
Without fluctuation in the center of the mixture of the vitalizing
And downward-voiding winds into one at the center of the six wheels,

May I rise for my own mind in a body of empty form
And the groups of demons of untimely death be suppressed.
Having attained well the power of control over all forms and vitality,
May I actually rise in a body of empty form

In father-mother union
From the innate bliss induced
By igniting again the fire of the fierce woman,
And may light rays of various colors spread out from my hair-pores.

May I perform meditation in which the immutable great bliss
Induced well by the power of the Seal –
Through union with a Great Seal
Of such empty form – is joined with emptiness.

Through the power of piling up the white and red constituents,
Twenty-one thousand six hundred in number,
Up and down throughout the central channel,
May the material constituents of my body be consumed as iron is by mercury.

May the twenty-one thousand six hundred immutable
Great blisses realizing emptiness
Cease that number of karmic winds, quickly purify
Obstructive predispositions, and I attain a Conqueror's exalted body.

May I easily achieve these wishes
Without hindrance, becoming a supreme captain
Releasing transmigrators through this supreme path
Into the supreme land of jewels of a Conqueror.

In short, through whatever collections of wholesome virtue,
As illustrated by this, have been accumulated,
May I quickly take birth in Shambhala, the treasury of jewels,
And complete the stages of the path in Highest Yoga Tantra.

4 *Daily Practice*

The initiations conferred have been the seven in the pattern of childhood. These authorize persons to hear, think about, and meditatively cultivate the stage of generation. Then, when students come to have the qualifications necessary to be a suitable vessel for cultivating the stage of completion, at that point the four high initiations and the fourth greatly high initiation are needed. Moreover, if someone not only cultivates the two stages – of generation and completion – which are the meaning of the *Kālachakra Tantra,* but also is to teach the entire tantra to others, that person also needs all four greatly high initiations as well as the initiation of a vajra master great lord. The initiations for the stage of completion are, for the time being, not needed; later, when such are appropriate in terms of students' development, they can be considered.

Since you have attained initiation, or authorization, for the stage of generation, your focus should be on cultivating that stage in practice. Furthermore, as much as the stage of generation is cultivated in a vast way, so much more profound is the practice. The most condensed version of meditative cultivation of the stage of generation is self-generation in a mandala of exalted mind, but even this is difficult for some. Thus, a very short self-generation as Kālachakra can be done in connection with the six session yoga.

Taking the practice of the precepts of the Bodhisattva vows

and the Mantra vows as the basis of your practice, you should cultivate the six session yoga. It is not absolutely necessary that you recite the words of the rite; it is sufficient to reflect on the meaning. The six session yoga is a compendium of all the practices that need to be performed three times during the day and three times during the night; you need to reflect on their meaning. This is like recharging a battery. If you leave it for a long time without recharging it, then on the day when you want to use it, it cannot help. Similarly, cultivation of the six session yoga does not necessarily bring about great progress but, at minimum, maintains what you have.

Thus, it will be good if you are able to recite and reflect on the six session yoga in connection with self-generation as Kālachakra. If, gradually, you ascertain the meaning of the topics, it is not absolutely necessary to recite the words; rather, you can do reflective meditation on the meaning of the topics, causing each of the topics to appear to your mind. Meditation that is a unification of stabilizing and analytical meditation is needed.

The main practice is deity yoga. When clear appearance as a deity and the "pride" of being that deity develop to the point where you are able to remain in such clear appearance and "pride" for four hours without interruption by other conceptions – given that you have no physical malady, etc. – you have developed the stage of generation well. At that point, on whatever object of observation in the body you set your mind, since wind and mind operate together, the winds gather at that place. Even now when we perform such imaginations in connection with the winds, the top of the head can start itching, and so forth.

When, in that way, the stage of generation is fully cultivated, you are to mix your mind entirely with cultivation of the stage of completion. The stage of completion in the *Kālachakra Tantra* is the six-branched yoga, which need not be explained here.

At the point of the sixth branch in the stage of completion, called the branch of meditative stabilization, one attains a union of immutable bliss and empty form. Twenty-one thousand six hundred periods of immutable bliss are gradually actualized, immediately after which the very subtle mind of clear light becomes an entity of an omniscient consciousness knowing all aspects of objects of knowledge. At that point, as the basis of immutable bliss, one has completed twenty-one thousand six hundred units of the essential constituent called the "mind of enlightenment", and in dependence upon that, one has actualized twenty-one thousand six hundred periods of immutable bliss, through which twenty-one thousand six hundred karmic winds have ceased and twenty-one thousand six hundred material factors of the body have been consumed. In the next moment the state of the Four Bodies of a Buddha is actualized.

To practice such paths of the stage of generation and the stage of completion, it is necessary first to attain pure initiation. To attain pure initiation, it is necessary to have experience of the altruistic intention to become enlightened. Also, the view of emptiness is needed since, as explained during the initiation, it is involved throughout the beginning, middle, and end of the process of initiation. When the view of emptiness is conjoined with the altruistic intention to become enlightened, the view of emptiness can serve as an antidote to the obstructions to omniscience.

To have such an altruistic intention to become enlightened – that is to say, to develop a wish to set all sentient beings in the state of Buddhahood in which all suffering and its causes are extinguished – previously it is necessary to develop in full form compassion that takes cognizance of the sentient beings who are tortured by suffering as well as to have full knowledge of the types of suffering through which they are tortured. Since this is the case, you need initially to identify, in terms of yourself, the general and specific types of suffering in cyclic existence and thereby develop a state of not wanting these sufferings. In order to develop a strong awareness not wanting such general and specific sufferings of cyclic existence and wishing to be liberated from them, it is necessary, as inner divisions of that process – the one being coarser than the other – to overcome attraction to the appearances of this lifetime before overcoming attraction to the appearances of future lifetimes.

This being the case, mental training must be done step by step. These initiations have brought together factors for the dependent-arising of your cultivating such an entire series of paths.

The most important thing is our daily life. As I always express, we as human beings now have a very good opportunity; thus, we must be good, honest persons. This is most important. Then, as practitioners we must sincerely practice what we believe; if we implement these ideas in our daily life, we will get the benefit whereas if they remain as mere knowledge, we will not benefit. Therefore, it is very important to put these into practice.

Also, a beginner should not expect too much right from the beginning. Too much expectation will lead to failure. At the start, you must realize that inner development will take time; it is not at all easy. According to my own experience, it takes time.

Then, determination – constant effort – is extremely important. Whenever we face an unsatisfactory situation, we should not lose our will, our courage. If we have courage, we can overcome any obstacle. Therefore, our own will and determination are very important.

If there were another way through which real permanent peace could be brought, the practice of dharma would not be very important. However, if we cannot find another means to bring ultimate happiness, then there is no alternative other than the spiritual way. We must make a strong determination to practice.

At the same time, we must have deep respect for non-Buddhist religions. All religions essentially have the same message of compassion and human improvement. Since the human mind has so many varieties, for certain persons religions such as Christianity, Judaism, Hinduism, Islam, and so forth will be more effective, more beneficial. Therefore, we must respect all religions, not feeling sectarian.

Then, among Buddhists ourselves, there are the Low Vehicle and the Great Vehicle, and within the latter there are minor differences, and within Tibetan Buddhism there are the so called Red Hats, Yellow Hats, Black Hats, and so forth. Actually, Shākyamuni Buddha had no hat, and thus his followers have become more concerned with fashion. If the real teaching were the hat, then Buddha would have had no teaching! We must realize that all Buddhists are followers of the same teacher, Shākyamuni Buddha.

Due to ignorance we sometimes develop feelings, "This is *my* tradition," "This is *my* religion," "This is *my* teacher." Such is very, very unfortunate; we must remain genuinely non-sectarian. As practitioners, we must blame ourselves rather than others. When some unfavorable thing happens, we should point inward, not outward, "They did this," "They did that." To blame the outside is absolutely wrong. Is this clear?

As Buddha said, "You are your own master." For instance, as far as I am concerned, my own future depends on myself. I cannot rely on others for my future; whether it is good or bad depends entirely on myself. If I do something wrong, I will face the ultimate consequences; Buddha cannot. Similarly, your future depends on yourself. Thus, we must be good, honest, sincere, truthful, courageous, and warm-hearted human beings. Through that, our future will be bright. If our minds become too weak, hesitant, and fearful, our future will be more difficult.

It is important not to expect too much right from the beginning but, in the meantime, to maintain great determination. With such an attitude, the future will improve.

Rites for Daily Practice: Three Versions of the Six Session Yoga

Introduction

Translated herein are three versions of the six session yoga – a system of daily practice that is conducted three times during the day and three times during the night, preferably at consistent intervals. The basic six session yoga, the second text, was formulated by the First Panchen Lama L̄o-sang-chö-ḡyi-gyel-tsen *(blo bzang chos kyi rgyal mtshan,* 1567?-1662). At the behest of His Holiness the Dalai Lama, this basic six session yoga was adapted to the practice of Kālachakra by his Senior Tutor, the ninety-seventh occupant of the throne of Gan-den, Tup-d̄en-lung-d̄ok-ñam-gyel-trin-lay *(thub bstan lung rtogs rnam rgyal 'phrin las)* known as L̄ing Rin-b̄o-chay *(gling rin po che,* 1903-1983). This considerably expanded adaptation is the first text.

Much of the first text is also borrowed from other Means of Achievement *(sgrub thabs, sādhana),* and it is unclear which portions were written by the Dalai Lama and by L̄ing Rin-b̄o-chay; in any case, the formulation of the text represents a system of practice advised by them for those who cannot fit in their daily schedule practice of a Means of Achievement of a complete mandala of exalted body, speech, and mind such as the Seventh Dalai Lama's *Means of Achievement of the Complete Mandala of Exalted Body, Speech, and Mind of the Supramundane Victor, the Glorious Kālachakra: the Sacred Word of Scholars and Adepts* or of merely an exalted mind mandala such as the Seventh Dalai Lama's *Means of Achievement of the Mandala of Exalted Mind of the Glorious Kālachakra: Good Vase of All Feats*. Though, as the Dalai Lama says in the notes to this translation, it is best to perform as extensive a version of such practice as is practicable, the text provides a fairly short system of practice that more than fulfills the requirements of the six session yoga. Nevertheless, a more vast version is required to fulfill the practice of the stage of generation.

The final text is a very brief rendition of the six session yoga for those who cannot manage to fit even the basic version into a day. Its brevity suggests that something is better than nothing and reflects a flexible attitude that takes account of individuals' capacities at this point of their development.

The six session yoga contains within it enactment of all facets of practice to which persons who have taken refuge in the Three Jewels, the Bodhisattva vows, and the Mantra vows and pledges have committed themselves. These are individually identified within the text in remarks separate from the process of meditation. The mode of practice is to cause the meaning of each section to appear to the mind, recitation of the words being used to stimulate reflection on the meaning. Emphasis is put on particular sections by inserting elaborations on that part into one's practice according to one's level of achievement.

1 *The Guru Yoga of Kālachakra in Connection with the Six Sessions in Completely Facilitating Form*

This text was formulated by His Holiness the Fourteenth Dalai Lama and versified by the Foremost Protector Ling Rin-bo-chay. It has been translated in accordance with instruction from His Holiness the Fourteenth Dalai Lama and Gan-den Tri Rin-bo-chay Jam-bel-shen-pen.

The text includes explanatory material, which is at the margin, and the actual meditation rite, which is the indented poetry. Further explanations by His Holiness the Dalai Lama given orally to the translator are provided in notes at the bottom of the page; several explanations by Gan-den Tri Rin-bo-chay Jam-bel-shen-pen are also in the footnotes, specified as being from him; notes by the translator are in brackets.

Namo guru-shrī-kālachakrāya.

Having bowed to the original Buddha,[1]

1 Jam-bel-shen-pen: "Original Buddha" is identified as "Buddha whose origin is the immutable bliss" or as the Complete Enjoyment Body in the sense that it is the basis of emanation of Emanation Bodies.

Union of the vajra of great bliss[2] with the aspectless Great Seal,
I will elaborate herein the mode of practising the very profound guru yoga[3]
In connection with the six sessions.

Those who want the good should not remain attached to the mere marvels of what appears during this lifetime as if such were the essence, but should, as their activity, achieve the great final aims of this and future lifetimes [liberation from cyclic existence and the great liberation of Buddhahood]. Also, to achieve the essence of the final aspiration, you should train in the paths that have an essence of emptiness and compassion.[4] For this, you should acquaint with and rely on a fully qualified spiritual guide properly, by way of both thought and deed. It is indispensable to take such guru yoga as the life of the path.

In addition, those who have entered into a mandala of any of the two higher tantra sets [Yoga and Highest Yoga Tantra][5] and have attained initiation should review[6] daily the root and secondary pledges and vows. In particular, if the pledges of the five Buddha lineages are not maintained in six sessions daily, one incurs a gross unseemliness. Since it is said that a

2 The "vajra of great bliss" is the immutable great bliss – method. The "aspectless Great Seal" is emptiness, whereas the aspected Great Seal is the consort Vishvamātā. The union of the vajra of great bliss and the aspectless Great Seal is the exalted wisdom of undifferentiable bliss and emptiness. The apprehension aspect *(bzung rnam)* of the exalted wisdom of undifferentiable bliss and emptiness appears as Kālachakra. Initial homage is made to such a Kālachakra.

3 Jam-bel-shen-pen: This is called a guru yoga because one is viewing one's lama *(guru)* as undifferentiable from Kālachakra.

4 There are different interpretations of the path having an essence of emptiness and compassion according to sūtra, the three lower tantras, Highest Yoga Tantra, and the *Kālachakra Tantra*. [See n.108 of the Introduction.]

5 Both of these involve taking Mantric vows, and thus the six session yoga must be done for both of these.

6 The meaning of "review" is to take each of these to mind, consider what is supposed to be done, and correct oneself.

gross contravention of Mantra is a heavier fault even than performing all four defeats of the vow of individual liberation, [killing a human, stealing, sexual misconduct and lying about spiritual attainments] maintenance of the six sessions without break is very important.

Here, with respect to how to practice guru yoga in dependence on the Supramundane Victor Kālachakra in connection with the six session yoga, stated in completely facilitating form,[7] the practitioner should have trained his or her continuum by way of the common path. Then, a yogi who, having attained pure initiation of this personal deity [Kālachakra], maintains properly the pledges and vows should clean well the place of meditation which has the qualifications mentioned in the [fourth] chapter on Achievement [in the *Kālachakra Tantra*]. Then, you should lay out well in front of an arrangement of bases of exalted body, speech, and mind [such as an image, a book, and a stūpa] whatever offerings can be obtained – the offerings not involving any faults of deceit in motivation, procurement, and so forth.[8]

7 Literally, *nag 'gros su 'god pa* "stated such that one could go in the dark" means that the meaning of the text bestows such clarity that one can proceed easily even, so to speak, in the dark. The text was composed so that it fulfills being a yoga of Highest Yoga Tantra and of being a brief self-generation of Kālachakra.

8 If religious articles are arranged for the sake of making a house or room beautiful, the motivation is faulty; if the articles have been acquired deceitfully from others or by way of wrong livelihood, the mode of procurement is faulty. About such deceit, Nāgārjuna's *Precious Garland* (stanzas 413-415ab) says:

> Hypocrisy is to control the senses
> For the sake of goods and respect,
> Flattery is to speak pleasant phrases
> For the sake of goods and respect.
>
> Indirect acquisition is to praise
> The wealth of others so as to win it,
> Artful acquisition is to deride
> Others in order to acquire their goods.
>
> Desiring to add profit to profit
> Is to praise previous acquisitions...

Sitting well on a concentration-cushion in the manner of the seven features of Vairochana,[9] you should imagine that surrounding you are sentient beings filling all of space, the main of whom are your parents of this lifetime. In fact, they are undergoing the sufferings of their respective type among the six transmigrations [hell-beings, hungry ghosts, animals, humans, demi-gods, and gods] but are [imagined] in the form of humans.

It is said that at the beginning and the end [of virtuous endeavour] there are the two activities [of adjusting your motivation and making dedication respectively]. Thus, at the beginning you should analyze your mental continuum and remove any motivation seeking peace and happiness for yourself alone, seeking the marvels of cyclic existence in this lifetime or the future, and so forth. You should contemplate the importance and difficulty of gaining leisure and fortune, contemplate death and impermanence, the sufferings of the bad transmigrations, refuge, actions and their effects, the three and six sufferings of cyclic existence,[10] and so forth,

See Nāgārjuna and Kaysang Gyatso, *The Precious Garland And The Song of the Four Mindfulnesses* (London: George Allen and Unwin, 1975), p.80.

9 [The seven features of the recommended posture are:

1 to sit on a soft and comfortable cushion in the full adamantine posture or half adamantine posture
2 to keep the eyes neither opened very wide nor closed tight, aimed at the point of the nose
3 to keep the body straight with the backbone like a pile of coins
4 to keep the shoulders level
5 to keep the head neither high nor low, unmovingly in a straight line from the nose to the navel
6 to set the teeth and lips as usual with the tongue set against the back of the upper teeth
7 to breathe quietly and gently.

Adapted from Geshe Lhundup Sopa and Jeffrey Hopkins, *Practice and Theory of Tibetan Buddhism* (London: Rider and Co., 1976), p.xvi.]

10 [The three sufferings are mental and physical pain, the suffering of change, and the pervasive suffering of being under the influence of contaminated actions and afflictions. The six sufferings are described in brief in *Practice and Theory of Tibetan Buddhism*, p.24.]

thereby generating as much as you can an attitude of intending to leave cyclic existence.

Then, making inference from your own experience, you should contemplate well how sentient beings throughout space – your old mothers – wander in limitless and endless forms of cyclic existence through the force of conceiving the impermanent to be permanent, the painful to be pleasant, and the selfless to be self. You should contemplate well how they are undergoing inconceivable suffering, strong and rough, and that they, from beginningless time, have acted as your mother and directly and indirectly extended great kindness – sustaining you with kindness as your mother and so forth. Seeing that the responsibility for freeing them from suffering, as well as its causes, and of causing them to possess happiness has fallen on yourself, you should develop the wish to actualize the state of union [of exalted body and mind, Buddhahood,] in just the short lifespan of the degenerate era in order to set those sentient beings in the supreme state of union which does not abide in the extremes of cyclic existence and [solitary] peace.

Conjoined with the force of this precious altruistic intention to become enlightened which involves the two aspirations [of seeking others' welfare and of seeking your own enlightenment as a means to achieve that], you should visualize well – in accordance with what appears in the quintessential instructions – the objects of refuge in space directly in front of yourself.[11] Fulfilling the causal collection for the

11 According to one system, there is a large lotus seat with five smaller seats on it. On the middle seat is Shākyamuni Buddha; in front is the Dalai Lama; on the right is Maitreya; on the left is Mañjushrī; and in back is Vajradhara. Surrounding them: in front are your direct and lineaged lamas; on the right are the lamas of the lineage of the vast altruistic practices; on the left are the lamas of the lineage of the profound view of emptiness, and in back are the lamas of the lineage of practice with magnificent blessings. Between and around them are personal deities, sky-goers, guardians of doctrine, heros, heroines, Buddhas, and Bodhisattvas. Or, in what is called the all-inclusive jewel system you can imagine just Kālachakra as an entity including all of the lamas, personal deities, Buddhas, Bodhisattvas, and so forth.

uncommon refuge of the Great Vehicle [that is, having concern for the condition of all sentient beings – their obstructions to liberation and to omniscience – and having conviction that the Three Jewels have the power to protect those beings], you should imagine that all sentient beings, yourself and those around you, go for refuge:[12]

> With [the faith of] the great clarity I go for refuge
> To the Buddha, the master from whom supreme initiation has been attained,
> To the doctrine of undifferentiable method and wisdom taught by them,[13]
> And to the two types of aspirants to virtue residing in that [doctrine].[14]

Then, generate an altruistic intention to become enlightened:[15]

> From this time until enlightenment
> I will generate the altruistic intention to become enlightened,
> Generate the very pure thought[16]

12 [This stanza is found in the Seventh Dalai Lama's *Means of Achievement of the Complete Mandala of Exalted Body, Speech, and Mind of the Supramundane Victor, the Glorious Kālachakra: the Sacred Word of Scholars and Adepts*, 29.1.]

13 According to the Kālachakra system, the undifferentiable two truths specifically are the supreme immutable bliss and empty form. Similarly, undifferentiable bliss and emptiness are the supreme immutable bliss and the great seal of emptiness. Obeisance is made to the doctrine of such undifferentiable method and wisdom.

14 Jam-bel-shen-pen: The two types of spiritual community are most likely those who have attained the path of seeing and those who have not.

15 [This stanza is found in the Seventh Dalai Lama's *Means of Achievement of the Complete Mandala of Exalted Body, Speech, and Mind of the Supramundane Victor, the Glorious Kālachakra: the Sacred Word of Scholars and Adepts*, 29.3.]

16 One might interpret the "altruistic intention to become enlightened" as the generation of an aspiration to highest enlightenment for the sake of others by way of the seven quintessential instructions of cause and effect and then take "the very pure thought" as the development of the same aspiration by way of the equalizing and switching of self and other.

And abandon the conception of [inherently existent] I and mine.

Repeating the refuge and altruistic mind generation [stanzas] three times, definitely suffuse your mental continuum with the attitude of refuge. This fulfills the statement that as a precept of refuge you should go for refuge three times during the day and three times at night and fulfills the Vairochana pledge of going for refuge to the Three Jewels. Then, repeat three times:

I will cultivate [love wishing] that sentient beings have happiness,
[Compassion wishing] that they be free from suffering,
Joy in their abiding forever in bliss,
And the equanimity of equality.[17]

The first line fulfills the Ratnasambhava pledge of the giving of love. [The rest] fulfills the Ratnasambhava pledge of the giving of non-fright. Then:

From henceforth until attaining Buddhahood
I will hold without forsaking, even if it costs my life,
The attitude of wishing to attain complete enlightenment
In order to release all transmigrators from the frights of cyclic existence and [solitary] peace.

This fulfills the statement that once one has ritually taken up the aspirational intention to become enlightened, one should generate the altruistic intention to become enlightened in six sessions over day and night. Then, to take the vow of the practical intention to become enlightened, imagine that you

17 Love is the wish that all sentient beings have happiness and the causes of happiness; compassion is the wish that all sentient beings be separated from suffering and the causes of suffering; joy is the wish that all sentient beings remain forever in happiness, and equanimity is the wish that all sentient beings remain in equal happiness.

are repeating the following three times after the Conquerors and their Children [Bodhisattvas] – the objects of refuge – who are in front of yourself:[18]

> Lamas, Conquerors, and their Children,
> Please take heed of me.
> Just as the earlier Ones Gone to Bliss
> Generated an altruistic intention to become enlightened
> And dwelt by stages in the learnings of Bodhisattvas,
> So I also for the sake of helping transmigrators
> Will generate an altruistic intention to become enlightened
> And train in stages in the learnings of Bodhisattvas.

Repeating that three times, take the vow of the practical intention to become enlightened, and then gather the objects of refuge [into yourself]. Cultivate joy upon generating an altruistic intention to become enlightened:[19]

> Now my life is fruitful.
> I have attained a good human existence.
> Today I have been born in the Buddha lineage.
> I have become a Buddha Child.

Cultivate conscientiousness:

> Now, whatever happens,
> I will act so as not to sully

18 [This passage, from the third line to the end, is taken from Shāntideva's *Engaging in the Bodhisattva Deeds*, III.22-23. See n.26 of the Commentary for the Sanskrit.]

19 [These two stanzas are taken from Shāntideva's *Engaging in the Bodhisattva Deeds*, III.25-26. The Sanskrit is:

> adya me saphalaṃ janma sulabdho mānuṣho bhavaḥ
> adya buddhakule jāto buddhaputro 'smi sāmprataṃ
>
> tathādhunā mayā kāryaṃ svakulochitakāriṇāṃ
> nirmalasya kulasyāsya kalanko na bhavedyathā.

See Vidhushekara Bhattacharya, ed., *Bodhicaryāvatāra*, Bibliotheca Indica, Vol. 280 (Calcutta: the Asiatic Society, 1960), pp.36-37).]

This flawless holy Buddha lineage,
Initiating actions concordant with this lineage.

Those two stanzas fulfill the statement that you should, as a precept of the aspirational intention to become enlightened, contemplate in six sessions the benefit of generating an altruistic intention to become enlightened. Then, generate [i.e., imagine] the field for the accumulation [of merit]:

Within the great seal of clear light devoid of the elaborations [of inherent existence],[20]
On the broad path of the immortal gods in front of myself
In the center of an ocean of offering clouds of Samantabhadra
Like five-colored rainbows[21] thoroughly bedecked,
There is a jewel throne raised up by eight lions.
On it, on a pleasant lotus with a thousand open petals
Are discs of [white] moon, [red] sun, [black] rāhu, and [yellow] kālāgni planets.
On them is my kind lama, composite in one
Of all the innumerable forms of refuge,
Undifferentiable from the Supramundane Victor, the great Kālachakra,
Bearing the brilliance of sapphire and blazing with magnificence,
With one face and two hands, holding vajra and bell.
To symbolize the uncommon path of the union of method and wisdom[22]

20 This is the emptiness of inherent existence, the objective clear light. Within actualizing and meditating on the great seal of clear light – the emptiness of inherent existence – Kālachakra appears, as described, in space in front of you. The "broad path of the immortal gods" is space.

21 [Literally, "picture of the bow of the senses."] Jam-bel-shen-pen: Just as there are five senses, so a rainbow has five colors.

22 Method here is immutable great bliss, and wisdom is knowledge of emptiness. The path of the supreme immutable bliss – a union of method and wisdom or a union of the two truths – is generated

He is in the manner of union with Vishvamātā
Who has the color of camphor and holds curved knife and skull.
His outstretched red right leg and bent white left leg
Sport in dance on top of Māra and Rudra [symbolizing the afflictive emotions].
With hundreds of such features he charms.
His body is adorned with many types of amazing adornments,
Dwelling in the midst of the five stainless lights ablaze
Like the expanse of space beautified by the constellations.
The three places in his body are adorned with the form
Of letters of the natural divine light of the three vajras.[23]
From the seed letter at his heart Vajravegas are emitted,[24]
Very fearful, holding various weapons;
They draw in well the groups of protectors dwelling in countless lands
Who become of the same taste as the pledge-being,[25]
Whereby he becomes a great being who is the composite of all refuges.

This fulfills the Akṣhobhya pledge of maintaining [consideration of] your master. Next is the first branch of the seven-branched service, obeisance:

or made known in dependence upon a consort of empty form. [Thus "symbolize" here has the sense of coming to know, of generating such a path.]

23 The three letters or three syllables are *oṃ āḥ hūṃ* which, respectively, are at the crown of the head, the throat, and the heart.

24 Vajravega is a fierce deity with four faces, twenty-six arms, and two legs.

25 [The imagined deity is called a "pledge-being" *(dam tshig sems pa, samayasattva)*, and the actual deity is called a "wisdom-being" *(ye shes sems pa, jñānasattva)*.]

Respectful obeisance to the lama of the undifferentiable Three Bodies,
The Body of Truth of great bliss primordially free from [dualistic] elaborations,
The Body of Complete Enjoyment having the five features which are self-appearances of exalted wisdom,
And the dance of Emanation Bodies in oceans of realms of transmigrators.

This is how to keep the mind from the first fault in relation to the Bodhisattva [discipline] and how to make obeisance to the lama in accordance with the statement in Ashvaghoṣha's *Fifty Stanzas on the Guru (bla ma lnga bcu pa, gurupañchāshikā)* to do so three times daily with supreme faith.[26] Then comes the branch of offering:

To please the kind lama, the supreme field [for accumulating merit],
I offer with a mind unattached, undiscouraged,
And free from conceptions of the three spheres [of the inherent existence of agent, action, and object]
Vast, undulating clouds of external, internal, and secret offerings[27]

26 [Eight lines of praise to Heruka and eight lines of praise to Vajrayoginī have been omitted at the suggestion of His Holiness the Dalai Lama.]

27 Jam-bel-shen-pen: External offerings are such things as oblation, foot-bath, flowers, lamps, fragrant water, offerings of pleasant visible forms, sounds, odors, tastes, and tangible objects, and so forth. Internal offering is to offer the five fleshes and five ambrosias in purified form to the lama. Secret offering involves emanating goddesses who are offered to the lama and thereupon enter into union with the lama, generating great bliss. With that bliss consciousness, the lama meditates on emptiness in the manner of associating the bliss consciousness with a wisdom consciousness realizing emptiness, and thus this is called the offering of suchness. Then, within realization of emptiness, the lama emanates various Form Bodies bringing about the welfare of sentient beings, and thus this is called the offering of union [of exalted mind and body].

Actually arranged or arisen from the sport of meditative stabilization,
Twelve attractive [goddesses] of fine body bestowing bliss –
Whose lotus hands are beautified with substances suitable for offering –
As well as common and uncommon offerings,[28]
My body, resources, and collections of virtues.

This is how to maintain the Amoghasiddhi pledge of offering. At this point, if there is time, offer mandala extensively. In short form, the offering of mandala is:

To the lama, personal deity, and Three Jewels I offer in visualization
The body, speech, mind, and resources of myself and others,
Our collections of virtue in the past, present, and future,
And the wonderful precious mandala with the masses of Samantabhadra's offerings.[29]
Accepting them through your compassion, please bless me[30] into magnificence.
Guru idaṃ ratna-maṇḍalakaṃ niryātayāmi. [I offer this jewelled mandala to the guru.]

This fulfills the precept set forth in Ashvaghoṣha's *Fifty Stanzas on the Guru* to offer mandala to the lama three times daily. Then comes the branch of disclosing faulty deeds:

28 As described in books on the Kālachakra system, common offerings are such things as flowers, incense, perfumed water, and so forth, and uncommon offerings are the body's flesh, skin, blood, bone, heart, liver, lungs, and so forth.

29 Jam-bel-shen-pen: "Samantabhadra" *(kun tu bzang po)* [literally, "all good"] in the Sūtra system refers, for instance, to emanating hundreds of thousands of bodies that make offering [just as the Bodhisattva Samantabhadra did] and in the Mantra system refers to offerings that are appearances of the exalted wisdom of undifferentiable bliss and emptiness [which is all good.]

30 Jam-bel-shen-pen: "Me" should be understood as all sentient beings.

With strong regret and an intention of restraint in the future
I disclose individually my faulty deeds in all respects –
All ill-deeds and infractions done by myself and by others upon my urging
Due to the horse of the mind, untamed from beginningless time,
Having been crazed by the beer of unconscientiousness of the three poisons,[31]
And in particular disturbing the mind of the vajra master, breaking his word, and so forth,
Contradicting the pledges of the five lineages in general and my own particular lineage,
And not keeping properly the twenty-five modes of conduct[32] and so forth.

In more extensive form, recite the *Disclosure of Infractions*, the *General Disclosure*, and so forth. Then come the remaining branches [of admiration, entreaty, supplication, and dedication]:

I admire the oceans of good deeds done by myself and others
Which create the thousands of bubbles of pleasant effects.
Please let fall the rain of doctrine of the three vehicles
In accordance with the interests and thoughts of low, middling, and supreme trainees.
May coarse Form Bodies remain steadily without disintegrating or changing
For hundreds of eons in the sight of those who are short sighted.[33]

31 [Read *dug gsum* for *dus gsum* (15.3). The three poisons are desire, hatred, and obscuration.]

32 [See pp. 231-2 and 412-413.]

33 The subtle body remains forever in that the very subtle wind [which is form] – and thus the fundamental innate subtle body – as well as very subtle mind remain forever. A Buddha's coarse Form Bodies appear and disappear, but here you are requesting that

My collections of virtue, illustrated by this, are dedicated
As causes for quickly attaining the state of Kālachakra.

In addition, when there is time, you should familiarize your mental continuum with the common paths in accordance with what appears in the [Seventh Dalai Lama's] *Self-Generation of Kālachakra:*[34]

From this time until enlightenment
I will generate the altruistic intention to become enlightened,
Generate the very pure thought,
And abandon the conception of [inherently existent] I and mine.

For the sake of the three collections [of merit, ethics, and exalted wisdom]
I will achieve the perfections of giving, ethics,
Patience, effort, concentration, wisdom,
Method, wishes, power, and exalted wisdom.[35]

I will cultivate [love wishing] that sentient beings have happiness,
[Compassion wishing] that they be free from suffering,
Joy in their abiding forever in bliss,
And the equanimity of equality.

Having called [students] well with the beckoning of giving,
I will make talk pleasant to hear

even coarse Form Bodies remain for many eons without disappearing.

34 [The Seventh Dalai Lama's *Means of Achievement of the Complete Mandala of Exalted Body, Speech, and Mind of the Supramundane Victor, the Glorious Kālachakra: the Sacred Word of Scholars and Adepts*, 29.3.]

35 The last four perfections are divisions of the perfection of wisdom.

And, having become self-composed through behaving with purpose,
Will offer the great advice of the fulfillment of aims.

I will abandon the ten non-virtues –
The three forms of physical actions,
The four forms of verbal actions,
And the three forms of mental actions.[36]

I will abandon the five defilements
Preventing the three trainings[37] –
Regret, lethargy, sleep,
Excitement, and doubt.

I will abandon the four afflictions
That serve as the root of cyclic existence –
Desire, hatred,
Obscuration, and pride.

I will abandon the four contaminants,
Causes of cyclic existence – the contaminant of desire,
The contaminants of [cyclic] existence[38] and of ignorance,
And the contaminant of [bad] views.

I will achieve complete enlightenment
Through the four doors of thorough liberation –
Emptiness, signlessness,
Wishlessness, and non-activity.

36 [The ten non-virtues are comprised of three physical non-virtues (killing, stealing, and sexual misconduct), four verbal non-virtues (lying, divisive talk, harsh speech and senseless chatter), and three mental non-virtues (covetousness, harmful intent, and wrong ideas).]

37 The three trainings are the trainings in higher ethics, meditative stabilization, and wisdom.

38 Jam-b̄el-shen-pen: All four contaminants are concerned with cyclic existence but desire for the Form and Formless Realms is called a contaminant of cyclic existence *(srid pa'i zag pa)* in order to emphasize that even the Form and Formless Realms, which many have considered to be states of liberation, are bound within cyclic existence.

Taking the meaning of these words to mind, also make a deep promise to train, according to the way, in those paths. Then, make a supplication:

> Supplication to the kind lama, composite of all three refuges,
> Greatest wish-granting source yielding, when relied upon,
> All virtue and goodness within cyclic existence and peace.
> Bless my continuum into magnificence.

Taking to mind the benefits of relying on a spiritual guide and the disadvantages of not doing so, and so forth, make a promise to rely properly on a spiritual guide by way of both thought and deed. This is the essence of how to rely on the spiritual guide and how to keep the pledges of Ashvaghoṣha's *Fifty Stanzas on the Guru*. Through reflecting on the good qualities of the lama's exalted body, speech, and mind you should plant the supplication firmly with strong faith and respect, not just from the mouth but from the depths of the heart. Within that, repeat as much as possible the name-mantra of the lama, together with imagination of the descent of ambrosia and purification through it:[39]

> Oṃ āḥ guru-vajradhara-vagindra-sumati-shāsana-dhara-samudra-shrībhadra sarva-siddhi hūṃ hūṃ.

Again, make a supplication for initiation:

> May the Lama, Kālachakra, please bestow
> Completely the initiations. Bless me into magnificence

39 [The name of the lama who confers the initiation, rendered in Sanskrit, is repeated. Here, *vagindra-sumati-shāsanadhara-samudra-shrībhadra* is the Dalai Lama's name, which in Tibetan is Nga-w̄ang-l̄o-sang-d̄en-dzin-gya-tso-b̄el-sang-b̄o *(ngag dbang blo bzang bstan 'dzin rgya mtsho dpal bzang po): vagindra (ngag dbang) sumati (blo bzang) shāsanadhara (bstan 'dzin) samudra (rgya mtsho) shrībhadra (dpal bzang po)*.]

So that the defilements of the four types[40] may be
purified
And so that I may attain the Four Bodies.[41]

Make the above supplication three times.

From the heart of Kālachakra are emitted
Ones Gone to Bliss, in father and mother aspect,
As well as the circle of the mandala.
The initiation deities bestow the initiations
Of water, crown, silk ribbon, vajra and bell,
Conduct, name, and permission.
Likewise, they bestow the two sets
Of high and greatly high initiations
As well as that of a vajra master.
Through these, the physical channels and winds
Become serviceable, and I am authorized to cultivate the two stages.[42]
I come to have the lot of actualizing in this lifetime
The great state of Kālachakra possessing the seven features[43]
In which the twenty-one thousand six hundred karmic winds

40 These are the defilements associated with the four drops [see pp. 102-122, 260-1]. Beings of all three realms – Desire, Form, and Formless Realms – have these drops though they differ in structure in the Formless Realm. With these four drops are factors producing material phenomena that are purified through practising the path; empty form is beyond matter.

41 Jam-bel-shen-pen: The Four Bodies in the Kālachakra system are particularly the Truth Body, Complete Enjoyment Body, Emanation Body, and Pristine Consciousness Body [Bliss Body]. The Kālachakra initiations are taken in the manner of blessings into magnificence. Without requiring all of the ritual objects such as vases, one receives blessings similar to the initiations.

42 The stage of generation and the stage of completion.

43 [These are qualities of the effect state as a Buddha; they are identified as complete enjoyment, union, great bliss, non-inherent existence, compassion, uninterrupted continuity, and non-cessation. See notes to Tsong-ka-pa's *Tantra in Tibet* (London: George Allen and Unwin, 1977), n.84.]

And all material factors of the body have been
completely consumed.[44]

If at this point you can do reflective meditation on the entire path by way of, for instance, the *Basis of Good Qualities (yon tan gzhi gyur ma)*,[45] it is very good. Then:

As I make supplication respectfully from my heart,
To the Lama, Great Vajradhara, essence comprised
Of all the manifold refuges,
Please bless my continuum into magnificence.
Through the power of petitioning with strong feeling this way
My root Lama, the great Kālachakra,
Comes well to the crown of my head
And, happily dissolving, becomes of one taste with me.
All phenomena – causes, effects, entities,
And activities – are empty of inherent existence
From the very start, like a magician's illusions and dreams.

Manifesting clearly whatever ascertainment of emptiness you have and setting in meditative equipoise on bliss and emptiness is the definitive guru yoga, [a means of] amassing the collection of exalted wisdom, the supreme of protections, and is how to keep the mind from the eleventh infraction, which is to conceive phenomena such as names, [meanings,] and so forth which are devoid [of inherent existence to exist inherently].[46]

44 Twenty-one thousand six hundred karmic winds and twenty-one thousand six hundred material factors are completely consumed through actualizing twenty-one thousand six hundred periods of bliss. Thereby, the state of a Kālachakra Buddha is attained.

45 [For a translation of this as the *Foundation of all Excellence* as well as a commentary on it, see Geshe Wangyal, *The Door of Liberation* (New York: Lotsawa, 1978), pp.172-200.]

46 Jam-bel-shen-pen: The infraction here is not just to conceive that phenomena exist inherently but rather is to do so through the force of systems of tenets; thus the reference is not to an innate consciousness conceiving inherent existence but to an artificial conception of inherent existence.

Like bubbles coming from within emptiness
Are discs of [white] moon, [red] sun, [black] rāhu, and [yellow] kālāgni planets.
On them in the center of a lotus with opened petals
Are [again] moon and sun,[47] entities of the white and red constituents,
The surfaces of which are beautified with the series
Of vowels and consonants, entities of the major and minor marks [of a Buddha].[48]
In the center are the syllables *hūṃ* and *hi,* [representing] wind and mind.
These mix together into the form of the syllable *haṃ.*[49]
Through its transformation I [appear as] Kālachakra,
Bearing the brilliance of sapphire and blazing with magnificence,
Having four faces and twenty-four hands, the first two
Holding vajra and bell symbolizing great bliss,
Supreme and immutable, and the actuality of emptiness,
The nature devoid of [dualistic] elaborations.
Holding these, I embrace the Mother.

Contemplation of this is how to keep the three Akṣhobhya pledges of vajra, bell, and seal.

The remaining hand-lotuses, right and left, are adorned
With hand-symbols – sword, shield, and so forth.
My outstretched red right leg and bent white left leg
Sport in dance on top of Māra and Rudra.

47 Here the sun is below and the moon above.

48 As is presented in the Seventh Dalai Lama's *Means of Achievement of the Complete Mandala of Exalted Body, Speech, and Mind of the Supramundane Victor, the Glorious Kālachakra: the Sacred Word of Scholars and Adepts,* there are thirty-two vowels and eighty consonants [two sets of forty] representing the thirty-two major marks and the eighty minor marks.

49 The syllable *haṃ* represents the exalted wisdom of great bliss.

With hundreds of such features I charm.
My body is adorned with many types of amazing ornaments,
Dwelling in the midst of the five stainless lights ablaze,
Like the expanse of space beautified by the constellations.
Facing the Supramundane Victor, Vishvamātā
Of saffron color has four faces and eight hands
Holding various hand-symbols, knife, skull, and so forth.
In the posture with left leg extended
She embraces the Supramundane Victor.
Surrounded by eight shaktis on the seats
Of the eight[50] auspicious petals in the main and intermediate directions,
The principal figure, situated well, emits from his heart
Vajravegas, very fearful, holding various weapons;
They draw in the groups of protectors dwelling in countless lands
Who become of the same taste as the pledge-being.
Initiation deities bestow initiation and make the seal-impression
Of the lineage lord on top of the heads of all the figures, principal and surrounding.

Then, with respect to repetition of mantra, think:

The seed-syllables at the heart of the principal and surrounding figures
Are surrounded by the series of their respective mantras
From which groups of mandala deities are emitted
Effecting the welfare of transmigrators and again gathering
And dissolving into the seed syllable at the heart.

50 The word *bkra shis* (luck) here means "eight", the connection being that there are eight renowned signs of luck.

Repeat as much as you can, without any of the eight faults of repetition,[51] the essence mantra of the principal figure and the mantra of the Mother as well as the mantras of the eight shaktis:[52]

> Oṃ āḥ hūṃ hoḥ haṃkṣhaḥmalaverava hūṃ phaṭ.
> Oṃ phreṃ vishvamātā huṃ hūṃ phaṭ.
> Oṃ dāna-pāramitā huṃ hūṃ phaṭ.
> Oṃ shīla-pāramitā huṃ hūṃ phaṭ.
> Oṃ kṣhānti-pāramitā huṃ hūṃ phaṭ.
> Oṃ vīrya-pāramitā huṃ hūṃ phaṭ.
> Oṃ dhyāna-pāramitā huṃ hūṃ phaṭ.
> Oṃ prajñā-pāramitā huṃ hūṃ phaṭ.
> Oṃ upāya-pāramitā huṃ hūṃ phaṭ.
> Oṃ praṇidhāna-pāramitā huṃ hūṃ phaṭ.
> Oṃ bala-pāramitā huṃ hūṃ phaṭ.
> Oṃ jñāna-pāramitā huṃ hūṃ phaṭ.
> Oṃ vajrasatva, samayam anupālaya, vajrasatva, tvenopatiṣhṭha, dṛḍho me bhava, sutoṣhyo me bhava, supoṣhyo me bhava, anurakto me bhava, sarva-siddhiṃ me prayachchha, sarva-karmasu cha me chittaṃ shrīyam kuru, hūṃ ha ha ha ha hoḥ, bhagavan-sarva-tathāgata-vajra, mā me muñcha, vajrī bhava, mahāsamaya-satva, āḥ hūṃ phaṭ. [Oṃ Vajrasattva, keep (your) pledge. Vajrasattva, reside (in me). Make me firm. Make me satisfied. Fulfil me. Make me compassionate. Grant me all feats. Also, make my mind virtuous in all actions. Hūṃ ha ha ha ha hoḥ all the supramundane victorious Ones Gone Thus, do not abandon me, make me indivisible. Great Pledge being, āḥ hūṃ phaṭ.]

51 Jam-bel-shen-pen: These are faults of pronunciation and elocution such as speaking too slowly or too quickly.

52 [Of the thirteen mantras the first is that of Kālachakra; the second is of Vishvamātā, and the next ten are of the ten shaktis, two of whom are united with Vishvamātā. The final mantra is the hundred syllable mantra, used here for making up for omissions and so forth in one's mantra repetition.]

With the [above] hundred syllable mantra, make up for omissions and excesses and make the blessings firm. Then, make offering to yourself generated [as Kālachakra], thinking:

> Goddesses of offering emitted from my heart make offering [to myself generated as Kālachakra].
>
> Oṃ shrī-kālachakra-saparivāra arghaṃ pratīchchha namaḥ. [Oṃ glorious Kālachakra and retinue, accept an oblation, homage.]
>
> Oṃ shrī-kālachakra-saparivāra pādyaṃ pratīchchha namaḥ. [Oṃ glorious Kālachakra and retinue, accept a foot-bath, homage.]
>
> Oṃ shrī-kālachakra-saparivāra prokṣhaṇaṃ pratīchchha namaḥ. [Oṃ glorious Kālachakra and retinue, accept sprinkling, homage.]
>
> Oṃ shrī-kālachakra-saparivāra aṃchamānaṃ pratīchchha namaḥ. [Oṃ glorious Kālachakra and retinue, accept water for the face, homage.]
>
> Oṃ shrī-kālachakra-saparivāra puṣhpe pratīchchha namaḥ. [Oṃ glorious Kālachakra and retinue, accept flowers, homage.]
>
> Oṃ shrī-kālachakra-saparivāra dhūpe pratīchchha namaḥ. [Oṃ glorious Kālachakra and retinue, accept incense, homage.]
>
> Oṃ shrī-kālachakra-saparivāra āloke pratīchchha namaḥ. [Oṃ glorious Kālachakra and retinue, accept lamps, homage.]
>
> Oṃ shrī-kālachakra-saparivāra gandhe pratīchchha namaḥ. [Oṃ glorious Kālachakra and retinue, accept perfume, homage.]
>
> Oṃ shrī-kālachakra-saparivāra naividya pratīchchha namaḥ. [Oṃ glorious Kālachakra and retinue, accept food, homage.]
>
> Oṃ shrī-kālachakra-saparivāra shabda pratīchchha namaḥ. [Oṃ glorious Kālachakra and retinue, accept music, homage.]
>
> Oṃ shrī-kālachakra-maṇḍala-saparivāribhyaḥ namaḥ.[Oṃ homage to the glorious Kālachakra mandala and retinue.]

With [the latter] make the internal offering. Then, make praise:

> Homage to the glorious Kālachakra,
> Whose essence is emptiness and compassion,[53]
> Who is without the production and disintegration[54]
> of the triple[55] cyclic existence,
> Body in which mind and object of the mind are the same.[56]
>
> Obeisance to Kālachakra,
> Body born from the immutable
> Though absorption of *āli* and *kāli*[57] and the syllables
> *Hūṃ, phaṭ*, and so forth have been abandoned.[58]
>
> Obeisance to the Great Seal Woman,
> Beyond the nature of material particles,
> Having the nature of a prophetic configuration,

53 Here "emptiness and compassion" refer to undifferentiable emptiness and bliss – emptiness being the ultimate truth that is the absence of inherent existence, the aspectless great seal, and compassion being the immutable great bliss.

54 The "production of cyclic existence" refers to the extreme of cyclic existence itself; the "disintegration of cyclic existence" refers to the extreme of [solitary] nirvana. Similarly, in the *Chakrasaṃvara Tantra*, there is reference to the extreme of permanence or cyclic existence and the extreme of annihilation or nirvana. The non-abiding nirvana of a Buddha is free from the two extremes of disintegration and production, or cyclic existence and [solitary] nirvana.

55 Jam-bel-shen-pen: The "triple cyclic existence" refers, not to the three realms, but to body, speech, and mind.

56 Here "mind" refers to the supreme immutable bliss, and "object of the mind" refers to the aspected great seal of empty form; such exalted mind and body are one undifferentiable entity, non-dual. Obeisance is made to such a Kālachakra.

57 Jam-bel-shen-pen: The white and red constituents are symbolized by the vowels and consonants, called *āli* and *kāli*.

58 Obeisance is made to Kālachakra who "is born from", that is, has a nature of, immutable bliss that is generated, not from an action seal [an actual consort], a wisdom seal [an imagined consort], or from movement within the channels, winds, and drops of essential fluid, but from the great seal of empty form.

Woman possessing the supreme of all aspects.[59]

Homage to Vishvamātā,
Progenitress of all Buddhas,[60]
Who has abandoned production and distintegration,
Endowed with all-good deeds.

Then, perform withdrawal [of all appearances]:

The shaktis, as well as their seats, melt
Into light and dissolve into myself.
I also melt into light and then from within the emptiness of unapprehendability
Again transform into the aspect of the great Kālachakra
With one face and two hands.

At this point, it is appropriate also to cultivate the stage of completion. Then:

For the sake of all sentient beings, my mothers,
From now on I give away without regret
My body, resources, and whatsoever masses
Of virtue of the past, present, and future.

This increasing of the attitude of generosity is the Bodhisattva practice of giving and is how to keep the two remaining pledges of Ratnasambhava – the giving of things, which is to give away body and resources, and the giving of doctrine, which is to give away roots of virtue. When there is time, you at least should review the pledges and vows by way of their

59 The body of Vishvamātā, the "Great Seal Woman," is beyond the materiality of particles. Like a configuration that appears in a mirror in a certain way of making prophecies, her body – from within the fundamental innate mind of clear light – is endowed with the supreme of all aspects. Obeisance is made to such a Vishvamātā.

60 Jam-bel-shen-pen: The definitive Vishvamātā is the exalted wisdom directly realizing emptiness; since it gives rise to all Buddhas, the goddess that represents it is the progenitress of all Buddhas. The provisional Vishvamātā is the appearance of that wisdom as a goddess in physical form.

individual compendia as given later [in this text]. In short form, observe mere mindfulness of the three vows:

> I will achieve in accordance with the Conqueror's word
> The precepts formulated for the vows
> Of individual liberation, Bodhisattvas, and Vajra Vehicle,
> Not transgressing the subtler ones even in dreams.

Thinking on this accomplishes the brief mode of observing mindfulness of the three vows, the Vairochana pledge of restraining ill-deeds in relation to the three forms of ethics, and the Amoghasiddhi pledge of possessing all three vows.

> In accordance with the thought of the Conqueror, I will assume well
> All without exception of the excellent doctrine – verbal and realizational –
> Contained within the three vehicles and the four tantra sets.

Thinking on this fulfills the three pledges of the lotus lineage to apprehend the doctrine of the three vehicles in the Sūtra class [Hearer, Solitary Realizer, and Bodhisattva], and the two external doctrines in the Mantra class – Action and Performance Tantra – and the two secret doctrines in the Mantra class, Yoga and Highest Yoga Tantra. It also fulfills the Vairochana pledge of maintaining the ethics that is the composite of virtuous practices.

> I will thoroughly liberate transmigrators through methods appropriate to them.

Thinking on this is how to keep the Vairochana pledge of the ethics of effecting the welfare of sentient beings. Then, make wishes for what is being sought and dedication of virtue to highest enlightenment:

> Just as those of the lineage of sages along with Ravi came to attain knowledge-wisdom from this [tantra],

So may sentient beings dwelling in the three forms of cyclic existence become the same through the kindness of the *Kālachakra* [*Tantra*].[61]

In just the way that my mind-vajra dwells throughout the earth for the sake of liberating sentient beings,

So may it dwell in the three forms of cyclic existence of sentient beings through the force of Kālachakra.[62]

May those beings who through evil friends always go in the darkness of untruth and whose path is degenerate

61 Just as many of the lineage of sages including the sage *(drang srong, ṛṣhi)* Sūryaratha *(nyi ma'i shing rta)* [mentioned as Ravi *(nyi ma)*] attained common and uncommon fruits of the path and became enlightened from this tantra, so may all sentient beings of the three levels of existence attain all common and uncommon feats through the kindness of this *Kālachakra Tantra*.

[These two lines are from the *Kālachakra Tantra* (V.253cd):
prajñājñānasya lābhī saravimunikulaṃ vai tathāsmadbabhūva
evaṃ sattvā bhavantu trividhabhavagatāḥ kālachakraprasādāt.
See the *Kālachakra-Tantra and Other Texts*, Part 1, p.377 for the Sanskrit and p.328.5 for the Tibetan which differs slightly but not importantly from that cited in this text. See also Bu-dön's *Easily Understandable Annotations*, volume 1, Collected Works, 294.7-295.1, where he identifies the "three forms of cyclic existence" as the Desire, Form, and Formless Realms and from which the bracketed additions are taken.]

62 [These two lines are from the *Kālachakra Tantra* (V.258cd):
sattvānāṃ mokṣhahetoḥ sakalabhuvigataṃ chittavajraṃ yathā me
sattvānām eva yātu trividhabhavagataṃ kālacharkraprabhāvāt.
See the *Kālacakra-Tantra And Other Texts*, Part 1, p.379 for the Sanskrit and p.329.8 for the Tibetan which differs slightly but not importantly from that cited in this text. See also Bu-dön's *Easily Understandable Annotations*, volume 1, Collected Works, 296.7-297.2, which renders the two lines as follows:

Just as in order that sentient beings may be liberated my, that is to say, Mañjushrīkīrti's, mind vajra – mind devoid of obstructions – dwells throughout the entire earth, so may the exalted mind vajra abide and become manifest for the three forms of cyclic existence – Desire, Form, and Formless Realms – of

Attain this path and come to the vajra-jewel house
in a not long time.[63]

Also:

Through the power of the wholesome virtues that
have come from this
May I, through the power of Vajradhara, not transgress
The boundaries of formulations in all lifetimes
And complete the stages of the path of the two
stages.[64]

In short, through whatsoever collections of whole-
some virtue,
As illustrated by this, have been accumulated,
May I quickly take birth in Shambhala, the treasury
of jewels
And complete the stages of the path of Highest
Yoga Tantra.

In all lifetimes may I enjoy the glory of the doctrine
Without being separated from true lamas
And, thoroughly completing the qualities of the
grounds and paths,
Quickly attain the state of a Vajradhara.

Make the seal-impression of such wishes and dedications. Then, adorn [the practice] with a final expression of auspiciousness:

sentient beings through the force of Kālachakra.

Mañjushrīkīrti is the person who put together the *Condensed Kālachakra Tantra;* this, like the preceding two lines, is a wish made by him at the end of the tantra.

In the *Guru Yoga of Kālachakra* (30.5 read *dag gi rnam* for *dag gis rnam* in accordance with Bu-dön and the tantra *(sattvānāṃ)* as given just above.]

63 May those who, under the influence of bad friends, always go upon the path of untruth of darkness and have fallen from a path of virtue, attain this good, unmistaken path and proceed quickly to the vajra-jewel house – the state of a Vajradhara.

64 [Stage of generation and stage of completion.]

May the Bodhisattvas above [the earth] who supremely frighten the demi-gods dwelling in the class of demons,
The wrathful kings as well as their consorts who dwell in the directions and intermediate directions in the worlds of humans,
And the kings of hooded serpents under the earth who at all times bind up the groups of evil spirits and unvirtuous ones –
May all of them protect unknowing worldly beings in all respects each day.[65]

The extensive review of the three vows begins, if you have the vow of individual liberation of full ordination, with reviewing the two hundred fifty-three rules. [This section is to be omitted by those who do not have the vows of a fully ordained monk]:

From among the five groups of infractions
Of the vows of individual liberation
I will abandon the four defeats,
The thirteen remainders, the thirty downfalls [requiring] abandonment,

65 May protective beings above, on, and below the ground protect all worldly beings from inauspiciousness, bringing them in accordance with virtue to an unmistaken path.

[These four lines are from the *Kālachakra Tantra* (V.260):
ūrdhvaṃ ye bodhisattvāḥ paramabhayakarā mārapakṣhe sthitānāṃ
daityānāṃ martyaloke dishi-vidishi-gatāḥ krodharājāḥ sabhāryah
pātāle ye phaṇīndrā grahaparamashubham sarvadā bandhayanti
te sarve pālayantu pratidinasamaye 'jñānalokaṃ samantāt.
See the *Kālacakra-Tantra And Other Texts,* Part 1, p.379 for the Sanskrit and p.329.8 for the Tibetan which differs slightly but not importantly from that cited in this text. See also Bu-dön's *Easily Understandable Annotations,* volume 1, Collected Works, 297.4-.7, where the unknowing worldly beings are identified as not knowing the meaning of reality *(yang dag pa'i don).*

In the *Guru Yoga of Kālachakra* (30.5) read *mi shes* for *mi shis* in accordance with Bu-dön and the tantra *('jñāna)* as given just above.]

The ninety mere [infractions], the four to be individually disclosed,
And one hundred twelve faults, and also infractions included within the [seventeen] topics, and so forth.

The review of the eighteen root infractions of the Bodhisattva vow is:

I will keep from the eighteen root infractions –
Praising myself and deriding others, not giving doctrine or wealth,
Not forgiving though someone apologizes, abandoning the Great Vehicle,
Stealing the property of the Three Jewels, abandoning the doctrine,
Stealing a saffron robe, the five deeds of immediate retribution,
Wrong view, destroying cities and so forth,
Teaching emptiness to the untrained,
Reversing [someone's] intention to become completely enlightened,
[Causing someone] to abandon [vows of] individual liberation, deriding the Hearer Vehicle,
Falsely claiming [to have realized] the profound, receiving the property of the Three Jewels,
Bad ethics, and giving up the attitude of altruistic promise.
For sixteen, all four thorough entanglements –
Not considering the disadvantages, not overcoming the wish to do it,
Taking pleasure and delight in it, and lack of conscience and shame –
Are needed for there to be a root infraction.
For two, wrong view and giving up the altruistic attitude,
All four are not needed [for a root infraction].

Review of the root infractions and so forth of the Mantra vow:

Risking my life, I will keep from the fourteen root infractions –
Scorning and deriding the lama, despising the precepts,
Speaking fault of vajra brothers and sisters, abandoning love,
Giving up the aspirational and practical altruistic intentions,
Deriding the doctrines of Sūtra and Mantra,
Proclaiming the secret to the unripened,
Despising my own aggregates, abandoning emptiness,
Relying on a poisonous friend, not recollecting the view,
Uprooting the attitude of one with faith,
Not observing the pledges, and deriding women.

Also, review the root infractions and twenty-five modes of conduct and so forth mentioned in the *Kālachakra Tantra:*

I will keep well and properly from
The root infractions and likewise the collections of faults
Set forth in the *Kālachakra Tantra:* the groups of root infractions –
Disturbing the mind of the lama, breaking his word,
Emitting the essential fluid, holding the emptiness of Sūtra and Mantra
Respectively to be superior and inferior and thus making derision,
Deceitful love, abandoning the immutable bliss,
And speaking fault of yogis.
The twenty-five modes of conduct are to keep from
The five ill-deeds – killing, lying, stealing,
Adultery, and drinking beer;
The five secondary ill-deeds – making bets, dice, and board games,
Eating impure flesh, speaking senselessly,

Performing sacrifice for paternal and maternal ancestors,
And killing animals for making bloody sacrifice;
The five murders – killing cattle, children, women,
And men and destroying bases of exalted body, speech, and mind;
The five wrong thoughts – non-faith in the Buddha doctrine,
Enmity toward friends, leaders, and the Spiritual Community,
And deceiving those who trust in myself;
And the five desires – attachment for visible forms,
Sounds, odors, tastes, and tangible objects.

Review of the secondary pledges:

I will keep, without exception, the secondary pledges –
To abandon the four roots,[66] beer, and non-activities,
To rely on a holy protector, to respect and serve friends,
To maintain the ten virtues, and to abandon causes
Of turning away from the Great Vehicle
As well as contempt for and stepping over [sacred articles].

Review of gross infractions:

I also keep properly from the gross infractions –
Using an unqualified Seal [consort], engaging in absorption without the three discriminations,
Showing secret articles to those who are not vessels,
Quarrelling and disputing at an offering-assembly,
Perversely answering a question of the faithful,
Staying seven days in the home of a Hearer,
Claiming to be a yogi though not really so,
Teaching the excellent doctrine to the faithless,

66 [Killing, stealing, sexual misconduct, and lying about spiritual attainments.]

Engaging in mandala activities without completing the approximation and so forth,
Purposelessly transgressing the precepts of individual liberation and Bodhisattva vows,
And contradicting [the precepts set forth in] the *Fifty Stanzas on the Guru*.[67]

Review of the uncommon pledges set forth in the Mother Tantras:

I will not look down on left-handed behavior,
Will make praises [of women/men],
Abandon absorption with the unqualified,
Not be devoid of the view when in union,
Take unchanging interest in using desire in the path,
Not disregard the two types of Seals,
Mainly work at external and internal methods,
Not emit the kunda, keep pure behavior,
And forsake nausea when taking the mind of enlightenment.

If wishes are made in more extensive form, they are:[68]

Through the power of the great increase of the vast lake
Of the collections of virtue upon the accumulation—again and again

67 [See *The Mahāmudrā Eliminating the Darkness of Ignorance Supplemented by Aśvaghoṣa's Fifty Stanzas of Guru Devotion*, translated and edited by Alexander Berzin (Dharamsala: Library of Tibetan Works and Archives, 1978).]

68 [This final section of wishes, except for the last stanza, is taken verbatim from the *Prayer-Wishes of the Glorious Kālachakra Together With An Expression of Auspiciousness (dpal dus kyi 'khor lo'i smon lam shis brjod dang bcas pa)*, 553-559.8, by the Buddhist monk Lo-drö *(shākya btsun pa blo gros)*. In the colophon, Lo-drö says that he composed the text, which has a section that is not used here, to fulfill a reference at the end of Kay-drup's *Rosary of Offering of Kālachakra (dus kyi 'khor lo'i mchod phreng)* to make extensive wishes and expressions of auspiciousness. The text is in the same volume with Kay-drup's *Mandala Rite*, Lo-sang-tsul-trim-den-

In the lake of my mind – of the stainless stream of meditation,
Repetition, and offering from the snow mountain of such pure special thought

And through the power of mentally gathering together
All the collections of virtues related with the past, present, and future,
May I be taken care of in life after life
By holy protectors, spiritual guides of the supreme vehicle.

From the instructions happily bestowed by them
May I come to know the way of gathering together the doctrines
Of the three vehicles and from practising their meaning
Ripen my mental continuum with the common paths.

Through attaining the seven pure initiations
May potencies for the seven grounds be well established,
The seven stains of the constituents and so forth be cleansed,
And I be empowered to practice the yoga of the first stage and achieve the common feats.

Through the four supreme initiations, mundane and supramundane,
May the seeds of the four vajras of the Four Bodies be established
And I be authorized to hear, explain, and cultivate

b̄ay-gyel-tsen's *Initiation Rite of Kālachakra, Stated in an Easy Way*, etc. with no publication data. The wishes are directed toward practising the full structure of paths of the stages of generation and completion of the Kālachakra system. An explanation of the stanzas requires a full explanation of the entire path structure of the tantra and thus will not be attempted here. I hope to publish a separate work on the Kālachakra stage of generation.]

The four branches of approximation and achievement of the second stage.

Sitting well on the throne of the four pure initiations
In the supreme inestimable mansion of the Vajra Vehicle
With the foot-stool of non-deteriorated vows and pledges
May I become a universal monarch of the doctrine of the two stages.

Through exalted body, speech, mind, and wisdom, cleansed and purified,
Through the yoga of meditating on the six lineages and the six branches,
And through the light of vajras set in individual places in the body,
Strongly blazing, may demons and obstructors be burned.

May mandalas of the four elements be generated
In the middle of the expanse of space
And from their combining into one may a five- and three-staged fence
As well as a palace with a seat be established.

In the center of that may I as the glorious Vajravega
Through the firm meditative stabilization of the King of Wrathful Ones
Put an end to external and internal demons and obstructors
By emitting a host of sixty guardians of the doors.

Considering that through the exercise of dispersal and gathering
The field of accumulation pervades the full expanse of space,
May the collections, powerful like waves, be thoroughly completed
Through performing the amassing of the accumulations – the preparation – according to the rite.

Through cultivating the pride of the Truth Body at the end
Of the dissolution of the six constituents just as in the stages of death
May I complete the meditative stabilization of the four doors of liberation
Bringing about full enlightenment instantaneously.

Through meditating on space, wind, fire, water, earth, and Mount Meru,
May I realize the status of vajra-body,
With channel wheels and so forth at the crown of the head,
Forehead, neck, heart, navel, and secret region.

Through meditating well on a vajra tent
On top of lotus, moon, sun, rāhu, and kālāgni,
May the collections of winds of the right and left channels be stopped
In the channel-with-conch through the supreme vajra yoga.

Through the power of meditating on an inestimable mansion
With the light of stainless jewels inside the vajra tent
May the land where I will be enlightened as a Buddha
Be purified and my physical support become free from defilement.

Through meditating on the twos – moon and sun, vowels and consonants,
Wind and mind, and the two letters – combining into one, the letter *haṃ*,
May great bliss be generated from the gathering together in the central channel
Of the white and red constituents and the subtle wind and mind.

Then through the power of meditating on the deities of the mandala of great bliss –

The exalted body of Kālachakra, complete in all aspects,
Having the nature of the great bliss possessing the supreme of all aspects
Together with his Knowledge Woman –

May [these meditations] serve as causes of generating
The supreme stages of completion in which the Great Seal
Of empty form is filled with the taste of immutable innate bliss,
Actually embraced[69] respectively by the aspected and unaspected Seals.

Through cultivating manifest enlightenment by way of the five aspects,
The supreme king of mandalas, the branch of approximation,
Generating from the seed of absorption of Father and Mother
The supreme complete circle of the deities in the womb

And setting them well in their respective places,
May I generate the supreme realizations of the path
Through purifying the aggregates, constituents, sense faculties,
Objects, action faculties, and activities.

With the vajric Supramundane Victor as well as a Knowledge Woman
Who abide in the lotus of the wheel of great bliss
And dwell in the form of a drop of great bliss
Through the force of having been melted by the fire of the fierce woman at the navel,

May I meditatively cultivate the branch of near-achievement, the supreme

69 [Read *'khyud pa'i* for *brgyud pa'i* (43.1).]

King of activities, by means of enlightenment in
twenty aspects –
The five arousals by the pleasant song of goddesses,
The five constructions, and the five comprised by
the five Fierce Ones

Drawing [the wisdom-beings] to the circle of
pledge-beings,
Entry, binding, being delighted, and becoming of
one taste –
And by means of bestowing initiation, seal-impression, and mindfulness of purity,
And thereby may the meanings of those be actualized.

Through the blazing upward in the central channel
Of the fire of the fierce woman incited by the
downward-voiding wind
Upon blessing the secret space into magnificence
and becoming absorbed
And, from that, the gradual descent of the mind of
enlightenment

Due to the melting of the letter *haṃ* at the crown of
the head
And the stopping of the movement of the winds in
the right and left channels,
May the yoga of the drops be actualized, the
supreme branch of achievement
Causing me to understand well the four joys of the
forward process.

Through the four joys of stability from below of the
passage
Upward again in the same procedure
May I bring to completion the branch of great
achievement,
The subtle yoga, and the manifest enlightenment
of the magical net.

In short, may I bring to completion the effort of
cultivating in four sessions

The supreme stage of generation purifying the external and internal bases of purification,
Water cleansing ordinary appearance and the conception of ordinariness,
The path ripening for the full generation of the stage of completion.

Also, may I ripen limitless transmigrators through unimpededness
In achieving the feats of final achievement
Of the highest type through striving
At repetition, burnt offering, and giving of offerings.

May I familiarize with the six-branched yoga:
The two virtues at the beginning – individual withdrawal and concentration,
The two virtues in the middle – the paths of vitality-stopping and retention,
And the two virtues at the end – mindfulness and meditative stabilization.

May my mind be set one-pointedly, free from laxity and excitement,
On the place where it is contemplated that a corner of the eyes
Enters inside the upper point of the central channel
Through the gaze of half-closed eyes, turned upward.

Through that may the four night signs – like smoke, mirage,
Fireflies, and butter lamp – be manifested,
Unmistaken signs of the gathering of the collections
Of the winds of the right and left channels in the central channel.

Also, through meditating well as before
In the manner of looking at space free from clouds,
May the six signs – blazing, moon, sun, rāhu,
Lightning, and drop – be completed.

Through the concentration of one-pointed observation of forms
According to my wish, upon the gradual withdrawal
Of the empty forms in the area of the body-drop,
May the bliss of physical and mental pliancy be induced.

Through the power of one-pointed familiarization with the two yogas
Of achieving empty forms in that way
And of making steady those achieved,
May I achieve the word of truth and the five clairvoyances.

Through familiarizing with the vitality-stopping of spontaneous vajra repetition
In which wind and mantra are inseparable in the path of rāhu
And the vitality-stopping of pot [-like wind control]
In which the upper and lower winds cease at the navel,

May the special signs of the collections of the winds
Entirely entering and remaining for a while
In the center of the wheel of emanation dawn
And the melodiousness praised by Bodhisattvas be actualized.

Through the yoga of holding my mind steadily at the end of generating
The four joys of descent from above and stability from below
Without fluctuation in the center of the mixture of the vitalizing
And downward-voiding winds into one at the center of the six wheels,

May I rise for my own mind in a body of empty form

And the groups of demons of untimely death be suppressed.
Having attained well the power of control over all forms and vitality,
May I actually rise in a body of empty form

In father-mother union
From the innate bliss induced
By igniting again the fire of the fierce woman,
And may light rays of various colors spread out from my hair-pores.

May I perform meditation in which the immutable great bliss
Induced well by the power of the Seal –
Through union with a Great Seal
Of such empty form – is joined with emptiness.

Through the power of piling up the white and red constituents,
Twenty-one thousand six hundred in number,
Up and down throughout the central channel,
May the material constituents of my body be consumed as iron is by mercury.

May the twenty-one thousand six hundred immutable
Great blisses realizing emptiness
Cease that number of karmic winds, quickly purify
Obstructive predispositions, and I attain a Conqueror's exalted body.

May I easily achieve these wishes
Without hindrance, becoming a supreme captain
Releasing transmigrators through this supreme path
Into the supreme land of jewels of a Conqueror.

In short, through whatever collections of wholesome virtue,
As illustrated by this, have been accumulated,

May I quickly take birth in Shambhala, the treasury of jewels,
And complete the stages of the path in Highest Yoga Tantra.

[End of recitation and meditation]

Colophon

Where else than in this profound path
Of divine guru yoga and the six session yoga
Is there the king of wish-granting jewels bestowing easily in one life
The vajra-body with an essence of emptiness and compassion!

Therefore this great fruit cluster of the all-inclusive [wish-granting tree] of ritual formulation
Grown well from the golden ground of special thought
Is offered as a cloud of offerings pleasing the one with lotus in hand,
As it is well contrived and resplendent with a hundred thousand moons.

May the great river of the priceless teaching of the One Gone to Bliss,
Beautified in all directions with series of waves of explanation and achievement,
Be exalted with the play of the three modes of scholarship[70]
By the kings of nāgas magnificent with the hoods of the three trainings.[71]

May he who has the nature of appearing as the one friend of all beings on the three levels,
Dance of compassion of the oceans of Conquerors pervading space,

70 Jam-b̄el-shen-pen: The three modes of scholarship are explanation, debate, and composition.

71 Jam-b̄el-shen-pen: The three trainings are the trainings of higher ethics, meditative stabilization, and wisdom.

Be firm in the sky of the mind of transmigrators
Subduing the darkness of troubles through the blazing warm rays of his activity.

Through this supremely superior good path may beings equal in number to particles
Thoroughly conquer over the combat of the four types of defilements
And actualize in not too long the state of Kālachakra
With the complete dexterity of the ten fearless powers.

This "Mode of Practicing Guru Yoga In Dependence Upon the Supramundane Victor Kālachakra In Connection With the Six Session Yoga, Fruit Cluster of the All-Inclusive Wish-Granting Tree" was very respectfully written down by the ninety-seventh occupant of the throne of Gan-den, the respectful servant, the Tutor Līng [Rin-b̄o-chay] called Tup-d̄en-lung-d̄ok-ñam-gyel-trin-lay *(thub bstan lung rtogs rnam rgyal 'phrin las)* at the behest of the supreme great refuge and protector [His Holiness the Fourteenth Dalai Lama], the divine crown jewel of cyclic existence and peace, who asked that, for the sake of sustaining the practice of his meditation, a rite be formulated upon his indicating the nature of the contents and how to arrange the order. May this which is offered serve as a cause of all transmigrators' being taken care of with pleasure by the pervasive lord and guru, Kālachakra.

2 *Six Session Yoga*

This text was formulated by the First Panchen Lama Lo-sang-chö-gyi-gyel-tsen (blo bzang chos kyi rgyal mtshan, 1567?-1662). Only the actual meditation rite has been translated, not the brief identifications of which vows, pledges, and so forth are being fulfilled, since these were given in the first text. The section at the end that reviews the vows individually appears to have been added by Pa-bong-ka (see p.135).

Until enlightenment I go for refuge to the Buddha,
The Doctrine, and the Supreme of Communities.
Through the merit of the giving and so forth that I have done
May I achieve Buddhahood in order to help transmigrators.
(3 times)

May all sentient beings, having become devoid of the attachment and aversion
Of [holding some as] close and [others as] distant, attain superior bliss.
Having become free from the ocean of suffering difficult to bear
May they never become separate from the bliss of excellent liberation.

From henceforth until attaining Buddhahood
I will hold without forsaking, even if it costs my life,
The attitude of wishing to attain complete enlightenment
In order to release all transmigrators from the frights of cyclic existence and [solitary] peace.

Lamas, Conquerors, and their Children,
Please take heed of me.
Just as the earlier Ones Gone to Bliss
Generated an altruistic intention to become enlightened
And dwelt by stages in the learnings of Bodhisattvas,
So I also for the sake of helping transmigrators
Will generate an altruistic intention to become enlightened
And train in stages in the learnings of Bodhisattvas.
(3 times)

Now my life is fruitful.
I have attained a good human existence.
Today I have been born in the Buddha lineage.
I have become a Buddha Child.

Now, whatever happens,
I will act so as not to sully
This flawless holy Buddha lineage,
Initiating actions concordant with this lineage.

On a mentally captivating jewel throne in space in front of myself
Upon discs of sun, moon, and opened lotus
Is my root lama, the Pervasive Master Vajradhara,
Blue in color, with one face, his two hands holding vajra and bell,

Embracing a consort like himself.
Blazing with the magnificence of the major and minor marks and wearing many precious adornments,
He wears clothing of divine substance captivating the mind.
Merely through taking him to mind, all distress is eliminated.

Essence containing all the supreme refuges,
He sits in the cross-legged posture, the three places [of his body]
Adorned with the three letters. Through the light of the letter *hūṃ*,
The lama Vajradhara [is invited] from his natural abode;
Jaḥ hūṃ baṃ hoḥ. They become non-dual.

I bow to the lotus feet of Vajradhara,
Lama like a jewel
Through whose kindness great bliss itself
Dawns in an instant.

I make offering with oceans of clouds of various
External, internal, and secret offerings,
Things held by owners and not held,
Things actually arranged and emanated with the mind.

To the lama, personal deity, and Three Jewels I offer in visualization
The body, speech, mind, and resources of myself and others,
Our collections of virtue in the past, present, and future,
And the wonderful precious mandala with the masses of Samantabhadra's offerings.
Accepting them through your compassion, please empower me with blessings.
[Idaṃ guru-ratna-maṇḍalakaṃ niryātayāmi. (I offer this jewelled mandala to the guru.)]

I petition the lama, precious one
Endowed with a Conqueror's deeds in innumerable lands
Through the sport of saffron of all the Ones Gone To Bliss of the three times
And ten directions, in accordance with what will subdue [trainees].

I petition the lama, precious one
Praised well as the excellent field surpassing

All the wheels of the manifold Conquerors
For the thought of those of low mind, [emanated] by Vajradhara.

Having seen that all without exception of the supreme and common feats
Follow after proper reliance on you, O Protector,
May I, disregarding body and life,
Be blessed to achieve only what is pleasing to you.

Through making such petitions, the supreme lama
Comes to the crown of my head, samājaḥ,
And happily becomes again of one taste with me.

All environments and beings, like magicians' illusions, dreams,
And the moon [reflected] in water, are empty of inherent existence.
Though not truly existent, appearances designated by names and thoughts
Appear like water bubbles coming forth in water.[1]

With the pride of being Vajrasattva,
Holding the symbols – the secret vajra of innate great bliss
And the secret bell of freedom from the elaborations of inherent existence –
I embrace the Female Supramundane Victor.

For the sake of all sentient beings, my mothers,
From now on I give away without regret
My body, resources, and whatsoever masses
Of virtue of the past, present, and future.

I will keep from the eighteen root infractions –
Praising oneself and deriding others, not giving doctrine or wealth,

1 This stanza is added, in accordance with instruction from His Holiness the Dalai Lama, from a work by Gung-tang Gön-chok-den-bay-drön may (*gung thang dkon mchog bstan pa'i sgron me*, 1762-1823).

Not forgiving though someone apologizes, abandoning the Great Vehicle,
Stealing the property of the Three Jewels, abandoning the doctrine,
Stealing a saffron robe, the five deeds of immediate retribution,
Wrong view, destroying cities and so forth,
Teaching emptiness to the untrained,
Reversing someone's intention to become completely enlightened,
Causing someone to abandon individual liberation, deriding the Hearer Vehicle,
Falsely claiming [to have realized] the profound, receiving the property of the Three Jewels,
Bad ethics, and giving up the attitude of altruistic promise.
For sixteen, all four thorough entanglements –
Not considering the disadvantages, not overcoming the wish to do it,
Taking pleasure and delight in it, and lack of conscience and shame –
Are needed for there to be a root infraction.
For two, wrong view and giving up the altruistic attitude,
All four are not needed [for a root infraction].

Risking my life, I will keep from the fourteen root infractions –
Scorning and deriding the lama, despising the precepts,
Speaking fault of vajra brothers and sisters, abandoning love,
Giving up the aspirational and practical altruistic intentions,
Deriding the doctrines of Sūtra and Mantra,
Proclaiming the secret to the unripened,
Despising my own aggregates, abandoning emptiness,
Relying on a poisonous friend, not recollecting the view,
Uprooting the attitude of one with faith,
Not observing the pledges, and deriding women.

I will keep, without exception, the secondary pledges –
To abandon the four roots, beer, and non-activities,
To rely on a holy protector, to respect and serve friends,
To maintain the ten virtues, and to abandon causes

Of turning away from the Great Vehicle
As well as contempt for and stepping over [sacred articles].

I will also properly keep from the gross infractions –
Using an unqualified Seal, engaging in absorption without the three discriminations,
Showing secret articles to those who are not vessels,
Quarrelling and disputing at an offering-assembly,
Perversely answering a question of the faithful,
Staying seven days in the home of a Hearer,
Claiming to be a yogi though not really so,
Teaching the excellent doctrine to the faithless,
Engaging in mandala activities without completing the approximation and so forth,
Purposelessly transgressing the precepts of individual liberation and Bodhisattva vows,
And contradicting [the precepts set forth in] the *Fifty Stanzas on the Guru*.

I will not look down on left-handed behaviour,
Will make praises [of women],
Abandon absorption with the unqualified,
Not be devoid of the view when in union,
Take unchanging interest in using desire in the path,
Not disregard the two types of Seals,
Mainly work at external and internal methods,
Not emit the kunda, keep pure behavior,
And forsake nausea when taking the mind of enlightenment.

I will achieve in accordance with the Conqueror's word
The precepts formulated for the vows
Of individual liberation, Bodhisattvas, and Vajra Vehicle,
Not transgressing the subtler ones even in dreams.

In accordance with the thought of the Conqueror, I will assume well
All without exception of the excellent doctrine – verbal and realizational –
Contained within the three vehicles and the four tantra sets.

I will thoroughly liberate transmigrators through methods appropriate to them.

Through the power of the wholesome virtues come from this
May I, through the power of Vajradhara, not transgress
The boundaries of formulations in all lifetimes
And complete the levels of the path of the two stages.

In short, through whatsoever collections of wholesome virtue,
As illustrated by this, have been accumulated,
May I quickly take birth in Shambhala, the treasury of jewels,
And complete the stages of the path of Highest Yoga Tantra.

In all lifetimes may I enjoy the glory of the doctrine
Without being separated from true lamas
And thoroughly completing the qualities of the grounds and paths
Quickly attain the state of a Vajradhara.

3 *Abbreviated Six Session Yoga*

This text was formulated by Lo-sang-den-dzin (blo bzang bstan 'dzin)

From my heart I go for refuge to the Three Jewels.
I will release all sentient beings from pain and set all in final bliss.
To do that, I will generate an altruistic intention to attain perfect enlightenment
And thereupon will train in the learnings of Bodhisattvas.

On a throne in space in front of myself upon discs of sun, moon, and lotus
Is my root lama, the Pervasive Master Vajradhara,
Blue in color, holding vajra and bell,
Embracing Vajradhātu-īshvarī and sporting with innate bliss.

The three places [of his body] are marked by the three letters.
With the light of the letter *hūṃ*, the wisdom-beings are invited and become of one taste [with the imagined beings].
Homage to the lotus-feet of Vajradhara.
I make offering with oceans of clouds of external, internal, and secret offerings
And with the unsurpassed offerings of Samantabhadra –
Mountains, lands, vases of jewel treasures, sun, moon, and so forth.

Having seen that all without exception of the supreme and common feats
Follow after proper reliance on you, O Protector,
May I, disregarding even body and life,
Be blessed to achieve only what is pleasing to you.

Through making such petitions, the lama comes to my crown
And dissolving into me becomes of one taste with me.
I am Vajrasattva, holding vajra and bell
And, embracing the Female Supramundane Victor, sport with innate bliss.

For the sake of my mothers, I give away without regret
My residence, body, resources, and collections of virtue of the past, present, and future.
Even if it costs my life I will not transgress the boundaries formulated
For the three vows – individual liberation, Bodhisattva, and Secret Mantra.

Having assumed well the doctrine – verbal and realizational – contained within the three vehicles
And the four tantra sets I will thoroughly liberate transmigrators through methods.

By this virtue may the wishes made by the Ones Gone To Bliss and the Bodhisattvas be accomplished.
I dedicate this virtue to the maintenance of the doctrine.
Through the ineluctable power of the magnificent blessings of the Three Jewels and of dependent-arising
May my good wishes be accomplished and I quickly attain Buddhahood.

Appendix

1 *Mantras in the Kālachakra Initiation, Stage of Generation*

As mentioned in the Introduction, the text of the initiations for the stage of generation in the Kālachakra system is Kay-drup's *Mandala Rite of the Glorious Kālachakra: Illumination of the Thought (dpal dus kyi 'khor lo'i dkyil chog dgongs pa rab gsal)* supplemented with material from Lo-sang-tsul-trim-den-bay-gyel-tsen's *Initiation Rite of Kālachakra, Stated in an Easy Way (dus 'khor dbang chog nag 'gros su bkod pa)*. Thus the mantras listed below are from those two texts.

Translations into Tibetan of several of the mantras as found in the *Means of Achievement of the Complete Mandala of Exalted Body, Speech, and Mind of the Supramundane Victor, the Glorious Kālachakra: Sacred Words of Scholars and Adepts (dpal bcom ldan 'das dus kyi 'khor lo'i sku gsung thugs yongs su rdzogs pa'i dkyil 'khor gyi sgrub thabs mkhas grub zhal lung)* by the Seventh Dalai Lama, Gel-sang-gya-tso *(bskal bzang rgya mtsho*, 1708-57) are also included. Reference also is made to the apparent source for the Seventh Dalai Lama's translations, Bu-dön Rin-chen-drup's *(bu ston rin chen grub) Commentarial Explanation of the "Initiation Chapter"* [*of the Kālachakra Tantra*], *Annotations to (Kulika Puṇḍarīka's) "Stainless Light" (dbang gi le'u 'grel bshad dri med 'od kyi mchan)* found in volume 2 of his Collected Works. Bu-dön's translations are almost exactly the same as those given in the Seventh Dalai Lama's text, but the latter has several that do not appear in Bu-dön's text.

Several variants are also listed, these being found in Bu-d̄ön's *Mandala Rite of the Glorious Kālachakra: Source of Good Qualities (dpal dus kyi 'khor lo'i dkyil chog yon tang kun 'byung)* in volume 5 of his Collected Works and his *Means of Achievement of the Supramundane Victor, the Glorious Kālachakra: Fruit Clusters of the Wish-Granting* [*Tree*] *(dpal dus kyi 'khor lo'i sgrub thabs dpag bsam snye ma)* in the same volume. Bu-d̄ön also has a text devoted to giving forty-one genealogies of the transmission of various schools of tantras (those of Kālachakra being at the beginning) as well as listing three hundred fifty-five mantras found in various tantras; it is called *Collection of the Retention* [*Mantras*] *of the Tantra Sets of Secret Mantra (gsang sngags rgyud sde bzhi'i gzungs 'bum)* and is found in volume 16 of his Collected Works.

The mantras are listed in order of appearance in the text, under the respective chapter heading. A tentative editing of the mantra is given first, followed for the most part by a tentative translation into English. Next are references to Kay-drup's *Mandala Rite* and/or L̄o-sang-tsul-trim-d̄en-b̄ay-gyel-tsen's *Initiation Rite,* with the Tibetan translation given if supplied; these, in turn, are followed by references to Bu-d̄ön's works along with the Tibetan translation if supplied. The word order of the Tibetan is sometimes awkward since it follows the Sanskrit word order. After the first version, variations are given in italics.

Several references are also made to L̄o-sang-tsul-trim-d̄en-b̄ay-gyel-tsen's *Explanation Of The Initiations Of The Supramundane Victor, The Glorious Kālachakra: Garland Of Rubies (bcom ldan 'das dus kyi 'khor lo'i dbang gi bshad pa padma ra ga'i phreng ba),* which has translations into Tibetan of several mantras not translated in the above works. These have been included at the end of the respective entries, using "Kang-s̄ar" to refer to the text (which is in volume 3 of his Collected Works), since he was also known as D̄re-wo Kang-s̄ar-ḡyap-gön Rin-b̄o-chay *(tre bo khang gsar skyabs mgon)* and to distinguish it easily from his *Initiation Rite of Kālachakra, Stated in an Easy Way*. There are also scattered references to the Seventh Dalai Lama's *Explanation of the Mandala Rite of the Glorious Guhyasamāja, Akṣhobhyavajra, Illumination Brilliantly Clarifying the Principles of the Meaning of Initiation, Sacred Word of*

Vajrasattva (dpal gsang ba 'dus pa mi bskyod rdo rje'i dkyil 'khor gyi cho ga'i rnam par bshad pa dbang don de nyid yang gsal snang ba rdo rje sems dpa'i zhal lung) as "Seventh Dalai Lama's *Explanation*". These latter two texts are particularly helpful not only for providing translations of the mantras but also for putting their meaning in context. It should be clear from these citations that not just the sounds of mantras but also their meanings are important to the conduct of these rituals.

The editing principles are conservative; almost all changes are supported by at least one edition.

I.4 TOOTH-STICK, WATER, KUSHA GRASS, AND THREAD

Oṃ āḥ hūṃ hoḥ haṃ kṣhaḥ vajra-danta-kāṣhṭha-chatur-vimokṣha-mukha-vishuddha-svabhāvaṃ kāya-vāk-chitta-jñāna-mukha-dantādi-malaṃ vishodhaya svāhā.

> "May the seed syllables of the six lineages – *oṃ āḥ hūṃ hoḥ haṃ kṣhaḥ* – and the tooth-stick having the nature of the purity of the four doors of liberation purify the defilements of the teeth and so forth of the faces of exalted body, speech, mind, and pristine consciousness *svāhā.*"
>
> Kay-drup's *Mandala Rite* 298.5: Oṃ āḥ hūṃ hoḥ haṃ *kṣha* vajra-danta-kāṣhṭha-chatur-vimokṣha, mukha-vishuddha-svabhāvaṃ kāya-vāk-chitta-jñāna-mukha-dantādi-malaṃ vishodhaya svāhā.
>
> Bu-dön's *Initiation Chapter* volume 2, 297.7: Oṃ āḥ hūṃ hoḥ haṃ kṣhaḥ *vajrā*-danta-kāṣhṭha-chatur-vimokṣha, mukha-vishuddha-svabhāvaṃ kāya-*vāg*-chitta-jñāna-mukha-dantādi-malaṃ *vishodhaya* svāhā (rdo rje so shing bzhi rnam par thar pa rnam par dag pa'i rang bzhin sku gsung thugs ye shes zhag dang po la sogs dri ma rnam par sbyang bar mdzod rnam par sbyang bar mdzod).
>
> Kang-ṡar, 382.2: rdo rje so shing rnam par thar pa *bzhi'i sgo* rnam par dag pa'i rang bzhin sku gsung thugs ye shes *zhal* dang po [so?] la sogs dri ma rnam par *sbyong.*

Oṃ hrīḥ suvishuddha-dharma-sarva-pāpaṃ nichāmasya shodhaya sarva-vikalpanā-apanaya hūṃ.

"*Oṃ hrīḥ* purify all ill-deeds of the aggregation by way of the thorough purity of phenomena, remove all conceptuality *hūṃ.*"

Kay-drup's *Mandala Rite* 298.6: Oṃ hrīḥ suvishuddha-*dharma*-sarva-*pāpa-nicha-asya* shodhaya sarva-*vikala-panā* apanaya hūṃ.

Bu-dön's *Mandala Rite,* volume 5, 187.3: Oṃ hrīḥ suvishuddha-dharma-sarva-*pāpa*-nichāmasya shodhaya sarva-*vikalpanāpanaya* hūṃ.

Kang-sar, meaning, 382.4: chos thams cad shin tu rnam par dag pas sgrib pa thams cad rnam par sol cig/ rnam par rtog pa thams cad sol cig.

Oṃ vajra-tīkṣhṇa baṃ.

"*Oṃ vajra* sharpness *baṃ.*"

Kay-drup's *Mandala Rite* 299.1: same.

Bu-dön's *Mandala Rite,* volume 5, 187.4: same.

Seventh Dalai Lama's *Explanation* 309.2: rdo rje rnon po.

Oṃ buddha-maitri-rakṣha rakṣha sarvān svāhā.

"*Oṃ* protect, protect against all [the unfavorable] with buddha-love *svāhā.*"

Kay-drup's *Mandala Rite* 299.2: same.

Bu-dön's *Mandala Rite,* volume 5, 187.4: Oṃ buddha-maitri-rakṣha rakṣha *sarvāṃ* svāhā.

Seventh Dalai Lama's *Explanation* 310.6: sangs rgyas byams pa srungs shig srungs shig thams cad.

I.5 SIX LINEAGES AND VAJRASATTVA

Oṃ ā ā aṃ aḥ vajrasatva-mahāsukha-vajra-kālachakra shiṣhyasya abhimukho bhava saṃtuṣhṭo bhava varado bhava, kaya-vāk-chittādhiṣhṭhānaṃ kuru svāhā.

"Vajrasattva, Vajra Kālachakra of great bliss, approach the student, thoroughly please. [the student], bestow the supreme, bless into magnificence exalted body, speech, and mind."

Kay-drup's *Mandala Rite* 299.3: Oṃ ā ā aṃ aḥ vajrasatva-mahāsukha-vajra-kālachakra shiṣhyasya abhimukho bhava *santuṣhṭa* bhava *rado* bhava, kaya-vāk-*chittādhiṣhṭhānaṃ* kuru svāhā.

Bu-dön's *Initiation Chapter,* volume 2, 298.3: Oṃ ā ā aṃ aḥ vajrasatva-mahāsukha-vajra-kālachakra shiṣhyasya abhimukho bhava santushto bhava varoda bhava, kaya-vāk-chittādhiṣhṭhānaṃ kuru *kuru* svāhā (rdo rje sems dpa' chen po bde ba rdo rje dus kyi 'khor lo slob ma'i mngon du phyogs par mdzod yang dag par mnyes par mdzod mchog stsol bar mdzod sku gsung thugs byin gyis brlab par mdzod).

II.2 OUTSIDE THE CURTAIN

Oṃ pravishaya bhagavān mahāsukha-mokṣha-puraṃ sarva-siddhi-sukha-pradaṃ paramasukha-uttamasiddhya jaḥ hūṃ baṃ hoḥ prasiddhyasva.

"Supramundane Victor, let me enter for great bliss
Into the city of liberation [the mandala],
The joyous bliss of all feats.
Through the feat of excellent supreme bliss
Make it be thoroughly accomplished *jaḥ hūṃ baṃ hoḥ.*"

Kay-drup's *Mandala Rite* 318.2: Oṃ pravishaya bhagavān mahāsukha-mokṣha-puraṃ sarva-siddhi-sukha-pradaṃ paramasukha-uttama-siddhya jaḥ hūṃ baṃ hoḥ *prasiddhyasvā* (dngos grub kun gyi bde ba nyams dga' ba// thar pa'i grong du bcom ldan bde chen 'jug// mchog tu bde ba dam pa'i dngos grub kyis// dzaḥ hūṃ baṃ hoḥ rab tu grub par mdzod).

Bu-dön's *Mandala Rite,* volume 5, 206.6: Oṃ pravishaya bhagavān mahāsukha-mokṣha-*suraṃ* siddhi-sukha-pradaṃ paramasukha-uttama-siddhya jaḥ hūṃ baṃ hoḥ prasiddhyasva.

Kang-ṡar, 378.5: oṃ 'jug pa bcom ldan 'das bde ba chen po thar pa grong du dngos grub kun bde ba rab tu dga' ba mchog tu bde ba dam pa dngos grub rab tu grub par mdzod. (Full translation, same as above, on 379.3).

Oṃ sarva-tathāgata-anuttara-bodhi-alaṃkāra-vastra-pūja-megha-samudra-spharaṇa samaya shrīye hūṃ oṃ vajra-rakṣha haṃ, oṃ vajra-uṣhṇīṣha hūṃ phaṭ.

"*Oṃ* the pledge issuing forth an ocean of clouds of offerings of garments as adornments of the highest enlightenment of all Ones Gone Thus *shrīye hūṃ*. *Oṃ* vajra protection *haṃ*. *Oṃ* vajra crown protrusion *hūṃ phaṭ*."

Kay-drup's *Mandala Rite* 318.4: Oṃ sarva-tathāgata, anuttara-bodhi-alaṃkāra-vastra-pūja-megha-samudra-spharana samaya shrīye *huṃ* oṃ vajra-rakṣha haṃ, oṃ vajra-uṣhṇīṣha hūṃ phaṭ.

Bu-dön's *Mandala Rite*, volume 5, 209.3: Oṃ *sarvva*-tathāgata, anuttara-bodhi-alaṃkāra-vastra-pūja-megha-samudra-spharana samaya shrīye hūṃ oṃ vajra-rakṣha *hūṃ*, oṃ vajra-uṣhṇīṣha hūṃ phaṭ.

Kang-s̄ar, 380.4: de bzhin gshegs pa thams cad kyi bla na med pa'i byang chub rgyan gos kyi mchod pa'i sprin gyi [text reads gyis] ni rgya mtsho 'phro ba'i dam tshig go// rdo rje'i bsrung ba// rdo rje'i gtsug tor.

Oṃ dvadasha-aṅga-nirodha-kāriṇi hūṃ phaṭ.

"*Om* making the cessation of the twelve branches *hūṃ phaṭ*."

Kay-drup's *Mandala Rite* 318.5: same.

Bu-dön's *Mandala Rite*, volume 5, 209.3: Oṃ *dādasha*-aṃga-nirodha-kāriṇi hūṃ phaṭ.

Kang-s̄ar 381.2: bcu gnyis yan lag 'gog pa byed pa.

Āḥ khaṃ-vīra hūṃ.

Kay-drup's *Mandala Rite* 318.5: *Ā* khaṃ-vīra hūṃ (but later as above).

Bu-dön's *Mandala Rite*, volume 5, 209.3: *A* khaṃ-vīra hūṃ.

Seventh Dalai Lama's *Explanation* 457.5: āḥ is the seed syllable of Vairochana; kha is the seed syllable of Amoghasiddhi; vī is the first letter of Vairochana's name; [ra] is the first letter of Ratnasambhava's name; hūṃ is the seed syllable of Akṣhobhya. Therefore, while saying that mantra give to each student a flower garland which arises from the appearance of what in entity are the exalted wisdoms of the five lineages as those letters and is marked with those letters producing [those deities] respectively. A certain [scholar] asserts that the meaning of the mantra āḥ khaṃ-vīra hūṃ is "hero of space" *(nam mkha'i dpa' bo).*

Oṃ sarva-yoga-chittaṃ utpadayāmi.

"I am causing the mind of all-encompassing yoga to be generated."

Kay-drup's *Mandala Rite* 320.2: same.

Bu-dön's *Mandala Rite,* volume 5, 209.7: Oṃ sarva-yoga-*chitta*-utpadayāmi.

Kang-sar 390.6: thams cad rnal 'byor sems bskyed par bgyi'o.

Oṃ surata-samayas tvaṃ hoḥ siddhya-vajra-yathā-sukhaṃ.

"*Oṃ* may you having the pledge of thorough joy achieve the vajra [of Buddhahood] as wanted."

Kay-drup's *Mandala Rite* 320.3: same.

Bu-dön's *Mandala Rite* volume 5, 209.7: Oṃ *surate* samayas tvaṃ hoḥ siddhi-vajra-yathā-sukhaṃ.

Kang-sar, meaning, 391.3: shin tu dga' ba'i dam tshig dang ldan pa khyod kyi ji ltar dga' ba'i rdo rje ste sangs rgyas bsgrub par bya'o.

II.3 SEEING THE MANDALA

Oṃ vighnāntakṛt hūṃ.

Kay-drup's *Mandala Rite* 320.5: same.

Bu-dön's *Mandala Rite,* volume 5, 210.2: Oṃ *vighnantakṛt* hūṃ.

Oṃ mahārata, sudriḍḍha sutoṣhyo, susuṣho, vajrasatva ādya-siddhya māṃ.

"*Oṃ* may great joy, thorough firmness, thorough happiness, thorough bliss, Vajrasattva, be established in me today."

Kay-drup's *Mandala Rite* 320.5: Oṃ mahārata, sudriḍḍha *sutoṣho,* susuṣho, vajrasatva ādya-siddhya māṃ.

Bu-dön's *Mandala Rite,* volume 5, 210.4: same as first version.

Kang-sar, meaning, 392.6: dga' ba chen po shin tu brtan// shin tu dgyes dang shin tu bde// rdo rje sems dpa' de ring ni// grub par mdzod cig bdag la'o.

Oṃ sarva-tathāgata-pūja-upasthānāya ātmānaṃ niryātayāmi, sarva-tathāgata-vajrasatva adhitiṣhṭhasva māṃ hūṃ.

"Since I offer myself for the worship and service of all Ones Gone Thus, may Vajrasattva, the entity of all the Ones Gone Thus, please bless me into magnificence."

Kay-drup's *Mandala Rite* 320.7: Oṃ sarva-tathāgata-pūja-upasthānāya ātmānaṃ niryātayāmi, sarva-tathāgata-vajrasatva *adhitiṣhṭhāsvā mā* hūṃ (de bzhin gshegs pa thams cad la mchod pa dang bsnyen bkur ba'i phyir bdag 'bul bas de bzhin gshegs pa thams cad kyi ngo bo rdo rje sems dpas bdag la byin gyis brlab tu gsol).

Bu-dön's *Mandala Rite,* volume 5, 210.4: final *hūṃ* omitted.

Oṃ sarva-tathāgata-pūja-karmaṇe ātmānaṃ niryātayāmi, sarva-tathāgata vajra-karma kuru māṃ.

"Since I offer myself for the activity of worshipping all the Ones Gone Thus, may all the Ones Gone Thus please grant me the vajra activities."

Kay-drup's *Mandala Rite* 321.2: Oṃ sarva-tathāgata-pūja-*karmaṇa* ātmānaṃ niryātayāmi sarva-tathāgata vajra-karma kuru māṃ (de bzhin gshegs pa thams cad la mchod pa'i las kyi phyir bdag 'bul bas de bzhin gshegs pa thams cad kyis bdag la rdo rje las mdzad du gsol).

Bu-dön's *Mandala Rite,* volume 5, 210.4: Oṃ sarva-tathāgata-pūja-karmaṇe *ātmanaṃ* niryātayāmi, sarva-tathāgata vajra-*karmma kuruta* māṃ.

Oṃ sarva-tathāgata-pūja-abhiṣhekāya ātmānaṃ niryātayāmi, sarva-tathāgata vajra-ratna abhiṣhiṃcha māṃ.

"Since I offer myself for the worship of all Ones Gone Thus and for conferral of initiation, may all the Ones Gone Thus please confer on me the vajra jewel initiation."

Kay-drup's *Mandala Rite* 321.2: Oṃ sarva-tathāgata-pūja-*abhiṣhekaya* ātmānaṃ *nīryātayāmi* sarva-tathāgata vajra-ratna *abhiṣhiñcha maṃ* (de bzhin gshegs pa thams cad la mchod pa dang dbang bskur ba'i phyir bdag 'bul bas de bzhin gshegs pa thams cad kyi[s] bdag la rdo rje rin chen gyi dbang bskur du gsol).

Bu-dön's *Mandala Rite*, volume 5, 210.5: Oṃ sarva-tathāgata-pūja-abhiṣhekāya *atmanaṃ* niryātayāmi sarva-tathāgata vajra-ratna *abhishinñcha* māṃ.

Oṃ sarva-tathāgata-pūja-pravaratanāya ātmānaṃ niryātayāmi, sarva-tathāgata vajra-dharma-pravarataya māṃ.

"Since I offer myself to all the Ones Gone Thus for the thorough turning [of the wheel of doctrine], may all the Ones Gone Thus please thoroughly turn [the wheel of] vajra doctrine for me."

Kay-drup's *Mandala Rite* 321.6: Sanskrit same (de bzhin gshegs pa thams cad la mchod pa rab tu skor ba'i phyir bdag 'bul bas de bzhin gshegs pa thams cad kyis bdag la rdo rje'i chos skor du gsol).

Bu-dön's *Mandala Rite*, volume 5, 210.6: Oṃ sarva-tathāgata-pūja-pravaratanāya *ātmanaṃ* niryātayāmi, sarva-tathāgata vajra-*dharmaḥ*-pravarataya māṃ.

Oṃ sarva-buddha-pūja-upasthānāya ātmānaṃ niryātayāmi, sarva-tathāgata-vajra-vairochana adhitiṣhṭha māṃ.

"Since I offer myself to all the Ones Gone Thus for worship and service, may Vairochana, the entity of all the Ones Gone Thus, bless me into magnificence."

Kay-drup's *Mandala Rite* 322.1: Oṃ sarva-buddha-pūja-upasthānāya ātmānaṃ *niryātayāma* sarva-tathāgata vajra-vairochana-adhitiṣhṭha 'māṃ (de bzhin gshegs pa thams cad la mchod pa dang bsnyen bkur ba'i phyir bdag 'bul bas de bzhin gshegs pa thams cad kyi ngo bo rnam par snang mdzad kyis bdag la byin gyis brlab tu gsol).

Bu-dön's *Mandala Rite*, volume 5, 210.5: Oṃ sarva-buddha-pūja-upasthānāya *ātmanaṃ* niryātayāmi sarva-tathāgata vajra-vairochana-adhitiṣhṭha māṃ.

Oṃ guru-charaṇa-pūja-upasthānāya ātmānaṃ niryātayāmi, sarvasatva-paritrāṇāya ātmānaṃ niryātayāmi.

"I offer myself for worship and service at the feet of the guru, I offer myself for the help of all beings."

Kay-drup's *Mandala Rite* 322.4: Oṃ guru-charaṇa-pūja-upasthānāya ātmānaṃ niryātayāmi, sarvasatva-*paritraṇāya,* ātmānaṃ niryātayāmi.

Bu-dön's *Mandala Rite,* volume 5, 210.7: Oṃ guru-*charṣhaṇa*-pūja-*upasthānaya ātmanaṃ* niryātayāmi, sarvasatva-*pariḍāṇaya ātmanaṃ* niryātayāmi.

Om vajra-udakaṭhaḥ.

"*Oṃ* drink the vajra water."

Kay-drup's *Mandala Rite* 322.3: same.

Bu-dön's *Mandala Rite,* volume 5, 211.4: Oṃ *pañca-amṛta*-vajra-udakaṭhaḥ.

Seventh Dalai Lama's *Explanation* 491.4: rdo rje chu 'thung zhig.

Oṃ shūnyatā-jñāna-vajra-svabhāvātmako' haṃ.

"I have an essential nature of indivisible emptiness and wisdom."

Kay-drup's *Mandala Rite* 323.6: abbreviated.

Oṃ āḥ ra ra ra ra, la la la la, vajra-aveshaya hūṃ.

"*Oṃ āḥ ra ra ra ra, la la la la,* may the vajras thoroughly descend *hūṃ.*"

Kay-drup's *Mandala Rite* 324.6: same.

Bu-dön's *Mandala Rite,* volume 5, 212.4: same.

Seventh Dalai Lama's *Explanation* 501.3: rdo rje kun tu phob.

Oṃ sarva-tathāgata-kula-vishodhani svāhā.

"*Oṃ* the purification of the lineages of all Ones Gone Thus *svāhā.*"

Kay-drup's *Mandala Rite* 325.6: same.

Bu-dön's *Mandala Rite,* volume 5, 213.6: same.

Bu-dön's *Initiation Chapter,* volume 2, 391.5: Oṃ sarva-tathāgata-kula-*vīshvadhani* svāhā (thams cad be bzhin gshegs pa rnam par sbyongs).

Kang-ṡar 405.1: de bzhin gshegs pa thams cad *kyi rigs* rnam par sbyong.

Oṃ pratigṛhnas tvaṃ imaṃ satva-mahābala.

"*Oṃ* Great Powerful Being, take care of this

[student]."

Kay-drup's *Mandala Rite*, 325.7: Oṃ *pratigṛhnastva* imaṃ satva-mahābala.

Bu-dön's *Mandala Rite*, volume 5, 214.1: same as first version.

Kang-sar, meaning, 405.3: sems dpa' stobs po che slob ma byang chub ma thob par rjes su zungs shig.

Oṃ divyendriyānudghaṭaya svāhā.

"*Oṃ* open the divine sense power *svāhā*."

Kay-drup's *Mandala Rite* 326.2: (unclear) Oṃ *devyintrāyaṇḍyiḍḍorahgha āya* svāhā.

Lo-sang-tsul-trim-den-bay-gyel-tsen's *Initiation Rite*, 488.4: Oṃ *devyintrāya-aḥ ṇṭudaghatāya* svāhā.

Bu-dön's *Mandala Rite*, volume 5, 213.7: Oṃ *divyendriyāṇuḍghaṭaya* svāhā.

Kang-sar 406.2: lha'i dbang po rab tu dbye bar mdzod.

He vajra-pashya.

"O, look at the vajra [mandala]."

Kay-drup's *Mandala Rite* 326.4: same.

Bu-dön's *Mandala Rite*, volume 5, 214.1: same.

Kang-sar 407.1: kye rdo rje ltos shig.

Seventh Dalai Lama's *Explanation*, meaning, 524.3: rdo rje dkyil 'khor la ltos.

Samaya hoḥ hoḥ hoḥ hoḥ.

Kay-drup's *Mandala Rite* 326.6: same.

Bu-dön's *Mandala Rite*, volume 5, 214.4: *hoḥ hoḥ hoḥ*.

III. ORIENTATION

Oṃ sarva-pāpaṃ dahana-vajrāya vajrasatvasya, sarva-pāpaṃ daha svāhā.

"*Oṃ* burn away all ill deeds for the sake of Vajrasattva's vajra burning all ill deeds *svāhā*."

Kay-drup's *Mandala Rite* 326.6: same.

Bu-dön's *Mandala Rite*, volume 5, 214.7: Oṃ sarva-pāpaṃ dahana-vajrāya vajrasatvasya, sarva-pāpaṃ *daha daha* svāhā.

Kang-s̄ar, meaning, 420.3: rdo rje sems dpa' rdo rje'i ched du sdig pa thams cad bsregs la gzhi tshugs.

III.1 WATER INITIATION

Oṃ haṃ hāṃ hiṃ hīṃ hṛṃ hṝṃ huṃ hūṃ hḷṃ hḹṃ ā ī ṛ ū ḷ vajra-ḍākiṇyau vajra-amṛta-ghaṭair abhiṣhiñchantu māṃ svāhā.

"*Oṃ haṃ hāṃ hiṃ hīṃ hṛṃ hṝṃ huṃ hūṃ hḷm hḹṃ ā ī ṝ ū ḷ* please may the Vajra Female Sky-Goers confer initiation on me with the vases of vajra ambrosia *svāhā*.

Seventh Dalai Lama's *Means of Achievement,* 56.3: Oṃ haṃ hāṃ hiṃ hīṃ hṛṃ hṝṃ huṃ hūṃ hḷṃ hḹṃ ā ī ṝ ū ḹ vajra-*ḍākinyau* vajra-amṛta-ghaṭair *abhiṣhañchatu* māṃ svāhā (rdo rje mkha' 'gro ma la rdo rje bdud rtsi'i bum pa rnams kyis mngon par dbang bskur du gsol).

Bu-d̄ön's *Initiation Chapter,* volume 2, 300.7: Oṃ haṃ hāṃ hiṃ hīṃ hṛṃ hṝṃ huṃ hūṃ hḷm hḹṃ ā ī ṝ ū ḹ vajra-ḍākiṇyau *vajrāmṛta*-ghaṭair *abhishiṣhchantu maṃ* svāhā (rdo rje bdud rtsi'i bum pa rnams kyis mngon par dbang bskur du gsol bdag la).

Bu-d̄ön's *Mandala Rite,* volume 5, 215.7: Oṃ haṃ hāṃ hiṃ hīṃ hṛṃ hṝṃ huṃ hūṃ hḷm hḹṃ ā ī ṝ ū ḹ vajra-ḍākiṇyau, vajra-amṛta-ghaṭair *ābhiṣhiñhchantu maṃ* svāhā.

Jaḥ hūṃ baṃ hoḥ hi.

"Be summoned, enter, become fused with, be pleased, and become of the same taste."

Kay-drup's *Commentary on the Initiation Chapter,* 604.5: dgug gzhug bcin mnyes par byed pa... ro mnyam du byed pa.

Vajra-bhairava ākarṣhaya jaḥ.

"Vajra Frightful One, summon *jaḥ.*"

Kay-drup's *Mandala Rite,* 328.3: same.

Bu-dön's *Initiation Chapter,* volume 2, 300.1, has a similar mantra: Vajra-*bhairavā* ākarṣhaya ... jaḥ (rdo rje 'jigs byed 'gugs par mdzod).

Gandhaṃ puṣhpaṃ dhūpaṃ dīpaṃ akṣhate naividye lāsye hāsye vādye nṛtye gītye kāme pūja kuru kuru svāhā.

"Make offering with perfume, flowers, incense, lamps, fruit, food, lower robe, smiles, music, dance, singing, and touch *svāhā.*"

Kay-drup's *Mandala Rite,* 271.7. See note 48.

Oṃ prajñāpāramitā huṃ hūṃ phaṭ.
Oṃ lochani huṃ hūṃ phaṭ.
Oṃ māmakī huṃ hūṃ phaṭ.
Oṃ pāṇḍarā huṃ hūṃ phaṭ.
Oṃ tāra huṃ hūṃ phaṭ.

Kay-drup's *Mandala Rite,* 328.6.

Oṃ ā ī ṛ ū ḷ pañcha-dhātu-vishodhani svāhā.

"*Oṃ ā ī ṛ ū ḷ* be founded in the purification of the five constituents."

Seventh Dalai Lama's *Means of Achievement* 56.4: Sanskrit same (khams lnga rnam par sbyong ma).

Bu-dön's *Mandala Rite,* volume 5, 217.4: Sanskrit same.

Bu-dön's *Initiation Chapter,* volume 2, 392.1: Sanskrit same (khams lnga rnam par sbyong *ba*).

Kang-sar, meaning, 428.4: yum lnga'i sa bon brjod pas de rnams kyi khams lnga rnam par sbyong ba la gzhi tshugs.

III.2 CROWN INITIATION

Oṃ aṃ iṃ ṛṃ uṃ ḷṃ sarva-buddha-vajra-mukuṭaṃ mama pañcha-buddha-ātmakaṃ bandhayantu huṃ hūṃ phaṭ.

"*Oṃ aṃ iṃ ṛṃ uṃ ḷṃ* please may all the Buddhas bind on me the vajra crowns having the nature of the five Buddhas *huṃ hūṃ phaṭ.*"

Seventh Dalai Lama's *Means of Achievement:* 56.5: Oṃ aṃ iṃ *ṛṃ* uṃ ḷṃ sarva-buddha-vajra-mukuṭaṃ mama pañcha-buddha-ātmakaṃ bandhayantu huṃ hūṃ phaṭ (sangs rgyas thams cad rdo rje cod pan bdag la lnga sangs rgyas bdag nyid can bcing du gsol).

Bu-dön's *Initiation Chapter,* volume 2, 300.7 and volume 5, 217.6 for Sanskrit: Sanskrit same as first version (sangs rgyas thams cad dang rdo rje cod pan bdag la lnga sangs rgyas bdag nyid can bcing du gsol).

Kang-ṣar, 430.5: oṃ mgo 'dren aṃ sogs lnga sangs rgyas lnga'i sa bon dang sangs rgyas thams cad kyis bdag la rdo rje cod pan sangs rgyas lnga'i bdag nyid can bcing du gsol.

Oṃ a i ṛ u ḷ pañcha-tathāgata-parishuddha svāhā

"*Oṃ a i ṛ u ḷ* be founded in the thorough purity of the five Ones Gone Thus."

Seventh Dalai Lama's *Means of Achievement* 56.6: Sanskrit same (de bzhin gshegs pa lnga yongs su dag pa).

Bu-dön's *Mandala Rite,* volume 5, 218.1: Sanskrit same.

Bu-dön's *Initiation Chapter,* volume 2, 392.2: Sanskrit and Tibetan same.

Kang-ṣar 433.3: de bzhin gshegs pa lnga yongs su dag pa gzhi tshugs.

III.3 SILK RIBBON INITIATION

Oṃ a ā aṃ aḥ ha hā haṃ haḥ phreṃ hoḥ sarva-pāramitā mama vajra-paṭṭaṃ bandhayantu huṃ hūṃ phaṭ.

"*Oṃ a ā aṃ aḥ ha hā haṃ haḥ phreṃ hoḥ* please may all the Perfection Goddesses tie on me the vajra silk ribbon *huṃ hūṃ phaṭ.*"

Seventh Dalai Lama's *Means of Achievement* 56.7: Sanskrit same (thams cad pha rol tu phyin ma bdag [la] rdo rje dar dpyangs bcing du gsol).

Bu-dön's *Initiation Chapter,* volume 2, 301.1: Sanskrit same (thams cad pha rol tu phyin *pa* bdag la rdo rje dar dpyangs bcing du gsol).

Bu-dön's *Mandala Rite,* volume 5, 218.5: Oṃ a ā

aṃ aḥ ha hā haṃ haḥ phreṃ hoḥ sarva-pāramitā mama vajra-*paṭṭāṃ* bandhayantu huṃ hūṃ phaṭ.

Kang-ṣ̄ar, 436.4: a sogs nus ma'i so bon dang pha rol tu phyin ma thams cad kyis bdag la rdo rje'i dar dpyangs bcing du gsol.

Oṃ a ā aṃ aḥ ha hā haṃ haḥ hoḥ phreṃ dasha-pāramitā pāripūraṇi svāhā.

"*Oṃ a ā aṃ aḥ ha hā haṃ haḥ hoḥ phreṃ* the Female Fulfillers of the ten perfections."

Seventh Dalai Lama's *Means of Achievement* 57.1: Sanskrit same (pha rol tu phyin ma bcu yongs su rdzogs ma).

Bu-d̄ön's *Initiation Chapter*, volume 2, 392.5: Sanskrit same (pha rol tu phyin ma bcu yongs su rdzogs *pa*).

Kang-ṣ̄ar 440.4: pha rol tu phyin *pa* bcu yongs su rdzogs ma (preferred reading).

III.4 VAJRA AND BELL INITIATION

Oṃ hūṃ hoḥ vijñāna-jñāna-svabhāve karuṇā-prajñā-ātmake vajra-vajra-ghaṇṭe savyetarakarayor mama vajrasatvaḥ saprajño dadātu huṃ hūṃ phaṭ.

"*Oṃ hūṃ hoḥ* please may Vajrasattva together with [his] Wisdom Woman bestow the vajra and vajra-bell that have a nature of consciousness and exalted wisdom [and] an essence of compassion and wisdom in my right hand and other hand *huṃ hūṃ phaṭ.*"

Seventh Dalai Lama's *Means of Achievement:* 57.1: Sanskrit same (rnam shes dang ye shes kyi rang bzhin snying rje shes rab kyi bdag nyid can rdo rje dang rdo rje dril bu g.yas pa dang cig shos kyi lag pa dag la rdo rje sems dpa'i shes rab dang bcas pa stsal du gsol).

Bu-d̄ön's *Initiation Chapter*, volume 2, 301.2: Oṃ hūṃ hoḥ vijñāna-jñāna-*svabhāva*-karuṇā-prajñā-ātmake vajra-vajra-ghaṇṭe savyetarakarayor mama *vajrasatva*-saprajño dadātu (rnam shes dang ye shes kyi rang bzhin snying rje shes rab kyi bdag nyid can rdo rje rdo rje dril bu gyas pa dang cig shos kyi lag pa dag la). Bu-dön adds, "The translation by Rva has: huṃ hūṃ phaṭ, and since it appears in all of them, above and below, it is suitable."

Bu-dön's *Mandala Rite,* volume 5, 219.3: Oṃ hūṃ hoḥ vijñāna-jñāna-svabhāve karuṇā-prajñā-ātmake vajra-vajra-*ghaṇṭai* savyetarakarayor mama vajra-satvaḥ saprajño dadātu.

Kang-sar 441.6 . . . vajrasatvaḥ . . .

Oṃ huṃ hoḥ sūrya-chandra-vishodhaka svāhā.

"*Oṃ huṃ hoḥ* thoroughly purifying sun and moon."

Seventh Dalai Lama's *Means of Achievement* 57.3: Sanskrit same (nyi ma zla ba rnam par sbyongs).

Bu-dön's *Mandala Rite,* volume 5, 219.4: Sanskrit same.

Bu-dön's *Initiation Chapter,* volume 2, 392.6: Sanskrit same (nyi ma zla ba rnam par sbyong *ba*).

III.5 CONDUCT INITIATION

Oṃ a ā e ai ar ār o au al āl aṃ aḥ sarva-bodhisatvāḥ sabhāryāḥ sarvadā-sarvakāma-upabhogaṃ vajra-prataṃ mama dadantu svāhā.

"*Oṃ a ā e ai ar ār o au al āl aṃ aḥ* please may all the Bodhisattvas with their consorts bestow on me the vajra conduct of thoroughly enjoying all desires at all times *svāhā.*"

Seventh Dalai Lama's *Means of Achievement* 57.4: Sanskrit same (thams cad byang chub sems dpa' btsun mo dang gcas pa thams cad kyi tshe 'dod pa tham cad nyer bar longs spyod pa rdo rje brtul zhugs bdag la stsal du gsol).

Bu-dön's *Initiation Chapter,* volume 2, 301.3: Oṃ a ā e ai ar ār o au al āl aṃ aḥ sarva-*bodhisatvaḥ sabhāryaḥ* sarvadā-sarvakāma-upabhogaṃ vajra-prataṃ mama dadantu svāhā (thams cad byang chub sems *dpas* thams cad kyi tshe 'dod pa tham cad nyer bar longs spyod pa rdo rje brtul zhugs bdag la stsal du gsol).

Bu-dön's *Mandala Rite*, volume 5, 220.2: Oṃ a ā e ai ar ār o au al āl aṃ aḥ sarva-bodhisatvāḥ *sabhāryaḥ* sarvadā-sarvakāma-upabhogaṃ vajra-prataṃ mama dadantu svāhā.

Oṃ a ā e ai ar ār o au al āl aṃ aḥ vishayendriya-vishodhani svāhā

"*Oṃ a ā e ai ar ār o au al āl aṃ aḥ* purification of the objects and sense powers *svāhā*."

Seventh Dalai Lama's *Means of Achievement* 57.5: Sanskrit same (yul dang dbang po rnam par sbyong ma).

Bu-dön's *Initiation Chapter*, volume 2, 393.2: Sanskrit same but see his remark that *aṃ āḥ* is not in the Indian text (yul dang dbang po rnam par *sbyong*).

Bu-dön's *Mandala Rite*, volume 5, 220.2: Oṃ a ā e ai ar ār o au al āl aṃ aḥ *viṣhayendraya*-vishodhani svāhā.

III.6 NAME INITIATION

Oṃ ha hā ya yā ra rā va vā la lā sarva-krodha-rājāḥ sabhāryā maitrī-karuṇā-mudita-upekṣhā-sarva-samatā-svabhāvaṃ vajra-pūrvaṃgamaṃ nāma me dadantu huṃ hūṃ phaṭ.

"*Oṃ ha hā ya yā ra rā va vā la lā* may all the Kings of Wrathful Ones with their consorts bestow on me the name preceding the vajra which has the nature of entirely equal love, compassion, joy, and equanimity *huṃ hūṃ phaṭ*."

Seventh Dalai Lama's *Means of Achievement* 57.6: Sanskrit same (thams cad khro ba'i rgyal po gtsun mo dang bcas pa byams pa snying rje dga' ba btang snyoms thams cad mnyam nyid rang bzhin rdo rje sngon du 'gro ba'i ming bdag la stsal du gsol).

Bu-dön's *Initiation Chapter*, volume 2, 301.4: Oṃ ha hā ya yā ra rā va vā la lā sarva-krodha-*rājaḥ sabhārya* maitrī-karuṇā-*mudati*-upekṣhā-sarva-samatā-svabhāvaṃ vajra-*pūrvagami* nāma me dadantū huṃ hūṃ phaṭ (thams cad khro ba'i rgyal po gtsun mo dang bcas pa byams pa snying rje dga' ba btang snyoms thams cad mnyam nyid rang bzhin sngon du 'gro ba'i ming bdag la stsal du gsol).

Bu-d̄ön's *Mandala Rite,* volume 5, 220.6: Oṃ ha hā ya yā ra rā va vā la lā sarva-krodha-rājaḥ *sadhādya* maitrī-karuṇā-mudita-upekṣhā-sarva-samatā-*svabhāvaṃ* vajra-*pūrvaṃgamāṃ* nāma me dadantu huṃ hūṃ phaṭ.

Oṃ ha hā ya yā ra rā va vā la lā chatur-brahma-vihāra-vishuddha svāhā.

"*Oṃ ha hā ya yā ra rā va vā la lā* the thorough purity of the four abodes of purity *svāhā.*"

Seventh Dalai Lama's *Means of Achievement* 58.1: Sanskrit same (tshang pa'i gnas bzhi rnam par dag pa).

Bu-d̄ön's *Initiation Chapter,* volume 2, 393.3: Sanskrit and Tibetan same.

Bu-d̄ön's *Mandala Rite,* volume 5, 220.6: Sanskrit same.

O, Vajra (your Mantra name) *tathāgata-siddhi-samayas tvaṃ bhūr bhuva[ḥ]svaḥ.*

"O, since you are able to realize the reality [of the three realms] below the ground, on the ground, and the heavens, you will be established as the One Gone Thus, Vajra (your Mantra name)."

Kay-drup's *Mandala Rite* 341.3: tathāgata-siddhi-samayas tvaṃ *bhūrabhuvasvaḥ*

Bu-d̄ön's *Mandala Rite,* volume 5, 221.6: Tathāgata-siddhi-samayas tvaṃ bhūr *bhubasvaḥ.*

Kang-s̄ar, meaning, 458.1: sa 'og sa steng mtho ris kyi 'jig rten gsum las 'das pa'i de bzhin gshegs pa khyod kyi grub pa'i dam tshig la gnas par byas so.

Seventh Dalai Lama 617.2: *siddhi* grub pa, *samaya* . . . bkabs 'dir rtogs pa yin la/ sus rtogs na *tvaṃ* zhes pa ste khyod/ gang rtogs na/ *bhūr* [text reads *bhūru*] rlung gi dkyil 'khor te de la sogs pa'i sa 'og/ *bhuva* sa steng/ *svaḥ* mtho ris srid rtse'i bar kyi khams gsum gyi de kho na nyid/ *aḥ* yig dgag tshig gis mtshon pa de rtogs nus pa yin no// zhes pa ste don go bde bar brjod na khyod kyis khams gsum gyi chos nyid de sa [text reads: des] rab tu dga' ba la sogs pa'i rim pas rtogs nus pas na/ de bzhin gshegs pa 'di zhes bya bar grub pa ste 'tshang rgya bar 'gyur ro// zhes pa yin nam snyam.

III.7 PERMISSION INITIATION

Oṃ evaṃ padma-vajra-chīhnau prajñopāyau maṇḍala-adhipati-vajra-sukha-jñānāṃgaṃ mama dadatāṃ haṃ haḥ hūṃ phaṭ.

"*Oṃ evaṃ* please may wisdom and method symbolized by lotus and vajra be bestowed on me as the branch of exalted wisdom of vajra bliss of a lord of the mandala *haṃ haḥ hūṃ phaṭ.*"

Seventh Dalai Lama's Means of Achievement 58.1: Sanskrit same (padma rdo rje mtshan ma shes rab dang thabs dag dkyil 'khor mnga' bdag rdo rje bde ba ye shes kyi yan lag la bdag la stsal du gsol).

Bu-dön's *Initiation Chapter,* volume 2, 301.5: Oṃ evaṃ padma-vajra-chīhnau *prajñopāyo maṇḍalādhipati*-vajra-sukha-jñānāṃgaṃ mama dadatāṃ haṃ haḥ hūṃ phaṭ (padma rdo rje mtshan ma shes rab dang thabs dkyil 'khor mnga' bdag rdo rje bde ba ye shes kyi *mnga' bdag* la bdag la stsal du gsol).

Bu-dön's *Mandala Rite,* volume 5, 222.1: Oṃ evaṃ padma-vajra-*chīhno* prajñopāyau maṇḍala-*adhipatī*-vajra-sukha-jñānāṃgaṃ mama dadatāṃ haṃ haḥ hūṃ phaṭ.

Oṃ haṃ kṣhaḥ dharma-chakra-pravartaka svāhā.

"*Oṃ haṃ kṣhaḥ* turner of the wheel of doctrine *svāhā.*"

Seventh Dalai Lama's *Means of Achievement* 58.3: Sanskrit same (chos kyi 'khor lo bskor bar byed pa).

Kay-drup's *Mandala Rite* 342.6: Sanskrit same with instructions for the following five.

Bu-dön's *Initiation Chapter,* volume 2, 393.6:

Sanskrit same (chos kyi 'khor lo *rab tu* bskor bar byed pa).

Bu-d̄ön's *Mandala Rite*, volume 5, 222.3: Oṃ haṃ kṣhaḥ *dharmmaḥ*-chakra-pravartaka svāhā.

Oṃ haṃ kṣhaḥ vajra-chakra-pravartaka svāhā.

"*Oṃ haṃ kṣhaḥ* turner of the vajra-wheel *svāhā.*"

Oṃ haṃ kṣhaḥ khaḍga-chakra-pravartaka svāhā.

"*Oṃ haṃ kṣhaḥ* turner of the sword-wheel *svāhā.*"

Oṃ haṃ kṣhaḥ ratna-chakra-pravartaka svāhā.

"*Oṃ haṃ kṣhaḥ* turner of the jewel-wheel *svāhā.*"

Oṃ haṃ kṣhaḥ padma-chakra-pravartaka svāhā.

"*Oṃ haṃ kṣhaḥ* turner of the lotus-wheel *svāhā.*"

Oṃ haṃ kṣhaḥ chakra-chakra-pravartaka svāhā.

"*Oṃ haṃ kṣhaḥ* turner of the wheel-wheel *svāhā.*"

Oṃ vajra-hetu maṃ.

"*Oṃ* vajra cause *maṃ.*"

Kay-drup's *Mandala Rite* 343.2: Sanskrit same.

Bu-d̄ön's *Mandala Rite*, volume 5, 222.6: Sanskrit same.

Kang-s̄ar 466.1: rdo rje rgyu.

Oṃ vajra-bhāṣha raṃ.

"*Oṃ* vajra speech *raṃ.*"

Kay-drup's *Mandala Rite* 343.3: Sanskrit same.

Bu-d̄ön's *Mandala Rite*, volume 5, 222.6: Sanskrit same.

Kang-s̄ar 466.2: rdo rje smra ba.

Oṃ āḥ hūṃ hoḥ haṃkṣhaḥmalavaraya hūṃ phaṭ.
Oṃ hrāṃ hṝṃ hrāṃ hṝṃ hruṃ hṛḷ hraḥ svāhā.
Oṃ shrī-kālachakra huṃ hūṃ phaṭ.

L̄o-sang-tsul-trim-d̄en-b̄ay-gyel-tsen's *Initiation Rite* 520.1: Oṃ āḥ hūṃ *ho* haṃkṣhaḥmalavaraya hūṃ phaṭ. Oṃ hrāṃ *hrī hṝ hūṃ hṝḷ* hraḥ svāhā.

Kay-drup's *Means of Achievement*, volume 5, 127.4: Oṃ āḥ hūṃ hoḥ haṃkṣhaḥmalavaraya *huṃ* phaṭ. Oṃ hrāṃ *hrī hṝm hrūṃ hṝḷ* hraḥ svāhā.

Bu-d̄ön's *Means of Achievement*, volume 5, 150:

Oṃ āḥ hūṃ *ho* haṃkṣhaḥmalavaraya hūṃ phaṭ.
Oṃ *hraṃ hrīṃ hṝ* hruṃ *hḹ* hraḥ *hūṃ phaṭ*.

Kang-s̄ar 468.4: all three same as the first version.

Oṃ vajra-naitra-apahara-paṭalaṃ hrīḥ.

"*Oṃ* remove the covering obstructing the vajra eye *hrīḥ*."

Kay-drup's *Mandala Rite* 344.4: Oṃ vajra-naitra-apahara-*paṭālaṃ* hrīḥ.

Bu-d̄ön's *Mandala Rite,* volume 5, 223.7: Oṃ vajra-naitra-apahara-paṭalaṃ *hriḥ*.

Kang-s̄ar 469.4: rdo rje'i mig gi sgrib g.yogs sol cig.

Seventh Dalai Lama's *Explanation* 608.6: Hrīḥ symbolizes generation of the wisdom realizing emptiness.

Oṃ divya-nayana-mudghātayāmi svāhā.

"I am thoroughly opening the divine eye."

Kay-drup's *Mandala Rite* 344.5: Oṃ divya-*niyana-mudghatāyami* svāhā.

Bu-d̄ön's *Mandala Rite*, volume 5, 223.7: Same as first version.

Bu-d̄ön's *Initiation Chapter,* volume 2, 391.6: Oṃ divya-nayana-*mudghaṭayāmi* svāhā (lha'i spyan rab tu dbye bar bgyi'o).

Oṃ sarva-tathāgatān anurāgayasva.

"*Oṃ* make all the Ones Gone Thus pleased."

Kay-drup's *Mandala Rite* 345.2: Oṃ sarva-*tathā-gata-anurāgayasvā*.

Bu-d̄ön's *Mandala Rite,* volume 5, 224.5: Sarva-tathāgatān *ānurāgayasva*.

Kang-s̄ar 471.1: de bzhin gshegs pa thams cad mnyes par gyis shig.

Oṃ sarva-tathāgatān anurāgayāmi.

"*Oṃ* I make all the Ones Gone Thus pleased."

Kay-drup's *Mandala Rite* 345.2: Oṃ sarva-*tathā-gata-anurāgayami*.

Bu-d̄ön's *Mandala Rite,* volume 5, 224.5: Sarva-tathāgatān *ānurāgayami*.

Kang-s̄ar 471.2: de bzhin gshegs pa thams cad mnyes par bgyi'o.

Oṃ mahā-vajra hūṃ.

"*Oṃ* great vajra *hūṃ.*"

Kay-drup's *Mandala Rite* 345.7: same.

Seventh Dalai Lama's *Explanation* 629.5: *mahā-vajra* ni rdo rje chen po/ *hūṃ* thugs mtshon byed yin pas rdo rje chen po sangs rgyas kyi thugs rdo rje de sgoms shig// ces pa'i don du rjes 'brang gi mkhas pa 'gas bshad la.

Oṃ sarva-tathāgata-sapta-abhiṣheka-sapta-bhūmi-prāpto 'haṃ.

"*Oṃ* through all the Ones Gone Thus manifestly bestowing the seven initiations I have attained the seven grounds."

Seventh Dalai Lama's *Means of Achievement* 58.4: Sanskrit same (thams cad de bzhin gshegs pa bdun mngon par dbang bskur bas sa bdun thob pa nga'o).

Bu-d̄ön's *Initiation Chapter,* volume 2, 301.7: Oṃ sarva-tathāgatā-saptābhiṣheka-sapta-bhūmi-*labdho* 'haṃ (thams cad de bzhin gshegs pa bdun *pa* mngon par dbang bskur bas sa bdun *pa* thob pa nga'o).

Bu-d̄ön's *Mandala Rite,* volume 5, 230.6: Oṃ sarva-tathāgatā-sapta-abhhiṣheka-sapta-*bhumi-prapto* 'haṃ.

Bibliography of Works Cited

Note

Sūtras and tantras are listed alphabetically by English title in the first section. Indian and Tibetan treatises are listed alphabetically by author in the second section; other works are listed alphabetically by author in the third section.

"P", standing for "Peking edition", refers to the *Tibetan Tripiṭaka* (Tokyo-Kyoto: Tibetan Tripiṭaka Research Foundation, 1956).

1 *Sūtras and Tantras*

Brief Explication of Initiations
shekhoddesha
dbang mdor bstan
P3, vol. 1
Commentary: Mario E. Carelli, ed., *Sekoddeśaṭīkā of Naḍapāda (Nāropā) being a commentary of the Sekoddeśa section of the Kālachakra tantra,* (Baroda: Oriental Institute, 1941)

Chakrasaṃvara Tantra
dpal 'khor lo sdom pa'i rgyud kyi rgyal po dur khrod kyi rgyan rmad du 'byung ba
shrīchakrasaṃbaratantrarājādbhutashmashanālaṃkāranāma
P57, vol. 3
Translation: *Shrīchakrasambhāra Tantra, a Buddhist Tantra.* Tantrik Texts, under the general editorship of Arthur Avalon, vol. vii. Ed. by Kazi Dawa-Samdup, (London: Luzac; Calcutta: Thacker, Sprink, 1919)

Condensed Kālachakra Tantra. See *Kālachakra Tantra.*

General Secret Tantra
sarvamaṇḍalasāmānyavidhiguhyatantra
dkyil 'khor thams cad kyi spyi'i cho ga gsang ba'i rgyud
P429, vol. 9

Guhyasamāja Tantra
sarvatathāgatakāyavākchittarahasyaguhyasamājanāmamahākalparāja

de bzhin gshegs pa thams cad kyi sku gsung thugs kyi gsang chen gsang ba 'dus pa zhes bya ba brtag pa'i rgyal po chen po
P81, vol. 3

Hevajra Tantra
hevajratantrarāja
kye'i rdo rje zhes bya ba rgyud kyi rgyal po
P10, vol. 1
Translation: *Hevajra Tantra*, Parts I and II. Ed. and tr. D.L. Snellgrove, (London: Oxford University Press, 1959)

Kālachakra Tantra/Condensed Kālachakra Tantra/Kālachakra, King of Tantras, Issued From the Supreme Original Buddha
paramādibuddhoddhṛtashrīkālachakranāmatantrarāja
mchog gi dang po'i sangs rgyas las byung ba rgyud kyi rgyal po dpal dus kyi 'khor lo
P4, vol. 1
Sanskrit edition: *Kālacakra-Tantra And Other Texts*, Ed. Prof. Dr. Raghu Vira and Prof. Dr. Lokesh Chandra, Part 1, (New Delhi: International Academy of Indian Culture, 1966).

Kāshyapa Chapter Sūtra
kāshyapaparivartasūtra
'os srung gi le'u'i mdo
P760.43, vol. 24

Perfection of Wisdom Sūtra in One Hundred Thousand Stanzas
shatasāhasrikāprajñāpāramitā
shes rab kyi pha rol tu phyin pa stong phrag brgya pa
P730, vol. 12-18
See E. Conze's *The Large Sūtra on Perfect Wisdom* (Berkeley: U. Cal., 1975)

Vajrapañjara Tantra
ḍākiṇīvajrapañjaramahātantrarājakalpa
mkha' 'gro ma rdo rje gur zhes bya ba'i rgyud kyi rgyal po chen po'i brtag pa
P11, vol. 6

2 *Sanskrit and Tibetan Works*

Abhayākaragupta ('jigs med 'byung gnas sbas pa)
Ornament to the Subduer's Thought
munimatālaṃkāra
thub pa'i dgongs rgyan
P5294, vol. 101.

Ba-sō-chö-ḡyi-gyel-tsen (ba so chos kyi rgyal mtshan, 1402-1473)
The Lam rim chen mo of the incomparable Tsong-kha-pa, with the interlineal notes of Ba-so Chos-kyi-rgyal-mtshan, Sde-drug Mkhan-chen Ngag-dbang-rab-brtan, 'Jam-dbyangs-bshad-pa'i-rdo-rje, and Bra-sti Dge-bshes Rin-chen-don-grub
New Delhi: Chos-'phel-legs-ldan, 1972
Great Instructions on the View of the Middle Way
dbu ma'i lta khrid chen mo
Mādhyamika Text Series, vol. 3.
New Delhi: Lha-mkhar yons-'dzin Bstan-pa-rgyal-mtshan, 1972ff.

Bu-d̄ön Rin-chen-drup (bu ston rin chen grub, 1290-1364)
Collection of the Retention [Mantras] of the Tantra Sets of Secret Mantra
gsang sngags rgyud sde bzhi'i gzungs 'bum
Collected Works, volume 16
New Delhi: International Academy of Indian Culture, 1966
Commentarial Explanation of the "Initiation Chapter" [of the Kālachakra Tantra], Annotations to (Kulika Puṇḍarīka's) "Stainless Light"
dbang gi le'u 'grel bshad dri med 'od kyi mchan

Collected Works, volume 2

Easily Understandable Annotations For the Condensed Glorious Kālachakra Tantra, Great King of Tantras Arisen from the Supreme Original Buddha

mchog gi dang po'i sangs rgyas las phyungs ba rgyud kyi rgyal po chen po dpal dus kyi 'khor lo'i bsdus pa'i rgyud kyi go sla'i mchan

Collected Works, volume 1

Extensive Explanation of (Ānandagarbha's) "Rite of the Vajradhātu Mandala, Giving Rise To All Vajras": Wish-Granting Jewel

rdo rje dbyings kyi dkyil 'khor gyi cho ga rdo rje thams cad 'byung ba zhes bya ba'i rgya cher bshad pa yid bzhin gyi nor bu

Collected Works, volume 11

Mandala Rite of the Glorious Kālachakra: Source of Good Qualities

dpal dus kyi 'khor lo'i dkyil chog yon tan kun 'byung

Collected Works, volume 5

Means of Achievement of the Supramundane Victor, the Glorious Kālachakra: Fruit Cluster of the Wish-Granting [Tree]

dpal dus kyi 'khor lo'i sgrub thabs dpag bsam snye ma

Collected Works, volume 5

Chandrakirti (zla ba grags pa)

Supplement to (Nāgārjuna's) "Treatise on the Middle Way"

madhyamakāvatāra

dbu ma la 'jug pa

P5261 vol. 98; P5262, vol. 98

Also: *Madhyamakāvatāra par Candrakīrti*. Publiée par Louis de la Vallée Poussin, (Osnabrück: Biblio Verlag, 1970)

French translation by Louis de la Vallée Poussin up to VI.165 in *Muséon* 8 (1907), pp.249-317; *Muséon* 11 (1910), pp.271-358; and *Muséon* 12 (1911), pp.235-328.

English translation of first five chapters by Jeffrey Hopkins in *Compassion in Tibetan Buddhism*, (London: Rider and Co., 1980)

English translation of the sixth chapter by Stephen Batchelor in Geshé Rabten's *Echoes of Voidness*, (London: Wisdom, 1983), pp.47-92.

Chö-g̅yi-gyel-tsen, Jay-d̄zun (rje btsun chos kyi rgyal mtshan, 1469-1546)
Biography of the Omniscient Kay-drup Composed by Jay-d̄zun Chö-g̅yi-gyel-tsen
mkhas grub thams cad mkhyen pa'i gsang ba'i rnam thar rje btsun chos kyi rgyal mtshan gyis mdzad pa
The Collected Works of the Lord Mkhas-grub rje dge-legs-dpal-bzan-po, Vol. a
New Delhi: Mongolian Lama Guru Deva, 1980

D̄ak-tsang-s̄hay-rap-rin-chen (stag tshang lo tsā ba shes rab rin chen, born 1405)
The General Meaning of Kālachakra: Ocean of the Teaching
dus 'khor spyi don bstan pa'i rgya mtsho
New Delhi: Trayang and Jamyang Samten, 1973

Dharmakīrti (chos kyi grags pa)
Commentary on (Dignāga's) "Compendium of Valid Cognition"
pramāṇavarttikakārikā
tshad ma rnam 'grel gyi tshig le'ur byas pa
P5709, vol. 130
Also: Sarnath, India: Pleasure of Elegant Sayings Press, 1974. vol. 17
Sanskrit edition: *Pramāṇavārttika of Acharya Dharmakirtti*, ed. Swami Dwarikadas Shastri, (Varanasi: Bauddha Bharati, 1968)

G̅el-sang-gya-tso, Seventh Dalai Lama (bskal bzang rgya mtsho, 1708-57)
Explanation of the Mandala Rite of the Glorious Guhyasamāja, Akṣhobhyavajra, Illumination Brilliantly Clarifying the Principles of the Meaning of Initiation, Sacred Word of Vajrasattva
dpal gsang ba 'dus pa mi bskyod rdo rje'i dkyil 'khor gyi cho ga'i rnam par bshad pa dbang don de nyid yang gsal snang ba rdo rje sems dpa'i zhal lung
New Delhi: Tanzin Kunga, 1972
Means of Achievement of the Complete Mandala of Exalted Body, Speech, and Mind of the Supramundane Victor, the Glorious Kālachakra: the Sacred Word of Scholars and Adepts
bcom ldan 'das dus kyi 'khor lo'i sku gsung thugs yongs su rdzogs pa'i dkyil 'khor gyi sgrub thabs mkhas grub zhal lung

The eleventh work in a volume of the same title, 477-532
No publication data

Means of Achievement of the Mandala of Exalted Mind of the Glorious Kālachakra: Good Vase of All Feats
dpal dus kyi 'khor lo'i thugs dkyil 'khor gyi sgrub dngos grub kun gyi bum bzang
The fifth work in a volume entitled: *dpal bcom ldan 'das dus kyi 'khor lo'i sku gsung thugs yongs su rdzogs pa'i dkyil 'khor gyi sgrub thabs mkhas grub zhal lung*, 159-257
No publication data

Ḡön-chok-ḏen-ḇay-drön-may, Gung-tang (gung thang dkon mchog bstan pa'i sgron me, 1762-1823

Practice In The Manner Of The Very Condensed Clear Realization Of The Supreme Superior, The Ocean Of Conquerors (Jinasamudra)
phags mchog rgyal ba rgya mtsho'i mngon rtogs shin tu bsdus pa'i tshul du nyams su len pa
Collected Works of Guṅ-thaṅ dkon-mchog bstan-pa'i sgron-me, Vol. 7
Ngawang Gelek Demo, 1975

Gyel-tsap-dar-ma-rin-chen (rgyal tshab dar ma rin chen, 1364-1432)

How To Practice the Two Stages of the Path of the Glorious Kālachakra: Quick Entry to the Path of Great Bliss
dpal dus kyi 'khor lo'i lam rim pa gnyis ji ltar nyams su len pa'i tshul bde ba chen po'i lam du myur du 'jug pa
Collected Works, volume 1
No publicaton data.

Jam-ȳang-shay-ḇa ('jam dbyangs bzhad pa, 1648-1721)

Great Exposition of the Middle Way/Analysis of (Chandrakīrti's) "Supplement to (Nāgārjuna's) 'Treatise on the Middle Way'", Treasury of Scripture and Reasoning, Thoroughly Illuminating the Profound Meaning [of Emptiness], Entrance for the Fortunate
dbu ma chen mo/dbu ma 'jug pa'i mtha' dpyod lung rigs gter mdzod zab don kun gsal skal bzang 'jug ngogs
Buxaduor: Gomang, 1967

Jang-gya (lcang skya, 1717-86)

Presentation of Tenets/Clear Exposition of the Presentations of Tenets, Beautiful Ornament for the Meru of the Subduer's Teaching grub mtha'i rnam bzhag/grub pa'i mtha'i rnam par bzhag pa gsal bar bshad pa thub bstan lhun po'i mdzes rgyan

Varanasi: Pleasure of Elegant Sayings Printing Press, 1970

Sautrāntika chapter translated by Anne Klein in *Mind and Liberation. The Sautrāntika Tenet System in Tibet: Perception, Naming, Positive and Negative Phenomena, Impermanence and the Two Truths in the Context of Buddhist Religious Insight as Presented in Ge-luk Literary and Oral Traditions,* (Ann Arbor: University Microfilms, 1981)

Svātantrika chapter translated by Donald Lopez in *The Svātantrika-Mādhyamika School of Mahāyāna Buddhism,* (Ann Arbor: University Microfilms, 1982)

Kang-s̄ar-ḡyap-gön. See L̄o-sang-tsul-trim-d̄en-b̄ay-gyel-tsen.

Kay-drup-ge-lek-b̄el-sang (mkhas grub dge legs dpal bzang, 1385-1438)

Mandala Rite of the Glorious Kālachakra: Illumination of the Thought

dpal dus kyi 'khor lo'i dkyil chog dgongs pa rab gsal

The Collected Works of the Lord Mkhas-grub rje dge-legs-dpal-bzaṅ-po, vol. 5

New Delhi: Mongolian Lama Gurudeva, 1980

Also the sixth work in a volume entitled: *dpal bcom ldan 'das dus kyi 'khor lo'i sku gsung thugs yongs su rdzogs pa'i dkyil 'khor gyi sgrub thabs mkhas grub zhal lung,* 259-383

No publication data

Also found in: *The Collected Rites of the Kālacakra By Mkhas-grub Rje Dge-legs-dpal-bzaṅ* (Title on boards: *dpal dus kyi 'khor lo'i cho ga mkhas grub zhal luṅ,* (New Delhi: Guru Deva, 1979)

Means of Achievement of the Complete [Mandala of] Exalted Body, Speech, and Mind of the Glorious Kālachakra: Sacred Word of the White Lotus

dus kyi 'khor lo'i sku gsung thugs yongs su rdzogs pa'i sgrub thabs padma'i dkar po'i zhal lung)

The Collected Works of the Lord Mkhas-grub rje dge-legs-dpal-bzan-po, vol. 6

Also the third work in a volume entitled: *dpal bcom ldan*

'das dus kyi 'khor lo'i sku gsung thugs yongs su rdzogs pa'i dkyil 'khor gyi sgrub thabs mkhas grub zhal lung, 13-157
No publication data
Stages of the Series of Offerings of the Glorious Kālachakra
dpal dus kyi 'khor lo'i mchod phreng gi rim pa
The ninth work in a volume entitled: *dpal bcom ldan 'das dus kyi 'khor lo'i sku gsung thugs yongs su rdzogs pa'i dkyil 'khor gyi sgrub thabs mkhas grub zhal lung*, 431-457
No publication data

Lo-drö, Buddhist monk (shākya btsun pa blo gros)
Prayer-Wishes of the Glorious Kālachakra Together With An Expression of Auspiciousness
dpal dus kyi 'khor lo'i smon lam shis brjod dang bcas pa
The thirteenth work in a volume entitled: *dpal bcom ldan 'das dus kyi 'khor lo'i sku gsung thugs yongs su rdzogs pa'i dkyil 'khor gyi sgrub thabs mkhas grub zhal lung*, 553-567
No publication data

Lo-sang-chö-gyi-gyel-tsen, First Paṇ-chen Lama (blo bzang chos kyi rgyal mtshan, 1567?-1662)
Six Session Yoga
(untitled)
Collected Works of Blo-bzaṅ-chos-kyi-rgyal-mtshan, the First Paṇ-chen Bla-ma of Bkra-śis-lhun-po, vol. 1, 707.2-803.1
New Delhi: Gurudeva, 1973
Wish-Granting Jewel, Essence of (Kay-drup's) "Illumination of the Principles: Extensive Explanation of (Kulika Puṇḍarīka's) 'Extensive Commentary On The Condensed Kālachakra Tantra, Derived From The Root Tantra Of The Supramundane Victor, The Glorious Kālachakra, The King Of All Tantras, The Stainless Light'"
rgyud thams cad kyi rgyal po bcom ldan 'das dpal dus kyi 'khor lo'i rtsa ba'i rgyud las phyung ba bsdus pa'i rgyud kyi rgyas 'grel dri ma med pa'i 'od kyi rgya cher bshad pa de kho na nyid snang bar byed pa'i snying po bsdus pa yid bzhin gyi nor bu
Collected Works of Blo-bzaṅ-chos-kyi-rgyal-mtshan, the First Paṇ-chen Bla-ma of Bkra-śis-lhun-po, vol. 3
New Delhi: Gurudeva, 1973

Lo-sang-tsul-trim-den-bay-gyel-tsen, Dre-wo Kang-sar Gyap-gön (blo bzang tshul khrims bstan pa'i rgyal mtshan, tre bo

khang gsar skyabs mgon, late 19th and early 20th centuries)
Explanation Of The Initiations Of The Supramundane Victor, The Glorious Kālachakra: Garland Of Rubies
bcom ldan 'das dus kyi 'khor lo'i dbang gi bshad pa padma ra ga'i phreng ba
The Collected Works of Tre-bo Khaṅ-gsar bLo-bzaṅ-tshul-khrims-btsan-pa'i-rgyal-mtshan, vol. 3, 369-488
New Delhi: T.G. Dhongthog Rinpoche, 1975
Initiation Rite of Kālachakra, Stated in an Easy Way
dus 'khor dbang chog nag 'gros su bkod pa
The eleventh work in a volume entitled: *dpal bcom ldan 'das dus kyi 'khor lo'i sku gsung thugs yongs su rdzogs pa'i dkyil 'khor gyi sgrub thabs mkhas grub zhal lung*, 477-532
No publication data
Also: The Collected Works of Tre-bo Khaṅ-gsar bLo-bzaṅ-tshul-khrims-bstan-pa'i-rgyal-mtshan
New Delhi: T.G. Dhongthog Rinpoche, 1975, 313-368

Maitreya (byams pa)
Ornament for Clear Realization
abhisamayālaṃkāra
mngon par rtogs pa'i rgyan
P5184, Vol. 88
Sanskrit text: Th. Stcherbatsky and E. Obermiller, ed., *Abhisamayālaṃkāra-Prajñāpāramitā-Updeśa-Śāstra*, Bibliotheca Buddhica XXIII, (Osnabrück: Biblio Verlag, 1970)
English translation: Edward Conze, *Abhisamayālaṃkāra*, Serie Orientale Roma (Rome: Is.M.E.O., 1954)
Ornament For the Great Vehicle Sūtras
mahāyānasūtrālaṃkāra
theg pa chen po'i mdo sde rgyan gyi tshig le'ur byas pa
P5521, Vol. 108
Sanskrit text: S. Bagchi, ed., *Mahāyāna-Sūtrālaṃkāra of Asaṅga*, Buddhist Sanskrit Texts, No. 13, (Darbhanga: Mithila Institute, 1970)

Mi-pam-gya-tso (mi pham rgya mtsho, 1846-1912)
Clarifying the Meaning of the Words of the Glorious Kālachakra Tantra, Illumination of the Vajra Sun
dpal dus kyi 'khor lo'i rgyud kyi tshig don rab tu gsal byed rdo rje nyi ma'i snang ba
Gangtok: Sonam Topgay Kazi, 1971

Nāgārjuna (klu sgrub)

Precious Garland of Advice for the King

Rājaparikathāratnavalī

rgyal po la gtam bya ba rin po che'i phreng ba

P5658, vol. 129

Sanskrit, Tibetan, and Chinese in: Michael Hahn, *Nāgārjuna's Ratnāvalī, Vol. 1, The Basic Texts (Sanskrit, Tibetan, and Chinese)*, (Bonn: Indica et Tibetica Verlag, 1982)

English translation by Jeffrey Hopkins in: Nāgārjuna and the Seventh Dalai Lama, *The Precious Garland and the Song of the Four Mindfulnesses*, (New York: Harper and Row, 1975)

Treatise on the Middle Way/Fundamental Treatise on the Middle Way, Called "Wisdom"

madhyamakashāstra/prajñānāmamūlamadhyamakakārikā

dbu ma rtsa ba'i tshig le'ur byas pa shes rab ces bya ba

P5225, vol. 95

Sanskrit text: Louis de la Vallée Poussin, ed., *Mūlamadhyamakakārikās (Mādhyamikasūtras) de Nāgārjuna avec la Prasannapadā Commentaire de Candrakīrti*, Bibliotheca Buddhica IV (Osnabrück: Biblio Verlag, 1970)

English Translations: F.J. Streng, *Emptiness* (Nashville and New York: Abingdon, 1967); K. Inada, *Nāgārjuna, A Translation of his Mūlamadhyamakakārikā with an Introductory Essay* (Tokyo: The Hokuseido press, 1970); etc.

Nga-w̄ang-b̄el-den (ngag dbang dpal ldan, 1797-?)

Illumination of the Texts of Tantra, Presentation of the Grounds and Paths of the Four Great Secret Tantra Sets

gsang chen rgyud sde bzhi'i sa lam gyi rnam bzhag rgyud gzhung gsal byed

rgyud smad par khang edition, no other data

Nga-w̄ang-l̄o-sang-gya-tso, Fifth Dalai Lama (ngag dbang blo bzang rgya mtsho, 1617-1682)

Instruction on the Stages of the Path to Enlightenment, Sacred Word of Mañjushrī

byang chub lam gyi rim pa'i khrid yig 'jam pa'i dbyangs kyi zhal lung

Thimpu: kun-bzang-stobs-rgyal, 1976
Puṇḍarīka, Kulika (rigs ldan pad ma dkar po)
Great Commentary on the "Kālachakra Tantra", the Stainless Light
vimālaprabhānāmamūlatantrānusāriṇīdvādashasāhasrikā-laghukālachakratantrarājaṭīkā
bsdus pa'i rgyud kyi rgyal po dus kyi 'khor lo'i 'grel bshad rtsa ba'i rgyud kyi rjes su 'jug pa stong phrag bcu gnyis pa dri ma med pa'i 'od ces bya ba
P2064, vol. 46
Shāntideva (zhi ba lha)
Engaging in the Bodhisattva Deeds
bodhi[sattva]caryāvatāra
byang chub sems dpa'i spyod pa la 'jug pa
P5272, Vol. 99
Sanskrit and Tibetan texts: Vidhushekara Bhattacharya, *Bodhicaryāvatāra*,
Bibliotheca Indica, Vol. 280 (Calcutta: The Asiatic Society, 1960)
English translation: Stephen Batchelor, *A Guide to the Bodhisattva's Way of Life*, (Dharamsala: Library of Tibetan Works and Archives, 1979); also by Marion Matics, *Entering the Path of Enlightenment*, (New York: Macmillan Co, 1970); contemporary commentary by Geshe Kelsang Gyatso, *Meaningful to Behold*, (London: Wisdom Publications, 1980)
Tok-may-sang-bo (rgyal sras thogs med bzang po, 1245-1369)
The Thirty-Seven Practices
lag len so bdun ma
Dharamsala: Tibetan Cultural Printing Press, no date.
Vasubandhu (dbyig gnyen)
Treasury of Knowledge
abhidharmakoshakārikā
chos mngon pa'i mdzod kyi tshig le'ur byas pa
P5590, vol. 115
Sanskrit text: P. Pradhan, ed., *Abhidharmakośabhāṣyam of Vasubandhu*, (Patna: Jayaswal Research Institute, 1975)
French translation. Louis de la Vallée Poussin, *L'Abhidharmakośa de Vasubandhu*, 6 vols., (Bruxelles: Institut Belge des Hautes Études Chinoises, 1971)

3 *Other Works*

Avedon, John F. *In Exile From the Land of Snows*. New York: Knopf, 1984.

Bernbaum, Edwin. *The Way to Shambhala*. New York: Anchor Books, 1980.

Berzin, Alexander, trans. and ed. *The Mahāmudrā Eliminating the Darkness of Ignorance Supplemented by Aśvaghoṣa's Fifty Stanzas Of Guru Devotion*. Dharamsala: Library of Tibetan Works and Archives, 1978.

Bhattacharyya, Benoytosh. Ed. *Niṣpannayogāvalī of Mahāpanditā Abhayākaragupta*. Baroda: Oriental Institute, 1972.

Bleeker, Dr C.J. *Initiation*. Leiden: E.J. Brill, 1965.

Eliade, Mircea. *Rites And Symbols Of Initiation, The Mysteries of Birth and Rebirth*. New York: Harper and Row, 1965.

Fujita, Hiroki. *The World of Tibetan Buddhism*. Japan: Gyosei Ltd., [1984].

Gyatso, Tenzin, Fourteenth Dalai Lama. *My Land and My People*. New York: McGraw-Hill, 1962; rpt. New York: Potala Corportion, 1977.

——. *The Buddhism of Tibet and The Key to the Middle Way*. London: George Allen and Unwin, 1975.

——. *Kindness, Clarity and Insight*. Ithaca: Snow Lion, 1984.

Hoffmann, Helmut. *The Religions of Tibet*. London: George Allen and Unwin, 1961.

Hopkins, Jeffrey. "A Session of Meditating on Emptiness". *The Middle Way*, Vol. 59, No. 1, May 1984.

——. *Meditation on Emptiness*. London: Wisdom Publications, 1983.

——. "Reason as the Prime Principle in Tsong kha pa's Delineating Deity Yoga As the Demarcation Between Sūtra and Tantra". *Journal of the International Association of Buddhist Studies*, vol. 7 no. 2, 1984, pp.95-115.

——. *The Tantric Distinction*. London: Wisdom Publications, 1984.

Lati Rinbochay, Denma Lochö Rinbochay, Leah Zahler, Jeffrey Hopkins. *Meditative States in Tibetan Buddhism*. London: Wisdom Publications, 1983.

Lati Rinbochay and Hopkins, Jeffrey. *Death, Intermediate State and Rebirth in Tibetan Buddhism*. London: Rider and Co., 1979.

Lessing, Ferdinand D., and Wayman, Alex. *Mkhas Grub Rje's Fundamentals of the Buddhist Tantras*. The Hague: Mouton, 1968.

Nāgārjuna and Kaysang Gyatso. *Precious Garland and the Song of the Four Mindfulnesses*. London: George Allen and Unwin, 1975.

Rabten, Geshe. *The Life and Teachings of Geshe Rabten*. Trans. and ed. by Alan Wallace. London: George Allen and Unwin, 1982.

Renou, Louis. *The Nature of Hinduism*. New York: Walker and Company, 1962.

Roerich, George N.. *The Blue Annals*. Delhi: Motilal Banarsidass, rpt. 1979.

Sangpo, Khetsun. *Tantric Practice in Nyingma*. London: Rider, 1982.

bSod nams rgya mtsho. *Tibetan Maṇḍalas, The Ngor Collection*. Tokyo: Kodansha, 1983.

Sopa, Geshe Lhundup, and Hopkins, Jeffrey. *Practice and Theory of Tibetan Buddhism*. London: Rider and Co., 1976.

Tsong-ka-pa. *Tantra in Tibet*. London: George Allen and Unwin, 1977.

——. *The Yoga of Tibet*. London: George Allen and Unwin, 1981.

Tucci, Giuseppe. *Tibetan Painted Scrolls*. Roma: La Libreria Dello Stato, 1949.

Turner, Victor. *The Forest Of Symbols*. New York: Cornell

University Press, 1967.
Wangdu, Sonam. *The Discovery of the 14th Dalai Lama*. Trans. Bhikku Thupten Kalsang Rinpoche, Ngodup Poljor, and John Blofeld. Bangkok: Klett Thai Publications, 1975.
Wangyal, Geshe. *The Door of Liberation*. New York: Lotsawa, 1978.

Notes

1 *Notes to the Introduction*

1 This chapter is adapted from a paper delivered at the second Buddhist-Christian Theological Encounter in Vancouver, British Columbia, in March, 1985 in response to a paper written by Professor David Tracy of the University of Chicago.

2 My sources are primarily, but not exclusively, texts and oral teachings of the Ge-luk-b̄a order of Tibetan Buddhism. This order was founded by the savant and yogi D̄zong-ka-b̄a (1357-1419) from the easternmost region of Tibet. It came to have great influence throughout a region stretching from Kalmuck Mongolian areas near the Volga River (in Europe) where it empties into the Caspian Sea, through what are now Outer and Inner Mongolia and the Buriat Republic of Siberia as well as many parts of Tibet and Ladakh. D̄zong-ka-b̄a established a system of education with large universities eventually in three areas of Tibet but primarily in Hla-s̄a, the capital, which was like Rome for the Catholic Church; young men came from all of the above-mentioned regions to Hla-s̄a to study, usually (until the Communist takeovers) returning to their native lands after completing their studies.

For further reading on the topics of the chapter, see my *The Tantric Distinction*, (London: Wisdom Publications, 1984) and *Meditation on Emptiness*, (London: Wisdom Publications, 1983).

3 *theg dman, hīnayāna*.

4 The Tibetan and Sanskrit for the four schools of tenets are:
Great Exposition School *(bye brag smra ba, vaibhāṣhika)*
Sūtra School *(mdo sde pa, sautrāntika)*
Mind Only School *(sems tsam pa, chittamātra)*
Middle Way School *(dbu ma pa, mādhyamika).*

5 I.18ab. The Sanskrit is:

chittotpādaḥ parārthāya samyaksaṃbodhikāmatā.

See Th. Stcherbatsky and E. Obermiller, ed., *Abhisamayālaṃkāra-Prajñāpāramitā-Updeśa-Śāstra,* Bibliotheca Buddhica XXIII, (Osnabrück: Biblio Verlag, 1970), p.4.

6 Defined more technically within the context of Chandrakīrti's *Supplement to (Nāgārjuna's) "Treatise on the Middle Way" (dbu ma la 'jug pa, madhyamakāvatāra),* an altruistic intention to become enlightened is:

a main mental consciousness, taking cognizance of others' welfare and [one's own] great enlightenment, that, having the aspect of wanting to attain those, is induced by non-dualistic understanding and great compassion.

In Tibetan:

dmigs pa gzhan don dang byang chub chen po la dmigs nas ched du bya ba sems can thams cad kyi don du rnam pa de thob par 'dod pa ngo bo gnyis med kyi blo dang snying rje chen pos drangs pa'i yid kyi rnam shes.

See Jam-ȳang-shay-b̄a, *Great Exposition of the Middle Way/Analysis of (Chandrakīrti's) "Supplement to (Nāgārjuna's) 'Treatise on the Middle Way'", Treasury of Scripture and Reasoning, Thoroughly Illuminating the Profound Meaning [of Emptiness], Entrance for the Fortunate (dbu ma chen mo/dbu ma 'jug pa'i mtha' dpyod lung rigs gter mdzod zab don kun gsal skal bzang 'jug ngogs),* (Buxaduor: Gomang, 1967), 32b.6.

7 *chos sku, dharmakāya* and *gzugs sku, rūpakāya.*

8 Chapter II:

sems kyi rang bzhin 'od gsal te//
dri ma rnams ni blo bur ba//.

Varanasi: Pleasure of Elegant Sayings, 1974), Vol. 17, 63.11. The Sanskrit is:

prabhāsvaramidaṃ chittaṃ prakṛtyāgantatro malāḥ.

See Swami Dwarikadas Shastri, *Pramāṇavārttika of Acharya Dharmakirtti* (Varanasi: Bauddha Bharati, 1968), Vol. 3, 73.1.

9 See the Dalai Lama's exposition of this, pp.271-4.

10 *rang bzhin gyis grub pa, svabhāvasiddhi.*

11 *gsal zhing rig pa.*

12 The source for this list is Kensur Yeshi Thupten, former abbot of the L̄o-s̄el-l̄ing College of Dre-b̄ung Monastic University, presently resettled in Mundgod, Karnataka State, South India. The contents of the list are common knowledge among Ge-luk-b̄a scholars.

13 See the Dalai Lama's explanation of this in his *The Buddhism of Tibet and The Key to the Middle Way* (London: George Allen and Unwin, 1975), pp.80-82.

14 The first part of this chapter, up to the section on the difference between the four tantra sets, is adapted from the first part of my article "Reason as the Prime Principle in Tsong kha pa's Delineating Deity Yoga As the Demarcation Between Sūtra and Tantra", *Journal of the International Association of Buddhist Studies*, vol. 7 no. 2, 1984, pp.95-115. For a detailed discussion of the distinction between sūtra and tantra, see Tsong-ka-pa, *Tantra in Tibet*, (London: George Allen and Unwin, 1977) and Jeffrey Hopkins, *The Tantric Distinction*, (London: Wisdom Publications, 1984). Since the presentation closely follows D̄zong-ka-b̄a's argument in and the Dalai Lama's introduction to *Tantra in Tibet*, detailed page references are given in the notes. (The variations in the spelling of D̄zong-ka-b̄a's name are due to different systems used by different publishers.)

15 *bya ba, kriyā; spyod pa, charyā; rnal 'byor, yoga; rnal 'byor bla med, anuttarayoga.*

16 *nyan thos, shrāvaka.*

17 *rang rgyal, pratyekabuddha.*

18 The Dalai Lama's introduction in *Tantra in Tibet*, pp.20-1.

19 The translation of *arhan* as "Foe Destroyer" accords with the Tibetan translation as *dgra bcom pa;* for discussion of the etymology and justification of the translation, see my *Meditation on Emptiness*, n.553.

20 The Dalai Lama's introduction in *Tantra in Tibet*, p.43.

Ḏzong-ka-ḇa also speaks of these two meanings of "vehicle", but the line was unintentionally deleted from *Tantra in Tibet*. The beginning of the last paragraph on p.106 should read: "About 'vehicle', there is an effect vehicle which is that to which one is proceeding and a cause vehicle which is that by which one proceeds. Due to proceeding [it is called] a vehicle. With respect to . . ."

21 *dbu ma thal 'gyur pa, prāsaṅgika-mādhyamika.*

22 The Dalai Lama's introduction in *Tantra in Tibet*, p.57.

23 The Dalai Lama's introduction in *Tantra in Tibet*, pp.38-41, and Ḏzong-ka-ḇa's own exposition, pp.98-99.

24 Ḏzong-ka-ḇa discusses this point in some detail in his commentary *(dgongs pa rab gsal)* on Chandrakīrti's *Supplement to (Nāgārjuna's) "Treatise on the Middle Way" (madhyamakāvatāra)*, the first five chapters of which are translated in *Compassion in Tibetan Buddhism* (London: Rider and Co., 1980), pp.174-5. (For justification of my translation of *madhyamakāvatāra* as *Supplement to the "Treatise on the Middle Way"*, see my *Meditation on Emptiness*, pp.462-9 and 866-9.) Ḏzong-ka-ḇa says (p.175):

> To establish that even a single phenomenon does not truly exist, Mahāyānists use limitless different reasonings as set forth in the *Treatise on the Middle Way*. Hence their minds become greatly broadened with respect to suchness. Hīnayānists use only brief reasoning to establish suchness by valid cognition, and since they do not establish emptiness the way Mahāyānists do, do not have a mind broadened with respect to suchness . . . This difference arises because Hearers and Solitary Realizers strive to abandon only the afflictions [the obstructions to liberation], and cognizing a mere abbreviation of the meaning of suchness is sufficient for that. Mahāyānists are intent on abandoning the obstructions to omniscience, and for that it is necessary to have a very broadened mind of wisdom opened to suchness.

25 The Dalai Lama's introduction in *Tantra in Tibet*, p.55.

26 *'khor ba, saṃsāra.*

27 *byang chub kyi sems, bodhichitta.*

28 *Tantra in Tibet*, pp.98-99.

29 *phar phyin kyi theg pa, pāramitāyāna* and *sngags kyi thegs pa, mantrayāna*. The term "Tantrayāna" has great favor in the West but does not appear to have been popular in Tibet. There the favored term is Guhyamantrayāna *(gsang sngags kyi theg pa)*.

30 *rlung, prāṇa*. This is one among many points that Jam-ȳang-shay-b̄a *('jam dbyangs bzhad pa*, 1648-1721) makes in defending the position that the Buddhahoods of sūtra and tantra are the same. See his *Great Exposition of "Tenets" (grub mtha' chen mo)*, (Mussoorie: Da Lama, 1962), ca 44b.6-47a.8.

31 *sngags bla med, anuttarayogamantra*.

32 See Lati Rinbochay and Jeffrey Hopkins, *Death, Intermediate State and Rebirth in Tibetan Buddhism* (London: Rider and Co., 1979), pp.69-73.

33 The Dalai Lama's introduction in *Tantra in Tibet*, pp.55, and D̄zong-ka-b̄a's own exposition, pp. 139-42.

34 The Dalai Lama's introduction in *Tantra in Tibet*, pp.55-7, and D̄zong-ka-b̄a's own exposition, p. 110.

35 The Dalai Lama's introduction in *Tantra in Tibet*, pp.57-58.

36 The Dalai Lama's introduction in *Tantra in Tibet*, p.58, and D̄zong-ka-b̄a's own exposition, pp. 100-101.

37 *lha'i rnal 'byor, *devatāyoga*.

38 The Dalai Lama's introduction in *Tantra in Tibet*, pp.61-65, and D̄zong-ka-b̄a's own exposition, pp. 115-116.

39 The source here is Jam-b̄el-shen-pen Rin-b̄o-chay, abbot of the Tantric College of Lower Hla-s̄a during the time of its re-location in South India; he is currently head of the Ge-luk-bá order and residing at Jang-d̄zay College at Gan-den in Mundgod, Karnataka.

40 The Dalai Lama's introduction in *Tantra in Tibet*, pp.60 and 62, and D̄zong-ka-b̄a's own exposition, p. 115.

41 See the Mongolian scholar Nga-w̄ang-b̄el-den's *(ngag dbang dpal ldan)* statement of this in Tsong-ka-pa's*Yoga of Tibet* (London: George Allen and Unwin, 1981), pp.211-12.

42 The Dalai Lama's introduction in *Tantra in Tibet*, pp.62-63.

43 The Dalai Lama's introduction in *Tantra in Tibet*, pp.22-23

and Ḏzong-ka-ḇa's own exposition, pp. 107-108.

44 This section is based on Ḏzong-ka-ḇa's own exposition in *Tantra in Tibet,* pp.156-164, the Dalai Lama's introduction, pp.74-76, and my supplement, pp.201-209.

45 (New Delhi: Tanzin Kunga, 1972), 17.2-18.2.

46 See *Tantra in Tibet,* pp.156-157.

47 (Sarnath: Pleasure of Elegant Sayings Press, 1970), 529.18-530.8.

48 For a detailed discussion of this position, see *Tantra in Tibet,* pp.203-206.

49 (rgyud smad par khang edition, no other data), 7b.4ff. This passage is cited in my brief explanation of this point in Tsong-ka-pa, *The Yoga of Tibet,* p.211.

50 See the section on Action Tantra in Tsong-ka-pa, *The Yoga of Tibet.*

51 *Tantra in Tibet,* p.163.

52 Ithaca: Snow Lion, 1984.

53 These citations are found in the practice text, with brief commentary in notes; see pp.407-8. The citations respectively are from V.253cd, V.258cd, and V.260.

53a Dharamsala: Tibetan Cultural Printing Press, no date.

54 This chapter is adapted from an article that first appeared in *The Middle Way,* Vol. 59, No. 1, May 1984, as "A Session of Meditating on Emptiness." The full name of the author of the source text is Nga-w̄ang-l̄o-sang-gya-tso (*ngag dbang blo bzang rgya mtsho,* 1617-1682), Dalai Lama V, and its full title is *Instruction on the Stages of the Path to Enlightenment, Sacred Word of Mañjushrī (byang chub lam gyi rim pa'i khrid yig 'jam pa'i dbyangs kyi zhal lung),* (Thimphu: kun-bzang-stobs-rgyal, 1976), 182.5-210.6. For an English translation of the chapter on the perfection of wisdom, see J. Hopkins, "Practice of Emptiness", (Dharamsala: Library of Tibetan Works and Archives, 1974). For a more extensive discussion of the selflessness of persons, see my *Meditation on Emptiness,* pp. 43-51 and 175-196.

55 *ngo bo gcig la ldog pa tha dad.*

56 *Clear Exposition of the Presentations of Tenets, Beautiful Ornament for the Meru of the Subduer's Teaching (grub pa'i mtha'i rnam par bzhag pa gsal bar bshad pa thub bstan lhun*

po'i mdzes rgyan), (Varanasi: Pleasure of Elegant Sayings Printing Press, 1970), 435.20-436.5.

57 For an account of his life and a sample of his teachings, see *The Life and Teachings of Geshe Rabten*, trans. and ed. by Alan Wallace, (London: George Allen and Unwin, 1982).

58 The source here is Geshe Thupten Gyatso of the Go-mang College of Dre-b̄ung Monastic University, currently staying at the Tibetan Buddhist Learning Center in Washington, New Jersey. According to another version, the *Kālachakra Tantra* was set forth a year before his death, but the first version seems to be favored.

59 George N. Roerich, *The Blue Annals* (Delhi: Motilal Banarsidass, rpt.1979), p.754 n.l. Dhānyakaṭaka is also identified as being three days travel across the sea from Bengal in eastern India; see *The World Of Tibetan Buddhism* (Japan: Gyosei Ltd., [1984]), p.96.

60 Tibetan: *zla ba bzang po*. That the Sanskrit is Suchandra and not Chandrabhadra is clear in the tantra itself; see the *Kālacakra-Tantra And Other Texts*, volume 1, edited by Prof. Dr. Raghu Vira and Prof. Dr. Lokesh Chandra, (New Delhi: International Academy of Indian Culture, 1966), I.lc, Sanskrit p.332; Tibetan p.53.4.

61 G. Tucci, *Tibetan Painted Scrolls*, (Roma: La Libreria Dello Stato, 1949), p.212. For a very interesting and valuable account of the legends of Shambhala, see Edwin Bernbaum, *The Way to Shambhala* (New York: Anchor Books, 1980).

62 Helmut Hoffmann, *The Religions of Tibet* (London: George Allen and Unwin, 1961), p.125.

63 *ibid*, p.126.

64 For an enumeration of the stanzas of each of the five chapters, see Professor Lokesh Chandra's introduction to the *Kālacakra-Tantra And Other Texts*, volume 1, edited by Prof. Dr. Raghu Vira and Prof. Dr. Lokesh Chandra, p.18.

65 *The Blue Annals*, p.753.

66 Lokesh Chandra's introduction to the *Kālacakra-Tantra And Other Texts*, volume 1, p.7. According to Roerich, the name is Cheluka, *The Blue Annals*, p.755.

67 See *The Blue Annals*, p.754-5.

68 Helmut Hoffmann, *The Religions of Tibet*, pp.126-127; see his citation of Padma-g̅ar-b̅o *(padma dkar po)*. Lokesh Chandra repeats this in his introduction to the *Kālacakra-Tantra And Other Texts*, volume 1, pp.7-8; Lokesh Chandra holds the view that Chilupā himself reintroduced the tantra to India.

69 Helmut Hoffmann, *The Religions of Tibet*, pp.127-128.

70 *ibid.*

71 *ibid.*

72 Helmut Hoffmann, *The Religions of Tibet*, pp.120 and 126-128. Hoffmann dismisses the Tibetan historian S̄um-b̄a-ken-b̄o's *(sum pa mkhan po)* statement that Pindo Āchārya perhaps was the person who re-introduced the *Kālachakra Tantra* to India because his being a student of Atīsha who already was initiated into the tantra makes such a sequence impossible.

73 Helmut Hoffmann, *The Religions of Tibet*, p.126; Lokesh Chandra's introduction to the *Kālachakra-Tantra And Other Texts*, volume 1, p.7.

74 Lokesh Chandra's introduction to the *Kālacakra-Tantra And Other Texts*, volume 1, p.6.

75 *The Blue Annals*, pp.755-765, presents the development of the Kālachakra tradition in India and its spread to Tibet according to the histories of four different lineages.

76 Lokesh Chandra's introduction to the *Kālacakra-Tantra And Other Texts*, volume 1, pp.8-10.

77 Helmut Hoffmann, *The Religions of Tibet*, p.126; Lokesh Chandra's introduction to the *Kālacakra-Tantra And Other Texts*, volume 1, p.7; Roerich gives 1027 in *The Blue Annals*, p.754.

78 Helmut Hoffmann, *The Religions of Tibet*, p.128.

79 This and the next paragraph are drawn from Helmut Hoffmann, *The Religions of Tibet*, pp.129-130.

80 *The Blue Annals*, p.755.

81 For a list see Lokesh Chandra's introduction to the *Kālacakra-Tantra And Other Texts*, volume 1, pp.11-12.

82 For a list see Lokesh Chandra's introduction to the *Kālacakra-Tantra And Other Texts*, volume 1, pp.13-14.

83 For a list see Lokesh Chandra's introduction to the *Kālacakra-Tantra And Other Texts*, volume 1, p.14.

84 In volume ka of his Collected Works.

85 Available in a recent edition, (New Delhi: Guru Deva, 1973).

86 See Lokesh Chandra's introduction to the *Kālacakra-Tantra And Other Texts*, volume 1, p.16, which refers us to his *Materials for a History of Tibetan Literature*, pp.556-559.

87 Helmut Hoffmann, *The Religions of Tibet*, pp.125-126.

88 The source for the remainder of this paragraph as well as the next paragraph is Geshe Thupten Gyatso; he is following Puk-ba-hlun-drup-gya-tso's *(phug pa lhun grub rgya mtsho)* interpretation of Kālachakra astrological calculation, in which Shākyamuni Buddha's death is put at approximately 880 B.C. instead of 483 B.C. or thereabouts as is done in the Southern Buddhist tradition. G. Tucci in *Tibetan Painted Scrolls*, p.599, and Lokesh Chandra's introduction to the *Kālacakra-Tantra And Other Texts*, volume 1, p.6, mistakenly speak of the war as having already taken place.

89 The above etymological discussion is drawn from the Seventh Dalai Lama Gel-sang-gya-tso (bskal bzang rgya mtsho, 1708-57), *Explanation of the Mandala Rite of the Glorious Guhyasamāja, Akshobyavajra, Illumination Brilliantly Clarifying the Principles of the Meaning of Initiation, Sacred Word of Vajrasattva, (dpal gsang ba 'dus pa mi bskyod rdo rje'i dkyil 'khor gyi cho ga'i rnam par bshad pa dbang don de nyid yang gsal snang ba rdo rje sems dpa'i zhal lung)*, (New Delhi: Tanzin Kunga, 1972), 70.1-73.2. The Seventh Dalai Lama gives as his source Bu-dön's *Method of Initiation of the Glorious Kālachakra (dpal dus kyi 'khor lo'i dbang gi lhan thabs)*.

My source for the following enumeration of the initiations is Gyel-tsap-dar-ma-rin-chen *(rgyal tshab dar ma rin chen*, 1364-1432), *How To Practice the Two Stages of the Path of the Glorious Kālachakra: Quick Entry to the Path of Great Bliss (dpal dus kyi 'khor lo'i lam rim pa gnyis ji ltar nyams su len pa'i tshul bde ba chen po'i lam du myur du 'jug pa)*, Collected Works, vol. 1, (no publication data), 4a.3-4a.6.

90 p.64.

90a The classification of action faculties and their activities is not traditional to Buddhism but to Sāṃkhya. In the Kālachakra system there is a good deal of self-conscious borrowing of terminology from non-Buddhist systems. This borrowing from Sāṃkhya does not require re-interpretation to fit within Buddhism, but the usage of the terminology of the six-branched yoga, found in classical Yoga, for the levels of the stage of completion is completely revamped in the Kālachakra system with exclusively Buddhist meanings. Note also that the goddesses surrounding Kālachakra and Vishvamātā in the mandala of great bliss are called Shaktis *(nus ma)*, a term otherwise not used, to my knowledge, in Buddhist tantra. The borrowing of terminology from other systems was perhaps an effort to acclimate non-Buddhists to a Buddhist tradition.

91 This paragraph is drawn from Bu-dön's *Extensive Explanation of (Ānandagarbha's) "Rite of the Vajradhātu Mandala, Giving Rise To All Vajras": Wish-Granting Jewel (rdo rje dbyings kyi dkyil 'khor gyi cho ga rdo rje thams cad 'byung ba zhes bya ba'i rgya cher bshad pa yid bzhin gyi nor bu)*, Collected Works, (New Delhi: International Academy of Indian Culture, 1966), volume 11, 190-.5-191.2.

92 The Apte Sanskrit-English dictionary identifies the feminine form of this word, *shālabhañjikā*, as a courtesan, and thus, perhaps, these are attendants of the goddesses.

93 These are demi-gods; they are called "semi-humans" probably because they look enough like humans that one might wonder whether they are humans. The literal etymology of their name *(mi 'am ci)* is "human or what?"

94 For the count, I am following the description given by the Dalai Lama on p.254. A description made under the supervision of the Council of Religious Affairs of H.H. the Dalai Lama in Hiroki Fujita, *The World Of Tibetan Buddhism* (Japan: Gyosei Ltd., [1984]), p.96, gives seven hundred two deities. In bSod nams rgya mtsho, *Tibetan Maṇḍalas, The Ngor Collection* (Tokyo: Kodansha, 1983), p.236, the mandala is said to have 634 deities. A great deal depends on how the count is done – that is, how many consorts are counted, etc.

95 Tibetan, *rnam pa thams cad pa*.

96 The following description is taken from the Seventh Dalai Lama's *Means of Achievement of the Complete Mandala of Exalted Body, Speech, and Mind of the Supramundane Victor, the Glorious Kālachakra: the Sacred Word of Scholars and Adepts (bcom ldan 'das dus kyi 'khor lo'i sku gsung thugs yongs su rdzogs pa'i dkyil 'khor gyi sgrub thabs mkhas grub zhal lung)*, [n.d., in the same volume as Kay-drup's *Mandala Rite*], 86.1-87.7.

97 The painting of Kālachakra on the 1984 calendar of the Tibetan Medical Center in Dharamsala shows three arrows, but the picture in the Madison booklet shows a single arrow. The word in Tibetan is *me'i mda'* which literally means "fiery arrow"; the *Tibetan Dictionary* by Geshe Chosdag identifies this as *phyag mda'* which I presume to be just the honorific of "arrow" and not "hand arrow" since, as will be seen, Kālachakra is also holding a bow. The term may mean that the arrow has the capacity of fire.

98 *ibid*. 87.7-88.2.

99 The description is taken from the Seventh Dalai Lama's *Means of Achievement*, 88.2-89.4.

100 See n.56 of the translation.

101 Rather than the sixteen deities enumerated here, in *The World Of Tibetan Buddhism* (Japan: Gyosei Ltd., [1984]), a total count of fourteen deities in this mandala is given. Only eight Shaktis are counted, the remaining two being replaced by the consorts of the deities in the crowns of Kālachakra and Vishvamātā. However, there is no mention of consorts for them at this point in the Seventh Dalai Lama's *Means of Achievement*, and the Dalai Lama's ritual master reported that Vajrasattva is here imagined in meditation as a deer.

102 The description is taken from the Seventh Dalai Lama's *Means of Achievement*, 90.2-91.7.

103 *ibid*. 91.7-93.6.

104 The Seventh Dalai Lama's *Means of Achievement* (93.4) gives only four items: curved knife and vajra in the right hands and skull and bell in the left hands. This conflicts with Ḹo-sang-tsul-trim-ḏen-ḇay-gyel-tsen's *Initiation Rite of Kālachakra, Stated in an Easy Way* which I am following

here; see p. 320 of the translation.

105 The description is taken from the Seventh Dalai Lama's *Means of Achievement*, 93.6-95.2.

106 In the Kālachakra astrological system, a year has only 360 days; every fourth year has a leap month to make up for the missing days. Brief identifications of the deities of the speech and body mandalas can be found in Benoytosh Bhattacharyya, ed., *Nispannayogāvalī Of Mahāpandita Abhayākaragupta*, (Baroda: Oriental Institute, 1972), pp.78-86.

107 The description is drawn from Lati Rinbochay and Jeffrey Hopkins, *Death, Intermediate State and Rebirth in Tibetan Buddhism*, pp.59-61. For very interesting discussions of initiation in relation to rebirth, see Mircea Eliade, *Rites And Symbols Of Initiation, The Mysteries of Birth and Rebirth*, (New York: Harper and Row, 1965). In his introduction (xiii-xiv), Eliade says:

> Initiatory death provides the clean slate on which will be written the successive revelations whose end is the formation of a new man ... This new life is conceived as the true human existence, for it is open to the values of spirit ...
>
> All the rites of rebirth or resurrection, and the symbols that they imply, indicate that the novice has attained to another mode of existence, inaccessible to those who have not undergone the initiatory ordeals, who have not tasted death ...
>
> Initiatory death is indispensible for the beginning of spiritual life. Its function must be understood in relation to what it prepares: birth to a higher mode of being.

Here also, the dissolution of all ordinary appearance in a manner that mimics dying is necessary for rebirth on new principles. About the new birth, Eliade (xiv) says:

> The initiatory new birth is not natural, though it is sometimes expressed in obstetric symbols. This birth requires rites instituted by the Supernatural Beings; hence it is a divine work, created by the power and will of those Beings; it belongs, not to nature (in the modern, secularized sense of the term), but to sacred

> history. The second, initiatory birth does not repeat the first, biological birth. To attain the initiate's mode of being demands knowing realities that are not a part of nature but of biography of the Supernatural Beings, hence of the sacred history preserved in the myths.

Here in Great Vehicle Buddhism, however, the knowledge requires is of the *natural* state of things without the distortions of ignorance and the other afflictive emotions. Thus, it seems to me that the initiatory birth does indeed repeat the biological birth but within knowledge of the mode of being of phenomena, such that subsequent life is formed, not out of distorted knowledge of nature, but out of distortionless knowledge of the nature of things. It is not, therefore, a mere repetition but one within new knowledge of the ultimate and conventional natures of mental and physical phenomena. Knowledge of such reality is not part of ordinary life, and the new mode of being as known in deity yoga does indeed require passage to a new, sacred mode of manifestation, but the realities known through initiation are fundamental to ordinary life, albeit unknown.

The Kālachakra initiation accomplishes "passage from the profane to a transcendent state", as Eliade (p.104) says in his chapter entitled "Patterns of Initiation in Higher Religions". In its highest form, it also accomplishes passage from profane distortion to the most *ordinary* state, the fundamental innate mind of clear light, naturally latent in all experience but needing to be made manifest. In this sense, the sacred or divine life is at the very essence of the profane, made profane only by distortion.

108 Similarly, the term "compassion" *(snying rje, karuṇā)* is sometimes used in Highest Yoga Tantra additionally to refer to "bliss", but this does not cancel out its other meaning as the wish that all beings be free from suffering and the causes of suffering.

Karuṇā is etymologized as "stopping bliss" *(bde 'gog)* by adding an anusvara *(ṃ)* to the first letter *k*, making *kaṃ*, which means "bliss" *(bde ba)* and taking *ruṇa* (not found in the Apte dictionary) as meaning "stopping" *('gog pa)*. With respect to the compassion that is common to both the Perfection Vehicle and the Mantra Vehicle, that one cannot bear that other sentient beings are tormented by suffering stops one's own comfort and happiness (bliss). With respect to the uncommon meaning of *karuṇā* in Highest Yoga Tantra and in the Kālachakra system, the great immutable bliss involves a stoppage of the bliss of emission. Thus, both compassion and bliss are, so to speak, cases of the "stopping bliss". For a brief discussion of this, see L̄o-sang-chö-ḡyi-gyel-tsen's *Wish-Granting Jewel, Essence of (Kay-drup's) "Illumination of the Principles; Extensive Explanation of (Kulika Puṇḍarīka's) 'Extensive Commentary On The Condensed Kālachakra Tantra, Derived From The Root Tantra Of The Supramundane Victor, The Glorious Kālachakra, The King Of All Tantras, The Stainless Light'' (rgyud thams cad kyi rgyal po bcom ldan 'das dpal dus kyi 'khor lo'i rtsa ba'i rgyud las phyung ba bsdus pa'i rgyud kyi rgyas 'grel dri ma med pa'i 'od kyi rgya cher bshad pa de kho na nyid snang bar byed pa'i snying po bsdus pa yid bzhin gyi nor bu),* Collected Works of Blo-bzaṅ-chos-kyi-rgyal-mtshan, the First Paṇ-chen Bla-ma of Bkra-śis-lhun-po, (New Delhi: Gurudeva, 1973), vol. 3, 35.5-36.1. See also the Dalai Lama's remarks on this etymology in his introduction to *Tantra in Tibet* (p.48):

> In another way, the syllable *man* in 'mantra' is said to be 'knowledge of suchness', and *tra* is etymologised as *trāya,* meaning 'compassion protecting migrators'. This explanation is shared by all four sets of tantras, but from the specific viewpoint of Highest Yoga Tantra, compassion protecting migrators can be considered the wisdom of great bliss. This interpretation is devised in terms of a contextual etymology of the Sanskrit word for 'compassion', *karuṇā,* as 'stopping pleasure'. When anyone generates compassion – the inability to bear sentient beings' suffering without acting to relieve it, pleasure, peacefulness, and relaxation are temporarily stopped. Thus, in Highest Yoga the word 'compassion' *(karuṇā)* is designated to stopping the pleasure of the emission of the vital essence and refers to the wisdom of great bliss *(mahāsukha).* It is the mantra of definitive meaning and the deity of definitive meaning.

(I have revised the translation of the third sentence above.)

In addition to that connection between compassion and bliss, as Guy M. Newland of the University of Virginia pointed out in a colloquium, according to Ge-luk-b̄a explanations, those Bodhisattvas who have the most compassion are most capable of experiencing the great bliss of Highest Yoga Tantra.

Consider also the term "the path that has an essence of emptiness and compassion" *(stong nyid snying rje snying po can gyi lam)* [see Nāgārjuna's *Precious Garland*, stanza 396, for something similar], which is interpreted in four ways. It is interpreted in a manner common to the Perfection Vehicle as the path of the realization of the emptiness of inherent existence and of the compassion that is the wish that sentient beings be free from suffering and the causes of suffering – these two aspects affecting each other but not present in the same consciousness. It is interpreted in a manner common to the three lower tantras as the deity yoga in which the ascertainment factor of the consciousness ascertains the absence of inherent existence and the appearance factor altruistically appears as a divine body – the two factors of wisdom and method thereby being present in one consciousness. It is interpreted in a manner common with all Highest Yoga Tantras as the exalted wisdom of undifferentiable bliss and emptiness – a fusion of a bliss consciousness and a wisdom realizing the absence of inherent existence. In an interpretation exclusive to the Kālachakra system, it is interpreted as the undifferentiable entity of empty form (form empty of, that is, without, material particles) and supreme immutable bliss. From the viewpoint of the Kālachakra system, all four interpretations are acceptable; it is not that just because the term has a meaning exclusive to the *Kālachakra Tantra*, it is limited to that meaning in the Kālachakra system.

109 See Tsong-ka-pa, *Yoga of Tibet*, pp.47, 58-59.

110 For mention of the nature, aspect, and function of the offerings, see *Practice In The Manner Of The Very Condensed Clear Realization Of The Supreme Superior, The Ocean Of Conquerors (Jinasamudra) ('phags mchog ba*

rgya mtsho'i mngon rtogs shin tu bsdus pa'i tshul du nyams su len pa), by Gung-tang Gön-chok-den-bay-drön-may *(gung thang dkon mchog bstan pa'i sgron me*, 1762-1823), Collected Works of Guṅ-thaṅ dkon-mchog bstan-pa'i sgron-me, Vol. 7, (Ngawang Gelek Demo, 1975), 226.3-228.4; my translation of this was distributed at the Jinasamudra initiation by the Dalai Lama in Los Angeles in 1984.

111 These identifications are from Nga-w̄ang-b̄el-den *(ngag dbang dpal ldan*, 1791-?), *Illumination of the Texts of Tantra, Presentation of the Ground and Paths of the Four Great Secret Tantra Sets (gsang chen rgyud sde bzhi'i sa lam gyi rnam bzhag rgyud gzhung gsal byed)*, (rgyud smad par khang edition, no other data), 79.2-79.3.

111a In the conduct initiation, the sense powers are paired not in accordance with their respective objects but in accordance with the lineage of the deities that represent them such that deities of the same lineage are coupled. Similarly, in the name initiation, the action faculties are paired not in accordance with their respective activities but in accordance with the lineage of the deities that represent them. See L̄o-sang-tsul-trim-d̄en-b̄ay-gyel-tsen *(blo bzang tshul khrims bstan pa'i rgyal mtshan*, late 19th and early 20th centuries), *Explanation Of The Initiations Of The Supramundane Victor, The Glorious Kālachakra: Garland Of Rubies (bcom ldan 'das dus kyi 'khor lo'i dbang gi bshad pa padma ra ga'i phreng ba)*, The Collected Works of Tre-bo Khaṅ-gsar bLo-bzan-tshul-khrims-bstan-pa'i-rgyal-mtshan, (New Delhi: T.G. Dhongthog Rinpoche, 1975), vol. 3, 447.5-447.6. L̄o-sang-tsul-trim-d̄en-b̄ay-gyel-tsen, known also as Dre-wo Kang-s̄ar Gyap-gön *(tre bo khang gsar skyabs mgon)*, is the author of the *Initiation Rite* used to supplement Kay-drup's *Mandala Rite*.

111b The descriptions of the correspondences and functions of the internal initiations are taken from L̄o-sang-tsul-trim-d̄en-b̄ay-gyel-tsen's *Explanation*, Collected Works, vol. 3, 422.5-422.6, 436.5, 445.3, 446.4, 460.4, and 479.4.

112 See, for instance, Louis Renou, *The Nature of Hinduism* (New York: Walker and Company, 1962), pp. 97-98.

Renou says that name-giving occurs on the tenth day; hair-cutting, at three years; "tonsure", at four; piercing the ears, some time later. If these are the same here, the seven would not be chronological; however, the over-all list of seven seems chronological, with washing the new-born baby first and being given reading and other activities of the family lineage last.

113 For a fascinating discussion of the transitional, or liminal, nature of initiation, see Victor Turner *The Forest Of Symbols* (New York: Cornell University Press, 1967), pp.93-111. Turner, among many other points, speaks of the potential of these inter-transitional states (p.97):

> Liminality may perhaps be regarded as the Nay to all positive structural assertions, but as in some sense the source of them all, and, more than that, as a realm of pure possibility whence novel configurations of ideas and relations may arise.

As we have seen, in the Kālachakra initiation, the students offer everything of value to the lama/Kālachakra, then dissolve everything, including themselves, in emptiness, out of which they re-appear in new altruistically directed, validly founded, dynamic being. The liminal period of disappearance in emptiness is indeed a period of "pure possibility" ready for "novel configurations of ideas and relations". The dissolution into emptiness evinces a principle emphasized by Turner (pp.98-99):

> A further structurally negative characteristic of transitional beings is that they *have* nothing. They have no status, property, insignia, secular clothing, rank, kinship position, nothing to demarcate them structurally from their fellows.

The situation is, therefore, a mixture of extreme poverty and richness of potential; Turner finds such ambiguity and paradox (p.97) to be integral to the transitional state of the initiant. I would add that theoretically the situation is paradoxical only from an ordinary viewpoint that does not understand the process of appearance from within emptiness and the need for a new style of purification; still, from the viewpoint of someone undergoing the process (with no matter how much theoretical training) there must be phases of confronting the harrowing "paradox" that gain can come only from loss. Though it is easy to *explain* that everything must be given up in a disappearance into emptiness in order to reappear in pure form, the process of actually doing so must, for a beginner, entail a difficult sense of loss. See the Fifth Dalai Lama's description of such a sense of loss for a beginner in chapter four of the Introduction, pp. 57-8.

Also, for discussion of many aspects of initiation, see Dr C.J. Bleeker, *Initiation* (Leiden: E.J. Brill, 1965).

114 This section on the four drops is drawn from Nga-w̄ang-b̄el-den, *Illumination of the Texts of Tantra, Presentation of the Grounds and Paths of the Four Great Secret Tantra Sets,* 80.1-81.4.

114a The identifications of the entities of the seven initiations are taken from L̄o-sang-tsul-trim-d̄en-b̄ay-gyel-tsen's *Explanation,* 428.6, 431.4, 440.4, 443.6, 452.1, 457.1, and 465.1.

114b L̄o-sang-tsul-trim-d̄en-b̄ay-gyel-tsen's *Explanation,* 479.4.

115 The text is found in The Collected Works of the Lord Mkhas-grub rje dge-legs-dpal-bzaṅ-po, (New Delhi: Mongolian Lama Gurudeva, 1980), vol. 5, 795-937. For the translation I primarily used another edition which is found on pp.259-383 in a volume that has on its cover the title of one of the works contained within it: *dpal bcom ldan 'das dus kyi 'khor lo'i sku gsung thugs yongs su rdzogs pa'i dkyil 'khor gyi sgrub thabs mkhas grub zhal lung,* this being Kay-drup's *Means of Achievement of the Complete Mandala of Exalted Body, Speech, and Mind of the Supramundane Victor, the Glorious Kālachakra: Sacred Words of Scholars and Adepts,* found on pp.13-156 of the volume; it has no publication data. Page numbers throughout refer to this latter edition. I also used a handwritten edition (with no publication data) that was run off in India in a mimeograph type printing; I refer to it as the "handwritten edition".

116 This text is found in the same volume as the second text described in the preceding note, pp.477-532. It is also

found in The Collected Works of Tre-bo Khaṅ-gsar bLo-bzaṅ-tshul-khrims-bstan pa'i-rgyal-mtshan (New Delhi: T.G. Dhongthog Rinpoche, 1975), 313-368. The introduction to his Collected Works reports that he was among the candidates for selection as the Thirteenth Dalai Lama and speaks of the lama's next two reincarnations; the latest is said to have remained in Tibet and was estimated to be in his twenties in 1974.

117 It is clear that Kay-drup follows the great S̄a-ḡya master Bu-d̄ön Rin-chen-drup's *(bu ston rin chen grub) Mandala Rite of the Glorious Kālachakra: Source of Good Qualities (dpal dus kyi 'khor lo'i dkyil chog yon tan kun 'byung)* found in his Collected Works, (New Delhi: International Academy of Indian Culture, 1966), volume 5, 169-260. Therefore, page numbers for the parts translated here are given both to Kay-drup ("Kay") and Bu-d̄ön ("Bu").

118 Collected Works of Blo-bzaṅ-chos-kyi-rgyal-mtshan, the First Paṇ-chen Bla-ma of Bkra-śis-lhun-po, (New Delhi: Gurudeva, 1973), vol. 1, 707.2-803.1.

119 15.4-16.6

120 The biographical material in these two paragraphs is drawn from the introduction to Ferdinand D. Lessing and Alex Wayman, *Mkhas Grub Rje's Fundamentals of the Buddhist Tantras,* (The Hague: Mouton, 1968), pp.11-12, and from G. Tucci, *Tibetan Painted Scrolls,* (Roma: La Libreria Della Stato, 1949), pp.120-122 and 410-417. Kay-drup ("Scholar-Adept") is also called Kay-drup-tam-j̄ay-kyen-b̄a ("the omniscient Kay-drup" *mkhas grub thams cad mkhyen pa)* and Kay-drup-m̄a-way-nyi-ma ("Kay-drup Sun Of Propounders" *mkhas grub smra ba'i nyi ma).*

121 Ba-s̄o-chö-ḡyi-gyel-tsen wrote a set of annotations to D̄zong-ka-b̄a's *Great Exposition of the Stages of the Path (lam rim chen mo)* and an important work of practical instructions on the view of emptiness. For the former, see *The Lam rim chen mo of the incomparable Tsong-ka-pa, with the interlineal notes of Ba-so Chos-kyi-rgyal-mtshan, Sde-drug Mkhan-chen Ngag-dbang-rab-brtaṇ, 'Jam-dbyangs-bshad-pa'i-rdo-rje, and Bra-sti Dge-bshes Rin-chen-don-grub,* (New Delhi: Chos-'phel-legs-ldan, 1972); for the latter, see his *Great Instructions on the View of the Middle Way (dbu ma'i lta khrid chen mo)* in Mādhyamika Text

Series, vol. 3. Some say that his fifth incarnation wrote the former text.

122 Ge-s̄hay Thupten Gyatso of the Tibetan Buddhist Learning Center in Washington, New Jersey, at my request, wrote out a short biography of Kay-drup and then amplified on it in two sessions. The following account is a mixture of his written and oral presentations. For the *Secret Biography* itself, see the *Biography of the Omniscient Kay-drup Composed By Jay-d̄zun Chö-ḡyi-gyel-tsen (mkhas grub thams cad mkhyen pa'i gsang ba'i rnam thar rje btsun chos kyi rgyal mtshan gyis mdzad pa)*, The Collected Works of the Lord Mkhas-grub rje dge-legs-dpal-bzaṅ-po, Vol. a, 421-493. The author says that he bases his work on the *Secret Biography* of Kay-drup written by Chö-den-rap-jor, whom he says (423.6) heard most of the material from Kay-drup himself and supplied additional material from his clairvoyance. In the Collected Works is another biography of Kay-drup by Day-lek *(bde legs)*, *Biography of the Omniscient Kay-Drup: Captivating the Wise (mkhas grub thams cad mkhyen pa'i rnam thar mkhas pa'i yid 'phrog)*, Vol.ka, 5-31.

123 This prior rebirth is mentioned later in the *Secret Biography* by Jay-d̄zun Chö-ḡyi-gyel-tsen (430.4) as being given in a list of Kay-drup's former lives in Day-lek's *Biography of the Omniscient Kay-Drup: Captivating the Wise*. In the latter text (7.4-8.1), a longer list is given: Subhūti, Mañjushrīkīrti, Bhāvaviveka, Abhayākaragupta, the Translator Gö Kuk-b̄a-hlay-d̄zay *('gos khug pa lhas btsas)* [not the author of the *Blue Annals*], S̄a-ḡya Paṇḍiṭa Ḡun-ga-gyal-tsen *(kun dga' rgyal mtshan)*, and Ȳung-d̄ön-dor-jay-b̄el-wa *(g.yung ston rdo rje dpal ba)* who was an adept of the N̄ying-ma Order and Kay-drup's immediate predecessor. According to this list, Kay-drup is at the end of a list that includes a disciple of Shākyamuni Buddha, a compiler of the *Kālachakra Tantra* who was renowned as an incarnation of Vajrapāṇi, the founder of an important school of Buddhist philosophy, an important scholar, an important translator, a great scholar of another order of Tibetan Buddhism, and a great adept of another order of Tibetan Buddhism. These same persons are also given as prior incarnations of Kay-drup

in a list of fourteen incarnations ending with the Fourth Paṇ-chen Lama; in that list, the Paṇ-chen lamas are traced back to Kay-drup who is traced back to those just given. See G. Tucci, *Tibetan Painted Scrolls,* pp.412-413.

Missing in the latter lists but in the much shorter list of the *Secret Biography* by Jay-d̄zun Chö-ḡyi-gyel-tsen is Rik-b̄ay-ku-chuk The Greater *(rig pa'i khu phyung che ba),* who provides the link to Chandrakīrti and Nāgārjuna.

124 P5294, vol. 101.

125 The *Secret Biography* by Jay-d̄zun Chö-ḡyi-gyel-tsen (425.3) also says that at a certain point Nāgārjuna visited Rik-b̄ay-ku-chuk the Greater, telling him that he should rely on Mañjushrī and that he himself would take rebirth in an outlying land (Tibet), at which time Rik-b̄ay-ku-chuk (as Kay-drup) would be foremost in his circle. Āryadeva, Shāntideva, and Buddhapālita also told him of Mañjushrī's intention to be reborn in such an area. As the *Secret Biography* concludes, these accounts implicitly show Mañjushrī, Nāgārjuna, and D̄zong-ka-b̄a to be of the same mental continuum.

126 According to Day-lek's *Biography of the Omniscient Kay-Drup: Captivating the Wise* (7.6) Kay-drup is a later incarnation of S̄a-ḡya Paṇḍiṭa Ḡun-ga-gyel-tsen. Thus, his defense amounts to a justification of his own earlier writings.

127 D̄zong-ka-b̄a's three main disciples were Gyel-tsap, Kay-drup, and Dul-wa-dzin-b̄a *('dul ba 'dzin pa);* see the *Secret Biography* by Jay-d̄zun Chö-ḡyi-gyel-tsen, 430.1.

128 430.5 and 469.6. On 496.6 he reports that others had different visions of Kay-drup's departure.

129 *My Land and My People,* first published by McGraw-Hill in 1962 and reprinted by the Potala Corporation in 1977.

130 John F. Avedon's *In Exile From the Land of Snows* (New York: Knopf, 1984) gives a particularly vivid and moving account of the period after the Chinese takeover.

131 *rje btsun 'jam dpal ngag dbang blo bzang ye shes bstan 'dzin rgya mtsho srid gsum dbang gyur mtshung pa med pa'i sde dpal bzang po.*

132 Translated by Bhikku Thupten Kalsang Rinpoche, Ngodup Poljor, and John Blofeld (Bangkok: Klett Thai publications, 1975).

2 Notes to the Commentary

1 The Sanskrit is:

piṭakatrayaṃ dvayaṃ vā saṃgrahataḥ.

See S. Bagchi, ed., *Mahāyāna-Sūtrālaṃkāra of Asaṅga*, Buddhist Sanskrit Texts, No. 13, (Darbhanga: Mithila Institute, 1970), p.55.

2 For a discussion of the qualifications, see Bu-dön's *Mandala Rite of the Glorious Kālachakra: Source of Good Qualities (dpal dus kyi 'khor lo'i dkyil chog yon tan kun 'byung)*, Collected Works, (New Delhi: International Academy of Indian Culture, 1966), volume 5, 184.3ff.

3 *Commentary on (Dignāga's) "Compendium of Valid Cognition"*, Chapter II: *brtse ldan sdug bsngal gzhom pa'i phyir// thabs rnams la ni mngon sbyor mdzad// thabs byung de rgyu lkog gyur pa// de 'chad pa ni dka' ba yin//*, (Varanasi: Pleasure of Elegant Sayings, 1974), Vol. 17, p.54.14. The Sanskrit is:

dayāvān duḥkhahānārthamupāyeṣhvabhiyujyate
parokṣhopeyataddhetostadākhyānaṃ hi duṣhkaraṃ.

See Swami Dwarikadas Shastri, *Pramāṇavārttika of Acharya Dharmakirtti* (Varanasi: Bauddha Bharati, 1968), Vol. 3, 50.3.

4 Each student is to imagine himself or herself as the chief student to whom the lama specifically speaks.

5 I.18ab. The Sanskrit is:

chittotpādaḥ parārthāya samyaksaṃbodhikāmatā.

See Th. Stcherbatsky and E. Obermiller, ed., *Abhisamayā-*

laṃkāra-Prajñāpāramitā-Updeśa-Śāstra, Bibliotheca Buddhica XXIII, (Osnabrück: Biblio Verlag, 1970), p.4.

6 In Kay-drup's *Mandala Rite of the Glorious Kālachakra: Illumination of the Thought (dpal dus kyi 'khor lo'i dkyil chog dgongs pa rab gsal),* (n.d.), 296.5, read *mnyam nyid pa* for *mnyam med pa* in accordance with Bu-dön, volume 5, 185.4.

7 Bu-dön (volume 5, 185.4) reads *dpa' bo rnams kyis* for *mchog rnams kyis* in Kay-drup's *Mandala Rite* (296.5).

8 In Kay-drup's *Mandala Rite* (296.7) read *zhib tu* for *zhig tu* in accordance with the hand-written edition (42b.4), the latter showing signs of having been corrected at the last moment.

9 In Kay-drup's *Mandala Rite* (298.1) read *sngags kyi* for *sngags kyis.*

10 Kay-drup's *Mandala Rite* (298.1) has a short *huṃ* as does the hand-writteṅ edition (44a.4).

11 Also written as *udumbara* or *uḍumbāra*. The Sarat Chandra Das Tibetan-English Dictionary identifies this as a fabulous lotus of immense size.

12 The "mandala" here is a square board divided into quadrants. The lineage and appropriate feat are determined by the direction in which the tooth-stick falls. Jam-b̄el-shen-pen Rin-b̄o-chay tentatively identified the five cow-products as the urine, feces, milk, yogurt, and butter of an orange cow that eats only grass, not given by humans, for a period of seven days without the urine and feces having touched the ground. These are said to have tremendous medicinal qualities.

13 These two stanzas are taken from the *Condensed Kālachakra Tantra,* chapter II.12-13. See the *Kālacakra-Tantra And Other Texts,* volume 1, edited by Prof Dr Raghu Vira and Prof Dr Lokesh Chandra, (New Delhi: International Academy of Indian Culture, 1966), 101.9-102.5. The Sanskrit, from p. 340, is:

> garbhe garbhasthaduḥkhaṃ prasavanasamaye bālabhāvo 'pi duḥkhaṃ
> kaumāre yauvane strīdhanavibhavahataṃ kleshaduḥkhaṃ mahadyat
> vṛddhatve mṛtyudukhaṃ punarapi bhayadaṃ ṣhaḍga-

tau rauravādyaṃ
duḥkhād gṛhṇāti duḥkham sakalajagadidaṃ mohitaṃ māyayā cha
saṃsāro mānuṣhtvaṃ kvachiditi hi bhaveddharma-buddhiḥ kadāchit
tasmadbuddha 'nurāgo bhavati shubhavashādādiyāne bravṛttiḥ
tasmāchchhīvavajrayāne kvachidakhilamatirvartate bhāvanāyāṃ
tasmādbuddhatvamiṣhṭaṃ paramasukhapade hā pravesho 'tikaṣhṭam.

In the first line, the variant reading *bālabhāve* accords more with the Tibetan translation.

Bu-dön's *Easily Understandable Annotations For the Condensed Glorious Kālachakra Tantra, Great King of Tantras Arisen from the Supreme Original Buddha (mchog gi dang po'i sangs rgyas las phyungs ba rgyud kyi rgyal po chen po dpal dus kyi 'khor lo'i bsdus pa'i rgyud kyi go sla'i mchan)* volume 1, Collected Works, 51.2, is without any annotations for these stanzas. See Bu-dön's *Commentarial Explanation of the "Initiation Chapter" [of the Kālachakra Tantra], Annotations to (Kulika Puṇḍarīka's) "Stainless Light" (dbang gi le'u 'grel bshad dri med 'od kyi mchan),* volume 2, Collected Works, 14.2-15.5.

14 Kay-drup's *Mandala Rite* (299.5) reads "woman" *(bud med)* which has been translated as "mate" so as to apply to both males and females.

15 The Dalai Lama pointed out that the cosmology of the *Kālachakra Tantra* differs from that in Vasubandhu's *Treasury of Knowledge (chos mngon pa'i mdzod, abhidharmakosha).* In the latter system, the Crying is the fourth of the eight hot hells; for a description of it see Lati Rinbochay, Denma Lochö Rinbochay, Leah Zahler, Jeffrey Hopkins, *Meditative States in Tibetan Buddhism,* (London: Wisdom Publications, 1983), p.27, and Khetsun Sangpo, *Tantric Practice in Nyingma* (London: Rider, 1982), p.66.

16 See n.11.

17 In Kay-drup's *Mandala Rite* (300.4) read *de ring* for *di'ing;* also in the hand-written edition (46b.4) read *de ring* for *di ring.*

18 In Kay-drup's *Mandala Rite* (300.7) read *ma rang* for *ma'ang* in accordance with the hand-written edition (47a.3).

19 A short mandala-offering is given as an illustration of the type of offering here and throughout the rite wherever it is indicated.

20 Shākyamuni is said to have "shown the manner of becoming enlightened" in order to indicate that he had already become enlightened eons earlier and was making a display for the sake of followers.

21 For discussion of this topic see the Dalai Lama's *Kindness, Clarity, and Insight* (Ithaca: Snow Lion, 1984), final chapter.

22 At this juncture, Kay-drup points out that the text for the seven initiations is written for a practitioner's performing self-entry into a mandala but that instructions for using the text for conferring initiation are added. Kay-drup's *Mandala Rite* says:

> Here, entering the mandala and the rites of the seven initiations are treated mainly in terms of self-entry, but the uncommon activities involved in conferring initiation on students will be specifically indicated. For, this is [being composed] to help those of low intelligence interested in performing self-entry [into the mandala] in order to refurbish the vows for themselves, etc., without conferring initiation on students. Since the higher initiations are not needed for self-entry, they will be expressed in the format of rites for conferring initiation on students.

The higher initiations were not included in the Madison ceremony and are not translated here.

23 Kay-drup's *Mandala Rite* (318.5) only refers to this material and does not repeat it. It has been added here for the sake of convenience and completeness.

24 See n.12.

25 Kay-drup's *Mandala Rite* (319.4) only refers to this material and does not repeat it. It is added here from the rite of enhancement. The text itself resumes with the twenty-five modes of conduct.

26 III.22-23. The Sanskrit is:

> yathā gṛhītaṃ sugatairbodhichittaṃ purātanaiḥ
> te bodhisattvashikṣhāyāmānupūrvyā yathā sthitaḥ

tadvadutpādayāmyeṣha bodhichittaṃ jagaddhite
tadvadeva cha tāḥ shikṣhāḥ shikṣhishyāmi yathākramaṃ.

See Vidhushekara Bhattacharya, ed., *Bodhicaryāvatāra*, Bibliotheca Indica Vol. 280 (Calcutta: the Asiatic Society, 1960), p.36.

27 See chapter one of that book.

28 The stanza on the pledges is from the *Condensed Kālachakra Tantra*, Chapter III.86. See *Kālacakra-Tantra And Other Texts*, volume 1, edited by Prof Dr Raghu Vira and Prof Dr Lokesh Chandra, 167.1-4. The Sanskrit, from p.351 is:

vajraṃ ghaṇṭāṃ cha mudrāṃ gurumapi shirasā dhārayāmīṣhṭavajre
dānaṃ dāsayāmi ratne jinavarasamayaṃ pālayāmyatra chakre
pūjāṃ khaṅge karomi sphuṭajalajakule saṃvaraṃ pālayāmi
sattvānāṃ mokṣhahetorjinajanakakule bodhi-mutpādayāmi

Bu-dön's *Easily Understandable Annotations For the Condensed Glorious Kālachakra Tantra*, volume 1, Collected Works, 108.1, is without any annotations for this stanza. See Bu-dön's *Commentarial Explanation of the "Initiation Chapter" [of the Kālachakra Tantra], Annotations to (Kulika Puṇḍarīka's) "Stainless Light"*, volume 2, Collected Works, 378.2ff.

29 The two stanzas on the twenty-five modes of conduct are from the *Condensed Kālachakra Tantra*, Chapter III.93-94. See *Kālacakra-Tantra And Other Texts*, volume 1, 169.1-5. The Sanskrit, from p.352, is:

hiṃsāsatyaṃ parastrī tyajsva paradhanaṃ madyapānaṃ tathaiva
saṃsāre vajrapāshaḥ svakushalanidhanaṃ pāpametāni pañcha
yo yatkāle babhūva tridashanaragurustasya nāmnā pradeyā
eṣhājñā vishvabharturbhavabhayamathanī pālanīyā tvạyāpi
dyūtaṃ sāvadyabhojyaṃ kuvachanapaṭhanaṃ bhūtadaityendradharmaṃ

gobālastrīnarāṇāṃ tridashanaraguroḥ pañcha hatyāṃ na kuryāt
droham mitraprabhūnāṃ tridashanaraguroḥ saṃgha-vishvāsanaṃ cha
āshaktistvindriyāṇāmiti bhuvanapate pañcha-viṃshad-vratāni.

In the last line, the variant reading *pateḥ* accords more with the Tibetan translation.

Bu-dön's *Easily Understandable Annotations For the Condensed Glorious Kālachakra Tantra,* volume 1, Collected Works, 109.6, is without any annotations for these stanzas. The bracketed material is drawn from Bu-dön's commentary on this in his *Commentarial Explanation of the "Initiation Chapter" [of the Kālachakra Tantra], Annotations to (Kulika Puṇḍarīka's) "Stainless Light",* volume 2, Collected Works, 385.1-386.5.

30 Kay-drup's *Mandala Rite* (319.4) reads "women" *(bud med)* but has been amended so as to apply to both men and women. Also, in that edition (319.4) and the handwritten edition (69b.4) read *gzhan gyi* for *gzhan gyis.*

31 *sdig pa (pāpa)* is translated as "ill-deed" rather than "sin" in order to avoid the connotations of a sin against a creator God which many in our culture unavoidably associate with "sin".

32 According to Bu-dön's *Commentarial Explanation of the "Initiation Chapter" [of the Kālachakra Tantra], Annotations to (Kulika Puṇḍarīka's) "Stainless Light"*, volume 2, Collected Works, 386.3, the last refers to destroying religious images, stūpas, and so forth.

33 Here, according to Bu-dön (see previous note), this term refers to Buddhas.

34 VIII.131. The Sanskrit is:

na nāma sādhyaṃ buddhatvaṃ saṃsāro 'pi kutaḥ sukhaṃ
svasukhasyānyaduḥkhena parivartamakurvataḥ.

See Vidhushekara Bhattacharya, ed., *Bodhicaryāvatāra,* Bibliotheca Indica Vol. 280 (Calcutta: the Asiatic Society, 1960), p.170.

35 In Kay-drup's *Mandala Rite* (320.5) read *khaṃ* for *paṃ* in accordance with the hand-written edition (71a.5).

36 Stanza 24. See *The Mahāmudrā Eliminating the Darkness of Ignorance Supplemented by Aśvaghoṣa's Fifty Stanzas of Guru Devotion,* translated and edited by Alexander Berzin (Dharamsala: Library of Tibetan Works and Archives, 1978), p.175.

37 As Nāgārjuna's *Precious Garland (rin chen 'phreng ba, ratnāvalī),* stanza 377, says:

General rules and their exceptions
Are highlighted in all treatises.

See Nāgārjuna and Kaysang Gyatso, *Precious Garland and the Song of the Four Mindfulnesses,* (London: George Allen and Unwin, 1975), p.73.

38 Kay-drup's *Mandala Rite* (323.6) indicates the description of Vajravega in an ellipsis. The material from here through "... a tiger skin" has been added from the Seventh Dalai Lama's *Means of Achievement of the Complete Mandala of Exalted Body, Speech, and Mind of the Supramundane Victor, the Glorious Kālachakra: the Sacred Word of Scholars and Adepts (bcom ldan 'das dus kyi 'khor lo'i sku gsung thugs yongs su rdzogs pa'i dkyil 'khor gyi sgrub thabs mkhas grub zhal lung),* [n.d., in the same volume as Kay-drup's *Mandala Rite*], 71.2-71.7. Throughout the rite, abbreviated descriptions have been expanded in this way.

39 In Kay-drup's *Mandala Rite* (323.7) read *lte bar* for *lta bar* in accordance with the hand-written edition (75a.2).

40 A brief passage (324.7-325.1) that indicates an internal contradiction in someone's interpretation has been omitted. It reads: *'bebs pa'i tshe slob ma 'od dpag med du bskyed pa 'gog pa dang/ phebs pa la 'dri pa'i tshe/ mgon po rdo rje chos chen po// snang ba mtha' yas bde ba che// zhes bos nas 'dri bar 'dod pa ni khas blangs dngos su 'gal ba'o.* This seems to say, "To deny that at the time of descent the student is generated as Amitābha and then to assert that at the time of questioning upon the coming [of the deity] one invokes [the deity with], 'O great Protector, Vajra Dharma,/ Amitāyus of great bliss,' constitute a case of explicitly contradictory assertions." Amitābha and Amitāyus are the same deity.

41 Bu-dön's *Mandala Rite* (volume 5, 213.1) identifies the first three syllables as method and the last three as wisdom. The

colors given in brackets are tentative.

42 In Kay-drup's *Mandala Rite* (325.7) read *bcings* for *bcangs* in accordance with the hand-written edition (77a.6).

43 As identified by the Dalai Lama for the Jinasamudra *(rgyal ba rgya mtsho)* initiation in Los Angeles in 1984, the mandala symbolized by it is the exalted wisdom of non-dual bliss and emptiness.

44 The translation of these three items in uncertain.

45 "Bliss" is indicated by the term *ye shes,* which in other contexts means exalted wisdom but here, in terms of the ordinary state, means the ordinary bliss or pleasure of orgasm, described as the melting of the essential constituent.

46 A short, representative mandala-offering has been added, here and throughout the text when appropriate, as an illustration of the type of offering made.

47 The mantra is indicated (327.7) by only its first three syllables; it has been augmented from Lo-sang-tsul-trim-den-bay-gyel-tsen's *Initiation Rite of Kālachakra, Stated in an Easy Way (dus 'khor dbang chog nag 'gros su bkod pa),* 490.3. Such supplementation is done throughout the ritual.

48 Kay-drup's *Mandala Rite* (328.4) only says, "Make offering with *gandhaṃ* and so forth." The remainder of the list of offerings has been added from the same text (271.7), which curiously has both the *e* ending and *aṃ* ending for the last seven items; the translation is edited to accord with what the Dalai Lama said during the Madison ritual, including *akṣhate* for *akṣhataṃ.* The Dalai Lama identified *lāsye* as lower robe; the Apte dictionary gives "dance" for *lāsyaṃ,* but dance appears later in the list as *nṛtye*. The Dalai Lama identified *akṣhate* as fruit; the Apte identification as any type of grain is close in meaning. The Dalai Lama identified *kāme* as objects of touch *(reg bya);*the Apte identification is objects of desire.

49 Kay-drup's *Mandala Rite* (328.7) reads "one's own" *(rang gi)* since this part of the rite concerning the seven initiations is written mainly for one doing self-entry into a mandala.

50 Kay-drup's *Mandala Rite* (329.1) abbreviates the description with an ellipsis as it does with all the others. The

material has been added from the respective description in L̄o-sang-tsul-trim-d̄en-b̄ay-gyel-tsen's *Initiation Rite of Kālachakra, Stated in an Easy Way*, 492.1. The descriptions of the other deities throughout the ritual for the remaining seven initiations are similarly augmented with the respective sections from L̄o-sang-tsul-trim-d̄en-b̄ay-gyel-tsen's *Initiation Rite*.

51 So that Kay-drup's *Mandala Rite* may be abbreviated for the later initiations, it (330.4) gives what is to be substituted in each. Instead of merely listing these here, the complete rite is given for each respective initiation later at the appropriate time.

52 For an extensive discussion by the Dalai Lama on how the Tibetan schools all come down to the same basic thought, see the final chapter in his *Kindness, Clarity, and Insight* (Ithaca: Snow Lion, 1984).

53 Kay-drup's *Mandala Rite* (332.2) gives the beginning of the mantra as "*oṃ a iṃ* and so forth". L̄o-sang-tsul-trim-d̄en-b̄ay-gyel-tsen's *Initiation Rite* (496.2) gives a full rendering as *oṃ aṃ i ra uṃ ḷṃ*, the *anusvāras* having half moons below the dot. The *Mandala Rite* proceeds to give the seed syllables of the five Ones Gone Thus individually as *a i ṛ u ḷ* and again collectively in the concluding mantra (333.2) as *oṃ a i ṛ u ḷ pañcha-tathāgata-parishudda svāhā*. Thus, it is clear that the seed syllables of the five male Ones Gone Thus are *a i ṛ u ḷ* just as the seed syllables of the five female Ones Gone Thus are the corresponding long vowls, *ā, ī, ṝ ū ḹ*. Remaining is the question of why the *anusvāra* is added to this mantra, especially since it is not added to the concluding mantra.

54 The material ranging from this sentence up to but not including the mantra is added here and in the remaining initiations from the water initiation so as to accord with the Dalai Lama's actual conduct of the rite and the format in L̄o-sang-tsul-trim-d̄en-b̄ay-gyel-tsen's *Explanation*.

55 The text reads, "Having conferred initiation also with water from the religious conch, utter the earlier mantra of the water initiation." The material to which it refers is added here and in the remaining initiations from the corresponding section of the water initiation.

56 The Apte dictionary identifies *siddharasa (grub pa'i ro)* as quicksilver.

57 Both texts (335.6 and 503.3) read *dar dpyangs skye ba'i gnas lngar gtugs;* the meaning of *skye ba'i* is unclear and therefore has been omitted in translation.

58 According to Jam-b̄el-shen-pen Rin-b̄o-chay, internal sun and moon are purified in that the red and white constituents in the right and left channels are cleansed, and also external sun and moon are cleansed in the sense that sun and moon no longer are capable of generating suffering.

59 The text merely reads "oneself" *(rang),* which the Dalai Lama in the process of the rite amended to "the students' sense powers and their objects."

60 Kay-d̄rup's *Mandala Rite* (339.5) and L̄o-sang-tsul-trim-d̄en-b̄ay-gyel-tsen's *Initiation Rite* (511.6) merely read "oneself" *(rang),* which the Dalai Lama in the process of the rite amended to "the students' action faculties and their activities."

61 In Kay-d̄rup's *Mandala Rite* (341.2) read *bton* for *bten* in accordance with L̄o-sang-tsul-trim-d̄en-b̄ay-gyel-tsen's *Initiation Rite* (515.1).

62 The *Mandala Rite* (342.3) and the *Initiation Rite* (517.2) merely read "oneself" *(rang),* which the Dalai Lama in the process of the rite amended to "the students' pristine consciousness aggregate and pristine consciousness constituent."

63 The Dalai Lama added this stanza during the Madison initiation. L̄o-sang-tsul-trim-d̄en-b̄ay-gyel-tsen says in his *Explanation* (466.3) to move this stanza from those after giving the bell to here; the bracketed material in the translation is from his commentary.

64 In the *Mandala Rite* (344.5) read *khyod kyi* for *khyod kyis* in accordance with the *Initiation Rite* (520.4),

65 "Apprehension aspect" is a term referring to consciousness itself. The wisdom of undifferentiable bliss and emptiness itself appears as the divine body. The consciousness is the basis of emanation of the deity.

66 In brief, Kay-d̄rup's point in this section is:

> The entity of the master initiation at this point in the *Kālachakra Tantra* is not the exalted wisdom of bliss

generated in dependence upon having meditated on embracing a consort, for such constitutes the vase initiation from among the higher initiations. Rather, the vajra master initiation at this point is the appearance of the wisdom consciousness of bliss and emptiness as a divine body; in this context, the "great seal" is such a divine body. Thus, to identify the vajra master initiation at this point as a bliss consciousness generated in dependence upon embracing a consort is a mistake and involves fallacies as Kay-drup indicates.

The passage cited from the *Kālachakra Tantra* (III.97a) is found in the *Kālacakra-Tantra And Other Texts,* volume 1, 170.2. The Sanskrit, from p.352 is:

...nijapatinājñā pradeyā samātrā.

Bu-dön's *Easily Understandable Annotations For the Condensed Glorious Kālachakra Tantra,* volume 1, Collected Works, 110.5, is without any annotations. See Bu-dön's *Commentarial Explanation of the "Initiation Chapter" [of the Kālachakra Tantra], Annotations to Kulika Puṇḍarīka's) "Stainless Light",* volume 2, Collected Works, 393.4ff.

67 The passage cited (III.97b) is found in the *Kālacakra-Tantra And Other Texts,* volume 1, 170.2-170.3. The Sanskrit, from p.352 is:

vajraṃ ghaṇṭām pradāya pravarakaruṇayā deshayechchuddhadharmam.

Bu-dön's *Easily Understandable Annotations For the Condensed Glorious Kālachakra Tantra,* volume 1, Collected Works, 110.5, is without any annotations. See Bu-dön's *Commentarial Explanation of the "Initiation Chapter" [of the Kālachakra Tantra], Annotations to (Kulika Puṇḍarīka's) "Stainless Light",* volume 2, Collected Works, 393.7ff.

68 This passage on the pledges is from the *Condensed Kālachakra Tantra* (III.97c-98); see *Kālacakra-Tantra And Other Texts,* volume 1, 170.3. The Sanskrit, from p.352, is:

kuryāt prāṇātipātaṃ khalu kulishakule 'satyavākyaṃ cha khaṅga
ratne hāryaṃ parasvaṃ varakamalakule 'pyeva hāryā parastrī

madyaṃ dīpashcha buddhāḥ susakalaviṣhayā sevanīyāshcha chakre

ḍombyādyāḥ karttikāyāṃ susakalavanitā nāvamanyāḥ khapadme
deyāḥ sattvārthahetoḥ sadhanatanuriyaṃ na tvayā rakṣhaṇīyā.
buddhatvaṃ nānyathā vai bhavati kushalatānantakalpair jinoktam.

Bu-dön's *Easily Understandable Annotations For the Condensed Glorious Kālachakra Tantra*, volume 1, Collected Works, 110.6-111.1, is without any annotations. See Bu-dön's *Commentarial Explanation of the "Initiation Chapter" [of the Kālachakra Tantra], Annotations to (Kulika Puṇḍarīka's "Stainless Light"*, volume 2, Collected Works, 395.3ff.

69 Kay-drup is criticizing someone for misinterpreting an instruction in the *Condensed Kālachakra Tantra* (III.99) to the person conducting the ritual as something that is to be spoken during the conduct of the ritual. See *Kālacakra-Tantra And Other Texts*, volume 1, 170.6-170.9. The Sanskrit, from p.352 is:

toyaṃ tārādidevyo mukuṭa iha jināḥ shaktayo vīrapaṭṭo
vajraṃ ghaṇṭārkachandrau vratamapi viṣhayānāmamaitryādiyogah
ājñāsaṃbodhilakṣhmīrbhavabhayamathanī kālachakrānuviddhā
ete saptābhiṣhekāḥ kaluṣhamalaharā maṇḍale sampradeyāh.

Translated, this reads:

The water is the goddesses, Tāra and so forth; the crowns are the Conquerors; the heroic silk ribbons are the Shaktis;
Vajra and bell are sun and moon; conduct is the yoga of love and so forth [through] the name ["so and so Vajra", purifying] objects [and sense powers];
Permission is [for teaching] the glorious enlightenment, destroying the frights of cyclic existence, knowledge of Kālachakra.
These seven initiations are to be thoroughly bestowed in a mandala.

Bu-dön's *Easily Understandable Annotations For the Condensed Glorious Kālachakra Tantra*, volume 1, Collected

Works, 111.1-.3, is without any annotations. The bracketed material in the translation is from Bu-d̄ön's *Commentarial Explanation of the "Initiation Chapter" [of the Kālachakra Tantra], Annotations to (Kulika Puṇḍarīka's) "Stainless Light"*, volume 2, Collected Works, 398.2-399.3.

70 The petitions, mantras for conferring initiation, and the mantra for assuming the pride of being the deity are abbreviated in this text; thus, Kay-drup refers the reader to his *Means of Achievement of the Complete Exalted Body, Speech, and Mind of Kālachakra: the Sacred Word of the White Lotus (dus kyi 'khor lo'i sku gsung thugs yongs su rdzogs pa'i sgrub thabs padma dkar po'i zhal lung)*, where they are set out in full; see volume cha of his Collected Works, (New Delhi: Guru Deva, 1981), 32.2-33.5. L̄o-sang-tsul-trim-d̄en-b̄ay-gyel-tsen put all of these in his *Initiation Rite of Kālachakra, Stated in an Easy Way*, which this translator has used to make Kay-drup's *Mandala Rite* complete.

71 This section is specific to the particular time and place of the initiation. Below is that given at the initiation in Madison, Wisconsin, in 1981.

72 These three and a quarter stanzas are from the *Kālachakra Tantra*, III.100d-103; see *Kālacakra-Tantra And Other Texts*, volume 1, 171.2-171.9. The Sanskrit, from p.352 is:

mūlāpattiṃ kadāchidvrajati shaṭhavashānnārakaṃ duḥkhameti

mūlāpattervishuddhirbhavati hi guṇinaḥ saptaseka sthitasya

kumbhe guhye kadāchidvrataniyamavashāduttare nāsti shuddhiḥ

mūāpattiṃ gato yo vishati punaridaṃ maṇḍalaṃ siddhihetor

ājñām labdhvā hi bhūyo vrajati gaṇakule jyeṣhṭha-nāmā laghutvam

mūlāpattiḥ sutānāṃ bhavati shashadharā shrīguro-shchitta-khedāt

tasyājñānaṃ ghane 'nyā bhavati khalu tathā brātṛkopā tṛtīyā

maitrītyāgāchchaturthī bhavati punariṣhubodhi-chittapraṇāshāt

ṣhaṣhṭhīsiddhāntanindā girirapi cha nare 'yāchite

guhyadānāt
skandhakleshādahiḥ syāt punarapi navamī shuddha-dharme 'ruchiryā
māyāmaitrī cha nāmādirahitasukhade kalpanā dik cha rudrā
shuddhe sattve pradoṣhādravirapi samaye labdhake tyāgato 'nyā
sarvastrīṇām jugupsā khalu bhavati manurvajrayāne sthitānām.

Bu-dön's *Easily Understandable Annotations For the Condensed Glorious Kālachakra Tantra,* volume 1, Collected Works, 111.4-112.2, is without any annotations. See Bu-dön's *Commentarial Explanation of the "Initiation Chapter" [of the Kālachakra Tantra], Annotations to (Kulika Puṇḍarīka's) "Stainless Light"*, volume 2, Collected Works, 400.2-405.4.

73 The bracketed material is from Bu-dön's *Commentarial Explanation of the "Initiation Chapter" [of the Kālachakra Tantra], Annotations to (Kulika Puṇḍarīka's) "Stainless Light"*, volume 2, Collected Works, 400.4.

74 The Dalai Lama pointed out that in Kay-drup's *Mandala Rite* (394.4) *ri bong* (rabbit) indicates the singular and thus "first"; that (349.5) *mda'* (arrow) indicates "five"; that (349.5) *ri bo* (mountain) indicates "seven"; that (349.5) *klu* (serpent) indicates "eight"; that (349.6) *phyogs* (direction) indicates "ten"; that (349.5) *drag po* (fierce one) indicates "eleven"; that (349.6) *nyi ma* (sun) indicates "twelve"; and that (349.6) *ma nur* (name of a mineral drug) indicates "fourteen". In Kay-drup's *Mandala Rite* (349.6) read *ma nur 'gyur te* for *ma 'gyur te* in accordance with *Kālacakra-Tantra And Other Texts*, volume 1, 171.9. The latter also reads *nges par ma nur 'gyur te* instead of *ces par ma nur 'gyur te*.

75 The translation from Kay-drup's *Mandala Rite* ends here (349.7). The remainder is from Lo-sang-tsul-trim-den-bay-gyel-tsen's *Initiation Rite* (525.3-4).

76 This stanza is similar to Shāntideva's *Engaging in the Bodhisattva Deeds*, III.25. Here the second line reads "My being alive is also fruitful," whereas the usual reading of Shāntideva is "I have attained a good human existence." For the

Sanskrit of the latter, see footnote 19 of the first practice text.

77 This concludes the initiation ritual as found in L̄o-sang-tsul-trim-d̄en-b̄ay-gyel-tsen's *Initiation Rite of Kālachakra, Stated in an Easy Way*. The remaining two sections are not found in the ritual texts but are additions by the Dalai Lama at the Madison initiation.

Index

Index

Abhayākaragupta, 140–41, 495
Ornament to the Subduer's Thought (munimatālaṃkāra), 141
Niṣhpannayogāvalī, 487
abhidharmakosha
See: Vasubandhu, *Treasury of Knowledge*
abhiṣheka
See: empowerment; initiation
absorption
entering into, 82, 120–21, 265
formless absorptions, 45
generating from the seed of absorption, 368, 418
action faculties
and their activities, 71–74, 115–117, 318, 485, 491, 506
generated as deities, 318, 325, 491
purifying activities of, 124, 318–20
activities
altruistic, 15, 32, 70, 130
authorization to perform, 279
contaminated, 165, 170, 386
activities *(continued)*
as empty of inherent existence, 190, 400
external, 38, 162
mandala activities, 414, 430
non–activity, 190, 397
student's, 105
adopting and discarding, 14, 171
afflictive emotions, 40, 42, 45–46, 170, 172, 188, 196, 230, 488
and lineage, 249
rebirth impelled by, 95, 97
and root infractions, 359
tantrists not dominated by, 31, 33
transmutation of, 126–27
aggregates
ascertaining not one/not different, 54–57
as deities, 71, 219–20
and five Buddhas, 111, 229, 271, 280–87
mental and physical aggregates, 54, 72–73, 106, 108, 281, 412, 429, 362

About Wisdom

Wisdom Publications, a not-for-profit publisher, is dedicated to making available authentic Buddhist works for the benefit of all. We publish translations of the sutras and tantras, commentaries and teachings of past and contemporary Buddhist masters, and original works by the world's leading Buddhist scholars. We publish our titles with the appreciation of Buddhism as a living philosophy and with the special commitment to preserve and transmit important works from all the major Buddhist traditions.

If you would like more information or a copy of our mail-order catalog, please contact us at:

Wisdom Publications
199 Elm Street
Somerville, Massachusetts 02144 USA
Telephone: (617) 776-7416
Fax: (617) 776-7841
Email: info@wisdompubs.org
Web Site: www.wisdompubs.org

THE WISDOM TRUST

As a not-for-profit publisher, Wisdom Publications is dedicated to the publication of fine Dharma books for the benefit of all sentient beings and dependent upon the kindness and generosity of sponsors in order to do so. If you would like to make a donation to Wisdom Publications, please do so through our Somerville office. If you would like to sponsor the publication of a book, please write or email us for more information.

Thank you.

Wisdom Publications is a non-profit, charitable 501(c)(3) organization and a part of the Foundation for the Preservation of the Mahayana Tradition (FPMT).